The

QUEST FOR LITERATURE

*A Survey of Literary Criticism and
the Theories of the Literary Forms*

By

JOSEPH T. SHIPLEY, PH.D.

RICHARD R. SMITH, INC.

NEW YORK - - - - - - 1931

PRINTED IN THE UNITED STATES

Speculations of this sort cannot give genius to those that have it not; nor are they of much help to those that have, genius being most frequently incapable of drawing aid from speculations. Of what good, then, are they? To lead toward the fundament of beauty certain folk who enjoy reason, and who like to draw into the realm of philosophy matters that seem most independent thereof, that are commonly considered prey to the whims of taste.

BERNARD LE BOVIER DE FONTENELLE.

NOTE

——not that cold, algebraic kind, which, under pretext
of explaining everything, expresses neither liking nor dislike, and strips itself of every trace of personality.

CHARLES BAUDELAIRE.

THE nature of this book makes it largely a conspectus of
what men through the ages have thought about literature.
I have, indeed, tried to prevent my own adherencies from
coloring the presentation; it is my hope, not to make con-
verts to any special theory, but in some measure to promote
a consideration of the work of art in which enthusiasm will
be supported by understanding. Save for a few suggestions
none other seems to have made, therefore, and for the
gathering and the arrangement of the material, an indebted-
ness too great for instant notice pervades the text.

Yet in treating of an activity whose influence is still at
work upon us, it is inevitable that the judgment and the
feeling of both writer and reader must at every moment
color the material. Upon the wide field of our venturing,
the paths are many, and the views diverse; and the same
studies as have led to this presentation might well, with
another, have resulted in quite different selection, treatment,
and emphasis, and perhaps led to fundamentally different
conclusions. The swift survey of the history of literary criticism is no more than a sketch, in which but a glimpse of the
many figures is allowed, as they partake of the age's movements; and in which any reader's friends will perhaps seem
poorly limned in scant profile. In extenuation I plead that
the true object of interest is the long current, not the objects bobbing in its course; the flow of ideas through the

ages, rather than the men who block them or press them on.

The bibliographies at the close of the volume indicate, for the respective sections, the authors who should receive credit for the ideas expressed, any of which may be pursued more lengthily in the source-book. It would be as presumptuous of me to thank these many writers as to proclaim my gratefulness to the pine-grove I see from my window, to the breeze that idles through it, to the restful blue of the bay and the sky beyond.

It may be more appropriate, however, in a work of this sort, to name in gratitude some of the teachers who have led me the long way to this writing. Gentle Abner Holley of a child's memory; Edwin Van Buren Knickerbocker who taught a ten-year-old that literature has life; at the College of the City of New York, A. J. Goldforb, biologist, who made a youth feel that all life has the imaginative reach of art, as Paul Klapper showed him one's seniors may meet one on common ground of intellectual striving, where he walked also with Morris Raphael Cohen; and as his interests centered, Charles F. Horne made him aware of scholarship, and (at Columbia University) Jefferson B. Fletcher revealed that the erudition of the scholar may in one man be blent with the explorer's enthusiasm and the artist's taste. These men are as widely present in the text as those whose names run through its pages.

CONTENTS

All things are determined by number.
ARISTOTLE.

CONTENTS

CHAPTER I

DISTINCTIONS AND PRECAUTIONS

"I know what you're thinking about," said Tweedledum, "but it isn't so, nohow."

"Contrariwise," continued Tweedledee, "if it was so, it might be; and if it were so, it would be; but as it isn't, it ain't. That's logic."

"I was thinking," said Alice very politely, "which is the best way out of this wood."

LEWIS CARROLL.

THE DEFINITION OF CRITICISM

> Some will splash in the Milky Way,
> Or bump on the moon—oh dear!
> Light the stars up, Gabriel,
> Because the night is here.
>
> ELEANOR FARJEON.

"LET us define our terms." With these wise words the Frenchman strikes at the root of argument. For all discussion that aims at convincing instead of persuading, that is predominately intellectual rather than emotional in its appeal, is essentially exposition. In order to justify and properly prolong the human delight in discourse, objectors immediately seek to lay the motion on the table.

"I hope I'm mature enough not to try to define", retorts an Englishman.

An American protests that "defining cannot be carried on at all, except on condition that it is made a game, or that one neglects most of the relevant facts". More seriously and more safely, another Frenchman declares: "Definitions are not set a priori, save perhaps in mathematics. In history it is from the patient study of reality that they insensibly emerge."

The fields of literature are rank with the weeds of controversy. "In æsthetics", as Anatole France words it, "that is to say, in the clouds, one can argue more and better than in any other subject . . . There is not a single opinion in literature one cannot easily fight with its exact opposite."

It is not surprising that the more brilliant—and the duller —thinkers of every age have tried to break light through —or find shelter in—the fog of literary criticism.

Bold spirits there are who will always rush to define. The man who prophesied that the nineteenth century would be known by his name bluntly said: "Is the work good or bad? That's criticism's domain"; scorning, however, to define the moot words in his question. More mildly it has been observed that "the history of criticism is the history of the world's changing taste"; and in the hope that through the record some demarcations may grow, it will be briefly traced. Before approaching such a study of what criticism is, however, some speculations as to why it is, and what it is not, may be surveyed.

THE VALUE OF CRITICISM

I saw within my troubled head a heap of thoughts appear.
THE EARL OF SURREY.

To SPEAK of the function of criticism would be to imply a purpose to which it is devoted; the reasons authors assign for their activity, even the known impulses to their work, bear often so little apparent relation to the result that it is wiser to ask, instead, what values may be extracted from this sort of writing. These naturally vary with the point of view from which criticism is considered, so that the justification of criticism will be raised with different emphasis by the public, by the author criticized, and by the critic himself.

To the critic, whatever his immediate incentive to write, criticism seems always a savouring. It is an activity entered upon (as were Shaw's early lectures) to extend or to clarify the critic's knowledge; he writes in order to understand, and to weave the new thread of understanding into the design that marks his universe. Or it is an attempt to express anew the emotions aroused by the work of art as the critic lives, in the play of his mind upon it, the intense exaltation the art itself has worked in him. He seeks to master a significant aspect of being, and to prove his control by setting it forth in a new form; to conquer (a mite of) the universe by creating it. To the critic his work has the value of all self-expression that is bound in self-control.

The author criticized may, if he be properly humble, be chastened by criticism. Manifestly, his errors will be laid bare before him; but lapses from taste, submission to the

5

tyranny of a fashion or to a period's prejudice, too idiosyn-
cratic a departure from the confines of communicable art:
the more neatly hidden pitfalls that wait in a writer's path,
may also be uncovered. It has been questioned whether
authors derive profit—or anything more than indignation—
from this type of criticism; but there is a positive, what
might be called a creative, criticism, of more appreciable
value. This is most frequent in the suggestions of fellow-
writers when an author is discussing a contemplated work,
or showing a first draft to a friend; yet occasionally it rises
in more impersonal form. An essay by Clayton Hamilton on
Writing a Play Backward helped Elmer Rice to his first
stage success. The creative work of many a literary school,
from the old to the new Pleiade, has begun with a critical
manifesto. From both destructive and constructive criticism,
the author may learn.[1] Horace neatly phrases this conception in the remark that the critic may serve as a whetstone,
which, though it cannot cut, can sharpen iron.

For the public, criticism may do many things. At its lowest, it serves as a form of gossip, giving information as to
books and authors so that he who rides in the subway may
read. It may, on a somewhat higher level, assume the role of
the priest, and teach what in literature—as he in life—is
good or bad. Many a critic plays Moses to his readers. More
quietly, through their own efforts to understand, critics may
prepare the public for an author, by their joy in him and its
expression leading others to understand and to enjoy. Such,
recently, has been the progress of Eugene O'Neill. In this
guise, too, the critic helps to maintain general culture at a
level likely to produce genius, and grant it fit reception, to
ensure—as Matthew Arnold emphasizes, as Alfred Zimmern says—"the presence of a sufficient proportion of civilized persons—that is, of men and women who have individu-
ally made the effort to absorb, and as it were to live over

again in their own wider experience, the thought of their predecessors in civilization". Again, the critic may act as Anatole France suggests, rambling about the literary universe, planting an arm-chair here, hanging a hammock there, that those that rest in them may look on beauty. And finally, criticism, whether of the slap-stick Mencken or the rouge-stick Huxley style, whether orotund with Arnold or purple-patched with Pater, may be enjoyed for its own sake, as any other form of literary art. Criticism may be read for the sake of its subject; it is reread for itself.

ATTITUDES TOWARD THE CRITIC

Lord help us all, it is the greatest thing God made!
R. L. STEVENSON.

THE values that theoretical consideration leads one to assign to criticism may be questioned in the light of the various attitudes toward the critic. Of themselves, many critics feel it the mission to teach the authors of their time, or at least to keep general culture at a level that will foster the generation and reception of artists; although one might have fancied no man later than Matthew Arnold would declare that an age is no greater than its critics, Lewis Mumford has recently stated that critics must supply contemporary artists with "a coherent framework for their experience". Many critics, on the other hand, for whom their work is primarily self-expression, approve of the connoisseur who asks "Is it a good painting?" and scorn the sitter who inquires "Is it a likeness?" This attitude bears the danger of distortion, of over-emphasis of one aspect of the original, or falsification, for the sake of self-display.[2] The public, in turn, looks upon the critic as one who is to provide a stimulant, in the form of information or entertainment—the usual goal of the public being power and pleasure. To the author, the critic is one who has had granted that fiendish prayer: O that mine enemy had written a book!

An anthology might be collected of the words of authors upon critics, of which a suggestive few are here provided.

Seneca tells us:

Didymus wrote four thousand books. I should pity him if he had merely read so many useless works. The list includes treatises

8

in which he discusses the birthplace of Homer, the true mother of Æneas, whether Anacreon was more of a rake than a sot, whether Sappho was a prostitute, and other questions the answers to which you ought to forget if you know them. And then people complain that life is short.

Leaping the centuries to the neo-classicists in England, we find Ben Jonson defending his tribe, against those who say "critics are a kind of tinkers, that make more faults than they mend ordinarily." Pope also has high regard for the critic:

> Both must alike from Heaven derive their light,
> Those born to judge, as well as those to write.

But Dryden is less respectful, affirming that the "corruption of a poet is the generation of a critic", and adding

> And malice in all critics reigns so high
> That for small errors they whole plays decry.

Sterne has his fling at the "tormenting cant of criticism", whose practitioners look only at the stop-watch. Swift, in the *Battle of the Books*, lengthily pictures the malignant deity, Criticism, aglint on a snowy peak in Nova Zembla. Momus, seeking her aid for the moderns, found her

extended in her den, upon the spoils of numerous volumes, half-devoured. At her right hand sat Ignorance, her father and husband, blind with age; at her left Pride, her Mother, dressing her up in the scraps of paper herself had torn. There was Opinion, her sister, light of foot, hood-winked, and head-strong, yet giddy and perpetually turning. About her played her children, Noise and Impudence, Dulness and Vanity, Positiveness, Pedantry, and Ill-manners. The goddess herself had claws like a cat; her head, and ears, and voice, resembled those of an ass; her teeth fallen out before; her eyes turned inward as if she looked only upon herself; her diet was the overflowing of her own gall; her spleen was so large as to stand prominent like a dug of the first rate; nor wanted excrescences in the form of teats, at which a crew of ugly monsters were greedily sucking; and, what is wonderful to conceive, the bulk of spleen increased faster than the sucking could diminish it.

Roused at the danger of her "devout worshippers, the Moderns", this Goddess begins to vent her wrath:

"It is I" (said she) "who give wisdom to infants and idiots; by me children grow grow wiser than their parents, by me beaux become politicians, and schoolboys judges of philosophy; by me sophisters debate and conclude upon the depths of knowledge; and coffee-house wits, instinct by me, can correct an author's style, and display his minutest errors, without understanding a syllable of his matter or his language; by me striplings spend their judgment, as they do their estate, before it comes into their hands. It is I who have deposed wit and knowledge from their empire over poetry, and advanced myself in their stead."

After this, it might seem pity would call truce; and Coleridge is content to say "reviewers" where Disraeli later declares critics are those who have tried creative work and failed; Emerson, too, takes up the cry "the critic is a failed poet"; Goethe grows more vehement: "Kill the dog, he's a reviewer!" Keats damns the whole tribe of "dank-haired critics"; Byron storms:

> . . . As soon
> Seek roses in December, ice in June,
> Hope constancy in wind, or corn in chaff;
> Believe a woman, or an epitaph,
> Or any other thing that's false, before
> You trust in critics. . . .

Still earlier is the picture of the critic as pest:

> Critics are like a kind of flies, that breed
> In wild fig-trees, and when they're grown-up, feed
> Upon the raw fruit of the nobler kind,
> And, by their nibbling on the outer rind,
> Open the pores, and make way for the sun
> To ripen it sooner than he would have done.

Not content with his warning, Byron describes the making
of a critic:

> A man must serve his time to every trade
> Save censure—critics all are ready made.
> Take hackney'd jokes from Miller, got by rote,
> With just enough of learning to misquote;
> A mind well skill'd to find or forge a fault;
> A turn for punning, call it Attic salt;
> To Jeffrey go, be silent and discreet,
> His pay is just ten sterling pounds a sheet;
> Fear not to lie, 'twill seem a lucky hit;
> Shrink not from blasphemy, 'twill pass for wit;
> Care not for feeling—pass your proper jest,
> And stand a critic, hated yet caress'd.

In somewhat milder tone, but in the same vein, the American Lowell takes up the call:

> Nature fits all her children with something to do,
> He who would write and can't write, can surely review;
> Can set up a small booth as critic and sell us his
> Petty conceits and his pettier jealousies.

The discrimination of the critic, his vaunted ability to trace
distinctions with medieval minuteness, is celebrated by the
first Samuel Butler:

> He could distinguish and divide
> A hair 'twixt south and south-west side.

while a less precise aspect of his functioning is characterized
by Sir Henry Wotton, in the remark that "critics are like
brushers of noblemen's clothes."

William Morris is surprised at the existence of the critical
activity: "To think of a beggar making his living by selling
his opinion about other people! And fancy anyone paying
him for it!"

Arthur Symons: "Like the industrious crow, the critic

hops after the sowers of beauty, content to peck up the chance grains dropped by genius."

Bernard Shaw: "Those that can, do; those that cannot, teach."

Clement Wood: "Most of all, see critics for the shrunken failures they are."

(At this point it seems well to interpose the temperate remark of Anatole France: "Let us agree that we are talking about ourselves, on such and such a subject.")

Also from the French is the anecdote of the first night of an excitingly controversial play. In his enthusiasm, one spectator tumbled from the balcony. An instant awareness took the theatre; then, through the hushed anguish till he strike, one voice uprose (the dramatist's, no doubt): Lord land him on a critic!

George Jean Nathan makes the critic himself join the condemning chorus:

Much of the layman's distrust of criticism is to be accounted for by the distrust of criticism by critics themselves, so often frankly and substantiatingly voiced. Even the more intelligent and meritorious critics at times produce criticism so hollow and absurd that the least intelligent and least meritorious have no difficulty in detecting its nonsense and, one fears, somewhat cockily, announcing it for all to hear. Under the circumstances it is not strange that the layman should grow skeptical of all criticism, just as he grows skeptical of all oysters if he happens to catch a single bad one.

Christopher Ward pictures America in the golden days "Before Columbus Came":

> And there were no reviewers then.
> No critic pushed a poison pen.
> No callow youngster, fresh from school,
> His proper seat a dunce's stool,
> Who yesterday but learned his letters,
> Assumed to praise or damn his betters.

> No little clique conspired to boost
> The bantam cock to rule the roost.
> Nor did th' Algonquin pundits' babble
> Befool the gaping long-eared rabble
> Who never know how much of fake
> Is in that game of give and take
> When logs are rolled•and backs are scratched
> And mutual fulsome praises matched.

Every age, of course, has its more personal notes, such as this from "A New Dunciad":

> There, to the glee of many a lettered moron,
> Van Doren brayed a blessing on Van Doren.

Speaking especially of writing about one's contemporaries, Jules Lemaitre says it is not criticism, but conversation; Brander Matthews adds the reasons: it lacks the touchstone of time, the perspective of distance, and the assured application of the eternal standards (though the second of these is but the first set in a figure; and if there be eternal standards, it is hard to tell by what their application is to be assured—unless by the touchstone of time, and the three reasons totter, a false trinity).

In all these blows heavily dealt the critic we may perceive the working of a poison that deadens their power. For they cry with the voice of violence, not reason; and they rise from the victims, potential or actual, of the critic's pen. Indeed, there is measure of truth in Swift's word that "if the men of wit and genius would resolve never to complain in their works of critics and detractors, the next age would not know that they ever had any." Their words, furthermore, though of an abusive order, are themselves criticism: the speakers are self-condemned. An attacked author were wiser to develop France's remark, pointing out that the critic uses him, as he a storm or a wedding, as an avenue of self-expression; that those interested in his work should read it, as perchance the critic did; and that still, as Elizabeth Barrett Browning reminds us, "the natural healthy eye turns toward the light, and the true calling of criticism remains the distinguishing of beauty".

THE QUEST FOR LITERATURE

CRITICISM AND BOOK-REVIEW

Woo not the world too rashly, for behold,
Beneath the painted silk and broidering,
It is a faithless and inconstant thing.
(Hearken to me, Mu' tamid, growing old.)

THE strictures of authors upon critics are more justly
leveled at book-reviewers, whose wide domain must be
marked off. About twenty thousand books are printed annually in English; almost two hundred and fifty newspapers
of America have regular sections for book reviews. Readers
of such pages, and of the literary magazines, are likely to
learn from them all they will ever know of most books and,
save as they subscribe to a "book of the month" association,
to depend on them in choosing the books that they will
read. The review may thus have more practical importance
than the criticism; in any case it is different.

"The difference between criticizing a book and reviewing
it", says the Literary Editor of the *Chicago Evening Post,*

may be stated very simply. If you read a book and write a
summary of its contents, telling the ground it covers, possibly
noting the style, you have written a review of the book. You have,
that is, informed the possible reader as to what is in the book.
You have done a job of reporting. And like the reporter you have
kept yourself out of the story. If, on the other hand, you talk
about the book in terms of your own point of view, if you say
whether you think the book is a good one or a bad one, giving
your reasons for so stating, you are writing criticism.

It seems strange that one in such a position should be
thus confused. If the question as to whether one can keep

oneself "out of the story" be waived, there remain the statement that every review contains a summary, the implication that there is but one task for criticism, the vague reference to style—in the wrong division, the redundancy of "summary of its contents" and "ground it covers", and the failure to consider some essential differences between criticism and the book-review.

There are certain surface conditions of the reviewer's task that help determine the nature of his product. His discussion is usually limited to one book of an author; it may, however, include several books in a wide field, as three studies of America in the 80's, or four volumes of verse that have chanced to reach the paper together. These, too, are almost always "hot off the press"; in the case of books for which a wide sale is hoped, advance copies are often sent forth, that the review may appear on the publication day. This review, appearing in a periodical, is likely to reach a public of one rough intellectual level. It is published, furthermore, in a paper that perhaps values the reviews for the sake of the advertising, rather than because of its readers' desire and demand.

The book-review must be fashioned to meet these conditions. It must take little knowledge of the book's author, or its field, for granted. It must present the theme and the range of the book in its field, indicating, for example, that the volume discusses the theory of relativity, beginning with Xenophanes and ending with the critics of Einstein—adding, moreover, that it is written, with copious illustrations, in words of one syllable. For perhaps the chief task of the reviewer is to indicate the emotional and intellectual level at which the book makes its appeal, and to suggest, with reasons, how successful that appeal is like to be. *War and Peace* is discussed in terms it would be travesty to apply to

If Winter Comes. Abie's Irish Rose—which blushes unseen at the breath of literature—achieved a triumph for which *Kosher Kitty Kelly* strove in vain. Some reviewers, who write regularly for one periodical, with readers largely on one level, tend to assume that theirs is the only taste, and praise or condemn as that taste is satisfied. But beyond this distinction and discussion, the reviewer will probably seek to establish a relationship between the work and his reader, and to help the prospective buyer select from the mass of books those he will be glad to have purchased. The reviewer may, indeed, keep in mind another sort of public, of whom one editor writes: "Nine review readers out of ten will not read the book. Make your article informative enough so that the nine can lie successfully about it"—if not to the tenth, one may add, at least to one another. . . . The reviewer consciously gives the public what it wants, information and entertainment.

Book-reviewing, while meeting these requirements, may of course take many forms. The opening usually makes bold bid for attention, particularly in newspaper reviews, which must entertain regardless of their subject. A striking quotation, an episode of "human interest", the seeds of a controversy, a link with current affairs, anything in the book that points to excitement, is likely to be stressed. A summary is seldom given, in the better reviews, though the general field of the work is bounded in a few sentences and often the plot of a novel is carried far enough to point its perilous course. Quotations are also rather infrequent, and always short; important books, indeed, sometimes come to an editor's desk with a note limiting the length of extracts. In the case of non-fiction, the accuracy of the author, the errors and omissions of a compiler, are usually mentioned—

assuming the reviewer competent to check. The questions
of form, in general, as also the space allotted the review, are
determined by the probable appeal of the book to the paper's
public, that "fickle herd" which—via the editor's chair—
is the most important element in the reviewer's mind.[3]

THE BASES OF CRITICISM

> Jack was a boy of excellent taste, as should appear by
> his pulling out a plum; it is therefore supposed that his
> father apprenticed him to a mince-pie maker, that he might
> improve his taste from year to year; none standing in such
> need of good taste as a pastry-cook.
>
> BENTLEY, On the Sublime and Beautiful
> (Mother Goose's Melody).

THE first question one usually asks in regard to a critic
is of his standards. If he claims to be restricted by none, to
insist on no fundamental principles in art, the critic is asserting the superiority of his taste over the author's and
over that of other readers. If he be not (perhaps unwittingly) so presumptuous, the critic must make clear on what
bases his standards rest. Anatole France speculates that if,
in another five hundred years, biology becomes an exact
science, ethics in an equal period may achieve like growth,
so that, still a millennium later, one may hope to have an
exact science of æsthetics . . . One may meanwhile continue
to question.

Longinus early declared that the judgment of literature
is the long-delayed reward of much endeavor; but a perusal
of much that has been written by, shall we say, venerable
professors bids us wonder whether it is not often delayed
too long. If experience, if constant contact with masterpieces,
bring power of discrimination, surely the watchman in the
museum is the best critic of painting! Pope must have been
moved by numberless examples of irremediable bad taste
to his remark that critics, as well as poets, are born, not
made.

Yet from the comparison of experiences, it seems, something may be gleaned. Even then difficulties are imposed. One may attempt to check and balance one's own observations, arriving at interesting conclusions—but inevitably bound by the individual response. A man may look at an etching and a brilliant seascape without knowing he is color-blind; another may read Dostoievsky and Laurence Sterne without recognizing his lack of a sense of humor. The effort to check one's individual responses by comparison with the responses of others is hindered by the fact that an experience evokes a different attitude in everyone that undergoes it. The simpler the object contemplated, indeed, the more varied the response. "Pony", to one person, may bring an image of the shaggy Shetland that pulled a child's cart; to another, of a somewhat terrifying but fascinating steed on whose back he was held by an hostler at an amusement resort; to a third, of the translation that helped him gallop his way through Vergil. Fortunately for human intercourse, the more complicated the experience, to a certain degree, the more nearly the responses approach identity. Even the most elaborate drama or poem, however, wakes in various individuals attitudes so different as to seem quicksand to any save the most aerial builder of theories. Offering a number of poems, for free comment in writing, to several groups, made up mainly of Cambridge undergraduates reading for honors in English, I. A. Richards shows that there exists an "inability, widespread even among educated readers, to grasp what, in the widest sense, a poem is about.... owing to communicatory deficiencies not in the poems but in the readers". If there is so little agreement as to the poem itself, what concord can be expected as to its value?

By these elusive criteria, nonetheless, is to be estimated the value of the work of art. Standards of value have, therefore, been pronounced or sought in every age, and through the history of criticism we shall trace the quest.

WHO IS THE BEST CRITIC?

> If the coat be ever so fine that a fool wears, it is still
> but a fool's coat.
>
> OLD SAW.

AMONG the preliminary questions we ask without hoping
for answer, is one as to what group is likely to give rise
to the soundest criticism. Three claimants appear: those
indefinite bodies we may refer to as the average reader and
the cultured amateur, and that more recognizable entity, the
writer himself.

Many an artist has been content to please the general
public. Moliere tested his plays by the reaction of his cook,
who in one sense presumably had good taste; William Gil-
lette accepted, as just dictator of the theatre, "the man in
the street"; and Tolstoi turned to the moujik, the simple,
pious, earthy peasant, as the final judge of all art. "Almost
all the great writers of the past", says Hugh Walpole, and
Clemence Dane makes the remark a book's motto, "if they
have not appealed to the Man in the Street, have won the
interest of the Plain Man, who to my thinking is the Man
in the Street, plus a little culture".

A composite psychograph of the average man reveals
that his emotions control his thought and action. He will
not long remain philosophical, judicially impartial. Not
only does he incline to take sides but, having chosen his
allegiance, he knows (with a desire stronger than cognition)
the king can do no wrong. The motto "Right or wrong, my
country" must, though for different reasons, seem ludicrous
to both the patriot and the jingo. The average reader has
no taste for grays; as his hero has stepped from the white-

wash pail, so does his villain leer from the ink-pot. Improbabilities do not stay him on his course, if the emotional sweep be sufficiently strong to carry him, if the adventures be swift-following and violent. The average reader is best observed in bulk, and the art that demands mass attention is the drama; it is not surprising, therefore, to hear Maeterlinck say:

It is only the life of violence, the life of bygone days, that is perceived by nearly all our tragic writers; and truly I may say that anachronism dominates the stage.

Of another type of perennial favorite, the shocker, Walter Scott seems to approve; he says that Horace Walpole's purpose in *The Castle Of Otranto* was "not merely to excite surprise and terror by the introduction of supernatural agency, but to wind up the feelings of his readers till they became for a moment identified with those of a ruder age." Why Scott should have thought such an object worth attaining is hard to tell; though a critic today might take the stand that thereby would be achieved a catharsis of impulses of cruelty and fear latent in all of us. For that "ruder age" is not something man has left behind, a skin he has sloughed with the season; but something he has managed to work inward, as the wasp enlarges his hive: scratch a gentleman and you reach a barbarian; it is indeed the nucleus of his growing. Which makes this Gentle Reader even more worthy of thought, if it be true, as many claim, that the reader, by his desire made manifest, summons the work of art. Yet Judy O'Grady may well be right, not understanding Browning, to say that she does not, and still be deluding herself quite impertinently when she draws the conclusion that he's unintelligible. Each may speak for himself as to whether he is pleased, but not as to the quality of the pleasure.

The cultured amateur as a judge of literary values may

advance in his support that, theoretically, this nation is governed by amateurs. This recommendation must be modified by the recognition that the amateur is subject to influences that act less readily upon the mass. When George III of England spoke of his greatest countryman as "that sad stuff, Shakespeare", it was the courtiers, not the commoners, that lifted their cultured countenances from the bard. Readers of Cabell, and of the new gossiping biographers, doubtless recognize their cultural superiority. There grows, indeed, a suspicion that every level of reader feels a stratum below, like the big fleas and the little fleas,* until one despairs of identifying this hypothetical cultured amateur. Shall we accept Henry Ford? Or Woodrow Wilson? His favorite reading, we are told, was of detective stories. These cultured amateurs, besides, insofar as they dwell in the world of "society", have what Bruntiere calls "an instinctive horror of all that is solemn or serious"; they deem the last word has been said if they pronounce the verdict: We are not amused. The effect of their attitude, the French critic feels, is so far-reaching that

if you wish to know why Racine or Moliere, for example, have not always attained the depth of thought we find in a Shakespeare or a Goethe; or again, why certain questions, as of human destiny, encompassed in a Hamlet or a Faust, seem to have remained foreign to them, *cherchez la femme*, and you will find that the failing lies in the influence of women and the salons.

Shall we accept the artist as judge of art? Whistler emphatically would have none but a painter evaluate his work. Pope as definitely demands:

> Let such teach others who themselves excel,
> And censure others who have written well.

Ben Jonson is even more of an extremist: "To judge of poets is only the faculty of poets; and not of all poets, but

* Big fleas have little fleas upon their backs to bite 'em,
Little fleas have littler fleas, and thus "ad infinitum."

the best." Standing against these opinions rears Aristotle, with wall of analogy:

It is not the builder alone whose function it is to criticize the merits of a house; the person who uses it, the householder, is actually a better judge; and similarly a pilot is a better judge of a helm than a carpenter; or one of a company of a dinner than the cook.

Johnson plays a variation:

You may abuse a tragedy, though you cannot write one. You may scold a carpenter who has made you a bad table, though you cannot make a table. It is not your trade to make tables.

Johnson's contemporaries condemn the author-critic on more personal grounds. Dryden speaks of the dramatist thus empowered:

Whom then would he exempt, and on what score?
All who (like him) have writ ill plays before.
For they, like thieves condemned, are hangmen made,
To execute the members of their trade.

And Congreve:

In shoals, I've marked them judging in the pit,
Though they're on no pretense for judgment fit,
Save that they have been damned for want of wit.

This is, of course, mere abuse. Nor are the analogies wholly relevant; for, while the householder may judge of the comfort of the home, the pilot of the balance of the helm, none other so well as a maker can estimate their soundness. A better case against the writer as judge could be drawn from the expressed opinions of writers; there are classical examples, such as Corneille's opinion of Racine, the reciprocal estimates of Richardson and Fielding; Byron's words on Keats—Byron who said "Homer sometimes nods; Wordsworth sometimes wakes"; Charlotte Bronte's thoughts of

Jane Austen; and—to provide one illustration, the strictures on his contemporaries of Peacock:

> While the historian and the philosopher are advancing in, and accelerating, the progress of knowledge, the poet is wallowing in the rubbish of departed ignorance, and raking up the ashes of dead savages to find gewgaws and rattles for the grown babies of the age. Mr. Scott digs up the poachers and cattle-stealers of the ancient border. Lord Byron cruizes for thieves and pirates on the shores of the Morea and among the Greek islands. Mr. Southey wades through ponderous volumes of travels and old chronicles, from which he carefully selects all that is false, useless, and absurd, as being essentially poetical; and when he has a commonplace book full of monstrosities, strings them into an epic. Mr. Wordsworth picks up village legends from old women and sextons; and Mr. Coleridge, to the valuable information acquired from similar sources, superadds the dreams of crazy theologians and the mysticisms of German metaphysics, and favours the world with visions in verse, in which the quadruple elements of sexton, old woman, Jeremy Taylor, and Emmanuel Kant, are harmonized into a delicious poetical compound. Mr. Moore presents us with a Persian, and Mr. Campbell with a Pennsylvanian, tale, both formed on the same principle as Mr. Southey's epics, by extracting from a perfunctory and desultory perusal of a collection of voyages and travels, all that useful investigation would not seek for and that common sense would reject.

It may be said that critics recruited from other fields as often err; but the writer is drawn by his own work toward certain extravagances of judgment. Dealing with an art that is his life-long work, perhaps his life-long love, he is likely to be too intense, too devoted, to maintain an open mind. If strong, he may, as has been observed, be intolerant of other modes of work than his own; if weak, jealous of other work in his mode. Being equipped technically, he will tend to stress formal details; it is the authors among critics who complain of Dreiser's style. On the other hand must be considered such a reflection as T. S. Eliot's, that the artist, "who completes the circuit of impression and expression in his art", will be the better critic, in that his criticism will not be the satisfaction of a suppressed creative wish.

Out of these groups the critic must emerge; yet he must endeavor to avoid the faults of all. While these groups are, for the reasons indicated, largely irresponsible critics, they are nonetheless self-assertive, and of considerable importance in establishing the ultimate judgment of art.

THE ULTIMATE JUDGMENT

This no tomorrow hath, nor yesterday.

JOHN DONNE.

BEFORE the casual reader opens a book of verse, or turns the pages of a novel, affective tendencies of all sorts, based on information as to the author or on intuitive assumptions from the very sound of his name and other external causes, have set in and established those predispositions and prejudices against which the critics seek to erect their ivory tower. Whether the book be the season's latest or the race's first, the anticipation is colored by factors that act in advance upon the temperament of the reader, and help to determine his feeling.

The surest judge of any art, we are often told, is therefore time. The verdict of posterity is appealed to as that of a jury, if not infallible, at least final, and as fair as an author can find. Yet the desire of future generations to deal justly with the works of the past does not afford an unfailing measure of their ability to achieve a true evaluation. It has been pointed out that, save for the vicissitudes of occasional revivals, the "posterity" of Shakespeare consists largely of school children and professors; surely, outside of poets and students, the present readers of Marlowe, Spenser, Milton, and their early fellows, are comparatively few. Yet this select group, it may be urged, is sufficiently detached from the clamorous concerns of the poets' times to view the works apart from the lives and factions of their creators, to approach them impartially, and on purely æsthetic ground. The reader of Poe no longer apologizes for his perusal, nor

27

does the lady of today thrill with a sense of daring, as she opens her gilt-edged copy of Byron.

The slightest reflection on the consequences of compulsory education, however, reveals that the writers whose works remain have been tucked into one or another of the pigeon-holes that render life more smooth, have been neatly caught in a phrase—nay, an adjective—whereto the schoolboy memory may cling. Certain books, certain poems, it is true, are presented directly to the fresh and curious mind of the child; these the teacher is supposed to "introduce" effectively, and too often it is on the glib re-echoing of the instructor's (similarly echoing) opinion that a high mark sets the seal of truth. Later, the youth is frequently subjected to one of the rapid surveys of the history of literature, that consists in reading as much about the writers of the race as time will allow, with but meager glances at the writings. Supplementary reading of the authors is usually, indeed, required, but the necessity of passing through the course, or the mere unconscious influence of the verdicts of text and professor, is likely to form the judgments of those students who are not invincibly bored. By a process not unlike this, probably every reader has made his approach to authors of earlier days; whether he accept or rebel against the received evaluations, they press an insidious and insistent attack upon his judgment, they form an invisible yet distorting lens through which he must seek true vision.

An appeal is often made to the readers of foreign lands as to a sort of "contemporary posterity", whose judgment is likely to anticipate the verdict of time. Posterity begins at the border. It might seem, indeed, that the foreigner is sufficiently removed from national interests and local affiliations, yet deeply enough imbued with the spirit of the age, to form an unbiased and presumably correct opinion of a work. In the case of the novel, where much personal characterization occurs, where the depicting of the life of the land is often preponderant, an outside estimate may well seem more likely to be accurate than the response of those whose neighbors or whose interests are touched. Our response to a Zola novel, the French attitude toward an *Elmer Gantry*, for example, might well be truer indication of its "real", its intrinsic merit, than the native judgment as indicated by the book's immediate reception. For proper consideration, however, the foreigner must be familiar with the entire field of such books in the language concerned. In the case of poetry, appreciative aspects minimize the advantages of removal. The reader of a translation finds another, a new, poem, by a contemporary of his own race; the translator cannot hold his version free from the spirit of his period and his people; it must be judged as any native poem. To appreciate a poem in the original, on the other hand, a foreigner must reach beyond the mere significance of words to grasp the racial associations, the racial rhythm, and the racial impetus; he must break through precisely those barriers that render him an alien, and therefore, presumably, a timeless, judge. The foreigner becomes capable of appreciation in the measure of his approach to the native; in equal measure he becomes incapable of detached judgment.

A further restriction upon the foreigner is imposed by the great number of books indiscriminately assembled for his choosing; any native arrangement and prior selection leaves him no longer free. The gathering of distinguished English authors that recently entertained an American writer here considered inconsequential (although popular among those whose reading inclines toward "true story" magazines and tabloids), indicates the difficulty judgments in one language experience in bridging an ocean; the impossibility of selecting the best in foreign tongues, or of comparing foreign and native literatures, lies displayed before whoever contemplates

the list of awards of the Nobel Prize for literature. One of
the most popular American writers in French translation is
James Oliver Curwood. Poets, here again, suffer more than
other writers: the simpler narrative, the wilder bizarre effect, are likely to win translation or publication abroad; and
foreign readers of Service or Cocteau may never hear of
Robinson or Jammes. How many who have reread the last
forty pages of Joyce's *Ulysses*, have glanced at Gilbert's *Bly
Market*, or Dujardin's *The Laurels Are Felled*? Drowning in
the ocean of domestic print, the reader can clutch at straws
dropped to him from abroad, only by translators selecting
what matches their own theories or taste, or by mistrustful
publishers issuing—often, as the vogue drives them—what
they hope will sell.

Since foreign judgment, insofar as it is competent, draws
its impulse from the creator's land, and since posterity must
take as a point of departure what has already been said, the
ultimate judgment of the general reader would seem to be
that contemporary opinion which by force or fortuity prevails. Between the vociferated feeling of the day and the
genuine merit of the work there may, of course, be slight accord; there seems to exist no way of ensuring a proper reception for masterpieces—or of agreement as to which work
is a masterpiece, though reviewers fondly hail. Political and
personal issues crowd too closely upon the work for a true
perspective; yet—save for the general tendency of all books
to fall from popular favor, and on their way to oblivion to
lapse from the edification of adults to the entertainment of
children, (as novels), or from the entertainment of adults
to the edification of children, (as poetry)—allowing for the
inevitable drift toward neglected bookshelves, the preponderant opinion of the day, in criticism, not in sales, seems
usually the verdict of the morrow.

How, then, does the general reader form his opinion of

the worth of his contemporaries? The effect on public opinion of the monthly reports of the selection committees of the "book-of-the-month" organizations cannot yet be estimated; but the influence of reviews, and of the comments of one's "circle" or one's "set", on what is said about a book, is unquestionably great.

That certain condescension formerly observed in foreigners is even more marked, though perhaps less conscious of itself, when the mind turns to our known coevals. A prophet is not without honor, save in his own country and in his own house. How many of his fellow-actors imagined that the former horse-boy* who was fitting obsolescent favorites to the taste of the day, and dramatizing popular stories, was the greatest of English playwrights? Who among his customers saw in the pale, consumptive drug-clerk one of our purest poets? Look at this thing he calls *Endymion:* the presumption and the outmoded allusion of its Greek title; its first line, that begins with one of the vaguest and most unpoetic nouns in the language, ends with a phrase stolen from a dozen popular songs, and fills the space between them with the most abused word in the history of art! . . . This lad who grew up beside me, fed upon the same food, learned the same lessons—and was, belike, no prizeman at the school!—now bids me hail him as a blossomed genius! . . . Something of this inability to escape the personal difforms our judgments of writers we chance to know.

Most authors are fortunate enough to escape the ball and chain of our acquaintanceship, and to be known to us only by reputation. This, however, suffices to shed on them a patina resembling that of their predecessors, and to establish our attitude of approach. The reader of poetry is as little likely to change his notion of, say, Alfred Noyes as his opinion of Shelley; and often, reading about a man seems to render supererogatory the task of reading him. What dif-

completely unsubstantiated legend

ferentiates our attitude toward the authors of today rises from our contact with the spirit they feel in the age. Manifested in our own lives are the surgings that stir a Sandburg and a Sinclair; we are perforce partisans; we add our voice to the chorus of praise or condemnation, as the writer yields the expected responses; and we thus play our part in creating that wide-spreading opinion which becomes the verdict of posterity.

Some writers, more obscure, remain unknown to us until we lift their volume from a shelf, or come upon their stories or their stanzas in a magazine. These, at least, might hope for a fresh, fair reading. Yet the very fact that the name is new seems—I repeat—an implication that the work is undistinguished; in the era of advertisement should we not have heard of the man, if he were worth hearing? Some readers are forever unable to overcome this predisposition to find little merit, are the constant victims of their expectation. Those on the other hand who, despite frequent confirmation of this likelihood, at length find long-sought treasure, come upon and recognize freshness and vigor and charm, are prone, through their surprise and the keener pleasure of rebounding eagerness, to overestimate their discovery. Such of the fulsome praise frequent in reviews as is not personally impelled springs mainly from this overemphasis of pleased surprise.

It seems, then, that the opinions of the general reader are formed by the admixture of roused expectation (that tends always to find what it seeks) and personal attitudes and limitations; if ultimate judgments are to rest upon anything more solid, their bases must be sought in the elucubrations of the critics who, remote from the hubbub of personal involvement, are forever rearing their ivory tower. As Johnson sums up the situation:

Though it should happen that an author is capable of excelling, yet his merit may pass without notice, huddled in the variety of things, and thrown into the general miscellany of life. He that endeavours after fame by writing, solicits the regard of a multitude fluctuating in pleasures, or immersed in business, without time for intellectual amusements; he appeals to judges, prepossessed by passions, or corrupted by prejudices, which preclude their approbation of any new performance. Some are too indolent to read anything, till its reputation is established; others too envious to promote that fame which gives them pain by its increase. What is new is opposed, because most are unwilling to be taught; and what is known is rejected, because it is not sufficiently considered, that men more frequently require to be reminded than informed. The learned are afraid to declare their opinion early, lest they should put their reputation in hazard; the ignorant always imagine themselves giving some proof of delicacy, when they refuse to be pleased; and he that finds his way to reputation through all these obstructions, must acknowledge that he is indebted to other causes besides his industry, his learning, or his wit.

We must turn, then, to the professed critics for final valuation. But a general view of their final words shows, rather, so great a variety of judgments, in all ages, on all writers, so wide a discrepancy in estimate and—even where verdicts agree—in elements emphasized and phrases stressed, that those who read opinions can readily select, as most cogent, a criticism that forwards their own prejudices and predilections:—a general view of the words of critics shows ideas so diverse and many-tongued, indeed, that it seems the ivory tower the critics endlessly rear was in an older age called Babel. In other words—and here philosophy and science lend comfort—the æsthetic ultimate, as all ultimates, seems unattainable . . . Therefore we continue its roundabout quest.[5]

AVENUES OF INQUIRY

Wretched is the mouse that hath but one hole.

OLD SAW.

IN FOLLOWING the course of criticism through the ages, the observer must note whether the various utterances of critics move, like a science, ever toward a greater harmony with the universe, or whether, like an art, their validity has little reference to their age. As Einstein has supplemented Euclid, must we expect T. S. Eliot to surpass Aristotle? Does each age build upon the achievements of its predecessors? Is there, indeed, any progress in criticism at all?

While it does not fall within the scope of a survey of criticism, it may be pointed out that the critic of any era will have to consider the influence of many apparently extraneous forces upon the taste and the productions of the period. The effect of the defeat of Xerxes, and of the conquest of Athens, upon Greek literature; of the Spanish Armada upon the Elizabethan writers; of the storming of the Bastille upon the romantics; must be recognized and taken into account. Similarly, scientific progress must be noted, as modifying the spirit and the form of literature; political theories, philosophical systems, as helping to determine its spirit; machinery, industrial strife, as giving impetus to its moving. One may profitably watch to discern the extent to which a critic takes the color of his time, and his ability to discriminate among the prejudices of his period, and to trace its many impulses to their source.

Criticism, being one form of self-expression and inquiry into reality through the individual, partakes of the nature of art; being an examination into the expression of another,

34

his methods and the effects thereby achieved, it partakes of *not at all !* the nature of science. The complications this duality involves are greatly increased in the criticism of literature, by the fact that the vocabulary there employed is not its own. The basic terms of literary criticism are borrowed from the visual arts. When one speaks of a colorful composition, of the form of a statue, the design of a cathedral window, the eye can take in the whole work, can return to verify its impression, can regain the form at any time. But in the literary arts such words have only a figurative application; the great "purple patches" appear in ordinary black print; and for even this figurative application one must depend upon the memory, which selects, interprets, emphasizes, distorts, at a second degree of removal from the object. A literary work, indeed, is less an object—the printed poem, the bound play —than a movement in time. The painting is the artist's product, but the written words—whether in script, or in Roman or Gothic type, or in Braille—are merely the symbols by which the author conveys his achievement to the reader. Every work of art, depending upon communication, is to some extent a collaboration between the artist and the receptor; of all artistic forms, this is most largely true of literature; and perilous therefore the paths of criticism.

There are, besides, many rocks and roots to trip the unwary, along these paths, and pitfalls neatly hidden. Before appreciation or criticism can come, the meaning of the work must be grasped, its imagery recognized, its sensuous effects, of rhythm and sound, be felt. Many sets of mental habits must be held in check, or closely watched, lest they interfere with proper examination and reception. The response may be exaggerated by sentimentality or lessened by inhibitions (heat and cold at pendulum-span); it may be led astray by communal attitudes, the stock summonings of familiar terms, or by irrelevant associations due to personal memories, by the receptor's beliefs and theories in any sphere of life (but particularly in social and religious matters) as they are touched in the work, or by his theories and expectations of the technique of the particular art. With all these prior impulses indeed, the reader, looking at a work of art, may construct a quite different work in his own mind, and attack the author for the flaws his own personality has produced.

Upon the paths of criticism move many types of man, as the well-known tale of the elephant suggests. Asked to prepare a study of the pachyderm, the Frenchman went to the zoological gardens, and mingled with the chatting crowd.[*] The Englishman equipped an expedition to the jungle, and hunted the elephant in his native wilds. The German went to the encyclopædias, and read about the elephant and all mammalia, from mastodon to man. The Russian walked upon the starlit steppes, and evolved the concept of the elephant from his inner consciousness. The American trained the beast and put him in a circus. In all these ways, and more, critics have tracked the white elephant of art.

* Another version states that the Frenchman wrote on "The Elephant; His Lovelife."

LANGUAGE

The vaporous exultation not to be confined!
P. B. SHELLEY.

AMONG the contributions of psychanalysis to our knowledge of ourselves, not the least has been the revelation of
the truism hidden in the epigram that language exists to conceal thought. Analysis has proceeded until we congratulate
ourselves (perhaps too soon) upon having rediscovered what
we are talking about.

At a meeting of The Poetry Society of America I once
heard a man, commenting on hypostatization in a poem, rebuked for his display of "sophomoric wisdom"—yet the fault
is as common, and as fraught with danger, as tuberculosis.
The assumption of, the belief in, such entities as loyalty,
goodness, beauty, when there are only innumerable events
from which these qualities are abstracted, makes convenient
coin of common intercourse, but makes, as well, for much
of the confusion in criticism and ethics, much of the potency
in war.

Closely allied to this is the fallacy of projecting the effect as a quality of its cause: what one calls an "ill wind"
may have wafted another to safety.

Three degrees of qualities have been distinguished: those
inherent in the object, dependent mainly upon its chemical
constituency, such as wood, iron; those experienced by the
ordinary sense organs, on which there will be general agreement, as redness, warmth, smoothness, loudness; and those
that are more largely subjective, dependent upon the response of the individual, as awkwardness, gracefulness, the
majesty of an aged oak, the dreariness of a rainy day.

37

So forcefully has this distinction come upon some today, that they limit the function of criticism to marking out these types, and indicating the reasons why a work of art evokes certain subjective responses. This would, however, confine the critic to a description of the object and its effects, the technical part of his analysis; perhaps the truly critical part of his task is to consider the value of the experience when one opens oneself to a particular work of art. From the failure to recognize these two sides of the critical activity, from the confusion of the critical and the technical elements involved in analysis, have risen many artistic aberrations. The observation that good technique leads to, or accompanies, good results, develops a tendency to regard technical accomplishment as a sign of the excellence or even as the excellence itself. That the absence of a technical element may in itself be deemed a sign of bad work needs no emphasis to anyone who thinks of the dramatic unities; and the too frequent use of alliteration in the 1890's explains the tendency of this century's first decade to decry all poems using the device.

Words in themselves are even more deceptive, to those who fail to distinguish between their two uses. At times all can recognize that an especial significance is being attached to a term: when one speaks of "the thirteenth chair", it is likely that something other is intended than merely the seat beyond the twelfth; when one hears the phrase, "And what is more, you'll be a man, my son", anticipatory pride swells at a prospect brighter than mere entrance upon adult malehood. The word "bolshevik" no longer means a member of the major political party in Russia; it is used to evoke an instant image, a complete picture tinged with feeling, an emotional attitude. This emotive use of words contrasts sharply with their purely symbolic use, in which the word is a sign of a precise idea, denotes a specific something, so that information, not feeling, is primarily conveyed. Obviously, words are used symbolically, or should be, in scientific presentation; in all persuasion, and in art, the connotations that have accumulated are drawn into use, to establish a (perhaps unconscious) bias in the listener. When an alarmed person cries "What's the matter!" what he desires first is reassurance; after that his curiosity may have play. Most persons exclaiming at the beauty of the seashore or the sunset are merely making a vocal gesture of approval. So extensive is this use of language that Lascelles Abercrombie declares "words are not to be thought of as a simple means of describing objects or thoughts—they are a symbolical equivalent of imaginative experience. . . not applied to the image but identical with it." And I. A. Richards warns that "all terms used in the vain attempt (vain because the question is nonsensical) to say what things are, instead of to say how they behave, state nothing. Many apparent questions that begin with the words 'what' and 'why' are not questions at all but requests for emotive satisfaction." The range and the validity of the emotive use of words may fitly be discussed with the general problems of diction in art*; but it is important that the critic both in his reading and in his writing discriminate in the use of words between the logical symbol and the emotional summoning.

* See page 267f.; also pages 347 and 384.

1. Only images are identical with images. Words are symbolic equivalents both for the image and the reality. However, the idealists insist upon the identity of the image with the reality.

2. in the etymological sense of λόγος?

LOGIC

*One can prove anything one wants to; the real difficulty
lies in knowing what one wants to prove.*

ALAIN.

Bright reason will mock thee.

SHELLEY.

As THE chief instrument of advancing knowledge is commonly assumed to be reason, that in its extensions marks man from the beast, it is important as a basis for any consideration of theory to be sure our logic is sound. Recent thinkers, unfortunately, have made this a difficult task, by undermining the very foundations of thought.

They have, in the first place, smiling past the hypotheses that underlie most of our notions of reality, looked at the axioms, the unquestioned "self-evident truths" of the ages, and have found these pregnant with error, as justly free from challenge as the famous "self-evident truth" that the sun moves around the earth.

They have looked at induction, the method of reasoning that has led man from the dark ages to the centuries of scientific progress, of industrial and political and social revolution—and they have seen it is a sham. For induction, which builds up the general principles deduction may then apply, begins with the recognition of two similar things—and behind all association deduction lies implicit. To attempt to generalize from observed individual cases, furthermore, is to depend upon a syllogism: Whatever is true of a large number of similar cases is likely to be true of all. This is true of a large number of similar cases. Therefore. . . . If it be pointed out that this is a leap every child takes, the

40

proper retort flashes that such a leap is the basis of primitive magic, and that induction is then no more than a rationalization of baby's not taking a second lighted match. Behaviorism has a deal to say of such conditioning.*

Accepting this mixed procedure as induction, we have other observations to make. Obviously, one cannot examine all instances (and if one could, with every particular case considered, the general rule would be unnecessary); there is therefore the ever-present possibility that some unnoticed feature (such as the recent discovery of white dwarf stars, or of relativity, such as the recent conception of quanta) may upset one fine theory to set up another. In the great universe of particular things, moreover, how is an open-minded person to determine which items to investigate? Is our knowledge the result of a series of blind strikes? It seems that only those reach a goal through induction, who knew whither they were going when they set forth. "All the thinking in the world", said Goethe, "does not bring us to thought; we must be right by nature, so that good thoughts may come before us like free children of God, and cry 'Here we are!'"

Deduction, being dependent for its major premise, the general principle it is to apply, upon its sister method, is of course of no greater absolute validity than induction. Furthermore, save sketchily in reference and association, its syllogistic apparatus is rarely applied. Bertrand Russell, who has reasoned in many fields, declares that he knows but one instance of its use: when a German professor, reading a humorous issue of the philosophical journal *Mind,* and unable to understand the advertisements, argued: Everything in this issue is humorous. The advertisements are in this issue. Therefore. . . . While we may suspect Russell of humorous exaggeration, we must recognize that reason is no longer

* See also Note 15.

despot of man's way. Chesterton, indeed, maintains that the absolute unreason of the universe is the most certain proof of God.

Russell's example, indeed, plays on the surface of the matter. It is true that the major premise is seldom employed, save in limited instances such as "all the members of this club" or in theoretical abstractions such as those of logic and the Euclidian postulates, and that in these cases the general rule is needed merely for the sake of completeness, as in a schoolboy's exercise. When an argument is forward, however, the crux of it most often lies in the absence of one applicable rule: what seems "perfectly simple" to one is to the other darkly complex, dependent upon a causal chain that link by link must be recaptured. Sometimes the dispute centers, not upon the general rule, but upon the question as to whether the particular case falls under that rule. All gold is valuable—but is this lump of metal gold? Again, in truth, such clear-cut simplification is rare. If, for instance, the gold is in ore from which it cannot be readily extracted, it may be worthless. In social and æsthetic fields the possibilities of complication are manifestly endless. "The whole difficulty is to discover whether the rule is trustworthy as applied in the particular argument". This recognition reduces the statement from the status of a general rule to that of an affirmation about the case in hand, so that once more attention must be centered upon causal sequences and details.

The reasoning of early oratory traced its development step by step, each stage of the demonstration assuming the establishment of all before; it advanced from proof to proof. In this way, it drew attention to but a portion of an object or event at any moment, whereas not only æsthetic contemplation but sound science must consider the whole. Aristotle felt the inefficacy of such a procedure: "of all philosophers, Aristotle argues the least". On the other hand, this greatest of Greek thinkers led nineteen centuries astray by teaching men to classify instead of to measure. And of recent centuries, between the specialization of the experimental scientist and the "spatialization" of the theoretical scientist, out of the friction of error and opposed confusions, enough light has sparked to make it clear that the riddle of the universe has still eluded the philosophers, the physicists, and the mathematicians.

It is gradually being recognized, also, that every mode of examination of the universe (such as mathematics, metaphysics, poetry, engineering) involves the use of a different set of symbols, of what may be called a different language; that no one of these sets of symbols is more than merely one way of viewing a problem—the carpenter who makes a table, the boy who ultimately makes a bonfire of it, and the physicist who reduces it not to ashes but to electrons, all equally valid in their interpretation of the wood; and that most efforts to discuss the "real meaning", the "true nature", of anything, consist in an erection of one set of symbols as ultimate. A "real" seat is as much a solid substance that upholds me as it is a great void shot with millions of tiny thrusts of energy that prevent my falling through; it may be both of these, and such a bower as a poet may sing, and a figure that can be caught in an equation, and as many other things as there are ways of viewing it, perhaps including some that no man yet can tell . . . At length, however, man can say he knows not, but he knows that he knows not: the first rung toward knowledge has been climbed. [*]

cf. Socrates — "The wise man is he who knows he knows nothing."

APPROACHING A WORK OF ART

When your eyes have done their part,
Thought must length'n it in the heart.
SAMUEL DANIEL.

BEYOND verbal distortion and logical confusion, a more pervasive mental attitude may hinder appreciation of a work of art. There is a tendency today* to preach that there exists no such isolate thing as a work of art, but that any thing may be the object of æsthetic contemplation, when viewed as an end in itself. It has longer been observed that in the approach to those particular objects or events commonly known as works of art, there can be two main attitudes. If one goes with a group of college classmates to a revival, let us say, of *After Dark, or Neither Maid, Wife, nor Widow*, that prize specimen of our ink-pot melodrama, after having supped at the one restaurant east of Milwaukee at which the beer is warranted of pre-war brew, there is little doubt that the evening will be merry. The man who takes his sweetheart to the show, and the man who, disappointed at the last minute, goes alone—with a belly-ache to boot, may be expected to have different opinions of the play. A person desirous of achieving more relevant responses to the work of art, will more consciously control his emotional state, seeking to establish a prior condition of calm expectancy, so that the æsthetic object will invoke the appropriate mood, and develop in his mind its intrinsic pattern. In other words, the sentimental approach changes the object, the æsthetic approach changes the spectator. From one point of view, it might be mentioned, sadism is the obverse of

* See page 191f.

44

sentimentality, pleasure in cruelty the opposite that meets
pleasure in pity.

Other perversions of the proper attitude toward art have
of course been suggested. Leo Stein yields to a universal
tendency, dividing them into three. There is what he calls
the expectant interest, that desires a solution, a happy ending, or working through the artist strives to satisfy by the
conclusion, as one watches a fisherman in constant hope of
a catch. There is also the inventorial interest, whereby attention, too weak to hold the structural or rhythmic whole,
turns upon the details of a work, so that the name of an
artist comes to denote a color of the hair. There is finally
the sentimental interest (of which the former two seem
subdivisions), whereby the spectator is transformed into a
partaker. In still other figure, it may be said that the sentimental approach views life as though it were "literature",
and literature as though it were life. This must, of course,
be distinguished from the current tendency, as in Havelock
Ellis' *The Dance of Life,* to extend Pater's advocacy of living as a fine art; or, as among the younger æstheticians, to
suggest an identity of the æsthetic attitude and intelligence;
the sentimental approach, by permitting the personal mood
to override the intelligence, rather removes the work from
the field of art.

The distinction between the æsthetic attitude and the
sentimental is applied by Rebecca West to the authors themselves, who are perhaps of greater concern to the critic.
"Giving formal expression to a work of art", she avers, "is
to interpret one's experience to oneself, so that one merely
permits the audience to look over one's shoulder. But to
condition the expression of one's experience out of regard
for the effect on one's audience's mind"—is arrant sentimentality. "The sentimental artist is becoming nothing, he
has eyes, he has ears, he is being intelligent, he is playing

a game, he is moving certain objects according to certain rules in front of spectators." That this is hardly an inclusive description will be manifest to anyone who considers —what Rebecca West herself elsewhere points out—the earnest and sincere activity involved in putting together a "best-seller", wherein, be it *The Rosary, If Winter Comes, Main Street,* or what you will, sentimentality finds its kingdom. But as reader, and in author, the critic must recognize the indications, and the results, of the various approaches to a work of art.

What is regarded as sentimental may be a result of any or all of several predispositions. It may consist in too easy, too great, an emotional response to a situation, the quantity of emotional outlay being more than the work should summon—as when the stock responses are elicited by such hallowed ideas as motherhood and patriotic devotion. Recognition of this type of sentimentality, of course, depends upon knowledge of what sort and what depth of response is appropriate to a work; the perplexing element of sincerity must also come into account. Often accompanying violence of emotion, but occurring also with milder evocations, is a qualitative sentimentality, a vagueness or crudity of the emotion, a blurred affection or passion, without precise direction or intent. Either in receptor or in author, tendencies to these distortions may lurk, in addition to the other predispositions that may lead to inappropriate or irrelevant responses.

Personal grounds of interference with æsthetic judgment, for example, may lie deeper, or be more subtly hidden, than the appetites or immediate desires. During the ages of religious controversy, when opinions meant, possibly death, and surely salvation, there were few in the Protestant countries whose estimate of Dante's poetry does it what we deem justice; Johnson the Tory gives but grudging praise to Milton's *Paradise Lost*, and damns his *Lycidas* roundly. Rare is the tolerance that can opening cry

> Just for a handful of silver he left us,

yet retain true measure of the spirit's worth in the creation.* Still more unusual, it seems, is the maintenance of impartiality toward the preceding generation, or the one growing after; or is the unbiased survey of the work of an opposing literary school. To note the distortions effected by such blind pressure—and to hold himself (as much as may be) immune—is not the smallest, nor the easiest, part of the critic's task.

* Browning in "The Lost Leader"

CRITICISM AND CREATION

A great while ago the world begon,
With hey, ho, the winde and the raine.
WILLIAM SHAKESPEARE.

AN OPPOSITION is often erected between criticism and creation, by those who do not recognize that in its analytical aspect (as an activity) criticism is the complement and companion of creation, while in its synthetical aspect (as a product) it is a subdivision of creative writing itself. The critic is embodied in the creator, as M. Jourdain talked prose before he knew the term.* Actual critical writing, of course, could come only after other words, as Adam could appreciate happiness only after the fall. The writer of non-critical books records the impressions made upon him by a selected group of events in life; the critic does precisely this, limiting his selection to the events known as works of art.

In a survey of criticism, however, the interrelation of criticism, and creation in the narrower sense, may be observed. Do great critics, it may be asked, precede, accompany, follow, or appear irrespective of, great periods of creation? To what extent has criticism influenced the authors of any age? Does negative criticism help correct? Do positive suggestions inspire? These are questions on which a history may throw some light.

It may meanwhile be observed, before we are ready to characterize good criticism, that bad criticism is likely to disturb a reader more than bad creation. A poor book we can easily refrain from rereading, or—as one need not eat a whole egg to know it's rotten—put aside soon to forget.

* in Molière's "Le Bourgeois Gentilhomme" - slightly inept allusion

48

But a poor criticism is as a smudge on a favorite painting; it is resented less for its own lack of logic and beauty than for its effrontery in holding a treasure in awkward hands.[*] Yet to declare a book poor is itself a more presumptuous venture than to call an egg rotten; and a lesson in humility may be read in the history of literary criticism.

So much has been said of things to look for in criticism, that a final warning may be timely, against expecting anything in art. One is likely to be considerably disappointed if one seeks and does not find, and to reject what is, because it refuses to become the expected. If the critic find himself an impotent Procrustes, he harbors no guest: it may be worse if he succeed. The great outcry against Rodin was raised because spectators had come to expect of all sculpture a rhythmically rounded body. Brancusi carries them still a farther journey. Many writers of fiction today must struggle against the tendency to demand of all novels a definite plot. The reader attempts to interpret in the usual way a work with a different aim; he may, if he likes it, succeed in persuading himself that it is what he has wanted, and thus achieve misunderstanding; if not, he may attribute the resultant confusion to the author, and in his quest of what was never intended, fail to discover the new, positive achievement there may be. The likelihood of such disappointment is greatest with primitive, exotic, or unconventional modern works; the critic may endeavor to keep his mind open and plastic, by constantly turning, in a spirit of sympathetic inquiry, to a variety of unfamiliar forms.[*2] Here, too, his way will be clearer in the light of history.

[*] or, much worse, swaddling a pig in "incunabula".

[*2] Then a critic must have no preferences (even extra-professionally) but merely understandings.

CHAPTER II

THE GROWTH THROUGH THE GREEKS

Everything's been said; but, as nobody listens, we must always begin over again.

ANDRÉ GIDE.

THE MORAL BIAS

By a hammer, grooved of dolomite, he fell;
And I left my views of art, barbed and tangled, 'neath the
    heart
Of a mammothistic etcher at Grenelle. . . .
Then I stripped them, scalp from skull, and my hunting dogs
    fell full,
And their teeth I threaded neatly on a thong;
And I wiped my mouth and said "It is well that they are
    dead,
For I know my work is right and theirs was wrong."

RUDYARD KIPLING.

THE earliest recorded thinkers, Xenophanes of the sixth century B.C., Parmenides and Empedocles of the fifth, were busy with life itself, developing from magic and "rope-stretching", the constructive efforts of earlier peoples, the beginnings of physics and mathematics, and out of their racial needs producing the ethics that through the ages was to strive for supremacy with the Semitic code.* Literature, though a part of life, had as yet developed no disturbing features, nor indeed any great body of works, so that it was accepted with little more than casual mention. The many versions of the *Iliad* and the *Odyssey,* culminating in what we loosely call the work of Homer, show that the critical faculty was at work; but the poems themselves make few remarks that can be interpreted as criticism. Outstanding is the description of the shield beaten for Achilles by Hephæstus, adorned with scenes of war and peace, among them one of farmers in spring, "and behind the plough the earth went black, and looked like ploughed ground, though it was made of gold; that was a very marvel of the work." This flash of appreciation stands alone; though references

53

* cf. Arnold's definition of Hebraism and Hellenism:

to the "divine minstrels" who "from all men on earth get
their meed of honor and worship" show the esteem in which
the poet and reciter of tales was held.

The Homeric poems were soon subjected to criticism,
however, by the brilliant iconoclasts, the Voltaires and the
Paines, the Russells and the Shaws, of early Greece. Xenophanes had protested that Homer's gods were all too human. Rational explanation of the stories countered allegorical fancy; meanings were read into the lines; from
early race records, or such natural interpretations as that
Apollo's arrows represent the sun's rays, to the moral notion that Circe and Calypso embody temptations of the soul,
and the rhetorical flight that Penelope's weaving corre-
sponds to the steps of the syllogism.

Rhetoric, indeed, was the chief concern of the earliest
grammarians (stirps of the critic); for power hung on the
lips of the orator. The Sophists were accused of corrupting
the youth of the land, by leading them to talk fluently, to
"make the worse the better reason". But in the small city-
state, where the voice of the demagogue echoed in the ears
of all the citizens, the potency of oratory was soon comparable to that of the modern press. Criticism developed,
on the one hand, a concern with the technique of oratory
and, on the other, an engrossing interest in its subject. The
speech would win praise or condemnation according to the
political or moral code of its maker; it was definitely a part
of the life of the time—tense, heady life, as fervent as that
of the Plymouth colonists and more impetuously flashing;
and literature naturally was judged by the standards applied to living. The fact that the other great literary form
in ancient Greece, the drama, rose directly from the religion of the people, strengthened this attitude toward literature, and wove all its criticism on a moral bias.

+ but why disease?

ARISTOPHANES

Aurora had but newly chased the night.

JOHN DRYDEN.

THE early barbs of criticism led to the retaliation of early censorship. In *The Acharnians,* the courageous Aristophanes (c. 444–c. 380 B.C.) belabors Cleon the tyrant the more heavily for the latter's having taken offence at an earlier play; in 421 a restrictive law was passed, and in *The Knights,* though the attacks on Cleon continue, the satire—save when spoken by the chorus, the shreds of whose religious cloak still robed them in immunity—sets its victims in pseudonym.

In Aristophanes, whose exuberant yet pointed wit pierced every aspect of Athenian life, literature is not neglected. Indeed, Greek comedy was rich in parodies of the serious playwrights, whose works at the annual contests stirred excitement scarce equalled by the World's Series today. The general regard for them may be seen in the fact that Sophocles, in answer to his son's suit charging incompetence, did no more than recite the chorus in praise of Athens from his *Œdipus at Colonus.* Prominent citizens, heads ·of the army, representatives of the various Greek cities, were chosen as judges of these contests, to remove any suspicion of double dealing. They nonetheless receive their share of the comic writer's attention. The chorus of *The Birds* chants:

To the judges of the contest, we may mention in a word
The return we mean to make, if our performance is preferred.
First, then, in your empty coffers, you shall see the sterling Owl
From the mines of Laurium, familiar as a common fowl,

Roost among the bags and pouches, each at ease upon his nest,
Undisturbed hatching and rearing little broods of interest.
If you wish to cheat in office, but are inexpert and raw,
You shall have a Kite for agent, capable to gripe and claw;
Cranes and Cormorants shall help you to a stomach and a throat
When you feast abroad. . . . But if you give a vile, unfriendly
    vote,
Hasten and provide yourselves each with a little silver plate
Like the statue of a god for the protection of his pate,
Else, when forth you ramble on a summer holiday,
We shall take a dirty vengeance, and befoul your best array.

Other moments of travesty in Aristophanes are more literary in their aim, as when he attacks the current realism by setting a real sacrifice, in burlesque, on the stage, or mocks the messenger, through whose intervention all violent deeds were kept from the Greek audience, or makes the chorus a parody of itself—over-obsequious in *The Acharnians*, silly in *Lysistrata*, unmanageable in *Peace*. But his most direct and severe blows are reserved for his contemporary Euripides, who is shown hiring claques to wrest from Æschylus the seat of honor in Hades. The chorus of frogs, in a burlesque of Euripides' style, hails him approaching:

The full-mouthed master of the tragic choir,
We shall behold him foam with rage and ire,
Confronting in the list
His eager, shrewd, sharp-toothed antagonist.
Then will his visual orbs be wildly whirled
And huge invectives will be hurled.
Superb and supercilious,
Atrocious, atrabilious,
With furious gesture and with lips of foam,
And lion crest unconscious of the comb,
Erect with rage—his brow's impending gloom
O'ershadowing his dark eyes' terrific blaze.
The opponent, dexterous and wary,
Will fend and parry:

> While masses of conglomerated phrase,
> Enormous, ponderous, and pedantic,
> With indignation frantic,
> And strength and force gigantic,
> Are desperately sped
> At his devoted head. . . .
> Then in different style
> The touchstone and the file
> And subtleties of art
> In turn will play their part;
> Analysis, and rule,
> And every modern tool,
> With critic scratch and scribble,
> And nice, invidious nibble,
> Contending for the important choice:
> A vast expenditure of human voice.

The two dramatists advance and, burlesquing each the other, make sharp attack. Euripides objects to the obscurity and uncertain grammar of his earlier rival (as Dryden corrected the Elizabethans); to his opening silence; to his high-sounding phrases. Æschylus in turn reproaches Euripides with the monotony of his meter, his demeaning of the language (in its realistic approach to common speech), his domestic details, the tricks and trivialities of his dramas. For Aristophanes disliked not only the sentimentality and the scepticism of the last of the three great Greek tragedians; on more purely literary grounds he objected to his naturalistic style. In still another of the comedies, a character who must appear before the judges, and wishes to win their compassion, appeals for aid to Euripides, who refuses to come from his room. The scene-shifter wheels the room around, to reveal the dramatist composing. The defendant wheedles out of Euripides the beggar's cup from this play, the rags from that, the staff from—he mentions properties from half a dozen dramas before Euripides flies into a rage and drives him off: "Fellow, you'll plunder me a whole tragedy!" The contest in *The Frogs* ends when Bacchus, who has weighed in his scales the verses each playwright has offered, returns a verdict in favor of Æschylus.

Perhaps it is the dramatic form that forces Aristophanes' analysis into concrete attack and illustration; virtually all of Greek classical criticism moves in the realm of theory.

ANTITHESES OF GREEK THEORY

> "You're thinking about something, my dear, and that
> makes you forget to talk. I can't tell you what the moral
> of that is, but I shall remember it in a bit."
> "Perhaps it hasn't one," Alice ventured to remark.
> "Tut, tut, child!" said the Duchess. "Everything's got a
> moral, if only you can find it."
>
> LEWIS CARROLL.

FROM three points of view, opposing attitudes arose in
early Greek criticism, which have determined the lines of
conflicting opinion through the centuries. For the Greeks,
though they no more than we could read the riddle of the
universe, seem at least to have known what questions to
ask. "What is truth?" asked the judicial Roman; "What is
art?" inquired the Russian mystic; such imponderable   *Tolstoi*
wholes—too large to be cupped in an answer—did not content the Greeks, who dissected them into segments of appreciable size—not hesitating to dismember their gods in
the process—that they might be studied with some hope of
ensuing knowledge. Aristotle, it is true, looked the wrong
way; but it may be urged that classification is sound preliminary to measurement—from which minds were lengthily
turned by the Roman formulation.

From the metaphysical aspect, the antithetical views of
art showed it as symbolism, or as imitation. The early quest
of allegory in Homer, however, was checked by the em-
phasis of Solon, who inaugurated the regular readings of the   *ῥαψῳδοί ?*
Iliad and the *Odyssey,* but who was so extreme an adherent
of the theory of imitation as to forbid the drama, as a harmful lie. Socrates, accepting this theory, questions whether
the invisible—mental states, emotions—can be imitated, and

59

suggests that the facial expression may serve to represent them. He moves, indeed, a step beyond, advancing the idea that natural elements of beauty may be combined in new forms. The Pythagoreans set forward the theory that number is the original of which things themselves are imitations. In consequence of this—beyond the inevitable emphasis on abstract analysis—art seems twice removed from reality. The theory was pursued to its extreme in the assertion that certain rhythms of poetry are imitations of types of life or temper; its chief æsthetic development is in the work of Plato. The hold this concept had upon the Greeks is illustrated by the well-known story of the Athenian artist who, praised because his representation of a boy with grapes was so lifelike birds came to peck at the fruit, replied that if the work had been good the boy would have kept them away.[6]

From the moralistic point of view, some see art as having a purely "æsthetic", others, a practical, interest. Many recent thinkers accept Kant's view that "beauty is the character of adaptation to a purpose without relation to an actual purpose". To Socrates, as to most Greeks, beauty exists only relative to a purpose. We have already seen that the part played by Greek literature (drama and oratory) in Greek life brought it inevitably to serve a moral end— or at least, to meet a moral standard; yet it should be observed that to many books of recent times, books "with a purpose", as *Uncle Tom's Cabin,* the novels of Dickens, the dramas of Galsworthy, it is also considered in their day that an ethical test applies. Plato, however bound by the moralistic approach, recognizes that some art exists to give pleasure. This, he condemns.

To what does the wondrous muse of tragedy devote herself? Is all her aim and desire only to give pleasure to the spectators, or does she fight against and refuse to speak of their pleasant vices,

and willingly proclaim in word and song truths both welcome and
unwelcome? There can be no doubt that tragedy has her face
turned toward pleasure and gratification.

It is the value of the experience that Plato emphasizes; his
complaint is that art "in attending upon pleasure never regards either the nature or the reason of the pleasure to
which she devotes herself". Yet both Plato and his disciple
Aristotle recognize a purer beauty, free from the intermit-
tent uneasiness of desire. The one: "I do not mean by the
beauty of form such beauty as that of animals or pictures,
which the many would suppose to be my meaning; but understand me to mean straight lines and curves, and the
plane and solid figures that are formed from them by turn-
ing-lathes and rulers and measurers of angles; for these I
affirm to be not only relatively beautiful, like other things,
but they are eternally and absolutely beautiful." The other:
"The main elements of beauty are order, symmetry, and
definite limitation, and these are the chief properties the
mathematical sciences draw attention to." *

The Greek emphasis on morals may seem less absurd,
or less extreme, as drawn back from these abstractions and
applied to their living, when we consider that to them morality meant less a conforming goodness, a refraining from the
commission of certain specified acts, than a high-minded-
ness, a thoroughness of purpose and a fortitude of will.
"Virtue is knowledge", Socrates declared; this set no easy
standard for Greek life—one that, had the centuries maintained it, might well have served for literature as well.

From the æsthetic standpoint, the duality in criticism *Must there be
consists in abstract classification, and concrete analysis. *a duality?*
While the Greek could pierce his opponent with a personal
dart, keenly directed, his predilection was largely for philosophical consideration, for the elaboration of theory. The
extent to which his speculations were made the basis of his

* cf. "Euclid alone has looked on beauty bare." by E. Millay
2. for concrete analysis of problem of desire in beauty as embodied in a typical instance of "Death in Venice" by T. Mann.

critical notions is shown by the influence of the Pythagoreans upon Plato. Indeed, the theorem of Pythagoras, leading to the golden section (which was known to Theodorus, who taught mathematics to Plato) points directly to "dynamic symmetry", studied in recent years as the basis of Greek plastic art.[7]

Through the centuries, the golden mean, in physical as well as figurative connotation, has been the center of mystic communing. The line which represents its proportions was called, in the middle ages, the divine section. It is represented in a mathematical series formed by adding two adjacent terms to make the next (0.1.1.2.3.5.8.13.21.34. 55...n) wherein with increasing exactness the lesser of any two adjacent numbers is to the greater as the greater is to the sum. Curiously, this proportion, which Euclid gives two methods of obtaining, is found in the whorl of sunflower seeds, in the spiral growth of shells, and elsewhere in nature, and in figures early employed by the surveyors of Egypt, of whom the Greeks were students. Merely as a number, the golden mean exhibits interesting characteristics. The ratio of one number to the next, in the series, is 1.618.. The ratio of alternate numbers is 2.618... This is, obviously, 1.618 plus 1; but it is also 1.618 squared. The ratio of every fourth member is 4.236, which is 1.618 cubed, which is 2.618 plus 1.618, which is 1.618 multiplied by 2, plus 1. These interrelations continue to infinity; but more relevant is the rectangle whose sides represent this ratio (1: 1.618). For if the diagonal of this figure be crossed by its perpendicular, a square is marked off; and continuing the process gives a series of "whirling squares".

Let us approach this figure by another path. On the diagonal of a square whose sides are unity, construct a rectangle whose altitude is unity. The base of this rectangle will be $\sqrt{2}$. Repeat this process, with the diagonal of the

new figure as base; continue; and the successive rectangles
will have as bases $\sqrt{3}$, 2, $\sqrt{5}$, etc. But the square root of
5 is 2.236.., which is the sum of 1.618.. and .618..—
which latter is the reciprocal of the whirling square proportion and therefore gives a similar figure; so that the root 5
rectangle consists of two rectangles of the whirling square.
It is the contention of those who have developed these relationships (which will be much.clearer if the reader but take
pencil and draw the figures) that proportions based on the
whole number, i.e. on the line, are static as compared to
those which rest upon the irrational number, that takes on
meaning with the area, and gives a "dynamic" symmetry to
the forms so developed; and that Greek art, growing out
of these figures from surveying and building, is mainly
dynamic. Vitruvius, a Roman commentator of the first century B.C., states that the Greeks based the symmetry they
were careful to apply to their works of art, upon the proportion between the members of the human body and the
structure of the whole. Assuming that this meant commen-
suration of line, not area or volume, the Roman and the
medieval artists developed a static art. However successfully this "grammar of the art" may be applied to
Greek architecture and the fine arts, it has influenced the
technique of modern commercial design, and is an element
in the work of many a contemporary artist. If it underlies,
as it seems to underlie, much of Greek art, it is another
instance of the practical application the Greek artists made,
from which the critics build their theories.

PLATO AND IMITATION

Love, that moves the sun and the other stars.
DANTE.

THE consequences of the theory of art as imitation involved Plato (c. 428–347 B.C.) in a curious dilemma. Greatly as he delighted in the works of the poets, he found himself logically compelled to ban them from his ideal republic. For art, being philosophically an imitation of nature, and not of any ultimate reality or essence of things, but of the secondary reality of sense perception, is inevitably inferior to nature and, while occasionally serviceable for purposes of instruction, is largely useless and often, because of its baneful mythology, morally bad. Then it becomes psychologically harmful; for imagination not only hinders "reminiscence" and approach to the ultimate reality, but it plays strongly upon the emotions, and is therefore a seduction for weak, and a weapon for unscrupulous minds.[8] But if the artists are "those who are gifted to discern the true nature of the beautiful and the graceful, then will our youth dwell in a land of health, amid fair sights and sounds, and receive the good in everything; and beauty, effluent from fair works, will flow into the eye and ear, like a health-bringing breeze from a purer zone, and insensibly draw the soul from earliest years into likeness and sympathy with the beauty of reason."

Since the image, even outside of this ideal realization, has the same type of effect as the object, and the work of art because of its emotional appeal may move more strongly than the real event, it must be judged by the standards

64

applicable in living—and Plato's logic has twisted the knife of moral judgment more deeply into the vitals of art.

The triumph of the theory of imitation in the metaphysical field thus plays upon the moralistic; it reaches over into the æsthetic as well. For as the central problem of Greek philosophy is the synthesis of the one and the many, it follows that beauty, imitating reality, is, to the Greek, the imaginative or sensuous expression of unity in variety.

Every discourse ought to be constructed like a picture of a living organism, having its own body and head and feet; it must have a middle and extremities, drawn in a manner agreeable to one another and to the whole.

ARISTOTLE

Hay, now the day dawis.

ALEXANDER MONTGOMERIE.

THE development of criticism before Aristotle may be summarized in the story of the growth of the drama, which he traced. By the time of Hesiod, in the eighth century B.C., early contests were held; one may assume that the voting audience, and later the chosen judges, were the first official critics. Not long after the closing of the theatres, about 560 B.C., by Solon, Pisistratus established the annual dramatic contests, in which three or five playwrights, chosen by the archon of Athens, each on a day presented three tragedies and a farce, of which he was author, composer, director, and (at first) leading player. That the critical spirit was active there are many signs. Over twenty revisions of plays survive: *The Persians* and *Agamemnon* of Æschylus; Sophocles' *Antigone;* the *Medea, Alcmeon, Hippolytus,* of Euripides. Many themes are employed time and again; the three great tragedians are among the eleven who told the story of Œdipus; there are nine serious versions, and five comic parodies, of Medea's tale. After the author's death, there were new acting versions of his pieces—though few plays save of the great three·were revived; until Lycurgus (390–325) had authoritative versions of their works set down, and statues set up in their memory.

By the time of Aristotle (384–322 B.C.) therefore, the greatest works had already been written and universally recognized; and the material for a body of critical theory was at hand, and partly formulated. In fact, Aristotle annotated a collection of the treatises of his predecessors, to

66

which Cicero refers. Aristotle accepted the theory of imitation, though he was inclined to exempt statues, as rather
indicating feelings through external symbols than directly
imitating them. He asserted that poetry, however, is more
scientific and serious than history, in that, being general
rather than individual, its imitation comes closer to the
essence of reality. One further step he took, in declaring
that an imitation is often agreeable, even though the object
imitated is disagreeable—the pleasure, he said, arising
from recognition of the object. (This pleasure, since
photography has supplied it, painting at least seems inclined
to let us forego.) Moreover, as nature moves ever toward
improvement, the artist in his mimic world carries forward
this progress, and art is "the idealizing imitation of reality".

In the consideration of morals in art, also, Aristotle advanced beyond his predecessors. "The good and the beautiful are different", he declares, "for the former is always
a property of action, while the latter extends to objects free
from motion". On the other hand, "the beautiful is that
good which is pleasant because it is good". The noting of
pleasure in the expression even of disagreeable objects is a
growth beyond the moral attitude. Yet, while he can win to
a recognition of a beauty apart from goodness, as in his
discussion of mathematics, and can sharply distinguish between sexual and æsthetic choice, Aristotle is involved in
the Greek moral concern. Plato objects to the arts because
by habit and contagion they intensify the spectator's emotions; Aristotle on the contrary approves of them because,
like revival meetings, they leave the spectator emotionally
exhausted, tranquil: "producing by the stimulation of pity
and terror the purgation of these emotions." (This clause of
the definition of tragedy, which has been a stumbling block
for many barked critical shins, seems to imply what we

have called the sentimental approach to a work of art—
recall that the Greeks judged art as part of life.

> If music be the food of love, play on;
> Give me excess of it, that surfeiting,
> The appetite may sicken, and so die.

Duke Orsino desires an emotional debauch. When the music
no longer stirs him, he stops it. The satisfaction he seeks is
in the emotion, not in the music, which merely assists in
the establishment and play of the personal mood. The object
is dissolved in the emotion, instead of the emotion's being
created by and absorbed in the object. The distinction
hinges upon whether one goes to the work for the sake
of the emotional indulgence—as women go to weep at the
cinema, or whether one is roused to emotion because of
one's interest in the work of art. At any rate, according to
the Aristotelian theory of catharsis, the spectator indulges
his emotions without the restraints or consequences of actual
life, and finds pleasure in the indulgence.)*

Though he gives concrete illustrations of his critical
points, the tendency to generalization and to dogma that
crystallized in the centuries after him is clear in Aristotle's
theory. His most famous utterance in the field of literary
criticism is his definition of tragedy. "Tragedy is an imitation of an action noble, complete in itself, and of appreciable magnitude, in language sweetened with each kind of
sweetening in the several parts, conveyed by action and not
recital, and producing by the stimulation of pity and terror
the purgation of these emotions." The many difficulties inherent in this definition may be discussed when tragedy is
considered; the mere fact of its framing is a critical advance. It should be here noted, however, that of the "dramatic unities" Aristotle emphasizes only that of action, casually
alluding to the unity of time (made generally advisable be-

* See page 44f. and, especially, page 326f.

cause of the presence of the chorus), and not so much as mentioning unity of place. In the analysis of his definition, he declares that action is of prime importance, as opposed to character; though here, too, reservations must later be made.

Aristotle makes many observations, both in the *Poetics* and in the *Rhetoric,* that have given impetus to controversies, or have set the tone of subsequent criticism. Meter alone, he observes, instancing Empedocles, does not make the poet. Of diction, the unfamiliar is elevated, the current is clear; yet one should not seek the far-fetched, the obsolete, the excessive. The style should be clear, and "lowered or raised according to the subject", with perspicuity and propriety; prose style should not have meter, not lack rhythm.

The most literary style is the epideitic, which is in fact meant to be read; next to it comes the forensic. It is idle to make the further distinction that style must be attractive or elevated. Why should these qualities be attributed to it rather than self-control, or nobility, or any other moral excellence? The qualities already mentioned will manifestly make it attractive, unless our very definition of good style is at fault. This is the sole reason why it should be clear and not mean, but appropriate. It fails in clearness both when it is prolix and when it is condensed. The middle course is clearly the fittest. Then attractiveness will result from the qualities already mentioned,—a suitable combination of the familiar and the unusual, rhythm, and the persuasiveness that is the outcome of propriety.

Of truth in literature Aristotle strikes well-bottom with the paradox that it is better to use probable impossibilities than improbable possibilities—one word on consistence in art that marks our best-sellers from our best books.*

In his consideration of the Homeric problems Aristotle becomes as pedantic as his predecessors. Some of the

* See page 358f.

queries he seeks to answer are: Why did Odysseus take off his coat? Why is Menelaus represented as having no female companion? Why is Pampetie represented as carrying to the Sun the news of the slaughter of his oxen, when the Sun knows everything? If the gods drank nothing but nectar, why is Calypso spoken of as "mixing" for Hermes?

That most of Greek and Latin criticism is either metaphysical, or devoted to triviality and carping detail, is attributed by some to paucity of vocabulary. E. E. Kellett, for example, states:

> The fact is that the critical faculty was then far ahead of the vocabulary which could express it; and the Greeks, struggling to put into words their obscure feelings and lacking the polyglot phraseology which comes so easily to critics in our age, appear to us less wide-minded and deep-thoughted than they really were . . . The Greeks, deprived of this verbal assistance to thought, were often compulsorily dumb on what they really felt, and vocal on points which, though comparatively unimportant, lent themselves easily to verbal expression.

If, however, the Greeks "really felt", if they had anything more than the haziest drifts of dim feeling, on such matters as the imagination, as the poignancy of this writer, the vision, the sublimity, of that—even in the mind such conceptions would be verbal, thought and word twin-born; not only do occasional critical remarks reveal, but Greek philosophical writing plainly shows, that what interested these thinkers, they could express.* It seems more natural to conclude—as other facts also indicate—that the Greek interest in literature (which the Romans sucked, with all else literary, from the Greek) was not primarily æsthetic. Metaphysics and ethics long overlaid art.

While Aristotle was the leader of the peripatetic school of philosophers, and the teacher of Alexander the Great, few comments give indication of any influence he exerted upon other ancient writers in the fields of rhetoric and æsthetics.

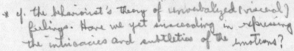

*cf. the behaviourist's theory of unverbalized (visceral) feelings. Have we yet succeeding in expressing the intricacies and subtleties of the emotions?

Horace does not mention him; no reference to him lies in
Quintilian; Cicero adduces him, among others, to prove that
dreams come true. All the middle ages, cherishing Horace,
overlook the Stagirite, so that he looms (like America) as a
discovery of the Renaissance.

Yet Aristotle made valid contribution in the growing
æsthetic concern and fruitful thought. He recognized that
pleasure is an end of art, that art deals not with the actual
but with the possible, and that beauty has not only a
separate, but a valid, existence. Still he is limited, as were
all of his time, in several fundamental ways. He lacked the
opportunity for comparison of the Greek with other literatures. He assumed that the literature he knew had attained
its ultimate growth; conceiving no other forms, (as, for
instance, the novel), he based his theories on oratory
(though ignoring his contemporary Demosthenes) and on
tragedy. Yet many of his observations seem sound today,
if we return to the mellower Greek, from the rigid rules
derived from him (often by misinterpretation) in the
twenty centuries that followed.

THE ROMAN FORMULATION

Clear thoughts are the most dangerous, for one dares not
change them—and that's an anticipation of death.

ANDRÉ GIDE.

WITH the collapse of their city-states, the high concerns
of the Greeks with morality and the social will lapsed to
more individual interests; instead of developing their philosophy and literature, they were called upon to teach these
to the other nations. Bleak tragedy was no longer concordant to their souls, and its reciprocal comedy dwindled to
the "new" social studies of Menander. The rhetoricians
began to formulate and classify; styles were distinguished
in a phrase—copious, medium, neat—so that each writer
might be labeled for the convenience of schoolboys; and
the practice of linking an epithet with a name, which Homer
had used of his men and gods—"the rosy-fingered dawn",
"the steadfast goodly Odysseus"—was extended to authors,
so that pupils might learn their qualities by rote. Manuals
of rhetoric became as popular in Alexandria, then in Rome,
as, recently, texts on the writing of short-stories or
scenarios.

Consequent upon the loss of civic consciousness and devoted loyalty, with the more personal centering, came an
era of realistic prose. The Stoics, with their "feeling of
reasonableness", even the Epicureans, who taught the
"reasonableness of feeling", increasingly scorned style. The
cynic Sextus Empiricus denied the value of grammar, by
declaring that poetry is good but as it conveys philosophy;
hence, useful poetry is clear, unfamiliar or epigrammatic
poetry is useless; in either case, grammar is unnecessary.

In condonement of his attack, it should be mentioned that at this time the technical terms of grammar, of the cases, the verb forms, were being developed.

Dionysius of Halicarnassus (died 7 B.C.), a teacher of Greek in Rome, may be termed the first professional critic. His occupation kept him from metaphysical abstractions, and centered his eye upon the work. To his frequent illustrations, indeed, we owe many treasures of Greek literature nowhere else preserved. While attacking the overadorned prose, the "senseless eloquence", of his time, Dionysius was sensitive to beauty in diction, and first stresses the value of variety as an element in style. In him we find an early insistence on *mimesis*, imitation, not of nature, but of the classical models.

From their Greek tutors the Romans were eager to learn. While they had the advantage of the opportunity of comparison of the two tongues and the two literatures, they availed themselves little of it, through their feeling that, save perhaps in oratory, the Greeks were their masters. Latin accentual poetry died under the press of Greek quantity; Latin drama was drawn directly from the Greek. By the first century B.C., the conquering nation had succumbed to the ideas of the conquered; the Greek view of beauty as the relation of the parts to the whole was commonplace. Cicero distinguished between masculine and feminine beauty—dignity and grace. The tendency to classify was developed in Horace, (65–8 B.C.) whose *Epistle to the Pisos*, known as the *Ars Poetica*, formulates into rules what Aristotle had observed as practices, and rivals the *Poetics* as the basis of critical thought for the next sixteen hundred years.

Probably written to dissuade a friend's son from turning versifier, the critical work of Horace, though perhaps based on a Greek treatise of Neoptolemus of Parium, and a

cf. A. Symonds "Blank Verse" for contention that all Latin popular poetry (vs. 'court' poetry) was accentual.

somewhat unmethodical miscellany—as Coleridge called it, is marked by a "singular felicity" of phrase, a mellowness of touch, and a gentleness in presenting its ripe wisdom, that have endeared the poet to the generations, and have helped to set him beside the more dispassionate, if more original, Aristotle.

"Let the Greek patterns be never out of your hands by night or day", he first advises. While insisting on the value of simplicity and unity—consistency, order, and proportion (which rhetoricians today call unity, coherence, and emphasis)—he warns against the deliberate quest of these, or of any, points of style:

Too many of us poets are deceived by a fallacious appearance of correctness: when we try to become terse we become obscure; the quest of smoothness leads to the failure of nerve and spirit; a man aims at grandeur and becomes turgid—if he plays too much for safety, and fears a storm, he grovels. In seeking to do a conjuring feat of variation on a single theme, there is danger of exhibiting a dolphin in the woods, in the floods a wild boar. The very desire to avoid faults produces fault, if art be lacking. Choose, O ye men of letters, a subject suited to your strength, and meditate long what your shoulders can bear, and what they cannot.

Horace had the gift of writing quotable phrases, maxims dear to those who find the observation of individual differences more tedious than the presenting of a general rule. Austin Dobson well challenges later times:

> Where can you show, among your names of note,
> So much to copy, and so much to quote?

The famous phrase of the "purple patch" is from his pages; many a drudge has found consolation in his advocacy of "the labor of the file". He mocks the man who mourns the good old days. His remark: "It is difficult to give proper expression to common things", keen observation as it is,

* cf. Irving's "Art is the representation of the obvious."

becomes the justification of later scorn of the "common". The comment on usage, "with which rests the arbitrament and right and law of speaking", is relied upon by the ages that glorify the conventional. The eighteenth century found itself forelightened in the phrase; "Of writing well right thinking is the beginning and the fount." And the artists of a century later attempted to realize the dictum that "as painting is, so is poetry". All ages are told not to reject a valid whole for a few blemishes in the parts; even "the good Homer nods". And all poets are counselled to keep their work unpublished, to let it lie enwombed, nine years; for "a voice let loose comes not back again." While he does not neglect the substance of the work, the emphasis of Horace is upon the perfection of technique.

The writers of the next century, Roman and Greek, were concerned with prose creation. Persius' satires show he might, today, have made a lively reviewer. Martial's epigrams frequently sting, and all scholars will rejoice in his disdainful query: "Shall I write hexameters of wars, that pedants may spout me, and good boys and fair girls loathe my name!" The Greek Plutarch, who employed in his "Lives" a method—of writing each essay on two men he might compare—that was later used in literary criticism, specifically avoided such criticism himself, in his study of Demosthenes and Cicero pleading ignorance of Latin. He did, however, take two steps beyond Aristotelian theory. Beauty and beautiful imitation, he declared, are distinct. We admire the imitation of the ugly not (as Aristotle felt) because of the pleasure of recognition, but because of an intelligent appreciation of the artist's cunning. We may, furthermore, admire in art not only what we think ugly, but what we deem morally bad, in life. Save for this contribution to theory, however, there is no elaboration of critical thought until Quintilian's *Institutes of Oratory*.

Quintilian (35?–96? A.D.) had the most advantageous position of all the ancient critics. Roman by birth, but well trained in Greek, he surveyed the two literatures after their great works had been written, yet before the barbarisms of the break-down had corrupted the tongues and destroyed appreciation. Recognizing the superior subtlety and grace of the Greek, he saw the compensating strength and variety of the Latin. He distinguished the succinct, vigorous, Attic style (founded by Empedocles, 5th Century B.C.) stripped of all superfluous, from the inflated, empty "Asiatic", (introduced by Hegesias, c. 300) lacking judgment and measure, and the balanced "Rhodian", (founded by Æschines, 330, when Demosthenes had defeated him in a contest) neither prolix nor terse: "the crystal fountains, turbid torrents, calmly flowing pools". He gave order to the critical terminology of the time. Submitting the rules, especially of prose, to intelligent question, he sought the devices most effective in convincing the reason, in persuading the emotions; the clarity and order of the design, and its success in concealing the artifice. *Ars est celare artem.* Insisting on clarity to the degree that it shall be impossible to misunderstand, Quintilian yet declares that correctness and clearness are mere preliminaries to good style; if the writer employ no artistic embellishment, he is but free from faults rather than perfective of style. Against the romantics of his day who were fighting the classical decline and increasing fixity by advocating spontaneous expression, he insisted: "That is most natural which nature permits to be done in the best possible way. How can anything be firmer when it is in disorder than when it is bound fast together and well arranged? As the flow of rivers is stronger in a sloping bed, which interposes no obstacle, than when the waters are broken by, and struggle with, rocky impediments, so is style that is connected and flows with full force better than that which is broken and interrupted. Why then should men think that vigor is impaired by beauty, when nothing is ever at its full power without art, and beauty is art's companion?" Yet his qualification, "true beauty is never divorced from utility", marks the hold of the moral attitude on Quintilian. *

*. It also marks the more utilitarian spirit of Roman thought than of the Greek.

AND LONGINUS

And yet he had a thomb of gold parde.

GEOFFREY CHAUCER.

A TRANSITION between declining Athens and rising Alexandria, we are told, is afforded by Demetrius Phalereus, who marks the movement from Attic philosophy and oratory to the Asian philology and grammar. Unfortunately, this Demetrius, who governed Athens from 317 to 307 B.C. and was invited by Ptolemy Soter to help form the great Alexandrian library, is not the author of the famous treatise *On Style* long attributed to him, but now convincingly shown to be of the first century before or after Christ.

Save for a possible dependence on the lost treatise of Theophrastus, the Demetrius who wrote *On Style* has given us the clearest and most original ancient handling of prose composition. He recognizes four degrees of style; of each of these he discusses the attainment through subject matter, composition, and diction; yet he considers the theme of least moment, for poor treatment will destroy the intrinsic charm of a subject, and good treatment will lend distinction to however forbidding a theme. The first style is the *elevated*: this is attained through the use of rounded periods; words of striking, even harsh combinations of sound; and frequent figures; its corresponding vice is frigidity. Thucydides is an exponent of the elevated style, which is akin to the sublime of Longinus, whose chief bogie is also the bombastic and the frigid. The *elegant* style, which Sappho and Xenophon exemplify, is marked by charm and gaiety of expression, by graces of diction and figure, smooth words, maxims; its exaggeration is the ridicu-

lous, the affected. The *plain* style, as in Lysias, is vivid and
clear, employing the language of daily life, direct and persuasive; yet ever in danger of aridity. Finally, the *forceful*
style by brevity, mordant wit, striking figures, and swift
rhythms achieves its potency; at the risk of lacking grace
and growing boorish. Most successful in the forceful style
is Demosthenes.

Demetrius looked with interest on other fields, as his passing comments on the actor's art attest; within the province
of style he was both subtle and keen. He knew the value of
omission:

All possible points should not be punctiliously and tediously
elaborated, but some should be left to the comprehension and in-
ference of the hearer, who when he perceives what you have
omitted becomes not only your hearer but your witness, and a
very friendly witness too. For he thinks himself intelligent because you have afforded him the means of showing his intelligence.
It seems a slur on your hearer to tell him everything as though
he were a simpleton.

Fine points of style do not escape him, as in his praise of
Homer's sentence:

"Nireus brought three ships, Nireus Aglæa's son, Nireus the
goodliest of men." Thus, though Nireus is hardly once mentioned
in the action, we remember him no less than Achilles and Odysseus,
who are spoken of in almost every line. The influence of the
figure is the cause. If Homer had said simply "Nireus the son of
Aglæa brought three ships from Syme", this would have been
tantamount to passing over Nireus in silence. It is with writing as
with banquets, where a few dishes may be arranged so as to seem
many.

Frequently indeed is this subtlety of Demetrius' analytical
powers instanced in his consideration of specific passages
and points:

The charge of garrulity often brought against Ctesias on the
ground of his repetition can perhaps in many passages be estab-

lished, but in many instances it is his critics who fail to appreciate the writer's vividness. The same word is repeated because this often makes a greater impression.

Here is an example: "Stryangaeus, a Mede, having unhorsed a Sacian woman (for the women of the Sacae join in battle like Amazons), was struck with the youth and beauty of the Sacian and allowed her to escape. Afterwards, when peace was declared, he became enamoured of her, and failed in his suit. He resolved to starve himself to death. But first he wrote a letter upbraiding the woman thus: 'I saved you, ay you were saved through me; and now I have perished through you'."

Here a critic who prided himself on his brevity might say that there is a useless repetition in 'I saved you' and 'you were saved through me', the two statements conveying the same idea. But if you take away one of the two, you will also take away the vividness and the emotional effect of vividness. Furthermore, the expression that follows ('I have perished' in place of 'I perish') is more vivid just because the past tense is used. There is something more impressive in the suggestion that all is over, than in the intimation that it is about to happen or is still happening.

Neatly (in anticipation) Demetrius punctures today's definition of a sentence:

The conveyance of two ideas in a sentence often gives a graceful effect. A writer once said of a sleeping Amazon: "Her bow lay strung, her quiver full, her buckler by her head; their girdles they never loose." At one and the same time the custom in regard to the girdle and its observance in the present case are indicated—the two facts by means of the one expression. And from this conciseness a certain elegance results.

Perhaps we should not pass from Demetrius without speaking of his sense of humor, which at times twinkles quietly in the best English tradition. Discussing metaphors, he instances:

It can correctly be said that a general pilots the state, and conversely that a pilot commands the ship. Not all metaphors can, however, be used convertibly like these. Homer could call the lower slope of Ida its foot, but he could never have called a man's foot his slope.

Some day a dissertation will be written to prove that Demetrius, like Shakespeare, was Irish!

Before the evening star that ushered in the Dark Ages, a few twilight gleams deserve notice. In the *Noctes Atticae* (c. 150 A.D.) Gellius presents an example at once of comparative criticism and of consideration of the concrete passage, unmatched in classical times:

I remember that the philosopher Favorinus, when in the heat of the year he had retired to his host's villa at Antium, and we had come from Rome to see him, discussed Pindar and Vergil somewhat in this way: "Vergil's friends and associates", said he, "in their memorials of his genius and character, say that he was wont to observe that he produced verse after the manner and fashion of a she-bear. For, as this beast produces its cub unformed and unfinished, and afterwards licks the product into shape and figure; so the results of his wits were at first rough-hewn and uncompleted, but afterwards, by rehandling and fashioning them, he gave them lineaments and countenance. Now", said he, "the facts prove that this quick-witted poet spoke with as much truth as frankness. For those things which he left polished and perfected—those on which he put the last touch of his censorship and his choice—rejoice in the full praise of poetical loveliness; but those of which he postponed the rescension, and which could not be finished owing to the interposition of death, are by no means worthy of the name and judgment of this most elegant of poets. And so, when he was in the grasp of sickness, and felt the approach of death, he earnestly begged and prayed of his dearest friends that they should burn the *Æneid*, to which he had not yet sufficiently put the file.

"Now among those passages that seem to have been most in need of rehandling and correction, that on Mount Etna holds the chief place. For, while he wished to vie with the verse of the old poet Pindar on the nature and eruptions of the mountain, he wrought such conceits and such phrases that in this place he has out-Pindared Pindar himself, who is generally thought to indulge in too exuberant and luxuriant rhetoric. To put you yourselves in the position of judges, I shall repeat, to the best of my memory, Pindar's verse on Etna . . . Now listen to Vergil's verses, which I should call begun rather than made." (Favorinus here recited

Pindar, *Pyth.* i 40-5; and Vergil, *Æn.* iii 570-584). "Now in the first place," said he, "Pindar, paying more attention to truth, says what is the fact—what actually happens there and what is seen by eyes—that Etna smokes by day and flames by night; but Vergil, while he laboriously seeks out noisy sounding words, confuses the seasons without any distinction. And the Greek said clearly enough that fountains of fire belched from the bottom, and rivers of smoke flowed, and twisted yellow volumes of flame rolled to the shore of the sea, like fiery snakes. But this good man of ours, by choosing to translate 'a burning stream of smoke' as 'a black cloud smoking with pitchy gusts and glowing ashes', has heaped things together coarsely and without moderation, and has harshly and inaccurately transposed what the other called fountains into globes of flame. Again, when he says it 'licks the stars', he has made an empty and idle exaggeration." [Note the criterion, imitation.] "Moreover, what he says about the black cloud, etc., is indescribable, and almost incomprehensible. For things that glow are not usually black or smoking—unless he has very vulgarly and improperly used the word *candente* of ash merely hot, not fiery and shining. For *candens* is said of the brightness, not the heat. But as for the stones and the rocks being belched and flung up, and the very same ones anon being liquefied, and groaning, and being conglomerated in air—all this was neither written by Pindar nor ever heard in speech, and it is the most monstrous of all monstrosities."

In Greek, the general observation still prevailed. Lucian, who wrote much personal satire, including a half-humorous analysis of his own work, flared into a diatribe against conceits and innovations:

Before all things, prithee remember me this, not to mimic the worst inventions of modern rhetoricians, and smack your lips over them, but to trample on them, and emulate the great classical examples. Nor let the wind-flowers of speech bewitch you, but, after the manner of men in training, stick to solid food. Sacrifice first of all to the goddess Clearness . . . Bid avaunt to bombast and magniloquence, to tricks of speech. Do not turn up your nose, and strain your voice, and jeer at others, and think that carping at everybody else will put you in the front rank. Nay, you have another fault, not small, perhaps your greatest, that you do not first arrange the meaning of your expressions, and then dress them in word and phrase; but if you can pick up anywhere some outlandish locution, or invent one that seems pretty to you, you try to tack a meaning onto it, and are miserable if you cannot stuff it in somewhere, though it may have no necessary connection with what you have to say.

The last words seem to many a warning that should ring today.

Philostratus (182–c. 250 A.D.)—from whom Ben Jonson translated "Drink to me only with thine eyes"— presents, in an imaginary conversation, the first definition of imagination.

EGYPTIAN: How do you know your Greek representations are truer? Did you go to heaven to copy the gods?
APOLLONIUS: There was another guide.
E.: You can mention no such thing, save imitation.
A.: It was imagination wrought these forms, a more cunning artist than imitation. Imitation will make what it has seen, but imagination will make what it has not seen, for she will suppose it according to the analogy of the real. Moreover, sudden disturbance will put out imitation's hand, but not that of imagination, which goes on undisturbed to what it has itself hypothetically conceived.*

The next contribution to critical theory is made by Plotinus (205–270 A.D.), who rises to defend the dignity of art against the Platonic condemnation: if a portrait give the mere features and nothing more, he declares, it is indeed an image of an image. But

if anyone condemns the arts because they create by way of imitation of nature, he must first observe that natural things are themselves an imitation of something further, and next he must bear in mind that the arts do not simply imitate the visible, but go back to the logos from which nature comes——

that is, art seeks beneath the particular for the universal—

and further, that they create much out of themselves, and add to what is defective, as being themselves in possession of beauty;

* Can it not be argued that imagination is but a sort of garbled or distorted version of the real or the experienced,— hence is a subdivision of imitation?

since Phidias did not create the Zeus after any perceived pattern, but made him as he would be if Zeus deigned to appear to mortal eyes.

There remains Longinus, *On the Sublime*. The poor schoolboy who, accepting a prompter's word, translated *poeta nascitur non fit* as "the poet is born mad" would have had Plato's sanction. He declares that

all good poets, epic as well as lyric, compose their beautiful poems not by art, but because they are inspired and possessed. And as the Corybantic revellers when they dance are not in their right mind, so the lyric poets are not in their right mind when they are composing their beautiful strains. . . . For the poet is a light and winged and holy thing, and there is no invention in him until he has been inspired and is out of his senses, and the mind is no longer in him.

It remained for the last Greek critic to make proper use of this theory of the first. We are told that Longinus was the Greek secretary of Zenobia, in the third century; we know him for his treatise on the sublime. In it he makes the first Greek reference to Hebrew literature, to "the legislator of the Jews"; he indicates his classical leaning by preferring the stricter form and deeper passion of the *Iliad* to the romantic unity, the sentimentality, the improbabilities (such as the foodless voyage) of the *Odyssey,* which he assigns to Homer's old age. He suggests that the writer should have the great works of the past always in mind, and should wonder how the future will adjudge his work—but for neither of these considerations should he hesitate to let himself go, when something "opportunely outflung" bears him to transport:

For a work of genius does not aim at persuasion, but ecstasy, lifting the reader out of himself. The wonder of it, wherever and whenever it appears, startles us; it prevails where the merely persuasive or agreeable may fail; for persuasion depends mainly on ourselves, but there is no gainsaying the sovereignty of genius.

It imposes its irresistible will upon us all. Where there is only skill in invention and laborious arrangement of matter a whole treatise, let alone a sentence or two, will scarcely avail to throw light on a subject. But the sublime at the critical moment shoots forth and tears all asunder like a thunderbolt, and in a flash reveals the author's full power.

The test of the sublime, then, is that it transports; and even though chewing-gum and "true-story" magazines were unknown to Longinus, he wisely added (as we have heard) that "the judgment of literature is the long delayed reward of much endeavor"; that, furthermore, the transport must recur when we reread, or there is not the true sublime.

Living in the ages of rhetoric, Longinus was preserved from the romantic's full yielding to inspiration. While nature supplies, art must regulate. The sublime—he suggests an analysis:

consists in a certain loftiness and consummateness of language, and it is by this and this alone that the greatest poets and prose writers have won pre-eminence and lasting fame . . . Beautiful words are in deed and in fact the very light of the spirit.

And the last words we hear before the dark ages are the first that will reach our ears in the new dawn.

CHAPTER III

THE RENAISSANCE

Oh, there's repristination!

ROBERT BROWNING.

THE DARK AGES

> Then began the Doctors over their cups to argue canon-
> ically concerning profundities. And the question arose,
> whether *magister nostrandus* or *noster magistrandus* is the
> fitter to denote a candidate for the degree of Doctor in
> Divinity.
>
> LETTERS OF OBSCURE MEN.

IN 313 was built the palace of Diocletian at Spalato, the
first example of western architecture not in the Hellenic
tradition. In 330, Constantinople became the seat of government of the Roman Empire. The Council of Carthage, in
398, forbade the bishops to read the pagan authors; few
others could read at all. About fifty years later, in a book
every library owned, *The Marriage of Philology and Mer-
cury*, Martianus Capella named the seven liberal arts: the
trivium, grammar, logic, and rhetoric; and the quadrivium
(named in Plato's *Republic;* basis of the degree Magister
Artium), arithmetic, music, geometry, and astronomy.
Whatever the worldly practice of individual priests, the
official doctrine of the church, renouncing this world, swept
aside the fine arts, as wasteful trifles, or as devilish lures.
Boethius (c. 470–c. 524) reports that he was visited by
a vision of Wisdom, who rebuked him for dallying with the
Muses, "wantons of the theatre". In 529 Justinian closed
the schools of Athens. Literature crept slowly through
hymns and humble ways, or slept in monastery schools,
until the goliards and the troubadours woke it again to love
and laughter. Drama, child of religion, was to be reborn
through the church. Criticism droned among the rhetorics,
awaiting new tongues, new books, new forms, and new
lovers of life—who would forget salvation watching the sun-

rise, and dare damnation for a lady's joy; who felt fresh brightness in the world around, and strove to snare its beauty.

Amid the incessant droning, a few voices may be distinguished. Over the numberless rhetoricians we may pass unheeding, though they include such churchmen as Isidore of Seville, Alcuin, and St. Augustine. But Sidonius Apollonius, at the end of the fifth century, recognizes, though he hardly approves, the new meters, and the imminent loss of Latin beneath "the rust of barbarism"; and he brings into one discussion pagan and Christian literature. Of a poet now unknown, he tells, the epigrams were "not seldom peppered, often honeyed, and always salt"; of the use of the epithet he offers perhaps the supreme example:

When he (Claudian) launches out against his adversary he claims, of right, the symbols of the characters and studies of either tongue. He feels like Pythagoras, he divides like Socrates, he expatiates like Plato, he is pregnant like Aristotle; he coaxes like Æschines, and like Demosthenes is wroth; he has the Hortensian bloom of spring, and the fruitful summer of Cethegus; he is a Curio in encouragement, and a Fabius in delay; a Crassus in simulation, and in dissimulation a Cæsar. He "suades" like Cato, dissuades like Appius, persuades like Tully. Yea, if we are to bring the holy fathers into comparison, he is instructive like Jerome, destructive like Lactantius, constructive like Augustine; he soars like Hilary, and abases himself like John; reproves like Basil, consoles like Gregory; has the fluency of Orosius, and the compression of Rufinus; can relate like Eusebius, implore like Eutherius; challenges like Paulinus, and like Ambrose perseveres.

Fulgentius, in the sixth century, renewed the wide application of allegory, divining it in pagan themes, and preparing the way for the acceptance of Plato and Vergil as anticipatory Christians. At the beginning of the next century, Latin versification having succumbed with Fortunatus, and rhymes having appeared in hymns, there was framed a regular Latin rhyming panegyric for Clotaire II in France;

and shortly afterwards, according to some scholars, "Leonine" verses were composed by Pope Leo II. (Others, however, attribute the name of these Latin rhyming verses to a twelfth century canon of Paris.) Bede, in the eighth century, was familiar with Anglo-Saxon, as his ecclesiastical history well shows; he helped its progress by ignoring it in his orthodox *Ars Metrica*.

Another four hundred years of rhetoric trudged by before the first treatise on the new forms. But during those centuries many slow changes grew to potency. The great heritages were absorbed, and intermingled, so that while the story-tellers copied, they freely interlaced: their heroes were as great as "Paris of Troy, or Absalom, or Partenopex"; the children of Rome became the fathers of Britain; and classical demigods, oriental heroes, and Christian paladins, hobnobbed with Celtic fairies. The corruption of Latin into the Romance tongues brought an ignorance, or at any rate an independence, of the classical restrictions. Drama, reawakening in the schools, and respringing from the churches, again claimed the people. Prose tales, fabliaux, were eagerly heard at tavern fireside and noble board; emprizing folk-lore, that humbler yet more homely mythology the classics had overlooked; and Christianity, having made woman a secret and a sin, provided fiction with the great element pagan literature largely lacked: love, and the wooing of woman, as the basis of romance.

It is, therefore, no coincidence that poetry should have its fresh reflowering in the land where courtship became as ceremonial as religion, and the knight's, or the troubadour's, lady was held as the earthly symbol of the Virgin Mother. And with the coming of the thirteenth century several Provençal treatises were devoted to the new forms. Continuing the practice of the early rhetoricians, of the illustrative quotation in which most of the treasures of the Greek anthology

—and here, of medieval verse—were preserved, these discussions disregarded the classical meters, substituting number of syllables (from four to fourteen) as the basis of the line, and admitting rhyme and assonance. The best of them, *Nova Poetria*, (1216), by Geoffrey de Vinsauf, is marked by the love of puns and other word-play that characterizes a self-conscious age; but it bears the first challenge to Horace, against the plea that one should not reject the whole for a few minor blemishes advancing the charge that "a little gall embitters a whole mass of honey, and one spot makes a whole face ugly." But of course the two were talking of different things: Horace had in mind the epics, the dramas, the swift moving orations, extensive works of the classics; before the Englishman (?) were the delicate lyrics, the patterned forms, of Provençal poetry. The conscious defence of the new against the old awaited another century—and a greater man.

DANTE

And in the midst of all, a fountain stood.

EDMUND SPENSER.

DANTE ALIGHIERI (1265–1321) sat on the mountain of the ages, looking back over the centuries of fixity and certitude, looking forward on the long vista of doubt and change. In his great creative work, *The Divine Comedy,* the "soul of the true church" is laid bare, and the ways of God and the devil, in a world where all knowledge has been attained, are vividly set forth. In his great critical writings, *De Vulgari Eloquentia* and *Convivio,* the growth of the new language is investigated, its possibilities studied, and its use justified. The work of art which is the greatest literary monument of the middle ages speaks with the tongue of the renaissance.

In his treatise *On the Vernacular,* Dante begins (as Diedrich Knickerbocker later opens his *History of New York* with the Creation) with the reasons why man alone has power of speech. Communication among the angels, we learn, is intuitive; the devils need none, setting God at naught, and requiring only recognition of their diabolic state; the animals act upon instinct alone;—man, having reason, must have words. Ready for man's use is an effective language all may learn: *grammatica,* Latin; but after what labor! How much more spontaneous that which the babe draws in with his nurse's milk! After classifying the languages of Europe (Teutonic-Slavonic, *Io;* Turanian; and Romance: *Oc,* of the Spaniards; *oil,* of the French; *si,* of the Italians), Dante considers the dozen and a half Italian dialects, sweeping each aside.

(The vulgar tongue of the Romans, or rather their hideous jargon, is the ugliest of all the Italian dialects; nor is this surprising, since in the depravity of their manners and customs also they appear to stink worse than all the rest . . . If the Genoese were through forgetfulness to lose the letter *z*, they would either have to be dumb altogether, or to discover some new kind of speech. Etc.)

For, speech being to the poet as his horse to the soldier, the best of all strains should be combined for his use. The best language is therefore composite: it should be "illustrious, cardinal, courtly, and curial". Its subject should be elevated: war, virtue, love—nor should inferior writers presume to employ its strains; but Dante passes quickly to what he considers the essence of poetry: diction. Almost as though the scholastic rhetorics had never been penned he handles the new forms. Canzoni should be composed in lines of, preferably, five, seven, or eleven syllables; even lines are rude (Italian, with its feminine endings, has still little use for them). There are four degrees of style: mere prose, which is insipid; sapid prose, which displays more care; ornate prose, which is charming as well; and language at once sapid, charming, and elevate, which is style achieved. Despite his choice of the vernacular, Dante is far from the language of the people Wordsworth advocates. Indeed, his examination of words distinguishes the childish, the feminine, and the manly; only the last are valid, and of those not the sylvan but the urban—of which again two types, the glossy and the rumpled, are discarded, leaving as suitable for high poetry only the combed-out and the shaggy. The detail of this analysis may be judged from a definition: combed-out words are

trisyllabic, without an aspirate, without an acute or circumflex accent, without double x or z, without the conjunction of two liquids, or the placing of them after a mute—which freedoms give a certain sweetness.

The shaggy are all others that, like the pronouns and the

articles, cannot be dispensed with; and others which, though not so combed-out, when mixed with combed-out words are ornamental. An example of the latter type is

sovramagnificentissimamente

which indeed rolls along the tongue.

The treatise breaks off in the midst of Book II; and the early wisdom of what was written bids us lament the loss. Dante's earlier book, *The Banquet,* (in Italian, since the prose is commentary on his Italian poems; the *De Vulgari* is in Latin) looks forward to the later discussion, but contains little consideration of purely literary problems. In it, though, the poet wisely objects to translations, on the ground that the original form cannot be preserved in the rendering.

In his emphasis on diction, in his defence—and eminent use—of Italian, Dante lays the cornerstone of the state-house of modern literature. He had himself, indeed, hung for a time undecided whether to write his great work in Latin hexameters; half a century later, Petrarch turned still to the classic tongues, and influenced the author of the *Decameron* to abandon the vernacular and devote himself to Latin genealogies of the gods and geographical treatises. But the new life was too youngly vigorous for the moribund speech; and into the tongue of that *vita nuova* Dante brought a grammatical regularity, a precision and loftiness of vocabulary, an order and a distinction, that helped make its first works lastingly its greatest. Poetry, said Plato, is a lovely falsehood; the middle ages stressed its falsity; Dante, its loveliness.

THE GREAT REBIRTH

Now the bright morning star, Dayes harbinger,
Comes dancing from the East.

JOHN MILTON.

IN ITS wider aspects, the whole renaissance is a critical
movement. Dissatisfaction is at least the step-mother of
invention, and sharp the wits of the ill-treated child. Those
who are not content with conditions seek ways to mend
them. They may for a time submit; then they will try either
to remove the objectionable features, or to move themselves.
The Crusades, in addition to the reward of eternal salvation, more immediately proffered a combination of these
two methods, and lifted from the soldier of the Cross the
triple burden of material, political, and religious domina-
tion. The spirit of adventure, surging out of earthly toil,
was whetted by the tales of the early travel-liars, whose
wildest word, in the light of trophies seen and riches
fancied, seemed pallid understatement. The merchants,
meanwhile, with wealth always one grasp beyond (and that
fell hand the noble's!) must seek their gain in safer or
shorter routes and farther gleanings; the invention of the
astrolabe and the mariner's compass, the discovery of new
worlds, were result and cause again of bolder dreaming,
bolder doing. Looking about them, men learned the color
of the sky by viewing the heavens, instead of hearkening
to the priest: observation checked and disputed authority.
Gunpowder gave the citizen a sense of his personality, as
printing gave him opportunity to make knowledge his; and
the return of the classics from their oriental rest strengthened the stand that came with the reading of the Bible,

against the sole, divine dictation of the Church. Within the Church, asserting personality organized the soldiers of Jesus, and announced the freedom of the individual will. Life being more turbulent, more intense, than for a thousand years, art in its new growth was held on the one hand as a precious joy, and on the other as a mighty weapon of earthly persuasion or of hellish lure. The puritan grew to power in the surge of the Reformation. The feudal system succumbed to the strong and confident bourgeois. National consciousness awoke; through three hundred years the bright Italian cities paled before French power and Spanish pride, until the island country became the Mistress of the Seas. Incidentally, these astute statesmen and warriors, these early scientists and thinkers, these ardent livers and lovers, produced the greatest body of literature time has known.

THE RENAISSANCE IN ITALY

"Gracious heavens!" he cries out, leaping up and catching hold of his hair, "What's this? Print!"

CHARLES DICKENS.

FROM the time of Boccaccio to that of Savonarola, it was a schoolboy's exercise to maintain, refute, evade the Platonic ban on poetry. In 1527 Marco Vida, Bishop of Alba, published in Latin a *Poetics* the influence of which lasted until Boileau and Pope. The classics had come into full recognition; Vergil is the model for Vida's discussion of form; by the appeal to "reason and to nature" he clearly intended the ancient practice and the ancient eye. "Steal" from the ancients, he advised.

Two years later appeared, in Italian, the first four parts of the *Poetics* of Trissino, who, in addition to the classical meters, considers such new forms as the sonnet, the ballata, the canzone. He indicates, as the main characteristics of diction, clearness, grandeur, beauty, and swiftness—rather a haphazard aligning; and he begins the great misunderstanding by adding to Aristotle's unity of action a unity of time the Greek had never intended.

After Trissino, throughout the century, important critical works appeared in great number, the eager study of the classics resulting in academic rivalries and consequent controversy. The published works, aside from countless lectures, took three main forms. There were the translations of Aristotle's *Poetics*, with more or less elaborate commentary. The book appeared in Latin in 1536, in the original Greek in 1548, in Italian in 1549. There were abstract discussions of poetry, such as Daniello's *Defence* in 1536, which listed

invention, disposition, and elocution, as the main elements
of the poet's art, and granted the writer free choice of
subject. And there was the formal *Ars Poetica*, which
carried on the methods of the medieval rhetoric. The
greatest concentration of activity occurred just after the
mid-century, when were published, besides many lesser
works, the Latin *De Poeta* of Minturno (1559), Victorius'
edition of the *Poetics* (1560), Scaliger's *Poetics* (1561), the
last two parts of Trissino's work (1563), Minturno's study
in Italian (1564), and the exhaustive *Poetics* of Castelvetro (1570). Robortelli should be mentioned, not merely
for his edition of Aristotle's *Poetics* (1548), but for the first
printing of Longinus (1554), and for the conjunction of
Aristotle and Horace in the *Explicationes* (1555), of which
the essay on Wit is foretaste of the renaissance salting.

In 1549 Lilius Giraldus, while preferring the Latin
writers, published a study *Of the Poets of Our Time* which
reached out to French and German authors, and mentioned
Chaucer and Surrey. Six years later, in a book on romance,
Cinthio endeavored to deduce rules from Ariosto as Aristotle had drawn them from Homer; for the "battle of the
books" had begun, and the new forms were forced to justify
their differences from the old. Minturno, paying greater
attention to the ancients, and but grudgingly admitting
Ariosto to the rank of poet, defended the dignity of the
poet, and the worth of his work, against gathering attack.
He carried the triune division into critical theory, discussing such topics as the matter, the instrument, and the mode;
manners, affections, and deeds; prose, verse, and mixed
narrative; words, harmonies (rhythms), and times
(meters). Perhaps it was the Procrustean bed of this number that led him to his greatest word: "It will be the business of the poet so to speak in his verses that he may teach,
that he may delight, that he may move." Two-thirds of this

injunction is drawn from Strabo, who declares that the good poet is perforce a good man, and whose description of poetry as a kind of elementary philosophy, which gives us pleasurable instruction, is called by Spingarn the keynote to the renaissance theory of poetry. Rather, these are the inheritance from the middle ages; the final third is the dower of the new times.

Julius Caesar Scaliger is the first after Quintilian, and with equally dispassionate air, to attempt a comparative survey of literature. While Aristotle is acceptable to him, he states that the best thing to do with Plato's ban on poets is to leave it unread; he objects (rightly enough, meseems) to Plutarch's attributing the number of the muses to the number of letters in their mother's name; and he is largely responsible for the establishment of the Vergil worship that held the next three centuries. His chief contribution to criticism, outside of the fulness of classification that he inaugurated, is the declaration that the material—not the form—of poetry, is verse, a conception that reaches toward what Paul Valéry and others are emphasizing today. By his emphasis on verisimilitude, however, Scaliger smoothed the path for the formulation of the three dramatic unities by Castelvetro.

The *Poetics* of Lodovico Castelvetro presents the Greek text of Aristotle, with a summary, a translation, and a commentary, in Italian. The drama is considered from the point of view of its performance, it being argued, for example, that verse is valid because it permits raising the voice without loss of dignity. While Castelvetro is impartial, in his discussion of literature, between the ancients and the moderns, and he prefers Vergil to Homer, he fixed the authority of Aristotle; he established the rule of decorum, and in pronouncing the unities of time and place, subordinated that of action. Even in him, however, the creative independence of the age at moments rears: "What do beginning, middle, and end matter in a poem, provided it delights?" Accused of heresy, Castelvetro fled the land.

The Aristotelian dogma was no longer disputed; only by challenging interpretations might innovators gain a hearing. Tasso, in *Jerusalem Delivered,* attempted an illustration of the classical and romantic unity harmonized. Toward the close of the century, indeed, two rash scholars ventured to breast the current. Francesco Patrizzi, pointing to inconsistencies in Aristotle's definition of verse, and to the general understanding of "poem" as "a work in verse", declared, first, that "verse is so proper and so essential to every manner of poetry that, without verse, no composition either can or ought to be poetry"; then, conversely, that "all the materials comprised in art, science, or study, can be suitable subjects for poetry, provided that they be poetically treated." After which, theory cut its last chain, with the sword of Giordano Bruno: "The rules are derived from the poetry, and there are as many kinds and sorts of true rules as there are kinds and sorts of true poets."

By the time, however, that the critics were winning their independence of the new-found Greek and Latin literature, the fresh flowers of the renaissance had bloomed and blown, and the seed of further creation fell upon soil worked and reworked by the rules of the classicists, and the daring sprouts outside the furrowed lanes were uprooted as rank weeds. The neo-classical age lay strait upon the lands.

THE RENAISSANCE IN FRANCE

Surely the stars are images of love.

PHILIP J. BAILEY.

OVER the Alps, as later across the Channel, a similar development took place. The attention of the nation was turning to letters; humanism entered the realm, and classical learning revived. The nature of the king had a widespread influence upon the habits of his countrymen, and the aged Louis XII had just been succeeded by Francis I, who was twenty-one and eager for power. After a brief and unsuccessful fling at warfare, the king turned to the easier glory of patronage; his sister, Margaret of Navarre, and the gentlemen of the realm, were quick to follow.

Several factors contributed to make the early renaissance struggle intense. Success meant, not merely reputation, but comfortable, even luxurious, years. Appointments to sinecures were worth going great lengths for, and in the wavering religious policy of the king the means were at hand. Those who were progressive in literary forms were likely to be radical also in ideas; what easier than to bring charges of heresy? A book, as soon as printed—even while circulating in manuscript—was public property; many garbled editions of popular works were issued, from which heresy openly grimaced. Rabelais, in a later issuing of *Pantagruel,* speaks of his own attacks on the church as printer's errors; he carefully removed all objectionable material—and immediately afterward appeared a reprint of the original edition in pristine strength! Despite the ten-year "privilege" granted by the king, Rabelais, who tells us he was a martyr "jusques au feu exclusivement"—up to the fire, found it

convenient (as twice before) to flee from France. The humanist Dolet was burned; Marot (head of the second literary
school) was twice censured for eating meat during Lent, and
died in exile; the Chambre Ardente was instituted for heresy
trials; and the Sorbonne began its *Index Expugatorius*—
with the first French version of the *New Testament* (1523),
Marot's *Psalms,* and *Pantagruel* and *Gargantua.* The king's
attitude toward the church held the liberals tense: at one
time he acceded to the massacre of the Vaudois or to the
burning of the friend of Erasmus; at another, he founded the
Royal Professorships against the wishes of the Sorbonne, or
allowed evangelical preachings in the Louvre all through
Lent. The sympathetic Margaret was once forced to dismiss
her secretary, doing her best to help him secretly. It was clear
that the poet or scholar, the potential secretary, curé, professor, or director of court entertainments, had not only
to address delicate compliments to his immediate patron, but
to indite an occasional epistle or sonnet that might be of
service in some later plight.

Though the struggle for reform swept across all expression, from theories of style to practical orthography, it was
on poetry that the conflict centered. When Rabelais was
leaving his convent, and Marot was finding his distinctive
style, there were born the two who carried the banner of the
new forces, and were chief by precept and practice to over-
turn the Marotic school. Pierre de Ronsard (1524–1585),
threatened with deafness, turned from arms to orders; he
began the study of Greek and dreamed of reforming French
poetry. When he was twenty-three, he encountered a similar
dreamer, Joachim du Bellay, (1525–1560), who had begun
his career as a law-student and then had turned to letters.
In 1548, Sibilet published a poetic theory based on the
school of Marot, and a year later du Bellay loosed his shafts
in the *Deffense et illustration de la langue françoyse.*

As later, in nineteenth century France, three schools followed one another in rapid succession. About 1523, as has been suggested, Clement Marot began the work that freed him from the earlier school of the rhetoriqueurs, their artificial forms, and their fashionable follies of allegory and rhythmical conceit. By 1525, four of the most prominent of the courtly artificers were dead, and with the publication of his collected works in 1532 the leadership of Marot was unquestioned. Naturally the old guard could not tolerate this usurpation. Their tradition was longest maintained in Toulouse and in Rouen, where annual poetic contests stemmed the tide of novelty. In the latter city, in 1536, a poet-priest named Sagon, seven-fold prize winner, jealous of Marot and zealous for the faith, savagely attacked the poetry, religion, and morals of the newer artist. Four of Marot's friends quickly responded; others rallied to the support of Sagon and, finally, Marot himself flayed his opponents. One Bucher addressed a poetic epistle to both the combatants, urging them as good Christians to stop the quarrel. They did.

The new group, trying to avoid the affected pedantry of the rhetoriqueurs, and the jargon and doggerel of the few followers of Villon, turned to the Latin and Greek classics. Marot's translations of Ovid, Vergil, and Moschus show little knowledge; but an ease that grows from the models is carried into his original work. He used many classical forms—epistle, elegy, eclogue—and of course the ballade, the rondeau, and other French forms of his day. Though he introduced the sonnet, he was not an innovator rhythmically; he was given to strained inversions and *chevilles*, words added for the sake of the meter or the rhyme. He was, however, different in that he came with no trumpeting, no razing theories, but by innate good sense almost unconsciously uprooted the pedantry of his predecessors and paved the way for the school to come.

It is the folly of the followers that often leads to the downfall of a leader. *Les jeunes* imitated the eccentricities of their master, the cough of genius; they adopted mottoes, chose noms de plume, wrote *blasons* (perpetual praise or continuous vituperation). In 1522, Fabri had proclaimed the first school in *Le Grant et vray art de pleine rhétorique,* reprinted five times before Sibilet's *Art poétique françois.* The very titles show the change that had come into the spirit of the writers: poetry is no longer a division of rhetoric. But, though Sibilet has seen the growth in Marot and his disciples, he is conservative, he clings to the older ideals. That these should be completely swept aside is the assumption of the manifesto of 1549.

Du Bellay's *Defence,* like many a manifesto, was not such a novelty as its sponsors dreamed. It is, for one thing, probably based on Sperone Speroni's Italian *Dialogue of the Tongues* (1542); but all that is best in art has a common grounding. Though detesting the moderation of Sibilet, this second sprouting of *les jeunes* was annoyed that he had stolen some of their fire. In the first part of his pronouncement du Bellay maintained that French wanted only cultivating to equal Greek and Latin for literary use [9], that translation was good, but that imitation (as Vergil of Homer) was better. He broke entirely with the old French forms—no French poetry before the sixteenth century, he declared, with the sole exception of the *Roman de la Rose,* is worth the reading.

Leave to the Floral Games of Toulouse and the contests of Rouen all the old French poetry; the rondeaux, ballades, virelais, chants royaux, chansons, and other rubbish that corrupt the taste of our language, and serve only to show our ignorance.

Of the many metrical forms he would introduce as substitutes, only the ode was untried: epigram, elegy, and the rest had been attempted by the school of Marot. It is not in novelty of precept that his importance lies, but in the vigorous, whole-hearted acceptance of the renaissance. The half-hearted Marotic school was disdained: Marot lacks the first element of good writing, namely, learning—his fame would have been doubled had his work been halved; Heroet is so poor in rhyme, so lacking in charm and adornment, that he is a philosopher rather than a poet; Saint-Gelais maintains his reputation as a writer by never writing; and Scève, in his desire to avoid the usual (shades of dada!) has attained an obscurity that not even the most learned can lighten. Thus du Bellay dismissed the poets Sibilet had hailed as models.

The new poets rallied under the shield of the manifesto. At once du Bellay issued *Olive,* a book of sonnets and odes, and Ronsard followed with the first four of his odes. With five others, they organized the Pléiade, or constellation of seven poets, in imitation of the Pleiad in Alexandria in the third century. The band was at once assailed in *Le Quintil Horatian* by a close friend of Marot, the leader of Trinity College at Lyons. This scholar raised the call for clarity against the Pléiade's over-learned appeal, and easily punctured the inconsistencies of du Bellay; but he was too much the irate schoolmaster to be effective. Sibilet responded more cuttingly, repeating his defence of translation, and implying that du Bellay himself was not greatly original. Autels more directly pointed out that the main difference between the schools was that the theory of imitation enabled you to omit what you were unable to translate. Du Bellay's answer refers to Vergil, Ovid, and Horace, whom he had not copied, but fails to mention Ariosto and other Italians, to whom the new school was turning, and on whom he had freely drawn. He rises in dignity: "If anyone wishes to revive the farce of Marot and Sagon he is at liberty to do so, only he must find someone else to play the fool with him"—and closes the controversy. The greatest defence of the new school must of course be its poetry; here the bellicose du Bellay yields place to Ronsard.

Hardly any other poet has been as great an innovator as Ronsard. Not merely did he maintain steadily, for the first time in French verse, a high standard of style, but he introduced over a hundred new meters (bringing the Alexandrine back into favor); he plumbed the resources of the language for sound combinations and colorings; and he gave the individual line a dignity it had not before attained. But, about this time, du Bellay had ripened sufficiently for satire; *Contre les Petrarchistes* withdraws his boast of having been first to write a Petrarchan sonnet in French, and mocks the outworn machinery and stock figures of the form. Then, in *Le Poète Courtisan,* he launches his full power against the remnants of the old school and its lingering champion, Saint-Gelais. His triumph was short-lived: two years later, the king died; Margaret, "the sole support and pillar of all my hope", left for Savoy; he had quarreled with his patron; he was growing deaf. Nor was it the end for du Bellay alone. The lavish expenditures of the court, and the ravages of the religious wars, had impoverished the country. The pressure of the Church, growing more and more insistent until it culminated in the massacre of St. Bartholomew's Day, drove many of the survivors out of the country, and was fatal to progress in jurisprudence, philosophy, and scholarship. The wars of the poets were ended; the lion lay dead with the lamb. The court was through with its trifling for a generation or so, and poetry was not yet a popular recreation. The poets had won the vernacular for literature; now—within the rules—the people won the literature. France was ready for an era of drama and of prose.

ELIZABETHAN ENGLAND

Far off I hear the crowing of the cocks.

HENRY WADSWORTH LONGFELLOW.

IN ENGLAND, which was bilingual till the end of the fifteenth century—and in literature, though with another language, into the seventeenth—the course that had been run in Italy and France worked into more definite grooves. The brilliantly bedecked young Englishmen, returning from a campaign on the continent or a plundering trip along the Spanish Main, full of round oaths and bearded like the pard, were aped in speech and costume by the gallants of the town. There was need for the warning of Thomas Wilson (1553), that "Favorinus the philosopher did hit a young man over the thumbs very handsomely for using over-old and over-strange words". From several sources might these impressive phrases be drawn: we hear of the "fine courtier who will talk nothing but Chaucer"; of the "far-journeyed gentlemen who powder their talk with over-sea" borrowings; and of the "strange inke-horne terms" the olden tongues supplied.

The work of Chaucer, in the fourteenth century, had not stabilized either the language or the poetry of the land; the poems of this courtly Londoner, in contact with the writings of France and Italy (where he was referred to as "the great translator") set a standard too high for turbulent England. The breakdown of the old forms, the loose and licentious doggerel of the century that followed Chaucer, made anyone sensitive to poetic beauty eager for new methods and devices. So low had the art fallen, and so close was the theatre to the trollop and the tavern, that there were gathering clouds of righteous Puritan ire. Lovers of poetry turned, with ardent hopes, to the classics.

In 1570, Roger Ascham recommended the classical meters; in 1586, Webbe declared that if the English had started aright, they might have equalled the ancients. But the classics, to minds accustomed to English usage, were strange in three respects. They were completely without rhyme. They permitted foot-substitutions within the line, variation and equivalence; whereas English verse had been built on syllable counting—which had prepared it, indeed, for submission to "the tyranny of the iamb". Classical verse, finally, was based upon, and regulated by, the rules of quantity; English forms had always been determined by the natural accent. About each of these differences fierce battle waged.

Ascham began the attack on rhyme with the claim that its misliking was no "newfangle singularitie". The device, he declared, had been tried by Simmias Rhodias, and had been so scorned that

the like folly was never followed of any many hundreds of years after, till the Huns and the Gothians and other barbarous nations of ignorance and rude singularity did revive the same folly again.

Gascoigne (1575) objects merely to "rime without reason . . . that your rime leade you not from your firste invention"; but Blennerhasset (1578) in the *Mirror For Magistrates* declares that rhyme alone brings Buckhurst, Tuberville, and Gascoigne nearer to Marot than to Homer, Vergil, and Seneca. He predicts an outcry over the "new poetry". Stanyhurst, in the preface to his translation of the *Æneid* (1582) quotes a rhyming jury-roll as equal to much verse, anticipating the examples in Nashe's *Anatomie of Absurditie:*

> The porter said, by my snout,
> It was Sir Bevis that I let out.

and

> Some lost a nose, some a lip,
> And the King of Scots hath a ship.

In the *Apology for Poetry* (circulated in manuscript c. 1581, published 1595) Sir Philip Sidney takes a middle course: "whether of these be the most excellent would bear many speeches"; though he maintains that "neither rhyming nor versing maketh a poet, any more than a long gown maketh an advocate". Puttenham (1589) devotes three chapters to proclaiming the antiquity and worth of rhyme, which "the American, the Peruvian, the very cannibal" spontaneously employed; yet he sets the two forms, "that one in the schole, this other in courts of princes, more ordinary and allowable". Thomas Campion, in his *Observations in the Art of English Poesie* (1602) made the last stand for the classical forms, observing that rhyme is a figure and therefore, like all tropes, "sparingly to be used, lest it offend the ear with tedious affectation". The death-blow was dealt the following year, by Samuel Daniel, whose *Defence of Rhyme to All the Worthy Lovers and Learned Professors Within His Majesty's Dominions* opens in challenging tone: "Rhyme, which both custom and nature doth most powerfully defend; custom that is before all law, nature that is above all art". The critic then proceeds to show that each of the "eight several kinds of new promised numbers" Campion had proposed, was an old English form, decked out in foreign terms.

Daniel, indeed, lifted a trumpet-blast against the dominant classics, that sounds with sincerity and power:

Me thinks we should not so soon yield our consents captive to the authority of Antiquity, unless we saw more reason: all our understandings are not to be built by the square of Greece and Italy. We are the children of nature as well as they; we are not so placed out of the way of judgement, but that the same sun of discretion shineth upon us. . . . Time and the turn of things brings about these faculties according to the present estimation; and *Res temporibus non tempora rebus servire oportet*. . . . It

is not books only but that great book of the world and the all
over-spreading grace of heaven that makes men truly judicial. Nor
can it but touch of arrogant ignorance to hold this or that nation
barbarous, these or those times gross, considering how this manifold creature man, wheresoever he stand in the world, hath always
some disposition of worth, entertains the order of society, affects
that which is most in use, and is eminent in some one thing or
other, that fits his humour and the times. . . . The Goths, Van-
dals, and Longobards, whose coming down like an inundation
overwhelmed, as they say, all the glory of learning in Europe,
have yet left us still their laws and customs, as the originals of
most of the provincial constitutions of Christendom, which being
well considered with their other courses of government, may seem
to clear them from this imputation of ignorance. And though the
vanquished never speak well of the conqueror, yet even through
the unsound coverings of maledictions appear those monuments
of truth as argue well their worth, and proves them not without
judgement, though without Greek and Latin.

The lines of English verse seemed, in the first half of the
sixteenth century, to have run amuck, and attention to the
question of syllable-counting as opposed to foot-division had
a most salutary effect. Puttenham declares that marking the
syllable is natural to English; Gabriel Harvey, advocating
the foot, gives a list of words of "indifferencie", which will
stand in any place, that seems to include most of the disylla-
bles in the language. As Harvey's concern shows, this problem
was absorbed in the greater one of quantity and accent; but
out of its consideration, despite our prosody's adoption of
the classical terms, came a return to a freedom within order,
in accord with the genius of the language.

The term *accent,* in prosody, may denote two things: the
stress, opposed to the foot, as the basis of line scansion—as
in Anglo-Saxon poetry; and the stress on the important
syllable within the foot. It is in the latter sense that the
Elizabethan used the term, in opposition to the classical observance of quantity. This aspect of Elizabethan critical
thought is of interest chiefly because the great poets were

caught by the lure of classical forms. Edmund Spenser's early work shows strained accents; he composed hexameters "extempore in bed", translating:

That which I eate did I joye, and that which I greedily gorgèd,
As for those many goodly matters left I for others——

and he wrote: "Why, a God's name, may not we, as else the Greeks, have the kingdom of our own language, and measure accents by the sound, reserving the quantity to the verse?" (Spenser did not know that Latin, before the Greek influence, was all accentual.)

For the poet's venturing, Harvey takes him roundly to task, in clear and effective tones:

In good sooth, and by the faith I beare to the Muses, you shal neuer haue my subscription or consent (though you should charge me wyth the authoritie of fiue hundreth Maister Drants) to make your Car*pen*ter, our *Car*penter, an inche longer or bigger than God and His Englishe people haue made him. Is there no other Pollicie to pull downe Ryming and set vppe Versifying but you must needes correcte *Magnificat*: and againste all order of Lawe, and in despite of Custome, forcibly vsurpe and tyrannize vppon a quiet company of wordes that so farre beyonde the memory of man haue so peaceably enioyed their seuerall Priuiledges and Liberties, without any disturbance or the leaste controlement? What? Is Horaces *Ars Poetica* so quite out of our Englishe Poets head that he muste haue his Remembrancer to pull hym by the sleeue, and put him in mind of *penes usum,* and *ius*, and *norma loquendi?* . . . I dare sweare priuately to your selfe, and will defende publiquely againste any, it is neither Heresie nor Paradox to sette downe and stande vppon this assertion (notwithstanding all the Preiuduces and Presumptions to the contrarie, if they were tenne times as manye moe) that it is neither Position, or Dipthong, or Diastole, or anye like Grammer Schoole Deuise that doeth or can indeed make either long or short, or encrease or diminish the number of Sillables, but onely the common allowed and receiued Prosodye, taken vp by an vniuersall consent of all, and continued by a generall vse and Custome of all. . . . It is the vulgare and natvrall Mother Prosodye that alone worketh the feate, as the onely supreame Foundresse and Reformer of Position, Dipthong, Orthographie, or whatsoeuer else: whose affirmatiues are nothing worth, if she once conclude the Negatiue: and whose *secundæ intentiones* muste haue their whole allowance and warrante from hir *primæ*. And therefore, in shorte, this is the verie shorte and the long: Position neither maketh shorte nor long in oure Tongue, but so farre as we can get hir good leaue.[10]

The practice of these men, fortunately, and of their colorful contemporaries [11], was more forthright than their speech. "I never heard the old song of Percy and Douglas that I found not my heart moved more than with a trumpet". So Sidney, in a truer moment; and when he hesitated over his own work, he tells us—

> Thus, great with child to speak, and helpless in my throes,
> Biting my truant pen, beating myself for spite:
> "Fool", said my Muse to me, "Look in thy heart, and write!"

("The heart is the mind's Bible", later said Keats.) Even at the time of his classical experiments, Spenser was pondering *The Faerie Queene*, which in its purely native stanza is one of the greatest contributions to English poetic form. And, in a field that fortunately—however it was scored by moral flaying—was deemed unworthy of critical concern till 'twas too late to mar, in the drama of Marlowe and of Shakespeare, rhyme was discarded, and in its stead there developed another triumph of English prosody: blank verse.

The defence of poetry and drama against the attack of the moralists took two main lines: an historical review, quoting the authorities in praise of literature; and a contemporary survey, admitting the evil, but demanding that it, not poetry, be destroyed. Ever the dignity of the poet's calling is emphasized. *Poeta nascitur, non fit;* and the process of making him fit, of rendering him worthy of his art, is further ennobling. Yet there had been sermons even against the miracle plays; Ascham found no merit even in *Morte Arthure:* "the whole pleasure of which book standeth in two speciall poyntes, in open mans slaughter, and bold bawdrie"; the attacks grew more frequent and more violent; in 1579 Stephen Gosson (who until the age of twenty-four had been a gallant and a playwright) addressed Sidney in the *School of Abuse*, damning the blasphemy and immorality of all pagan literature, and asserting that the theatre played procurer to the brothel. The answer, Sidney's *Apology*, recognizes the faults in the literature of the time, definitely assailing the "mongrel tragi-comedy"; but it boldly asserts the prime worth of poetry:

Firstly, truly, to all them that professing learning inveigh against poetry may justly be objected that they go very near to ungratefulness, to seek to deface that, which in the noblest nations and languages that are known, hath been the first lightgiver to ignorance, and first nurse, whose milk by little and little enabled them to feed afterwards of tougher knowledges: and will they now play the Hedgehog, that being received into the den, drave out his host? or rather the Vipers, that with their birth kill their parents?

As his enthusiasm rose, Sidney suggested that poetry may be one of the means of leading man back to happiness after the fall.

The crowding hordes of defences and attacks grew ever more abusive and insistent, until—after Elizabeth had given way to the Stuarts—with the rising power of the Puritans, in 1642 the theatres were closed.

Two later Elizabethans stand above the crowd. Francis Bacon (1561–1626) presents no criticism in his essays, save the general comment of the famous *On Studies*. Nor does the *Advancement of Learning* deem literature worth much attention. Three centuries before the study of crowd psychology, however, Bacon points out that drama has been regarded "by learned men and great philosophers as a kind of musician's bow by which great minds may be played upon.

And certainly it is most true, and one of the great secrets of nature, that the minds of men are more open to impressions and affections when many are gathered together than when they are alone". Of poetry, his views are mainly classical, combining the æsthetic and the ethical demand. He does, however, oppose allegorical interpretation, pointing out that usually the fable grows first, and the moral is afterward devised. Regarding the arts as "learning licensed in imagination", he traces the sources of imaginative pleasure, to a "more ample greatness, more perfect order, more beautiful variety". Like Montaigne, he had little faith in the stability of the modern tongues; like Plato, he indicates the power of words to lead astray. Accepting the traditional reference of history to the memory, philosophy to the understanding, and poetry to the imagination, Bacon followed the Spaniard Huarte, rather than the ancients, in finding less madness than creative fire in the imagination—which transforms while presenting life, whether in the past as in the epic, in present action as in the drama, or through allegory and symbol in "parabolic" poetry. These divisions of poetry, be it noted, all present the outer world; the subjective types, the lyric, Bacon sets rather in the domain of philosophy and rhetoric, where the metaphysicals pressed them toward the neo-classical neglect. (The metaphysical mood is matched, in criticism, by Henry Reynold's *Mythomystes*.) But soon Bacon declares poetry is but a character of style, "and belongeth to arts of speech"—and turns his attention to philosophy.

The plays of Ben Jonson (1573–1637), *Every Man in His Humour, The Poetaster*, present large fragments of orthodox critical thought; in his *Conversations* with Drummond of Hawthornden, and in the collection *Timber*, he elaborates his support of the classical doctrines, urging the unities, and the "nothing too much" of the Greeks, upon an overflowing time.

At first following Sidney, Jonson was confirmed in his classical leaning by the work of the Dutch critic Daniel Heinsius (1580–1655), who held to the sane medial way while Europe else was leaping toward the precious, the pedantic, or the prodigious, who was therefore hailed by the classicists of every land, and whose very words are frequent in the final pages of *Timber*.

Many of Jonson's particular judgments are striking, as that Shakespeare, whom he admired as much as any man this side idolatry, "wanted art", that the sonnet was a Procrustean bed; that (though he warned against snap judgments) "the water-rhymer would find more suffrages than Spenser"—which was, indeed, likely, as Service today would outvote Robinson. He naturally attacked the romantic drama, "the Tamerlanes and Tamerchams of the late age, which had nothing in them but the scenical strutting and furious vociferation to warrant them".

The equipment of the poet is described by Ben Jonson. The first essential is, of course, inspiration. This must, however, be supplemented by industry; as the best writers "obtained first to write well, and then custom made it easy and a habit". As, however, "words and sense are as the body and soul", exactness of study and multiplicity of reading aid in the process, for the poet must "be able to convert the substances or riches of another poet to his own use". In proper respect for scholarly attainments and craftsmanship—the oars of genius—Jonson declared of the poet's product that "things wrote with labor deserve to be so read." Fortunate for the reader when he, like the great Elizabethans, may feel that art is a labor of abounding life and love.

CHAPTER IV

RULE AND REVOLT

"You see, the earth takes twenty-four hours to turn on
its axis——"

"Speaking of axes," said the Duchess, "chop off her head."

LEWIS CARROLL.

THE REIGN OF RULE

Around the ancient track marched, rank on rank,
The army of unalterable law.

GEORGE MEREDITH.

WHILE renaissance art, in the exuberance of its personal growth, had been welling in romantic freedom and variety, renaissance criticism, in the enthusiasm of its discovery of the ancients, had been organizing in classical uniformity and order. At first a servant of its time, called upon to justify the very existence of poetry, then the use of the vernacular, for an age that was disputing the authority of the Church in religious affairs it proceeded to erect an imaginary yet infallible Aristotle for æsthetic. Helpless against the creative urge of the times, though serviceable in checking the euphuistic extravagances of the extremists, in that great name was gathering an undertow of orthodox pronouncement that, when the great tide of the renaissance had ebbed, drew all writers into the back-sweep of neo-classical thought.

Consideration of every prominent critic of the age would run too lengthily on, for this was a period of prose and of self-consciousness; the writers knew what rules they were observing and to sustain their position set them down again. The regularity of the repetition, however, makes it necessary, after the first presentation, to note only the individual variations of the classical theme.

The French most rigidly developed the literary regulations, and longest observed them. The crystallization of Francis Malherbe (1555–1628) was almost unbroken till Hugo. Objecting to the freedom of the Pléiade, Malherbe set definite rules for the Alexandrine (which is to French poetry and drama as blank verse to English); he set upon their pedestals the idols of the age: propriety; the criticism of each work after its "kind"; and good sense. He dwelled much on details of technique, and verbal criticism, protesting—as Milton against Hall's "teach each"—against such lines as

> Mais vous, belle tyranne, aux Nérons comparable

where a sense of humor might spoil the effect by unburying the comment "tira nos nez"—"pulled our noses"; as it melts into a closing pun the lines of Frost:

> Before I built a wall I'd want to know
> What I was walling in or walling out,
> And to whom I was like to give offence.

There was an impulse toward rebellion against the tightening classical hold, as when Mathurin Regnier declared that "reason may deceive, as well as the senses"; as when Francis Ogier said that the better way of imitating the Greeks was by giving heed "to the tastes of our own country and the genius of our own language, than by forcing ourselves to follow step by step both their intention and their expression"; as when Corneille wrote *Clitandre*, a play "obeying all the rules of the drama, but having nothing in it". But the influence of Italian critical ideas, the growing rationalistic philosophy, and the reaction against the Pléiade, carried conformity: a year before its official inauguration, the French Academy, established (1637) to "ascertain the vocabulary of the language, fix its grammar, and reform its style", condemned Corneille's *Le Cid*. The attack on the play was led by Cardinal Richelieu; and, though the public enjoyed the drama—witness Boileau's

> In vain 'gainst *The Cid* does a minister league,
> All Paris views Chimène with the eyes of Rodrigue.
> In vain as one man The Academy sneers;
> The obstinate public, rebellious, reveres——

everyone succumbed to the new dictatorship. Chapelain, a member of the Italian Accademia della Crusca, held the pen for this attack; he it was who popularized the three unities in France—latest land to conquer but longest to bind; he, who wrote—and, though his time admired, betrayed himself to the ages by writing—*La Pucelle* to demonstrate how knowledge of the rules, without *trop grand élévation d'esprit*, can enable one to produce a work of art. For the "laws" a work must obey, drawn from the work, were drawn into "rules" for creating new pieces in the kind. Says Scudéry:

Now from the study of all these precepts and the reading of all these heroic poems, here are the rules I have formed, rules derived from those of Aristotle, from Tasso and these other great men, and therefore infallible, provided they are followed.

The quarrel of the Ancients and the Moderns—in England curiously headed by Temple, and by Bentley whose *Dissertation on the Epistles of Phalaris* is the first English essay in scientific criticism—gave vent to controversial vehemence, until Dryden pointed out that Ovid is less classical than Chaucer, and discrimination began to replace blind categories. Much disputatious fire was kindled over the matter of borrowed themes; Marin declared that what is "scholarship in regard to the ancients is theft when moderns are concerned"; and Dryden compared the adaptor of a play to a watch-maker: the metals are not his own, but "the price lies wholly in the workmanship". The battle of the books had effects unseen by these classicists. In a wider circle of readers, which included many women, it helped popularize criticism; it insinuated into an unready world the notion of relativity in literature; and it hatched—*Graecorum ab ovo*—the idea of evolution, which the Abbé Dubos in his *Critical Reflections on Poetry and Painting*, in 1719, and Montesquieu in *The Spirit of the Laws*, a generation later, fledged before it soared through Taine and Brunetière.

The civil wars of England, with many of the courtiers long exiled in France, established an intimate contact that bore theory swiftly over the Channel; the pedantries of the Jesuit René Rapin (1621–1687) were translated, and equalled, by Thomas Rymer (1646–1713), whom Pope called "one of the best critics we ever had", but whom Macaulay—with typical insularity—distinguished as "the worst critic that ever lived". A specimen of the criticism that rises from observance of the "kind" is Rymer's comment on Shakespeare's Iago:

> He would pass upon us a close, dissembling, false, insinuating rascal, instead of an open-hearted, frank, plain-dealing soldier—a character constantly worn by them for some thousand years in the world. . . . Philosophy tells us it is a principle in the nature of man to be grateful.

What Aristotle had proffered as convenient classification in his *Rhetoric* becomes æsthetic certitude in Rymer. This author of *Tragedies of the Last Age, Considered and Examined By the Practice of the Ancients, and By the Common Sense of All Ages* assures us that

> many, perhaps, of the tragical scenes in Shakespeare might do yet better without words. Words are a sort of heavy baggage that were better out of the way at the push of action, especially in his bombast circumstance, where the words and action are seldom akin, generally are inconsistent, at cross purposes, embarrass or destroy each other; yet to those who take not the words distinctly, there may be something in the buzz and sound, that, like a drone to a bagpipe, may serve to set off the action.

Despite these pedantries, or worse, Rymer is perhaps the first English critic to survey literary history and, with few predecessors elsewhere, to employ the comparative method in adducing specific passages, and to examine these quotations æsthetically, studying rather "the niceties of Poetry than any of the little trifles of Grammar", seeing the drama as a thing live in the performance, endeavoring—however blinded by reason—to analyze the poetic qualities and to determine their source. The forcefulness of Voltaire and the influence of Jeremy Collier owe something to the methods of this too despised critic. Indeed, as Spingarn points out, the shift in respect to Rymer was due to the very movement he forwarded: his age admired a critic for his principles; the ages after judged him by the application. Rymer, though his comments were disastrous, was one of the first to take the specific regard.

John Dryden (1631–1700)—whom Johnson preferred, wrong, to Rymer right; though Johnson's censure of Shakespeare for the tragic fate of Cordelia and other innocent figures binds him as straitly to the notion of poetic justice—John Dryden was saved by an independent nature from so servile a "common sense" and concern for "poetical decency"; though generally classical in the enunciation of principles, he turns with fresh vision to each work he views. While he recognized that "Shakespeare had a larger soul of poesy than any of our nation", he deemed him therefor worthy of being translated out of his barbarous tongue into the English of the civilized age. Yet he defended tragi-comedy, asseverating:

It is not enough that Aristotle has said so, for Aristotle drew his models of tragedy from Sophocles and Euripides; and, if he had seen ours, might have changed his mind.

He also takes the first great, open stride beyond the didactic attitude, in his declaration that delight is "the chief, if not the only, end of poetry".

Other countries at this time present little that is new. The creator of Don Juan, in Spain, attacked the unities by declaring that comedy to the eye, as history to the understanding, comprehends *multum in parvo*—the problem being to make the events probable as shown. But this defence by Tirso de Molina (1585–1648) did not keep Lope de Vega Carpio (1562–1638) from boasting that six of his twenty-two hundred plays obey the rules. (Only no one has been able to discover which six!) Cervantes, even when Don Quixote attacks romances, seems undiscriminating in his literary satire; though in *The Blessed Vagabond* he does make Comedy proclaim: "It matters nothing to the listener that I pass in a moment from Germany to Guinea without leaving the stage; for thought is winged, and by it he can accompany me where I go"; but with Gongora Spanish literature grew into an extravagance that painted the Lyly—until the land itself grew sterile with vain pride.

In Germany, the most backward of European lands because of internal conflicts, the first critical writing in the new tongue, *The Book of German Poetry* (1624) by Martin Opitz, helped effect the prosodic transfer from quantity to accent, brought the influence of Ronsard to German literature, and urged attendance upon French models—advice that, when the close of the Thirty Years' War permitted its being taken, brought in the full regularity of the neo-classical school.

The most influential of the later French neo-classicists was Nicolas B. Despréaux Boileau (1636–1711), followed in his own land by the vehement Voltaire (1649–1778) and the biting Buffon (1707–1788). Boileau attacked the importations from Italy with bourgeois love of clarity; he reproved the bookish and the artificial writers of the time, insisting that nature be the artist's model, and reason his guide. Only the Jansenists, laughing at the imbecility of human reason, would have mocked him; but each age by "nature" means its own, and Boileau proved but to be giving support to Malherbe, for the one thing that makes us sure of the reasonableness of the rules, he continued, is their constancy—and once again we are with the ancients. Why the rule of the three unities? (I follow Brunetière's paraphrase):

Because it's not natural to confine to two or three hours an action the real duration of which would fill months, years, centuries; because, furthermore, it's not reasonable to spread through space or time a subject the effect of which, by hypothesis or definition, depends upon its concentration.

Voltaire, at first hesitant, saw the inability of the moderns to match the ancient works, their erroneous conception of progress—standing on Vergil's shoulders!—and the reasonableness of Boileau's argument; and after his early rebellion he gave his force to the classics. Buffon made one progressive, and famous, remark, developing the fact that only well written books last, for information can be transferred; fact becomes public property; novelty ceases to be novel: "These things are outside the man; the style is the man himself". *Le style est l'homme même.* But the prestige of these other men sufficed to hold the century to their rules, which La Harpe helped fix upon the land by his, the first, history of literature, "a reasoned history", as his preface explains, "of all the arts of the wit and the imagination from Homer to our day, excluding only the exact and the physical sciences"; but a history peevishly personal, by the man—fellow to him who, on beholding a rhinoceros, exclaimed "There is no such creature!"—who cried out upon the "inconceivable pronunciation" of English.

In England—save when the moral purpose, as in Jeremy Collier's *Short View of the Profaneness and Immorality of the English Stage* (1698) blunted the literary, or when Dryden's defence of the romantic drama was echoed by Pope: "To judge Shakespeare by Aristotle's rules is like trying a man by the laws of one country who acted under those of another"—the formulation of Boileau was expressed or implied, with various modifications of personal style, by all who wrote criticism, notably the mild-mannered Addison, the caustic Swift, and the ponderous, dogmatic Johnson, whose strictures on Milton's versification adorn many pages of *The Rambler.* This is the period, too, in which "the characters proper to literature" were set down; although John

Erskine, who has written an essay with that title, says even today that "the body is a fit subject for literature, but not in detail", and suggests that the faraway—Cromwell or, better, King Arthur, not Roosevelt—is the best theme.

A few of the time, indeed, made contribution to æsthetic theory. Hobbes and Locke gave the imagination a measure of philosophical attention, which Addison endeavored to present more popularly. "Time and education", said Hobbes, "begets Experience; Experience begets Memory; Memory begets Judgment and Fancy; Judgment begets the strength and structure, and Fancy begets the ornaments, of a poem". *Fancy* and *wit* were to Hobbes synonymous, though to the Elizabethans *wit* meant intellect as opposed to will; with Dryden the term came to signify "propriety of thought and words", what Pope called "sense"—changing with literary taste, and destroying Hobbes' distinction. Edmund Burke attempted an analysis of certain æsthetic elements. He attributed differences in taste to the varying degrees of experience in life and art that men may have. The judgment, he declared, is analytical; imagination is the constructive faculty in man. The exaltation we derive from tragedy (for "pleasure" is too paltry a term) arises from an exercise of the spiritual elements within us, and is comparable to the bodily exhilaration after muscular exercise. Outside of such physiological or metaphysical speculations, however, the tyranny of the kind, of propriety, of good sense, pressed ever more tightly upon the country, through schools and academic papers in France, through the rapidly increasing periodicals in England, drowning the first murmurs of the romantic revolt. Yet it should be noted, on leaving as on entering this period, that the age was one of important concerns; religious, then political and social revolutions were gathering their power in old maladjustment and in new philosophical theory; minds busied with such problems, as were many of the critics', especially in France, found it less troubling to accept what was handed down in the relatively unimportant field of art. There, for other tension and turmoil, were security and repose. Poised for their satire was a settled form. When the revolutions came, æsthetics was not last to know the change.

THE "ROMANTIC" WORLD

The old order changeth, yielding place to new,
And God fulfils himself in many ways,
Lest one good custom should corrupt the world.
                                    ALFRED, LORD TENNYSON.

MANY critics feel that the neo-classical age was but a long
breathing-spell in the onward march from the dark ages:
while the liberators rested, the very weapons of their
triumphant progress—the great works of the ancients—were
trained against them, were used to line them into lock-step.
Then, in the romantic rebellion, the advance-guard of freedom broke once more through the bonds, to final victory.
Others think the romantics more akin to the blind Samson,
and—led by T. S. Eliot—lament the repose and order of
eighteenth century philosophy and art. Fear of discipline has
been suggested as at the core of most uneasiness in the face of
set forms, as during the French Revolution, as in the post-
war unrest of today; although the great artists seem always
to have welcomed a certain measure of limitation against
which to strive, the weaker move either toward complete
reliance upon imposed standards, or toward utter anarchy.
As, among our writers of today, many insist upon the full
freedom of a Gertrude Stein or a James Joyce, crying the
"revolution of the word", and many (Renan, Eliot, Benda)
mourn the surety of Catholicism and eighteenth century rule,
so the romantic rushed to his extreme. The new era was, indeed, rooted in the renaissance; the rise of the sense of personality, the development of the scientific method, the growth
of the questioning spirit, all stirred uneasily beneath the
Augustan order, and broke free once more in the changes that

came, with the closing century, upon every aspect of man's being.

Political oppression, class differences, material discomfort or want, seemed less endurable in the light of a thousand new candles science was supplying with taper, philosophy was dipping, and industry was bringing the match. The "outrageous stimulation" of the epoch—"things are in the saddle and ride mankind"—led to an anti-intellectualist movement then as now; our age presses harder to prick a blasé shell: we'd "give Kant plus Spinoza for Aspasia's memoirs"; the romantics sought a return to the simplicity of nature. Rousseau preached "so eloquently that he almost persuaded us to go on all fours"; but our "primitives" as well as the Romantic "naturals" are pierced by Lowell's barb (read the whole of his essay on Thoreau):

I do not believe that the way to a true cosmopolitanism carries one into the woods or the society of musquashes. Perhaps the narrowest provincialism is that of Self; that of Kleinwinkel ["Main Street"] is nothing to it. The natural man, like the singing birds, comes out of the forest as inevitably as the natural bear and the wildcat stick there. To seek to be natural implies a consciousness that forbids all naturalness forever. It is as easy—and no easier—to be natural in a salon as in a swamp, if one do not aim at it, for what we call unnaturalness always has its spring in a man's thinking too much about himself.

The desire to withdraw from a mechanical civilization, marked even in the extremists of today, as in Eugene Jolas' *Cinema*, as in *Erewhon* or in "back to nature" cults, is declared by others akin to the quest of the comfort and assurance of the womb. Man cannot master machines by destroying them—for too many benefits accrue from their employment, but only by continuing their development while preserving his human integrity. "I don't think machines matter much"; says old Mrs. Thurlow in St. John Ervine's *The Ship;* "it's people who matter. Guns don't usually go off

by themselves, and anyhow a peasant's spade is a machine."
Later she remarks "You think, because you see the confusion of a half-completed job, that it's a bungled job", and
points out that those who refuse to acclaim, advance, make
use of, mechanical improvements are not progressive but
reactionary. So severe a critic of his age as the author of
Sartor Resartus admonished Emerson:

A man has no right to say to his own generation, turning quite
away from it, "Be damned!" It is the whole Past and the whole
Future, this same cotton-spinning, dollar hunting, canting and
shrieking, very wretched generation of ours. Come back into it,
I tell you.

Of our time more strongly.... Accept the material movement, but keep the spirit pure.... A shrewd logic might wonder by whom are set the eternal standards that bid the body
move with the times and yet the soul stand steadfast. Perhaps evolution, the life-force, God, has willed a general
march.

The movement from the country to the towns, and to the
slums of cities; the accumulation of great fortunes, and the
consequent extremes of poverty and wealth; the assertion,
philosophically then politically, of the rights of the individual—checked, in the face of a tortured world, by the
development of organized altruism, by humanitarian activities, by socialism, communism;* the volcanoes of armed
revolution, and the more glacier-like inexorable slow stream
of industrial change; the smashing of codes and creeds, with
God overthrown and morals flung at the feet of discarded
religion—the more neglected in practice by those who still
rendered lip-service and clung to a pallid faith in forgiveness
hereafter:—these are the striking manifestations of the years
the romantics felt before them, whose further grim development our generation has known, and whose far culmination
times yet to come shall see.

* Does not an organized humanitarianism differentiate
between individuals far more effectively than its
opposite, organized barbarism?

GERMANY RISES

Still thou knowest that in the ardor of pursuit men often
lose sight of the goal for which they have started.
JEAN-CHRISTOPHE FRIEDRICH SCHILLER.

THE middle ages were still near enough, in a Germany that
retains its Oberammergau mystery and inaugurates its
Weimar festival, for the romantic spirit to seem less a revival
than a continuation. The classicist J. C. Gottsched com-
plained, in 1750, that

> while I, after treating poetry in general, have dealt with all its
> kinds, and given its own rules to each, so that beginners may turn
> them out impeccably, the Zurich poetic has done nothing of the
> sort. One can, from its books, learn to make neither an ode nor a
> cantata, neither an eclogue nor an elegy, neither a verse epistle nor
> a satire, neither an epigram nor a song of praise, neither an epic
> nor a tragedy, neither a comedy nor an opera.

Yet Bodmer, thus attacked, twenty years before Percy's
Reliques gave specimens of the old Swabian poetry, of the
Minnesinger's fables, of the *Nibelungenlied*.

Johann Joachim Winckelman (1717–1768), though a
classicist in expression, seems, more than his French and
English contemporaries, concerned with the spirit:

The more tranquillity reigns in a body, the fitter it is to draw the
true character of the soul, which, in every excessive gesture, seems
to rush from her proper center, and being hurried away by extremes becomes unnatural.

His concern with archeology and the visual arts pointed the
way for Gotthold Ephraim Lessing (1729–1781), who in
Laocoon [12] (1766) developed the differences between painting and poetry. Simonides had early declared that "Painting

131

is silent poetry; poetry, painting that speaks." Many critics
—Plutarch—Jonson—Fénelon—Croce—have repeated his
words. Robert de Montesquiou has turned the idea:

> But especially, under leaves aswarm,
> Reflection, the echo of a form . . .
>
> But even more, in wooded ground,
> Echo, reflection of a sound.

The symbolists declare that their aim is to lead poetry the
pathway back to its source in music. Lessing maintains, on
the contrary, that each of the arts, because of its medium,
its instruments, and its consequent technique, yields different
impressions, must result in different effects. A picture is
spatial and instantaneous; a poem is a movement in time.

In the two years of his play-reviewing, the *Hamburgische
Dramaturgie*, Lessing further endeavored to penetrate to the
principles behind the immediate work; he was wise in warning a race that had just awakened to Elizabethan freedom
against too easy a neglect of the past; yet he was equally
wise in observing that every work of genius is its own rule.

The first of the four Schlegels (Johann Elias, 1719–1749),
had inaugurated the German study of Shakespeare; the
others made many effective analyses of particular works,
showing their scorn of the metaphysical in the remark that
æsthetics is "the salt which dutiful disciples are going to
put on the tail of the ideal—as soon as they come near
enough"; yet Friedrich ventured to define literature as "the
comprehensive essence of the intellectual life of a nation".
The thought that "æsthetics is absolutely independent of
poetry" was also enunciated by Novalis (Friedrich von Har-
denberg, 1772–1801), who made many a memorable epigram,
as "Every Englishman is an island". The critical comments
of Schiller, when they were not abstract, were likely to be

ill-natured; the preëminent personality in criticism, as in other forms of literature, was one who, as Hugo later in France, lived through an ardent rebellion to a calmer age.

Johann Wolfgang von Goethe (1749–1832) reveals in his criticism an eclectic ranging. He insisted that "in art and poetry, personality is everything"; the poet must grasp what is individual, through this he may attain the universal. "The writer's style", he paraphrased Buffon, "is a true expression of his inner self." While this may be true of the unconscious style, however, Goethe warned against its affecting the treatment: "Poetry of the highest type manifests itself as altogether objective; when once it withdraws itself from the external world to become subjective, it begins to degenerate." (Such an understanding is the criterion of George Moore's *Anthology of Pure Poetry**.) And Goethe is thoroughly classical in pointing out the limitations imposed by the artist's materials, though he seems more inclusive in the remark that "a work that is good all through will surely be a classic". His early insistence that the artist have no creed derived from or in fealty to the intellect, while it mellowed with the urge of implicit standards, remained throughout Goethe's life a recognition that the function of the artist is not to imitate, nor to organize nature, not to wrangle or reason, but to create. That is all the artist's concern; though later the value of his product will depend partly upon its wisdom and its ardor. "Nature organizes a living, indifferent being; art a dead but significant being". It is curious to discover so experienced a craftsman judging Shakespeare (at the opposite extreme from Lamb) from the standpoint of the stage only; in general, his criticism seeks to follow the process of creation with the author. From Goethe's practice, indeed, with Coleridge's word, springs the most popular formula of recent

* See page 258.

criticism: to discuss what the author has tried to do, how or to what extent he has done it, and whether it was worth doing. From his catholicism rises, too, the current feeling that there is no question of degree of merit in art; there may be many kinds of beauty, but each of them is best.

THE ENGLISH SOAR

Such fire was not by water to be drowned.

LODOVICO ARIOSTO.

SOME poets of eighteenth century England—Thomson; Gray; Shenstone, who planned the *Reliques of Ancient English Poetry* (1768) with Thomas Percy, and who anticipated Poe in the romantic pronouncement that "the words 'no more' have a singular pathos, reminding us at once of the past pleasure and the future exclusion of it"—moved toward artistic freedom. In 1775 Tyrwhitt made Chaucer's beauty live again, by indicating the value of the final 'e'. Warton's study of the earlier English poets freshened men's view; the work of Dr. Hickes in Icelandic and Anglo-Saxon, Percy's *Runic Poetry*, Gray's *Descent of Odin:* the cult of the medieval, of Norse literature, of "Ossian"; the rise of the Gothic romance, and the appearance of the border ballads of Scott and the fresh lyrics of Burns, cleared the path for the conscious enterprise of the early nineteenth century poets.

Awake to the portentous moment wherein they dwelt, these writers were both poets and champions of their work, of its fresh return to the sources of inspiration, in nature and in the deeps of man. Sir Joshua Reynolds, at the opening of the Royal Academy in 1769, had deemed it necessary to urge upon the students

an implicit obedience to the Rules of Art, as established by the practice of the great masters . . . Every opportunity should be taken to discountenance the false and vulgar opinion, that rules are the fetters of genius; they are fetters only to men of no genius, as that armor, which upon the strong is an ornament and a defense, upon the weak and misshapen becomes a load, and cripples the body it was meant to protect. . . . How much liberty may be taken to break through these rules and, as the poet expresses it,

> To snatch a grace beyond the reach of art,

may be a subsequent consideration, when the pupils become masters themselves. It is then, when their genius has received its utmost improvement, that rules may possibly be dispensed with. But let us not destroy the scaffold, until we have raised the building.

(One is reminded of Brander Matthews' frequent remark: "First learn the rules; then you may break them".) Throughout his discourses the painter emphasizes that novelty is false lure, and beauty based on custom, and that "perfect form is produced by leaving out particulars and retaining only general ideas".

At the margin of this observation, William Blake (1757–1827) passionately scrawled: "To generalize is to be an idiot; to particularize is the great distinction of merit". To this he added "Unity is the cloak of folly"; "Invention depends altogether on execution", and other remarks that pointed his individual and mystic career. Picturing himself dining with Ezekiel and Isaiah, he asks: "Does a firm persuasion that a thing is so make it so?" and answers, before the pragmatists: "All poets believe that it does". More directly attacking the moribund age, Blake placed unity, and morality, outside the province of poetry as philosophy's concern; and declared that "We do not want either Greek or Roman models if we are but just and true to our own imaginations". [Here he anticipated that other prophet, Walt Whitman, speaking in the same tongue beyond the waters, who completed the democratization of poetry, establishing free verse, in spirit and in name; who cried forth:

Come Muse, migrate from Greece and Ionia.
Cross out, please, those immensely overpaid accounts;

That matter of Troy and Achilles' wrath, and Æneas', Odysseus'
    wanderings;
Placard "Removed" and "To Let" on the rocks of your snowy
    Parnassus. . . .

and who declared:

I was looking a long while for a clue to the past for myself and
    for these chants—and now I have found it:
It is not in those paged fables in the libraries (them I neither
    accept nor reject);
It is no more in the legends than in all else;
It is in the present—it is this earth today;
It is in Democracy (the purport and aim of all the past);
It is the life of one man or one woman of today—the average man
    of today;
It is in languages, social customs, literatures, arts;
It is in the broad show of artificial things, ships, machinery, poli-
    tics, creeds, modern improvements, and the interchange of
    nations,
All for the average man of today.]

The more deliberate advance of the romantic power was
made by William Wordsworth (1770–1850) and Samuel
Taylor Coleridge (1772–1834), who in their joint *Lyrical
Ballads* (1798) sought the dual goal—Wordsworth, to make
the familiar poetical, exciting sympathy by the truths of
nature; Coleridge, to make the unfamiliar acceptable,
awakening the interest of novelty through imaginative color.
Disappointed at the reception of the volume, Wordsworth,
who had written most of the poems, prepared for the second
edition, two years later, a preface in which he enunciated his
poetic creed. Poetry, he declared, is truth "carried alive into
the heart by passion", but ordered by reflection: "the spontaneous overflow of powerful emotion, recollected in tranquillity." There should be no difference, he maintained, between the language of poetry and that of prose; both should
employ the diction, as the events, of everyday life. These
ideas forced Wordsworth to the stand that verse is but an

accident of poetry; Coleridge, whose poems in the same volume made him seem also sponsor for the theories, courteously refrained from immediate difference, but in the *Biographia Literaria* (notes from 1800–1817) made clear his belief that meter is the proper form for poetry, that Wordsworth's "real life" is selected and therefore unreal, his words—if ordinary in choice—poetic in arrangement, and his poems best when they most contradict his theory.

The unorganized and fragmentary thoughts of Coleridge include many of the most brilliant illuminations of critical theory. He called attention to the "willing suspension of disbelief" all art demands. He emphasized the "union of deep feeling with profound thought" that characterizes the highest creations of man. "For poetry is the blossom and the fragrancy of all human knowledge, human thoughts, human passions, emotion, language". From direct poetic experience combined with wide sympathetic reading, and metaphysical speculation he later deemed too protracted, Coleridge characterized the "esemplastic imagination", that shapes into one the variety within the event contemplated by the artist, and through the proferring of beauty communicates immediate pleasure. For he accepted the Greek theory of beauty, wherein "the many, still seen as many, becomes one". Of style, he asserts that it is, "of course, nothing but the art of conveying the meaning appropriately and with perspicuity, whatever that meaning may be, and one criterion of style is that it shall not be translatable without injury to the meaning" (a conception carried a stage farther by Arnold Bennett:

Style cannot be distinguished from matter. Ideas are conceived only in words. To say that a writer polishes up his style is merely to say that he is polishing up his idea, that he has discovered faults or imperfections in his idea and is perfecting it. An idea exists in proportion as it is expressed; it exists when it is expressed, and not before.

Croce extends this conception to the notion that the forming of the mental image is expression. But anon.) Despite the self-tormenting and self-portraying of the Romantics, Coleridge insisted upon the "utter aloofness of the poet's own feelings, from those of which he is at once the painter and the analyst." This, indeed,—even "the choice of subjects very remote from the private interests and circumstances of the writer himself"—he considers one sign of the born genius, whose innate qualities consist, besides, in "the sense of musical delight, with the power of producing it", a predominant passion, and depth and energy of thought.

The sanity of Southey, the catholicity of Leigh Hunt, the friendliness of book-lover Lamb, the color of De Quincey, to whom we owe the famous distinction between the "literature of knowledge" and the "literature of power"—science and art, the concrete discussions of too-well-read Hazlitt, all gave a mellower tone to the new spirit, which the sober and learned dogmatism of the many writers for the great reviews (Jeffrey and his "anti-enthusiasts") could not restrain; and which flamed in Shelley's pæan of ecstasy and inspiration. Percy Bysshe Shelley (1792–1822) declared that "poetry is something divine . . . the perfect and consummate surface and bloom of all things . . . the record of the best and happiest moments of the best and happiest minds". He is happier in the examples of his own work than might be some he turns to, however, when he praises spontaneity, and says "I appeal to the greatest poets of the present whether it is not an error to assert that the finest passages of poetry are produced by labor and study". Coleridge would probably have retorted as did Whistler when asked how he could justify so heavy a charge for a few hours' work; or as Webster, who, complimented on his excellent extempore reply to Haine, said "All my life has been a preparation for that speech". For the frequent response to the more frequently advanced theory of inspiration is, that the poet, through depth of experience, wide and loving acquaintance with literature, and constant practice of the art, must be ready, must be worthy of the lightning moment when it comes.

FRANCE BREAKS THE CHAINS

We have changed all that.

JEAN BAPTISTE POQUELIN (MOLIERE).

THE "Latin" genius was most harmoniously prolonged among the French, on whom the ideas of Aristotle, formulated by Horace and established in the new tongue by Malherbe and Boileau, most tightly straitened, and were longest fixed. Only a few in the eighteenth century—when, indeed, the revolutionists were busy in other fields—ventured variations from the orthodox code. Fontenelle declared that progress is an illusion, that every home of man has the same follies, of which, while the distribution varies, the sum remains. Diderot attempted an interrelation of the arts, and in his criticism reached his theories from the work; but his chief romantic characteristic was his occasional over-enthusiasm, as in his praise of the novelist Richardson. Chateaubriand, who lived through the revolutions—poiitical and literary—contributed little more than a figure for the critical imagination: "oars of the intellect and wind of the spirit". Joseph Joubert (1754–1824) is more definitely a forerunner: he recalls Longinus in his emphasis on the word, and in the dictum "Nothing that does not transport is poetry; the lyre is in a sense a winged instrument"; but he points clearly ahead with the remark: "One can find poetry nowhere unless it's in oneself." His definition of criticism is also forward-looking; he calls it "a methodical exercise of discernment".

The Romantic manifesto appeared in 1827, as the preface to *Cromwell*. Here Victor Hugo (1802–1885) proclaimed the new freedom, accepting Aristotle's original unity of action, but insisting that every work of art be viewed with unbound eyes. The young writers gathered ardently around their leader, with the oriflamme of Gautier's (apocryphal) red waistcoat in the van. Among those who carried the weapons of criticism in the romantic campaign was Charles Augustin Sainte-Beuve (1804–1869), who for several years had been contributing to *Le Globe,* a periodical that had attracted Goethe's attention. To this writer the critical spirit seemed "a large, clear river that winds and flows about the works, the monuments, of poetry". In the series of portraits he made for *Le Revue des deux mondes,* and in his *Monday Causeries,* Sainte-Beuve developed a form that has been the model of many subsequent critical essays. Spurred by his recognition that before judging one must understand, and that knowledge of the author is an aid to appreciation of the work, he began his essays (which magazine use limited to six or eight thousand words) with a biographical sketch. While indicating the family and background of the writer, he paid particular attention to the developing associations and literary influences, watching especially the critical period of late adolescence and early ripening of powers. Following this with a concrete study of books and passages, he came to an end with a comparison of the author and others whose traits offered interesting points of distinction. Influenced by the high hopes the period placed in science—though in truth the science of the romantics was an oddly intuitive, ideal structure—Sainte-Beuve looked forward to a critic-specialist, a scientist at once and an artist, who might determine the genera and species of literary minds. This Parthian arrow of neo-classical formulation, however, was blunted against the shield of his independence, as in his annihilation of Beyle in a satiric portrait of the "ideal critic", and when he declares that the art of the critic consists in two things: "to know how to read a book well, estimating it en route, not ceasing to savour it"—and to compare.

The consideration of environment, important for Sainte-Beuve, was quintessential to Hippolyte Taine (1828–1893), who illustrated in his *History of English Literature* his famous formula for judging the work through the social forces that had impelled it: the race, the milieu, the moment. The obvious refutation to Taine is that both Carl Sandburg and Scarface Capone have come from Chicago, that, as Brunetière lessons him, Venice produced both Tintoretto and the gondoliers.

Many of the French, however, impatient of all formulas, and of the ages of art for the sake of living, followed Théophile Gautier (1811–1872) into the fragrant meadows of art for art's sake. Chiseled perfection of style; the quest of the one, inevitable word—on which Flaubert took Maupassant; writing to please oneself, indifferent to all else—though at times deliberately to shock the bourgeois; the attempt to use sound as in music, and color as in painting—after Baudelaire's

Color and sound and fragrance correspond;
such efforts and such concerns in art itself swing pendulum-wide from the implicit or expressed didacticism of the centuries.

In still another direction, Zola drew romanticism to the dregs, according to some, though he maintained that "Romanticism is the initial, troubled period of Naturalism".* While tolerance, if not full freedom, had temporarily been won, the controversies wakened through those pulsing years are among the critical problems of today.

* See page 403f.

CHAPTER V

THE WIDENING VIEW

"Would you tell me, please, which way I ought to go from here?"

"That depends a good deal on where you want to get to", said the Cat.

"I don't much care where—" said Alice.

"Then it doesn't matter which way you go", said the Cat.

"—so long as I get *somewhere*", Alice added as an explanation.

"Oh, you're sure to do that", said the Cat, "if you only walk long enough."

Alice felt that this could not be denied, so she tried another question. "What sort of people live about here?"

"In *that* direction", the Cat said, waving its right paw round, "lives a Hatter, and in *that* direction", waving the other paw, "lives a March Hare. Visit either you like; they're both mad."

"But I don't want to go among mad people", Alice remarked.

"Oh, you can't help that", said the Cat. "We're all mad here. I'm mad. You're mad."

"How do you know I'm mad?" said Alice.

"You must be," said the Cat, "or you wouldn't have come here."

THE REVEREND CHARLES LUTWIDGE DODGSON.

THE VICTORIAN INTEREST

Com, no more,
This is mere moral babble, and direct
Against the canon laws of our foundation.
JOHN MILTON.

WHEREAS French writers had been more rigidly bound by æsthetic regulations, literature in England had been more closely watched by the puritans, and still another period of moral preoccupation came upon the heels of the romantics. The returning sobriety, after the early effervescence, is manifest in Landor's prescription:

I would seriously recommend to the employer of our critics, that he oblige them to pursue a course of study such as this: that, under the superintendence of some respectable student from the university, they first read and examine the contents of the book— a thing greatly more useful in criticism than is generally thought; secondly, that they carefully write them down, number them, and range them under their several heads; thirdly, that they mark every beautiful, every faulty, every ambiguous, every uncommon expression. Which being completed, that they inquire what author, ancient or modern, has treated the same subject; that they compare them, first in smaller, afterwards in larger portions, noting every defect in precision and its causes, every excellence and its nature; that they graduate these, fixing *plus* and *minus,* and designating them more accurately and discriminately by means of colors stronger or paler. For instance, purple might express grandeur and majesty of thought; scarlet, vigor of expression; pink, liveliness; green, elegant and equable composition; these, however, and others as might best attract their notice and serve their memory. The same process might be used where authors have not written on the same subject. Thus Addison and Fontenelle, not very like, may be compared in the graces of style, in the number and degree of just thoughts and lively fancies; thus the dialogues of Cicero with those of Plato, his ethics with those of Aristotle, his orations with those of Demosthenes. It matters not if one be found superior to the other in this thing and inferior in that: the qualities of two authors are explored and understood and their distances laid down, as geographers speak, from actual survey. The *plus* and *minus* of good and bad and ordinary will have something of a scale to rest upon; and after a time the degrees of the higher parts in intellectual dynamics may be more nearly attained, though never quite exactly.

Among the writers in other fields who attempted criticism, Macaulay followed the Sainte-Beuve model with cock-sure emphasis—later requesting that his critical writings be destroyed; Carlyle was vehement, and quick to hail the Germans, but carried off into metaphysical speculation; Thackeray was more conservative, and more catholic, in his views—though bold in parody. For this generation, as Coleridge had been for the first of the century, and as Pater was to be for the last, the leader was Matthew Arnold.

In his earlier critical writing, Matthew Arnold (1822–1888) was interested primarily in the work of art, offering both his delineation and his delight. Feeling that his own age was "wanting in moral grandeur", he demanded a total impression, through effective architectonics, building, as the bee its wax and honey (the figure borrowed from Swift), into sweetness and light, and achieving the "grand style", which "arises in poetry when a noble nature, poetically gifted, treats with simplicity or with severity a serious subject". The classical attitude, manifest in his quest of the mean, the union of good sense and continence with passion and exaltation, "the serenity which always accompanies true insight", is iterate in the statement that the artist should "see life steadily and see it whole". Feeling that poetry is, at bottom, a criticism of life, Arnold sought earnestly and tolerantly for truth.

To try to approach truth on one side after another, not to strive or cry, nor to persist in pressing forward, on any one side, with violence and self-will—it is only thus, it seems to me, that mortals may hope to gain any vision of the mysterious Goddess, whom we shall never see except in outline, but only thus even in outline.

Later, Arnold turned his attention to the critic. The reader of literature, he felt, should avoid the historic opinion, and on the other hand a too personal estimate, of the work, by steeping himself in the best writings; one should strive to have "always in one's mind lines and expressions of the great masters, and to apply them as a touchstone to other poetry." Once he sees things as they are, however, it becomes the duty of the critic to impart his understanding to the great body of readers, and to prepare the leaven of culture in the world, against the coming of the master-baker. Of course, no one can see the object as it really is; but, with due caution, the critical power

tends to establish an order of ideas, if not absolutely true, yet true by comparison with that which it displaces; to make the best ideas prevail. Presently these ideas reach society; the touch of truth is the touch of life, and there is a stir and growth everywhere; out of this stir and growth come the creative epochs of literature.

The critic is tempted on all sides, and must avoid all prejudice—chiefly, the narrowness of the "barbarian", the polite but limited aristocrat; the emotional and incoherent stir of the "populace"; and the false standards of the "philistine", the bourgeois who values all things as they contribute to his ease. Against these forces in society, the critic must (as Goethe felt) be champion of culture, must help spread the best that is known and thought in the world, must make the world safe for the artist.

The social concern of Arnold developed, in William Morris, into an activity that ranged from the invention of new type-fonts and comfortable chairs through the advocacy of socialism to the retelling of Norse tales; but the exclusively moral aspect of the age found its fullest critical exposition in John Ruskin, who said of the fine arts that "they must be didactic to the people, as their chief end". To justify this stand, Ruskin supposes a duality of stimulation from art: "æsthesis—mere animal consciousness of the pleasantness", present with all art; and theoria—"the exulting, reverent, and grateful perception of it", wakened only by the great, which is the good, which is the gift—and the revelation—of God.

In his moments of purer literary consideration, Ruskin is more trenchant. The old doctrine that *ars est celare artem* he bends to new significance in the thought that a great work carries us on wings of fancy till in the vision we forget the magic carpet whereon we fly: "the test of utmost fineness in execution in these arts is, that they make themselves be forgotten in what they represent". On degrees of artistic merit he is equally modern: "I admit two orders of poets, but no third; and by these two orders I mean the creative (Shakespeare, Homer, Dante) and reflective or perceptive (Wordsworth, Keats, Tennyson). But both of these must be *first*-rate in their range, though their range is different; and with poetry second-rate in *quality* no one ought to be allowed to trouble mankind."

THE "PATHETIC FALLACY"

Why has not Man a microscopic eye?
For this plain reason, Man is not a Fly.
ALEXANDER POPE.

PERHAPS Ruskin's most interesting contribution to criticism, one as frequently misunderstood as Emerson's remark about hitching a wagon to a star, is his analysis of the pathetic fallacy.

The spendthrift crocus, breaking through the mould,
Naked and shivering, with his cup of gold. . . .

These lines, observes Ruskin, are pleasurable but untrue. Can we reconcile our pleasure with the theory that beauty is truth?

There are two types of pathetic fallacy—(which, contrary to general opinion and the implication of the term, is only at times to be considered a fault): that, first, in which nature's mood is made to correspond with human activities or emotions, as in Lowell's *The Vision of Sir Launfal* and when the elements announce the dire events in Shakespeare; and that in which inanimate things are given other than their natural attributes:

The one red leaf, the last of its clan,
That dances as often as dance it can.

It is of the second type (akin to personification) that Ruskin speaks. For his elucidation, he distinguishes four types of men. There are, first, those that feel weakly, and see truly: to these the primrose by the river's brim is nothing more. There are, secondly, those that feel strongly, but think

Wordsworth's "Peter Bell"

151

weakly, and therefore see untruly: to these the primrose is a star, or a sun, or a fairy's shield, or a forsaken maiden. Beyond these are the first order of poets, who feel strongly, think strongly, and see truly. "Only"—last—"however great a man may be, there are always some subjects which *ought* to throw him off his balance; some, by which his poor human capacity of thought should be conquered, and brought into the inaccurate and vague state of perception, so that the language of the highest inspiration becomes broken, obscure, and wild in metaphor, resembling that of the weaker man, overborne by weaker things". These moments of prophetic inspiration, and the trivial devices of wilful fancy, with no expectation of belief, are, the ones above, the others beneath, condemnation. Of what he deems the objectionable pathetic fallacy, Ruskin gives instance from Pope, balancing with similar moods from Homer and Keats.

Odysseus speaks in Tartarus:

"Elpenor? How camest thou under the shadowy darkness? Hast thou come faster on foot than I in my black ship?"

Pope makes him question:

O, say, what angry power Elpenor led
To glide in shades, and wander with the dead?
How could thy soul, by realms and seas disjoined,
Outfly the nimble sail, and leave the lagging wind?

Keats (in *Hyperion*):

And there was purport in her looks for him
Which he with eager guess began to read:
Perplexed the while, melodiously he said
"How cam'st thou over the unfooted sea?"

It must be noted, however, that behind Ruskin's condemnation lies implicit the conviction that clear thinking and deep feeling, and their lofty presentation, are the only allowed ends of serious poetry.

APPROACHING OUR DAY

Now is the time when all the lights wax dim.
ROBERT HERRICK.

THE many conflicting views of the later nineteenth century still perplex the critics of today; much of our theoretical writing, indeed, is an effort to supply a rational basis for beliefs then ardently advanced on more emotional grounding. A few of the German writers may be mentioned: Heine, the sharp point of whose critical foil was buttoned with charm; Schopenhauer, who felt that taste was innate, and logical discrimination merely the rationalization of impulse—as for the critical faculty, "there is for the most part no such thing". Grillparzer proclaimed his direct attack upon the work:

My plan in these annotations is, without any regard to system, to write down on each subject what seems to me to flow out of its own nature. The resultant contradictions will either finally clear themselves away, or, being irremovable, will show me that no system is possible—

an admirable procedure, no doubt, provided the critic's appreciation be infallible. Spinoza made one observation—

We endeavor after nothing because we deem it good; but, on the contrary, we deem a thing good because we endeavor after it—

that requires pondering in any consideration of æsthetic taste. Nietzsche advanced his distinction of Apollonian and Dionysian, which some have sought to identify with classic and romantic, for by the terms he contrasts order and exuberance, calm reason and emotional fire, the serenity of Apollo and the orgiac zest of the wine-god. In Italy, the critical comments of De Sanctis were preparing the way for the æsthetics of Croce, who transposes the romantic recognition that all art is expression into the doctrine that all expression is art.

The emphasis on pleasure as the end of art is ingeniously, if not convincingly, extended to all aspects of living by Edgar Allan Poe (1809–1849):

But is it?

> It is a truism that the end of our existence is happiness; if so, the end of every separate part of our existence—everything connected with our existence—should still be happiness. Therefore the end of instruction should be happiness; and happiness is another name for pleasure—therefore the end of instruction should be pleasure. . . . He who pleases, is of more importance to his fellow-men than he who instructs, since utility is happiness, and pleasure is the end already obtained which instruction is merely the means of obtaining.

Assuming the 1st premise, are pleasures so measurable— Can pleasures of mind be ranked to those of senses?

The cultivation of art for art's sake indulged in by Théophile Gautier, Barbey d'Aurevilly, and other French "aristocrats of the mind", was given deeper tone by Charles Baudelaire (1821–1867), whose poetic principles and practice, whose early recognition and championship of such then scorned or detested, now admired or beloved, geniuses as Poe, Wagner, Whistler, Delacroix, Manet, whose inner poignancy and outer polish, make him so much the forerunner of our times as to justify Elie Faure's calling him

> the æsthetic apostle toward whom must converge the several manifestations of painting, music, and poetry, that are so many variations of the mysterious throbbings of the conscience and tragedies of the heart.

Agreeing with Jonson that only the poet is capable of entering into the spirit of another poet—"as though my brain were yours", is Flaubert's comment on Baudelaire's analysis of *Madame Bovary*—Baudelaire continues:

> I have tried more than once to shut myself, like all my friends, within a system from which I could preach at ease. . . .

And always my system seemed beautiful, broad, all-inclusive, suitable, neat, and, above all, smooth. And always a spontaneous creation of the universal will came to give the lie to my childish and senile system. . . . To escape the horrors of these philosophical apostasies, I proudly resigned myself to the humility of being content with feeling; I sought shelter in the impeccability of my naïveté.

In his essay *On Cosmetics*, Baudelaire maintained that nature is evil, and is made good by art:

The greater number of errors relative to the beautiful date from the eighteenth century's false conceptions of morality. Nature was regarded in those times as the base, source, and type of all possible good and beauty. . . . If, however, we consent to refer simply to the visible facts, we see that nature teaches nothing, or almost nothing. That is to say, she forces man to sleep, drink, eat, and protect himself, well or ill, against the hostilities of the atmosphere. It is she also who moves him to kill and eat or imprison and torture his kind; for, as soon as we leave the region of necessities and needs to enter into that of luxuries and pleasures, we see that Nature is no better than a counsellor to crime. . . . Religion commands us to nourish our poor and infirm parents; Nature (the voice of our own interest) commands us to do away with them.——[Baudelaire did not know this was the practice of many primitive tribes.]—Pass in review, analyze, all that is natural, all the actions and desires of the natural man, and you will find nothing but what is horrible. All beautiful and noble things are the result of calculation. Crime, the taste for which the human animal absorbs before birth, is originally natural. Virtue, on the contrary, is artificial, supernatural, since there has been a necessity in all ages and among all nations for gods and prophets to teach virtue to humanity; since man alone would have been unable to discover it. Evil is done without effort, naturally and by fatality; good is always the product of an art. *

This notion, wherein the later romantics swept away from the early nature-worship of Rousseau and the poets, was carried by Oscar Wilde (1856–1900) to the paradox that the "imitation" of the Greeks and most subsequent critics is

* However, evil being a human conception entirely originates solely in the mind of man (i.e. in his attitude toward a judgement of the phenomena of nature). Nature itself is neutral entirely, possessing the naïve cruel-likeness of the butcher bird and the uglinesness of the slimy swamp. (note man's regard for the dump-heap (Carl Sandburg) as beautiful).

really reversed, that life strives to be art. Walter Pater (1839–1894) is at once advocate and example of the painstaking devotion of this group to the minutiæ of the craft, declaring, in opposition to the theory that art pleases "by a fine excess", that its secret "does but consist in the removal of surplusage"—as the sculptor reveals the statue within the block. So Buffon advised that "the inner persuasion be not marked by over-enthusiasm; that everywhere there be more candor than confidence, more reason than warmth". It is such a notion that leads critics of this school (again following Jonson) to declare Shakespeare our greatest genius, but not, properly speaking, a good artist. Pater, modifying the French doctrine in another way than Wilde, sought to approach life as a fine art, anticipating the writers of today who declare that the æsthetic attitude is applicable—and should be applied—to all living.

Michael Angelo

Every man, Pater tells us, has his higher and lower moods; the appreciative reader must learn to discriminate between them. For the serious artist deserves a serious, cultured reader; "in his self-criticism, he supposes always that sort of reader who will go (full of eyes) warily, considerately, though without consideration for him, over the ground". Of the work itself, Pater is equally precise:

Just in proportion as the writer's aim, consciously or unconsciously, comes to be the transcribing, not of the world, not of mere fact, but of his sense of it, he becomes an artist, his work fine art; and good art (I hope ultimately to show) in proportion to the truth of his presentation of that sense.

Not, it will be observed, truth to nature; but sincerity, truth to himself—though it is hard to tell how the artist can reach the world, or "mere fact", save by his sense of it. Pater feels, too, that the discerning critic will penetrate to the essential virtue of works of art, possibly "hidden away, in part, under

* He meant that the artist points out to the observer thru his product which selects hitherto unnoticed, hence unseen elements in nature, unperceived phases. (cf Irving's — function of art is to point out the commonplace.)

those weaker elements . . . which for some minds determine their entire character."

The painter James MacNeil Whistler (1834–1903) is the most vehement of the English æsthetes of what has been called the fin-de-siècle decadence. He rises against the notion of democracy in art. "Listen! There never was an artistic period. There never was an art-loving nation!" Always the great artist stood isolate, alone, and imposed his work upon indifferent ages: "The master stands in no relation to the moment at which he occurs, having no part in the progress of his fellow-men." He pounds his fist on the table at this conception of progress: "Art is limited to the infinite, and beginning there cannot progress." And he shakes his fist at Ruskin and the declaration that art must follow nature: "Nature contains the elements, in color and form, of all pictures, as the keyboard contains the notes of all music"[1]—the rage of simile is upon him—"To say to the painter that nature is to be taken as she is, is to say to the player that he may sit on the piano". . . . The multiplicity of theories today, the contradictions and inconsistencies often traceable in the writings of one school, or of one man, make some think that in our time, literary criticism—and creation—have been playing blind-man's buff with the alphabet. The Germans have been most clear-eyed in recent study; by separate consideration of the receptor's psychology and of that entity, the work of art, they have at least begun to build with the blocks of critical thought.

[1] But it does not — (e.g. Oriental music)

SOME THOUGHTS OF TODAY

And there is nothing left remarkable
Beneath the visiting moon.

WILLIAM SHAKESPEARE.

MANY critics today seem to feel the need of defining the critic's task, and modern conceptions of criticism may well be traced through these attempts at definition. A few more general observations, however, may first be brought to mind.

Remy de Gourmont has called attention to the literary mode he named "dissociation of ideas", which may be said to operate like pinwheel fireworks. If every theme be regarded as a central node of thought, with ideas in concentric whirl (somewhat as the planets or the fancied electrons), there will be a constant tendency to fly off at a tangent. In the solar system, and in the usual work of art, this tendency is almost always exactly balanced by the centripetal force; but as in the atomic universe electrons frequently shoot forth on journeys of their own, so a novelist may choose to set out on some of these tangential flights of thought, for the joy of the questing. Such journeying is found in the many analogies of Proust; inside the minds of the characters we are shown when the "stream of consciousness" is presented; in Sterne's *Tristam Shandy*, in much of Joyce's *Ulysses*—much, indeed, of contemporary fiction and poetry, and even in the more necessarily direct form, the drama.

The juxtaposition of Sterne and Joyce brings to mind another critical principle now set forth, namely, that all art is contemporaneous, and contemporary. Says Norman Foerster:

Upon the assertion "the dead writers are remote from us because we know so much more than they did", the only sensible comment is that of T. S. Eliot: "Precisely, and they are that which we know". Perhaps we are beginning to suspect, as our interest in outlines and stories of philosophy, science, history, etc. would seem to indicate, that "that which we know" is never remote and irrelevant, but always present and serviceable.

The work of art, once experienced, "returns to the world of nature"; it becomes a vital part of the present environment, of the available avenues and events of life. This view of art as an extended garden among whose plants, all equally blossomed, the stroller may cull, suggests a many-colored, fragrant stroll; and a keen historical sense may combine with wide knowledge to reawaken in a receptor traditions moribund. But no reader of today, however scholarly and imaginative, can read Vergil or Swift as a contemporary; the centuries intervening have added to us their lore. With the passage of time, improved implements in the various arts, social changes, the drift of language, have lessened the emotional intensity of works of art, by the same tokens increasing their formal aspect. Words rich with feelingful associations to a troubadour's lady make now a pattern of meaning and sound. What is fraught with emotion to a contemporary (not merely direct references, but the age's mood) pales with the period; the work's self-contained values persist. That is, in part, why Edmund Spenser—for an instance —is "the poet's poet".

Two of the most respected critical writers of today carry this doctrine of form as power almost to a denial of emotion in art. The poet, says T. S. Eliot, seeks not expression of his emotions, but release from them; nor is his personality significant for his poetry: "Impressions and experiences which become important in the poetry may play quite a negligible part in the man, the personality". Why should I not write love poems, protests the young poet of today, since it's my trade to make poems; do they ask of an architect, before he's commissioned to plan a station, that he shall feel like riding on the train? Even the critic should be shorn of all emotions save those immediately induced by the work of art, "and these are, when valid, perhaps not to be called emotions at all. The end of the enjoyment of poetry is a pure contemplation from which all the accidents of personal emotion are removed: thus we aim to see the object as it really is and find a meaning for the words of Arnold." This is achieved, Eliot declares, largely by a labor of the intelligence. Similarly, Leo Stein identifies the æsthetic with the cognitive attitude; the essentials of art—we shall hear him say—are that it be known, that it have meaning only when known as an entity, and that it be not consumed by use, i.e., that it be the same each time it is contemplated. Irwin Edman maintains that "experience may achieve lucidity and vividness, intensity, and depth. To effect such an intensification and clarification is the province of art"; later, he adds "interpretation", and declares that the faculty so stimulated by the work of art is the intelligence.

Benedetto Croce, whose theoretical presentations have been even more influential than the ideas of T. S. Eliot, also declares that the artist writes after overcoming his personal feelings; but, instead of the active, formulating intelligence, he posits an immediate, intuitive grasp of the experience. Following the line of thought behind De Quincy's distinction of the literature of knowledge and the literature of power, the logical and the intuitive, Croce—with a reasoning as inexorable as Taine's—states that as soon as the event has been intuitively grasped, seen as a whole, it has been expressed, even within the artist's mind—and even there is art. Claudel grapples the basic psychological union here implied: "Every feeling is pregnant; and all conception is idea." *(Toute sensation est une naissance; toute naissance* *est co-naissance.*) Others, including C. J. Ducasse, limit the concept of art to "consciously objective self-expression". The actual work of art is, then, no more than a physical stimulant, helpful to revive the original impression in the artist and—it is hoped—to awaken it in the reader.* Despite Croce's statement that the work of art is thus a phenomenon of the practical world, and therefore properly subject to economic, ethical, and other considerations, his theories have been misinterpreted or extended to justify all extremes of personal presentation, without regard to the communicative aspect of art. The artist first claimed the right to self-expression; then assumed that any thing he might wish to say—however incomprehensible to others—was so justified; finally he felt it as a duty to express every thing in his mind. James Joyce has remarked that when Odysseus tried to conceal his identity from the Cyclops (becoming "Odys"), with him it was as inevitably with all men: it was the "Zeus", the divine in him, he sloughed—and "no man" that remained.

* In his consideration of the imagination, Alain develops the opposing theory. See page 232f.

THE CRITIC'S TASK

To rekene as wel his goodness as beautee.
GEOFFREY CHAUCER.

·PRAY, tell me on what particular grounds a poet should claim admiration." So Æschylus to Euripides, in *The Frogs*.

If we survey the efforts at criticism through the ages, we discover that the attempt to meet this request has chiefly inspired them. Recently, however, the existence of "grounds" on which all poets stand has been disputed; and criticism, according to the writer's personality, has found two other moulds.

The old, and still the most frequent, type of criticism, is "judicial". Whether it be Boileau, accepting only the classical standards, or the many who increasingly accept rules drawn from modern works—though one so late as Johnson, defending Shakespeare against the unities, adds:

I am almost frightened at my own temerity; and when I estimate the fame and strength of those who maintain the contrary opinion, I am ready to sink down in reverential silence—

or whether indeed there be an approach to the laws by way of the living literature, the judicial critic assumes that his task is not merely to recognize and to praise, but to appraise, to take or to find the relevant principles of art, and estimate the extent to which the particular work has successfully built upon them.

The "appreciative" critic, on the other hand, assumes differences of kind, but not of degree, in works of art. He endeavors to enter into the individual work from its creator's viewpoint, and thence proceed with the development, tracing the theme and its treatment, in the words of Pater, so as "to feel the virtue of the poet, to disengage it, to set it forth".

The "impressionistic" critic is concerned less with the work of art than with its effect upon him. I am, he admits, "talking about myself on such and such a subject"; his intellectual and emotional experience is what he seeks to record. Among the critical comments of our time, his writings will perhaps be least informative, and most entertaining.

The "function", or task, of the critic, has been set down in many variations of these modes. Anatole France seems at one moment appreciative, as when he states that the critic roams the world placing arm-chairs where subsequent journeyers may sit and look upon beauty; and impressionistic in the more definite remark:

As I understand criticism, it is, like philosophy and history, a kind of novel for the use of discreet and curious minds. And every novel, rightly understood, is an autobiography. The good critic is he who relates the adventures of his soul among masterpieces.

Poe, on the other hand, is impressionistic in the remark that "true criticism is the reflection of the thing criticized upon the spirit of the critic"; and judicial in his prospectus for the *Penn Magazine:*

It shall be a leading object to assert in precept, and to maintain in practice, the rights, while in effect it demonstrates the advantages, of an absolutely independent criticism;—a criticism self-sustained; guiding itself only by the purest rules of art; analyzing and urging these rules as it applies them; holding itself aloof from all personal bias; acknowledging no fear save that of outraging the right; yielding no point either to the vanity of the author, or to the assumptions of antique prejudice, or to the involute and anonymous cant of the Quarterlies, or to the arrogance of those organized cliques which, hanging like nightmares upon American literature, manufacture, at the nod of our principal booksellers, a pseudo-public-opinion by wholesale. . . . It will endeavor to support the general interest of the republic of letters, without reference to particular regions—regarding the world at large as the true audience of the author.

Most writers more consistently manifest a single trend. Albert Mordell, analyzing the critic, suggests that "the literary works we like best are those that tell of the frustration of wishes like our own". One might have expected him to say, considering the number of shopgirls who read in "true-story" magazines of millionaires' marrying shopgirls, the *fulfilment* of wishes like our own. Rebecca West applies psychanalysis in her presentation of the critic's task as appreciative:

> To identify the nature of a work of art, to discover of what conflict it is an attempted resolution, is not possible unless one owns the diligence to study history and the memory to record one's studies. That one may see how far the artist followed the fashion, and how far he wrote of what was in him, and how far the problems that interested him were of time or of eternity, and to determine how far the work is a resolution of that particular conflict and how much or how little the artist has resorted to such weak means of sublimation as sentimental interpretation or suppression of the facts, one must be as sensitive as a bird dog and be able to fight against one's own conflicts like a successful Laocoon in order to achieve an attitude of detachment. . . . It is the business of the critic to synthesize a million glances at his subject that will tell the onlooker at one glance the truth about him, as ultimate as he can get it.

After penetrating this psychanalytical jungle of jargon, one may still wonder whether it is not "in" some writers to follow the fashion; also, one may be perplexed as to just how one is to arrive at "the facts" in an author's life, to determine whether in his work he has suppressed them. Ben Jonson, furthermore, it may be stressed, and Pater, would hardly be content with Miss West's "one glance", that he who flies may read.

Saintsbury, whose long study of criticism should qualify

him at least to state the problem, sets also an appreciative end: "What idea of the original would this criticism give to a tolerably instructed person who did not know the original?"

De Sanctis, adding to Taine and Brunetière, asks—granted the race, the milieu, the moment, the passions of the poet: what has he done with his material? How has he constructed poetry out of reality? T. S. Eliot states that

the true generalization is not something superimposed upon an accumulation of perceptions; the perceptions do not, in a really appreciative mind, accumulate as a mass, but form themselves as a structure; and criticism is the statement in language of that structure; it is a development of sensibility.

The proponents of judicial criticism, perhaps because of its tendency to formulation, present a more formidable body of argument. Matthew Arnold, who conceived of criticism as ploughing and sowing seed for the creator's harvest, declared that by seeing the object in itself as it really is, criticism "tends to make an intellectual situation of which the creative power can profitably avail itself." Criticism is thus "a disinterested endeavour to learn and to propagate the best that is known and thought in the world."

Norman Foerster makes the most complete analysis of the critical method of this "modern humanism". Its first step, he declares, is historical understanding; but the critic must supplement this

understanding born of knowledge with the understanding born of sympathy. Holding his standards of judgment in abeyance, he must endeavor to read the book not only as if he were a contemporary of the author but as if he were the author himself. . . . Having come to understand the book as fully as possible, he will proceed to the specific task of criticism: judgment of the book's value.

First, "its value, its beauty", is judged quantitatively:

in what degree has the artist succeeded in carrying out his æsthetic intention? . . . Secondly the critic will judge of beauty qualitatively, asking, What kind of beauty does the book have? . . . The criterion in this case is not the artist or the critic but truth or nature—the nature of things, things as they really are.

The problem of value, the significance of the work of art to society, burdens the critic of this type. Arnold's "disinterested activity" is to govern the critic so that his inquiries may, as J. Middleton Murry says they must, "be modulated, subject to an intimate, organic governance, by an ideal of the good life". Such concerns make strong contrast with Goethe's declaration:

I am more and more convinced that, when one has to vent an opinion on the notions or the writings of others, unless this be done from a certain one-sided enthusiasm or from a loving interest in the person and the work, the result is hardly worth gathering up.

Beside this, the language of Landor sounds passionately impartial:

In what volume of periodical criticism do you not find it stated that, the aim of the author being such and such, the only question is whether he has attained it? Now, instead of this being the only question to be solved, it is pretty nearly the least worthy of attention. We are not to consider whether a foolish man has succeeded in a foolish undertaking: we are to consider whether his production is worth anything, and why it is, or why it is not. A perfect piece of criticism must exhibit where a work is good or bad, why it is good or bad, in what degree it is good or bad; must also demonstrate in what manner and to what degree the same ideas or reflections have come to others, and, if they be clothed in poetry, why, by an apparently slight variation, what in one author is mediocrity, in another is excellence.

The periodical criticism to which Landor refers was probably a perversion of what H. L. Mencken has called the "Goethe-Carlyle-Croce-Spingarn theory". This theory consists of Coleridge's three questions: What has the author tried to do? How, and how well, has he done it? Is it worth doing? Despite its popularity among those who talk critical theory, this avenue of inquiry proves a blind-alley for venturers. Carlyle states that "we have not read an author till we have seen his object, whatever it may be, as he saw it." But, the author's word as to his intent being notoriously unreliable, the only place to find his purpose is in the work; to judge from the work how well he has reached an end deduced from that work seems complicated and curious vanity. Sensing some such confusion, Joel Elias Spingarn elaborates the theory:

The poet's aim must be judged at the moment of the creative act, that is to say, by the art of the poem itself, and not by the vague ambitions he imagines to be his intentions before or after the creative act is achieved. For to create a work of art is the goal of every artist; and all questions in regard to his achievement resolve themselves into this: has he or has he not created a work of art?

As the three queries were intended, however, to help us decide whether or not the product *is* a work of art (if the author has done well something worth doing, his product is art), this explanation completely begs the first two questions. The problem of value remains. Clemence Dane tries to sweep that aside: "as soon as a critic criticizes the aims themselves he becomes a humanist criticizing the writer as a fellow-creature, not as a creator." That the critic, willy-nilly, is fronted by the question of value is emphasized in the words of I. A. Richards, who states that the critic must be

adept at experiencing, without eccentricities, the state of mind relevant to the work of art; able to distinguish experiences from one another, as regards their less superficial features; a sound judge of values.

In truth and in fine, he continues, "to set up as a critic is to set up as a judge of values". . . . . It is time we considered how criticism has dealt with the problem of value in art.

THE PROBLEM OF VALUE

"Lord, what fine notions of virtue do we women take
up upon the credit of foolish old philosophers! Virtue's its
own reward, virtue's this, virtue's that—Virtue's an ass,
and a gallant's worth forty on't."

SIR JOHN VANBRUGH.

WHEN Aristophanes makes Æschylus pose the question,
he has Euripides answer that the poet deserves admiration
"if his art is true and his counsel sound; and if he brings help
to the nation, making men better in some respect."

Even the most hardened individualist will recognize that
art has a definite value, inasmuch as the work would never
have come into existence were it not at least partial fulfilment of its creator's desire or need. What critics often overlook is that even the most hardened individualist is likely to
recognize a value that art has for the receptor. It is less from
the moral value implicit in, accidental to, art, than from the
moral lesson explicit, the didactic aim, that the practitioners
of art for art's sake withdraw. The cult of a beauty without
moral concern is the response to a moral concern without
beauty.

The earliest Greeks accepted the singer as sent by the
gods for man's delight. Alcinous, in the *Odyssey*, commands:
"Bid hither the divine minstrel, Demodocus, for the god hath
given minstrelsy to him as to none other, to make men glad
in what way soever his spirit stirs him to sing". From the
very divinity that shaped their drama, however, and from the
intimate relationship between oratory and civic affairs, the
Greeks inevitably judged their literature as life, praising or
condemning it by moral standards. This direct relation, which
existed to some extent in Rome also—where oratory equally

flourished, and where the drama (during Aristotle's lifetime) was introduced among other rites to check a plague—has never again been so intimate. To the Greeks, moreover, morality meant no such resignation, such will to abstain and to endure, as it came to signify to the men of sequent ages. The virtue of the Athenian, of the Spartan, even of the Roman, lay in a more positive strength of character, a thoroughness even in villainy that seems often more admirable (and is surely more dramatic) than the pusillanimous goodheartedness of Mr. Meanwell. "Christianity", Machiavelli pointed out, "places the supreme good in humility, meekness, and the contempt of worldly things, while Paganism sees it in a greatness of soul, strength of body, and all the qualities that make a man formidable." When Aristotle expects the hero of a drama to be of noble nature, he wants no more— yet no less—than a man able to stand defiant beneath the blows of the gods.

The Renaissance emphasis on the value of the arts in teaching the good life was doubtless largely due to the earlier intolerance, the puritan suspicion, of earthly delights as lures of the devil. Against a man who seeks to destroy the drama, the most telling argument is that it teaches what is good. By the time of the neo-classicists, however, the arts were less subject to such basic question; Dryden could place delight as the primary end of poetry: "Instruction can be admitted but in the second place; for poesy only instructs as it delights".

With the Victorians, the moral aspect of art rose to new significance. Popular education, the spread of periodicals and other reading matter, especially in the seductive form of the novel, gave literature a social significance deepened by the problems of the factories and slums. The novelists and the poets of the time—Dickens, Tennyson, Browning—exemplified in their works the theories of Schoolmaster Arnold.

Ruskin indicated the three functions of art: to enforce the religious sentiments of men, to perfect their ethical state, to do them material service. William Morris continued the emphasis on the last two of these; the first two were further stressed by the Russian Victorian, Tolstoi.

The penetrating French thinker, Alain, remarking that Æsop's fables are complete allegories, suggests that the "moral" was probably appended by a later grammarian. Scott compares the moral at the end of a tale to the mendicant who hobbles after a parade, hoping that the good spirits of the spectators will reach out to him. Surely no one takes as seriously intended the "lesson" of *The Ancient Mariner*—that, for what a sportsman would call a good shot, a ship's crew is slain, and the culprit, after enduring "life-in-death", must spend his days inflicting his tale on thoughtless strangers; any more than the moral of *The Pied Piper of Hamelin*, which the author himself burlesques in the rhyme:

> And, whether they free us from rats or from mice,
> If we've promised them aught, let us keep our promise.

The chief objection to the work of art that aims to teach is raised by Baudelaire, in his comment on Millet's paintings:

> Whether they harvest or sow, whether they are sending the cows to pasture or shearing the sheep, they all seem to be saying, "disinherited ones of the world though we be, nonetheless it is we who make it fruitful! We fulfil a mission, we exercise a priesthood." Instead of simply extracting the natural poetry of his subject, Millet must at any price add something to it. In their monotonous ugliness, all these pariahs have a philosophical, melancholy, Raphaelesque pretension. This misfortune, in the paintings of Millet, spoils all the good qualities that first draw one's attention towards them.

The answer of those who demand the freedom of art from moral or didactic aim is made, for the romantics, in Shelley's *Defence Of Poetry:*

The whole objection, however, of the immorality of poetry rests upon a misconception of the manner in which poetry acts to produce the moral improvement of man. Ethical science arranges the elements which poetry has created, and propounds schemes and proposes examples of civil and domestic life: nor is it for want of admirable doctrines that men hate, and despise, and censure, and deceive, and subjugate one another. But poetry acts in another and diviner manner. It awakens and enlarges the mind itself by rendering it the receptacle of a thousand unapprehended combinations of thought. Poetry lifts the veil from the hidden beauty of the world, and makes familiar objects be as if they were not familiar; it reproduces all that it represents, and the impersonations clothed in its Elysian light stand thenceforward in the minds of those who have once contemplated them, as memorial of that gentle and exalted content which extends itself over all thoughts and actions with which it co-exists. The great secret of morals is love; or a going out of our nature, and an identification of ourselves with the beautiful which exists in thought, action, or person, not our own. A man, to be greatly good, must imagine intensely and comprehensively; he must put himself in the place of another and of many others; the pains and pleasures of his species must become his own. The great instrument of moral good is the imagination; and poetry administers to the effect by acting upon the cause. Poetry enlarges the circumference of the imagination by replenishing it with thoughts of ever new delight, which have the power of attracting and assimilating to their own nature all other thoughts, and which form new intervals and interstices whose void for ever craves fresh food. Poetry strengthens the faculty which is the organ of the moral nature of man, in the same manner as exercise strengthens a limb. A poet therefore would do ill to embody his own conceptions of right and wrong, which are usually those of his place and time, in his poetical creation, which participates in neither. By this assumption of the inferior office of interpreting the effect, in which after all he might acquit himself but imperfectly, he would resign a glory in a participation in the cause. There was little danger that Homer, or any of the eternal poets, should have so far misunderstood themselves as to have abdicated this throne of their widest dominion. Those in whom the poetical faculty, though great, is less intense, as Euripides, Lucan, Tasso, Spenser, have frequently affected a moral aim, and the effect of their poetry is diminished in exact proportion to the degree in which they compel us to advert to this purpose.

Lest it be assumed that words of the "immorality of poetry" were unnecessary by Shelley's time, hear Ruskin again, developing Plato's objection: "But the best romance becomes dangerous, if, by its excitement, it renders the ordinary course of life uninteresting, and increases the morbid thirst for useless acquaintance with scenes in which we shall never be called upon to act." Or D. S. MacColl, in our century discussing the growth of orchestral music:

An art that came out of the old world two centuries ago, with a few chants, love songs, and dances, that a century ago was still tied to the words of a mass or opera, or threading little dance movements together in a "suite", became, in the last century, this extraordinary debauch, in which a man who has never seen a battle, loved a woman, or worshipped a god, may not only ideally, but through the response of his nerves and pulses to immediate rhythmic attack, enjoy the ghosts of struggle, rapture, and exaltation with a volume and intricacy, an anguish, a triumph, an irresponsibility, unheard of.

The answer of the devotees of art for art's sake is made by Pater:

The idea of justice involves the idea of right. But at bottom rights are equivalent to that which really is, to facts;[*] and the recognition of his rights, therefore, the justice he requires of our hands, or our thoughts, is the recognition of that which the person, in his inmost nature, really is; and as sympathy alone can discover that which really is in matters of feeling and thought, true justice is in its essence a finer knowledge through love. . . . It is not always that poetry can be the exponent of morality; but it is this aspect of morals which it represents most naturally, for this true justice is dependent on just those finer appreciations which poetry cultivates in us the power of making, those peculiar valuations of action and its effect which poetry actually requires.

* rather, equivalent to that which should be, to ideals.

"The business of the poet", William Griffith sets his credo, "is not essentially to save souls, but to make them worth saving." Pater continues:

That the end of life is not action but contemplation—*being* as distinct from *doing*—a certain disposition of the mind: is, in some shape or other, the principle of all the higher morality. In poetry, in art, if you enter into their true spirit at all, you touch this principle, in a measure. . . . To treat life in the spirit of art, is to make life a thing in which means and end are identified: to encourage such treatment, the true moral significance of art and poetry.

Censorship has probably been, on the whole, and even considering the English and American bias, more frequently religious and political than moral; similarly, there are other things than ethical systems the arts can be called upon to teach, or seen as inculcating. Despite Professor Lathaby's dictum:—"Art is best conceived as beneficent Labor which blesses both him who gives and him who receives. Beauty is its evidence. Beauty is virtue in being"—the current tendency is to feel that "when nature is used as a pulpit, she revenges herself and becomes a preacher", art straying into rhetoric and persuasion. Other sorts of uplift doctrines, more subtly disguised in emotive phrasing, replace the manifest moral. J. Middleton Murry appeals to the idealist, with the declaration that the artist "but guides the world to the achievement of its own design. He penetrates and seeks to identify himself with this timeless progress, in order that he may become, as it were, the taproot of the spirit which is at work in the world he contemplates." George Santayana makes appeal to the more intellectual, declaring that "to turn events into ideas is the function of literature . . . it comes to clarify the real world . . . Literature has its piety, its conscience; it cannot long forget, without forfeiting all dignity, that it serves a burdened and perplexed creature, a human animal struggling to persuade the universal Sphinx to propose a more intelligible riddle. Irresponsible and trivial in the abstract impulse, man's simian chatter becomes noble as it becomes symbolic; its representative function lends it a serious beauty, its utility endows it with moral worth." Without bothering to throw a placebo to those who seek a "moral" purpose, Irwin Edman similarly states (I repeat) the function of art to be "intensification, clarification, and interpretation of experience", and describes a symphony, a drama, or a poem, as "foretaste of what an ordered world might be". Ezra Pound builds a similar conclusion on more purely verbal basis, on a sense of the close link between diction and thought; literature, as he views it,

> has to do with the clarity and vigor of "any and every" thought and opinion. It has to do with maintaining the very cleanliness of the tools, the health of the very matter of thought itself. . . . In proportion as his work is exact, i.e. true to human consciousness and to the nature of man, as it is exact in formulation of desire, so is it durable and so is it "useful"; I mean it maintains the precision and clarity of thought, not merely for the benefit of a few dilettantes and "lovers of literature", but maintains the health of thought outside literary circles and in non-literary existence, in general individual and communal life.

The many who talk of the function of art, the purpose of poetry, the aim of the drama, have opposed to them the body of contemporary thought, which* protests that the word function begs the question by assuming something *to do*, whereas the end of art is *to be*. Just as we may ask, however, what value for man resides in the mountain, or the mouse, without implying an anthropocentric universe; so, granting the existence of events called works of art, it is legitimate to inquire into their value.

It must be recognized that there are two ways in which books may enter fields of human activity not primarily directed

* See page 191f.

toward the awakening of pleasure, or of the purely æsthetic attitude. Such works as the *Psalms*, the *Divine Comedy*, as *Gargantua* and *Pantagruel*, build upon systems of thought —as indeed what lengthy work does not?—upon religious or ethical or social creeds and codes that are the author's and that the reader must comprehend (if not temporarily accept) for a full appreciation of the work. Such books, too, as *Uncle Tom's Cabin*, as some of Dickens' novels and Galsworthy's plays, rise heatedly out of current and local issues or evils, and are clearly to be judged, in part, by the truth of their portrayal, or their power in producing a correction of the abuse. So difficult is it to distinguish between art and what we may call advertising, the presenting of personal desires and concerns (as Elbert Hubbard extensively indicated) that it has been said every work of art is propaganda for the personality and ideas of the artist.

* * * * * * * *

The moralist finds his values in conformity to some abstract conception of truth, reality, or goodness*, or in some concrete code of conduct. However drawn, such a code, declares the dweller in a world of relativity, tends at once to be obsolete, through the very fact that the sun does not stand still with the formulation. Life, being dynamic, is in process of continuous change, if not progress; and any fixity fails to keep abreast of man's varying states and attitudes, whatever spiral or circular path they may be tracing. Can we read Shelley adequately if we believe his ideas are moonshine?

> Safe upon the solid rock the ugly houses stand;
> Come and see my shining palace, built upon the sand.

These shifting sands the moralist views from safe retreat in his Mighty Fortress, on the solid rock of the eternal verities.
How, then, does the modern arrive at a theory of value?

* See page 205f.

Consciousness seems to depend upon how complex and how novel an experience is. The simple and the familiar become unreflective acts; the greater the number of possible alternatives among which one must choose, or the more unusual and strange the circumstances amid which one must act, the more alert, the more keenly conscious will one be. Even a familiar act, if set in a new situation, will call for readjustment, for reflection, for the awakening of tendencies, incipient emotions, impulses to action. Emotion is the outward sign, the conscious manifestation, of an attitude, a tendency to a particular action: part of the surge toward expression, in nerve and muscle, beats into the brain as feeling.

The ease with which one who is absorbed in a ghost story will startle, the shriek of an uncontrolled woman at a mystery play, are obvious instances of the tendency to action evoked by the work of art. Though its elements are sometimes strange, and often familiar, every work provides them with a new setting—"makes familiar objects be as if they were not familiar"—and calls upon the reader for new adjustments, awakening appropriate attitudes. The value of the work of art lies thus in the attitude aroused in the reader, not the momentary feeling, but the readiness for behavior that remains. "To evoke in oneself a sensation", says Tolstoi, "which one has experienced before, and having evoked it in oneself, to communicate this experience in such a way that others may experience it also . . . so that other men are infected by these same experiences and pass through them: in this does the activity of art consist". To which I. A. Richards rejoins that all experience "is filled with incipient promptings, lightly stimulated tendencies to acts of one kind or another, faint preliminary preparations for doing this or that . . . It is in terms of attitudes, the resolution, interanimation, and balancing of impulses (Aristotle's definition of tragedy is an instance) that all the most valuable effects of poetry must be described." More specifically, after developing the idea that anything is valuable that satisfies—or, he implies, that arouses—an impulse, he declares the importance of an impulse to be measured by the disturbance of other impulses within the individual the thwarting of that impulse involves; by the degree of coördination of activities within the individual, that is; by the reduction of fruitless, incoherent, frustrate, human stir.

Our investigation of the value of art thus brings us ever back to ethics. Whether one asks, in considering the value of art to man, the degree to which it promotes conformity to certain principles of conduct, or the degree to which it stimulates individual attitudes, one is left to determine along lines other than æsthetic which principles and which attitudes are best. Attitudes that tend to reduce waste and frustration—in the individual? or in society? Principles—of personal freedom? or of the limiting of that freedom for the general good? When this great ethical opposition has been brought to harmonious end, when the supreme artist-in-ethics has wrought this dilemma into unity, the effects of a work of art may then be studied with the hope of arriving at an estimate of its value that will not at once bring discordant voices. Meanwhile, our innate and developed prejudices and predispositions will continue to effect the choice that we call taste or judgment and wrap in reasoned summonings. The heart hath reasons reason knoweth not. In truth, applied standards are so often indistinguishable in the swift activity of taste that their abstract formulation may be little more than a logician's exercise. The discreet critic may shelter himself behind Blake's word, that unity and morality—value—are concerns of philosophy, not of art. He will, however, walk, though a safer, yet a lonely road.

THE CRITIC'S MATERIAL

Come and take choice of all my library.
WILLIAM SHAKESPEARE.

ACCORDING to the material with which he chiefly concerns himself, the critic's writings may be classified. They seem to fall into four main groups; but, like all systems drawn from the works, these issue no prior commands to the critic, who freely intertwines the various æsthetic concerns.

The first division we may call the history of art. In this would be included the classification of literary forms, the genesis of the various types, the development of different styles. Here also we may place general theoretical essays that, like Dryden's *Essay On Dramatic Poesy*, tend to avoid specific writings, while seeking the fundamental principles of the art. It is this type of writing that made it easy for the eighteenth century critic to judge a work: he assigned it to its "kind", then observed whether or not it obeyed the rules enjoined upon that kind. Johnson employs the method in his study of *The Metaphysical Poets*. A modern critic, investigating the history of a literary form, is less likely to take a Mosaic than a Darwinian point of view, such as is employed by Fernand Brunetière in *The Evolution of Genres in Literary History*. Perhaps under this head should also be included, in the study of an individual, the survey of other estimates of his work, as forms part of J. M. Robertson's consideration of Poe and all of Caroline F. E. Spurgeon's three volumes of collected *Chaucer Criticism and Allusion,* essay and anthology.

A second division is the psychology of art. Herein lies biographical criticism, which traces the life of the author that his work may be more readily and more fully comprehended. Carlyle's essay on Burns—written as a review of Lockhart's life of the poet—is an effective instance of this type. A more recent development is the psychanalytical essay, which seeks to explain the author's product, not by the surface events of his life, but through his inner frustrations and "subconscious" desires. Pioneer in this field was Van Wyck Brooks' *The Ordeal of Mark Twain*. As an offshoot of this type of consideration may be regarded the "new" biography (at least as old as Plutarch) set in current vogue by Lytton Strachey's *Eminent Victorians*, abetted by views through the "mirror" of Washington or of Downing Street (more alluring than the peep-shows of penny arcades) and by the dust of scandal raised now from many brooms.

[The tendency to "debunk" history that consists in revealing *The Private Life of Helen of Troy*, or the fact that George Washington enjoyed egg-noggs and dancing, is gently spanked by Berton Braley:

> Although, as through the world he plodded,
> It's said that Homer sometimes nodded,
> Note this about that poet-roamer—
> It wasn't nodding made him Homer!
>
> Napoleon was given to
> Doing some things he shouldn't do.
> These were his weak and phony part—
> They didn't make him Bonaparte!

Similarly it should be observed that "poetic license" indicates a fault, tolerated because of counterbalancing virtue:

> And though few tyros seem to know it,
> It's not one's license makes one poet!]

This particular brand of biographical criticism Gamaliel Bradford would trace to Sainte-Beuve, who said "I am a naturalist of souls". Bradford borrows the term Saintsbury used of the French critic, psychography, emphasizing the need of correctly interpreting a shoulder-shrug, a casual remark (no remark is casual), in building the victim's personality for new portrayal. As history, however, too seldom reports the shoulder-shrugs of even the most prominent figures, the critic is prone to lifting his hero's eyebrows when he would raise his own—and sends us to paraphrase the old Italian saying, as: Portrayal is Betrayal*.

Beyond this field stretches the domain we may call the sociology of art. As the previous division concerned itself with the problems of artistic perception and creation, the relation of the artist to the work of art; so here interest is directed toward the problems of the inception and of the communication of the work, the relation between the work of art and the society for which, or in which, it is produced. The environmental study of Taine finds prominent place in this group; here also belongs the work of Lewis Mumford, who in *Sticks and Stones* and *The Golden Day* is perhaps first to attempt a converse process, largely deriving the milieu and the race from its art. Interpretative essays may also be placed here, efforts to convey the meaning, the "message", of an artist, as Lowell in his study of Dante, as Shaw in *The Perfect Wagnerite*, as countless members of Shakespeare or of Browning societies. The studies of Arnold and of Ruskin present a variety of this type, seeking an ethical significance in the works that they consider. The more recent endeavors of such writers as Upton Sinclair in *Money Writes,* and V. F. Calverton, develop the environmental doctrine of Taine along the lines of economic determinism, seeking to trace, much more fundamentally than Taine suspected them, the factors that, if they do not produce the work of art, help to shape the artist. The fullest study along these lines, out-

* See Note 32

side, perhaps, of works untranslated from Germany and Soviet Russia, is Joshua Kunitz' survey of *Russian Literature and the Jew.*

The last division of critical consideration deals with the morphology of art, with the component materials of the work. Its scholarly aspect is textual criticism, the correction of errors in variant versions, the establishment of dates and authorships, the attribution of parts in collaborations, and other laborious and serviceable preliminaries to criticism—involving themselves, be it noted, considerable sensitivity and critical discernment. Perhaps the greatest single achievement in this field is Tyrwhitt's rediscovery of the fact that the final 'e' is valued in Chaucer's poetry; our understanding has been enlarged, and much beauty reclaimed, by such bodies of scholars as The Early English Text Society. Jules Romains states that from a study of the punctuation marks in his works, one critic reached sound psychological conclusions as to the author. More truly critical, in this group, is the great body of technical criticism, which studies the verse forms, the diction, the particular devices by which authors achieve their ends. Among the more colorful discussions of this sort is De Quincy's famous *On the Knocking at the Gate in 'Macbeth'*—though many seem to have mistaken the postscript for the essay. Another effective piece of technical analysis is *The Four-fold Problem of Diction,* in John Drinkwater's study of Victorian literature; Ruskin's consideration of the "blind mouths" of Milton's *Lycidas* is one more of the host of studies of this aspect of the work of art.

Recent activity has endeavored in many ways to employ in this technical consideration the general methods of modern science. The problems of artistic creation have always lured, as they have always baffled, the psychologist. What theory you will, of environment, of sublimation, fails to explain why

in "Sesame and Lilies"

one youth develops into a sot, and his neighbor, his brother, into a genius. Works of art, therefore, have been subjected to various statistical analyses; students have been requested to report their responses, in questionnaires directed to multitudinous ends—as though the muses could be caught with a kymograph. A favorite activity is to determine how often this color or that has been mentioned by a poet. Thus Karl Groos finds that while Schiller's youthful lyrics have twice as many optical references as Goethe's, both poets employ *red* less, and *green* more, as they grow older. Professor Edith Rickert shows, by a proportioned circle of the color-references in his writing, that William Sharp makes, in this respect at least, no considerable transformation when he signs himself Fiona Macleod. June Downey tells us, studying Keats, Shelly, Poe, Swinburne, and Blake, that Poe excels in auditory suggestions; Shelley, in olfactory; Keats, in cutaneous. Other investigators, like Nicolas Kostyleff, or Marguerite Wilkinson in *The Way of the Makers,* (women seem to be pioneers along these lines), seek the testimony of the artists themselves as to their methods, their secrets of the craft. Too often their words, or the reports of the students, or the works themselves, are accepted literally; possible rationalization of authors must be guarded against; the desire of students to seem wise or clever or helpful must be allowed for; "purple grapes" and "purple passion" must be distinguished. But such warnings are being issued by the investigators themselves, in comment upon one another's studies; and there are doubtless great possibilities latent in this pursuit of the essence of art through the laboratory.

One type of questionnaire tests the critic's appreciative powers, by presenting for his discrimination, say, as in the Abbott-Trabue series, a selection of poetry and three variations, one with the rhythm broken or made less subtle, one with the imagery made commonplace, one with the mood over-emphasized, made somehow sentimental. By the reader's choice among a number of such sets, his prejudices and predilections may be, to some extent, determined and counterbalanced.[13]

So prosaic a field as bibliography, Professor Daniel Mornet has shown, may through the survey of the number and dates of the editions of a book reveal interesting facts of readers' inclinations and changing tastes. Other varieties of scientific criticism aim more directly at the author. Numberless students, in advanced courses in literature or psychology, are being asked to record the images evoked by given selections, or to help compute the frequency and variety of sensory appeals in various writers. A new development, with its possibilities not yet explored, is the application (by Catherine M. Cox) of the methods of the intelligence test to authors through their works. We are told that the IQ (intelligence quotient: 100 equals the norm) of Bunyan as a child was 105, as a youth, 120; of Raphael, 110 and 150; of Kant 135 and 145; of Goethe, 185 and 200.[*] [Hegel, incidentally, says "Kant spoke the first rational word concerning beauty;" Bertrand Russell: "Kant has the reputation of being the greatest of modern philosophers, but to my mind he was a mere misfortune".]

The value of an intelligence rating of genius may be difficult to see; there is more perceptible reason for the painstaking study, by Vernon Lee and others, of the relation between materials and results; comparing, for instance, the prose of several writers as to the proportion of nouns, verbs, and adjectives, in the selections, as contributing to the quality of the writing; and in many ways indicating that such methods, while too detailed, perhaps, for general application, can be of great value in particular studies. Indeed, as a point

& absurd – if at all valid the I. Q. is constant throughout life.

of inquiry into the "secrets" of creation, more than the listing of types and rules, than biographical gossip or sociological speculation, this technical analysis is likely to prove illuminating to interested readers, and serviceable to artists in their craft.

THE CRITIC'S QUALITY

So I conjure you that you disquiet not yourself overmuch in this matter, for a broken spirit drieth the bones.
LETTERS OF OBSCURE MEN.

HAVING thus far considered that with which the critic
deals, we may give room to brief discussion of the characteristics of a good critic, or of good criticism. If we are examining
the critical essay, we may, wisely, observe not only its conclusions, but how they have been reached, the varieties and
quality of the argument or proof, the stated or implied
standards of judgment. The manner in which the immediate
occasion of the essay has affected the treatment should be
noted; and the general structure and particular qualities of
style subjected to analysis. From his various writings, one
may draw conclusions as to the quality of the critic.

Pater has said: "What is important, then, is not that the
critic should possess a correct abstract definition of beauty
for the intellect, but a certain kind of temperament, the
power of being deeply moved by the presence of beautiful
objects". While this leaves beautiful objects still to be defined, it is a sane insistence on immediate sensitivity. Valuable as such a quality may be, however, it is but the first step
toward criticism. With this appreciative power three other
elements of the critic's equipment must combine, to make his
offering worth while. Macaulay insisted that "no one ought
to set up as a judge of English who had not the Authorized
Version at his finger-ends". What André Gide says of all
artists is pertinent here of the critic: he "must not prefer
himself to the truth he would express: that's his whole
morality; nor the word nor the phrase to the idea it would

convey: that's his whole æsthetics". Irving Babbitt would have the critic approach the "golden impossibility", by combining the "feminine" virtues of comprehensiveness and sympathy with the "masculine" judgment, insight, and elevation. More modestly, as I say, three other aspects of the good critic may be suggested.

Personally, the critic should be marked by sincerity, fairness, candor; a freedom from rancor such as Byron bore; from malice—though mischief may have its moment; from the flippancy of many of our columnists—though a weighty argument may gain from lightness of touch; a boundless curiosity. As Baudelaire exclaims, so all true critics feel, in the presence of "something new that I was powerless to define, and this impotence irritated, held, and delighted me all at the same time, in a strange manner. . . . I resolved to discover why, and to transform my sensations into knowledge." "Question yourself when you laugh", said Stendhal; sweep that remark over every human activity, and you approach the spirit of the critic.

Intellectually, the critic must be doubly equipped. He should have a command of the relevant facts of life and art for use with each new work, such knowledge as would have prevented Dryden from speaking of Chaucer's "thousands" of imperfect lines (though Johnson had "reason to believe" the 'e' had once been vocal), or Lamb from telling us Shakespeare should be read, not acted. He should have, as well, logic and consistency in his reasoning, so that he may not, with Arnold, posit as a standard something he cannot define. He should be able to regulate his enthusiasm with the valve of common sense. [This balance should not, many feel, hold the critic from a predisposed fervor, such as Goethe insists upon; Oscar Wilde remarks scornfully that only an auctioneer can admire all schools of art; the present writer's volume of translations of modern French poets was scored with the phrase "One man cannot translate Hugo and Cocteau"; and Baudelaire states that the best criticism is partial and passionate. Perhaps the ideal critic would have a "predisposed fervor" for the best in every school.]

Formally, the critic must be able to express himself persuasively, if not convincingly; by the methods of the artist, symmetry and order, aptness, clarity, and proportion, unifying his impressions in a rounded whole, effecting the most seductive communication of his thought.

And again, emotionally, the critic must make manifest the depth of his sensitivity, the subtlety and suppleness and fineness and fulness with which he responds to the work of art. When Gide gives us this picture of Proust:—

Madame B . . . told me the other day that she had always had poor sight; her parents did not become aware of this at once, and it was not until she was almost twelve that she began to wear glasses. "I have the most vivid memory", she said, "of my joy when, for the first time, I could distinguish the separate pebbles in the courtyard."—When we read Proust, we suddenly begin to perceive details where before was only mass.

—we feel that Gide is enabling us to make finer distinctions. When Alain, in his *propos* on *Holly-Green,* pictures the reluctance of beauty to reveal its full blossom, we feel that he has blown to us some fragrance of the flower. When Francis Thompson reaches out to Shelley, we are aware of the presence of two poets as we read.

CHAPTER VI

NATURE AND ART

What I speak, my fair Chloe, and what I write, shows
The difference there is betwixt nature and art:
I court others in verse, but I love thee in prose;
And they have my whimsies, but thou hast my heart.
                                        MATTHEW PRIOR.

Devil take all theory!
FRANZ GRILLPARZER.

WHAT IS ART?

We should play all our lives, and never be entirely in
earnest.

SIMONIDES.

IN ATTEMPTING to recognize its characteristics, care must
be taken not to confuse art with beauty, its concomitant.
Beauty occurs, of course, in nature; but of those objects or
events called works of art, it is invariably product, and often
regarded as sign. Frequently, therefore, those seeking to
define art shift from one concept to the other as convenience
leads them. Every means to, or concomitant of, a desired end
may come itself to be an end of man's desiring. As Sybarites
protract the pleasures that are properly accompaniments of
sound bodily functioning, as Lucullans linger over the palatal
delights that may characterize our absorption of energy, so
æsthetes may wander from the trail of art on the quest of
naked beauty. They should remember that "Euclid alone has
looked on beauty bare"—and what he beheld was an abstraction!

An even more inviting web, in which the most influential
of contemporary critics, Croce, is entangled, is that spread
from the dome of art to the columns of artistic appreciation.
There has been a recent shifting of emphasis in critical consideration, after the period of art for art's sake and with the
new rise of a social consciousness and conscience, from the
work of art to the æsthetic attitude of the receptor. (Similarly, beauty comes to be defined, no longer in terms of the
object, but in terms of its effect.) During the transition from
one point of stress to the other, a measure of confusion might
be expected to arise . . . With these two cautions in mind,

we may proceed to see what has been meant by a work of art.

Defining—marking the limits or confines of a subject—involves comparison, setting it off from something else. The other great field, from which art must be separated, is nature. Longinus offered the key to this distinction, in the remark that nature supplies, art regulates. For in all the applications of the word "art", however far from fine art they may venture, as in the physician's art of diagnosis, the mechanic arts, the street-praise that "The way that man handles the bones is an art!"—there is the denotation of human activity, of human control, of man molding his environment. And in every reference to "nature", be it human nature, or the nature of the artist's materials (that he must know), there is the indication of something independent of human activity, beyond man's control—of the forces man's art cannot alter. Art is man added to nature. "Nature is the limit set to man." But Anatole France was anticipated by one greater: *

> Over that art
> Which you say adds to nature, is an art
> That nature makes. You see, sweet maid, we marry
> A gentler scion to the wildest stock,
> And make conceive a bark of baser kind
> By bud of nobler race: this is an art
> Which does mend nature, change it rather, but
> The art itself is nature.

The work of art, once it is an object, becomes a phenomenon of the natural world.

How set off what we call art from the other products of man? First, what distinction is traced between the fine arts and the useful arts? Leo Stein attempts to wave the matter aside. "The distinction between the fine arts and the others should not, in my opinion, have currency . . . It is much better to call everything art which is deliberately produced by man,

* Shakespeare

and not to be too fussy about the deliberation". But he is thus summary because eager to approach his own "very different" distinction of "pure and applied æsthetics".

The useful arts group themselves with science, in that they provide the instruments for other, later, satisfactions; they are weapons for carving comfort or delight: whereas works of art "provide instant satisfactions that are in an immediate sense present". Irwin Edman, indeed, calling art an exercise of the intelligence, points to "a very close resemblance between art and science, a resemblance so close that we might say that art is science, only more scientific." He elaborates this paradox by explaining that if a man explores human nature using himself and his neighbors as the guinea pigs of his psychological laboratory, he will (as O'Neill's *Strange Interlude* attests) falsify the presentation, to make himself more attractive, or because of narcissism, sadism, masochism, whatnot; whereas, if he chooses imaginary subjects, he may be disinterested, and aim at truth. Thus science is the process of collecting information about life through real material; art, the process of collecting information about life through imaginary material. Mr. Edman seems unaware that many an artist has real persons definitely in mind while creating his "imaginary" work; it is hard to see, furthermore, how these distinctions would apply to a symphony, or a landscape, or even to lyrics as personal as *The Skylark* or the *Ode to the West Wind*.

Approaching art through beauty, Kant calls that quality "the character of adaptation to a purpose without relation to an actual purpose." This rather clumsy effort at definition has been better put—beauty is its own excuse for being—in the statement of R. G. Collingwood, that "a work of art is a construction with no reference to anything outside its own internal structure." When we consider a machine it is, ordinarily, its efficiency we have in mind; a scientific law is usually thought of for its application or—when challenged— in its harmony with all relevant knowledge; a work of art is considered in terms of its inner clarity, and unity, and proportion. From this it follows that every object may be contemplated as art: the sailing craft, the automobile, may be viewed as a graceful body; the locomotive, as an object of self-contained restraint and power; the scientific law, as a splendid simplification, unification, of its theme. Did not Copernicus (for Galileo's later proof) arrive at certainty the earth went round the sun by consideration of the simplicity, the "unity in variety", the harmonious ordering, such a supposition gave to the mathematics and the music of the spheres? Every human construction, it may indeed be claimed, is art first, and is then drawn to its utility. The scientific law, the invention, exists in the mind as a concordant whole, part responding to part, each segment meaningless save with the rest, put to the one test of its inner harmony. Then there comes the application, the adjustment of this organized unit to an end, in science, industry, statesmanship. In the course of inspiration, man gets an idea; it seems good because of its self-sustaining rhythm; then he sees what ends it will subserve. The fine arts are art pure and simple: in other activities man adds the use.

This differentiation was perhaps glimpsed by Schopenhauer, when he linked knowledge with the æsthetic, and will with the practical, aspect of man's living: the apple as color and form, the apple as food. To attain this æsthetic consideration, to view the automobile, or the surgical operation, as art, it is necessary to withdraw from the object, to remove the elements of personal emotion, to replace concern with contemplation, to renounce doing and practice seeing. Every work of art is set in some sort of picture frame, achieves this "psychic distance", which each of the arts—as the verse in poetry, the stage in acted drama—has its own ways of winning.

Psychic distance consists in somehow setting the work of art off from other, more personal, more utilitarian, aspects of man's activity, so that, however deeply the emotions are stirred, they remain without bias of personal application. Some writers—of mystery plays, of romances—seek, on the contrary, to invite the reader into the work, to make him participant; as when the audience at a theatre are made the jury, or "Extras" detailing the stage-crime are distributed during intermission. Some moods or events,—the devotion of a mother, the consummation of passion—are more difficult than others to set at a psychic distance, to remove from insistent personal tuggings. Finding on their victim a photograph of his mother, the soldiers in Lawson's *Processional* stand in reverent salute—before continuing to maul him. The feeling thus satirized is so strong, however, that when a painter, at his mother's death-bed, sees her changing face in terms of portraiture, we deem him "inhumanly" cold, instead of adjudging that he is capable of distancing his own experiences to a degree we are too egocentric to attain. Many artists work their own lives—more, their neighbors'—into books.

Beyond the means inherent in its general form, the devices by which a work of art may be distanced are various and subtle. A cold atmosphere, remoteness of time or place, may serve to set off (not diminish) intensity of feeling in the tale; there is other ground than its divine inspiration for accepting in the *Bible* incidents elsewhere by some deemed pornographic or obscene. Many writers have found their land-dwelling readers properly distanced by the sea. Failure to achieve correct distance—every reader's requirements are different—will make the work seem too near, unduly sordid in its realism, too photographic for art; or will set it too far, as artificial, improbable, straining for its effects. Every work of art, however, achieves this sense of psychic distance for those who regard it as a work of art; because of it they tolerate, they may even approve, much that in ordinary life they would condemn—as Aristotle was perhaps not first to observe; through it they are able to view the work of art as self-dependent, self-contained. Of such a distancing, a "willing suspension of disbelief" is concomitant; though Coleridge's term implies a conscious activity, whereas an emotional acquiescence in the mood, properly induced, merely keeps the question of intellectual belief from rising. The work of art is judged in reference, not to all human knowledge, but to its own coherency of structure.

From the work of art as product we have been drawn to consider the work of art as a cause—in other words, the æsthetic attitude. When Croce says that anything taken intuitively into the mind, seen as a complete and unified image, is art, he (who Leo Stein says "reduces æsthetics to naught") means precisely what Leo Stein and others mean when they speak of the æsthetic attitude. All are concerned, not with the outward product, the work of art, but with the effect of something upon the receptor's mind.

An object is viewed æsthetically, says Leo Stein, when it is "known, unified, and enduring". When known, the object is seen as a whole, as an image or picture; furthermore, it is understood, not desired or disliked; it acts as a catalyst: "the object is not altered by being known, but the knower is". Goethe makes much the same statement in the field of the will, saying of Winckelman: "You do not learn anything when you read him, but you become something". In being apprehended as unified, the object is so seen that it has meaning only as a whole; the removal, alteration, or shifting of the parts destroys the object. The elements in works of art are fused as in chemical compounds; you can describe a picture in terms of its elements no more accurately than you can describe water by giving the qualities of hydrogen and oxygen. If enduring, an object is not destroyed by use; it has the same effect each time it is viewed. Leo Stein's "known" seems not precise, for æsthetic contemplation implies always a to-be-known. It is only when one has surpassed the powers of a work that he feels it as finally known; and indeed Mr. Stein makes the amendment, pointing out that few regard Shakespeare as known, but many read Longfellow with a sense of mere recall.

Mr. Stein then speaks of a pure æsthetic state: that of indefinitely continued exploration in the work of art (which runs the risk of lapsing into the inventorial attitude*) and of an applied æsthetic state, which has three variations. When one contemplates an object in any of these three ways, it does not stand by itself; it needs completing. As Virginia Woolf says of the books of Bennett, Galsworthy and Wells:

In order to complete them it is necessary to do something—to join a society or, more desperately, to write a check. That done, the restlessness is laid, the book finished; it can be put upon the shelf, and need never be read again. . . . *Tristram Shandy* or *Pride and Prejudice* is complete in itself; it is self-contained; it leaves one with no desire to do anything, except indeed to read the book again, and to understand it better.

There may be distinguished such attitudes as that toward a fox-trot, which leads us to dance, or to day dream, or (more desperately) desire to rewrite; toward an ax, which we use; and toward knowledge that we acquire to feed our ego, as Little Jack Horner (like many politicians equally successful) vaunted his intelligence . . . although the moral bias appears in some versions, wherein he exclaims "What a *good* boy am I!"

* See page 45.

In the insistence upon a proper æsthetic attitude in the receptor, there has come into criticism an ordered consideration of what men like Longinus or Pater implied when they asked that reader as well as writer be informed, be serious. To have great poets there must be great audiences too. At the basis of this appreciation lies intelligence, of course, understanding of the writer's theme and methods, acquaintance with the relevant background; less easily acquired is the equally essential sympathetic grasp, the intuitive leap that takes in the artist's theme, and the work of art, as a whole. As Theseus says when the horny-handed men offer their labored play: "The best in this kind are but shadows; and the worst are no worse, if imagination amend them". And alas, how often must we echo Hippolyta's reply: "It must be your imagination, then; not theirs"! But as true love seeks neither return, nor merit in the beloved, as to the greatest lover (the Christ) all is lovable, so perhaps by the greatest artist—the most æsthetically receptive—all things are seen as works of art.

ART AMONG MAN'S ACTIVITIES

> We may illustrate the course by which thought has hitherto run by likening it to a web woven of three different threads—the black thread of magic, the red thread of religion, and the white thread of science, if under science we may include those simple truths, drawn from observation of nature, of which men in all ages have possessed a store. Could we survey the web of thought from the beginning, we should probably perceive it to be at first a chequer of black and white, a patchwork of true and false notions, hardly tinged as yet by the red thread of religion. But carry your eye farther along the fabric and you will remark that, while the black and white chequer still runs through it, there rests on the middle portion of the web, where religion has entered most deeply into its texture, a dark crimson stain, which shades off insensibly into a lighter tint as the white thread of science is woven more and more into the tissue.
>
> SIR JAMES GEORGE FRAZER.

THERE may be further clarification of the relation of art to man, if an attempt be made to place it amid the other human processes. Clayton Hamilton suggests that there are, first, the scientific discovery of truth, which realism stresses, and which is exemplified in the works of Jane Austen and of Zola; then philosophic understanding, sought if not attained in George Eliot and Tolstoi; finally, artistic expression, whereon romance lays emphasis, as in Irving and d'Annunzio. The examples given are, perhaps, less peculiar than the order Hamilton presents, which runs counter both to such knowledge as we have, and common sense.

A development at once more logical and more thorough is carried through by R. G. Collingwood. He begins by reminding us of perhaps the commonest fallacy in general thought, the error of abstraction, and its frequent companion, the separation of the subject from the object, good from evil—

any of the "distinct but inseparable" extremes of a gradual and unlimited series. Try to sever top from bottom of a stick; you have but doubled your problem.[14] Proceeding from this reminder, the analyst considers the various phases of man's mental activity, seeing in each much good, yet fundamental error that keeps it from yielding full truth—until the last.

Art, he places first of man's impulses. (Alain traces the psychology of the savage who, after having made a figure, awed by its immutability, its independence of law and change and question, feared, then worshiped it.) Art is man's flying leap into the dark, the flight of his imagination in quest of reality. Conceive it, if you will, as man's flight from reality, or as "the knowledge science cannot reach"; it remains a venturing in the province of the imagination. The man who dwells therein is a lunatic (or a lover); he who plays there, a poet. As Gilbert Murray remarks, the artist is "moving in an imaginary world and playing there as children play". But the artist, creating as many worlds as there are works of art, fails to achieve one comprehensive cosmos.

Religion rectifies this shortcoming of art; it draws these myriad worlds into a single system. The nymphs and hama-dryads, the goddess rising from the sea at dawn, the thunder, and the springtime, and the generating sun, become appropriate parts of a story of creation and the universe. But while art peoples the grove and the fountain, religion believes in and prays to these embodiments; it accepts the symbol for the fact; it fails to distinguish the world of imagination from the world of reality.

Science marks the transition from the fields of imagination—of intuition, of faith—to the province of thought. But science has been carried astray in quest of the general rule, the abstraction—which, however convenient in conversation and in science, is false. Of late, indeed, science has recognized this limitation; not only does it speak frankly of its basic structures as hypotheses [15], content to dwell wholly in a world of shadowy symbols; but it turns, on the other hand, to emphasize less truth than usefulness. When it speaks of hypotheses, however, science is no longer accepting merely abstractions, which are necessarily false, but is rearing its structures on imaginary abstractions. And its turning toward utility is but turning in a circle, for *use* is a term of the scientific sphere; art is not, nor religion, concerned with the concept. But indeed, science cannot really escape, by talk of probabilities, its tendency to seek the general rule.

History carries thought back to the world of particulars. (In much of its experimentation and recording, of course, science uses the methods of history.) But the concept of history admits a world wherein every event is conditioned by every other event. Since it is impossible to know all the facts relevant to any occurrence (i.e. all facts), it is manifest that history cannot bring men to truth. The recorder of any event, furthermore, must for both fulness and impartiality of observation be outside the thing that he records; such an assumption, underlying the writing of history, makes false separation of subject and object (and, incidentally, accounts for the errors, only recently recognized, due to the "personal element" in scientific observations).

Philosophy has too often been tangled in the errors of the earlier forms, has been a variant (as well as a handmaid) of science or religion. True philosophy is "the activity of the self-conscious mind", wherein, since the subject embraces the object, the universe too assembles; and the more completely one achieves obedience to the command: Know thyself, the more fully one wins knowledge of all reality. He who pursues the proper study of mankind is also scanning God.

For each problem of man's being the cycle is renewed.

Art—granting always what Collingwood unquestioning presupposes: that the purpose of all man's mental activities
is alike the attainment of knowledge, the lighting of the dark
ways of life [16]—art is the questioning edge of the imagination, the first sensing of unfound truths, asserted as beauty.
Religion follows, attempting to order these imaginatively
glimpsed truths into an acceptable explanation of the universe, accord with which is goodness. Science is the questioning edge of thought, which leaps ahead like art, and seeks to
order like religion. History walks behind amid the concrete
facts of life, observing, checking. Philosophy accomplishes
the synthesis; this mote of reality (still floating in the random air) is tentatively assigned its landing-place. Then the
process starts anew. And ever the artistic impulse, religious
fervor, scientific curiosity, historical exactness, farther advance upon the great unknown, and challenge the ultimate
darkness.

This picture gives new meaning to Wordsworth's remark
that the first and last of all knowledge is poetry.

* * * * * * *

Among the avenues of man's dim explorations, the new
way of psychanalysis has led to thoughts of art. The
Freudian theory of suppressed desires makes art a ready
sublimation, an ideal wish-fulfilment. The emphasis upon a
sense of inferiority, instead of, or in addition to, sex, hardly
alters this conception; and the classification of men as introvert and extrovert merely adds another adjective for cross-
classification of the artist. Of the variations played upon
this theme, that of Rebecca West, as of one who has also
produced works of art, may be surveyed:

> Every man is in a state of conflict, owing to his attempt to rec-
> oncile himself and his relationship with life to his conception of
> harmony. This conflict makes his soul a battlefield, where the

forces that wish this reconciliation fight those that do not, and reject the alternative solutions they offer. Works of art are attempts to fight out this conflict in the imaginative world.

I suppose Miss West would answer one objection with the retort that day-dreams, the delusions and the scrawlings of the insane, and the false conceptions of the overwrought, are efforts to avoid this conflict; yet every attempted resolution is equally flight. It becomes even more difficult to follow, through the fighting forces that "wish" or spurn reconciliation, to her picture of art as a sort of entity, within yet beyond the individual artist, a sort of "super-cortex . . . whose business it is to pick out of the whole complexity of the environment those units which are of significance, and to integrate those units into an excitatory complex". But often, when amateur psychanalysts (and their masters) talk of complexes, the language grows too complex for mere intelligence to unravel to sound meaning.

Attempting to define the work of art in terms of the impulse to create, as the labors of the psychanalysts show, is perilous if not futile. For there is often little visible relationship between any known impelling force—such as an assignment from an editor: Paul Valéry was once told precisely how many type-spaces an article was to fill—and the completed work; while the assertion of a universal compulsion raises new difficulties, as to why only certain men become artists, and leaves unanswered old questions as to the judgment of their works. The effort of Valéry to achieve an emotionless definition of art, as something deliberately constructed, as "a machine designed to excite and combine the individual formations" of a particular level of readers, one "category of minds", and adding that "enthusiasm is not a state of mind for an artist"—makes neither the process nor the product more comprehensible. As we have seen, moreover, there is an increasing, almost an overwhelming, movement toward describing art, and beauty, in terms neither of the artist, nor of his product as an entity, a *Ding an sich,* but of the ones who are to receive, to appreciate, to enjoy the work of art.

THE GOOD, THE TRUE, THE BEAUTIFUL

Come you from heaven or hell,
What matter, Beauty!
CHARLES BAUDELAIRE.

MORALS have a shadow-like way of clinging. Straining through the darkness of mazy discussion, we think we have, if not disposed of, at least dispensed with, the problem of value. We venture toward the light, and behold! still it trails us. Nay, it has gathered reënforcements; we must strive to part the serried ranks of the good, the true, the beautiful.

The number three has through the ages exercised a strange influence over men. Long before the Christian trinity gave it wide circulation, it had acquired esoteric significance. While *three* may not be company, it certainly has crowded the pages of magic and of mystic recording. Almost anything seems to fall "naturally" into a tripartite division: a yardstick and a tragedy have a beginning, a middle, and an end; a circle may be described in terms of center, radius, circumference; time has its past, present, and future, its ancient, medieval, and supremely modern. Masson's essay on De Quincey ends with the remark:

It is a permanent addition to the mythology of the human race. As the Graces are three, as the Fates are three, as the Furies are three, as the Muses were originally three, so may the varieties and degrees of misery that there are in the world, and the proportions of their distribution among mankind, be represented to the human imagination forever by De Quincey's Three Ladies of Sorrow.

What will not prove susceptible of trisection? Thus there has been listed the trinity of man's responses: *will* (moral strength, goodheartedness, desire), *feeling* (pleasure, non-

205

pleasure, displeasure), and thought (conception, association, memory). And when truth is obviously the end of thought, and goodness manifestly the goal of human will, what more "natural", more inevitable, than to find equal intimacy between emotion and beauty! [17]

Unfortunately, the perfect parallel fails at this point; beauty steals from truth Antæan powers, and rises ever insistent. The confusion meanwhile has led to two confoundings. There have been efforts to define beauty in terms of an emotional absolute, an essential, intrinsic, "æsthetic emotion"; some who have drawn away from this temptation have defined it in negative terms, as anything that is not thought or will—that is neither inquisitive nor acquisitive, that does not question, and does not seek to use. In vehement withdrawal from such tendencies, those that feel folly in a completely emotional description of beauty have often—led of course by other considerations as well—linked the beautiful either with the good or with the true.

Of the identity of beauty and virtue much has already been said. Even Poe made proper obeisance, though he, as later Baudelaire and Pater, shifted the emphasis. Poetry, he says,

is not forbidden to depict, but to reason and preach of virtue. As of this latter, conscience recognizes the obligation, so intellect teaches the expediency, while taste contents itself with displaying the beauty: waging war with vice merely on the ground of its inconsistency with fitness, harmony, proportion—in a word with το καλόν.

Gilbert Murray makes an even more precise presentation:

It looks as if beauty might have greater claim than either happiness or virtue to be in itself the solution, or the nearest man can approach to a solution, of the ultimate secret of the world. Happiness is a terribly frail foundation on which to build any theory of life; and it seems to the plain man that happiness cannot be the ultimate goal because it has so often to be sacrificed for something better than itself. Virtue, or moral goodness, is too purely human a thing; and has too much the air of a means to an end beyond itself. Beauty is in things human and non-human, and seems almost omnipresent in the natural world. Now, if we ask Aristotle or Plato why a man should act righteously, or why he ought sometimes to sacrifice his happiness or to welcome martyrdom, they will answer, in language which to a Greek is perfectly simple though possibly strange to us, that he should do so ἕνέκα τόῦ καλον, for the sake of the beautiful.*

In these words we hear a ring quite other than that which sounds when J. Middleton Murry assures us the identity "which Plato established between the good and the beautiful" is "axiomatic, absolute, irreducible." Not goodness is beautiful, but beauty is good.

Those who are not content to hear that beauty lies in virtue, even when the word comes in the form that virtue consists in beauty, have often sought to link art with that other desideratum and far goal of man's questing, truth. Despite Poe's dictum that it is hopeless to "reconcile the obstinate oils and waters of poetry and truth", despite the implications of Coleridge's remark that all art involves a suspension of disbelief, critics as well as poets, since Plotinus sought the essence of reality behind Plato's "imitation" of life, have told us that

> "Beauty is truth, truth beauty": that is all
> Ye know on earth, and all ye need to know.

"All beauty", says Pater, "is in the long run only fineness of truth, or what we call expression, the fine accommodation of speech to that vision within." And while Pater limits his intent to the truthful conveying of the artist's vision, without regard to the degree of accuracy with which that vision captures any outer reality, the wider insistence is more usual. J. Livingston Lowes surveys many works to reach his

* From *The Classical Tradition In Poetry*, copyright by the President and Fellows of Harvard College.

moderate conclusion that "beauty is truth, presented through
illusion, tinged with emotion". Our "younger generation",
less reluctant to rush in, cries out (let Irwin Edman be
spokesman):

Truth is always propositional; it is a statement about a fact. But
facts are data of immediate experience, and it is the special
privilege of the fine arts to reveal immediate data with a clarity,
intensity, and purity that promotes them as it were to a special
degree of reality. . . . The "things" in a painting have more
purity and precision and intensity than the things as seen by the
routine practical eye. The characters in a novel have more urgency
and clarity than the people we brush against in our daily contacts. The place to seek for reality is not in some metaphysical
formula, but in the unimpeachable realities in works of art.

Of such a presentation, several criticisms at once rise. Why
do pleaders of a cause often state their case unfairly, by setting up a dummy opponent, to destroy in a phrase? It takes
no potent breath to blow down a straw man. Why must the
"unimpeachable realities in works of art" (if they exist) be
balanced against "some metaphysical formula", instead of
what some may deem not wholly impeachable realities in
nature and in life? If the "things in a painting have more
purity and precision and intensity than the things as seen
by the routine practical eye", is the logical conclusion that
they are truer? Has not the artist, perhaps, enabled us to
see with more "purity" precisely because he has simplified
the presentation, has singled out, isolated, certain elements,
has therefore falsified (and inevitably falsified) to gain this
purity and precision and intensity? Has not the artist, furthermore, in his capacity as man, first had the vision he now
conveys? What is there in the nature of his processes as an
artist, what differences mark him from other men, to warrant our believing that his vision of reality is more accurate
than that of the scientist—who examines the data of immediate experience with trained eye, or of the philosopher—

who seeks to draw these facts into a unified system, or even of the statesman, the merchant, the man in the street—who, like the artist, intuitively organize these data into separate visions of their own?

To state that art reveals truth, or produces (by developing or demanding) virtue, is, furthermore, mere characterization, listing of incidental attributes; from such a declaration we draw no knowledge that will enable us to distinguish art from the kymograph or the employment bureau. If we state that a work of art is that product of man's activity which reveals truth or produces virtue without intending to, we have framed a definition which not merely sounds trivial, but may include such human products as a letter left lying, or the last train home. Perhaps, therefore, while recognizing that virtue is good, and truth useful, and that art (along with all other of man's functionings, and nature's phenomena) may be basis of ethical or scientific deductions, it may be well to set these temporarily apart from the criteria we are seeking, and to ask if essential attributes of art may else be found. Having already speculated upon the object, the work of art, let us turn to its concomitant, beauty.

WHAT IS BEAUTY?

A thing of beauty is a joy forever.

JOHN KEATS.

O Lady! We receive but what we give!

SAMUEL T. COLERIDGE.

BEAUTY has been bound in so many empty nets of words that one begins to think it too wide a conception for any one definition to comprehend, or too impalpable, or too Protean, for all defining. Since we must, however, make, before we abandon, the attempt, we may even presume a suggestion of our own, after examining what others have had to say. We shall, at least, fail in good company.

The sixteen most commonly offered definitions of beauty have been gathered and studied by Messrs. Ogden, Richards, and Wood. While the details of their arrangement may in some instances be questioned, their main tripartite classification seems valid. Beauty, through the ages, they declare, has been considered as essence, as relation, or as cause.

Anything is beautiful, it might be said, that possesses the simple quality, beauty. And if you think it unlikely this should be said, hear Professor John Laird:

Human actions are good or bad in a moral sense, a value or its opposite belongs to them, in the same sense as redness belongs to a cherry. For similar reasons the values of beauty or its opposite belong to certain things in certain connections, just as objectively as any other qualities.

And lest you should think that in these days of relativity, such absolutes will be postulated only by out-of-date pedants, consider that a similarly intrinsic, though formal, quality is held to be the basis of beauty, by some of the most popular critics of our day. Vernon Lee declares that "a relation entirely *sui generis* between visible and audible forms and ourselves" can be deduced from the fact that given proportions, shapes, patterns, compositions, have a tendency to recur in art. The English trio is content to remark that tennis tends to recur in summer without anyone's ever trying to establish a *sui generis* relation! Clive Bell devotes a book to emphasizing that "either all works of visual art have some common quality, or when we speak of 'works of art' we gibber"; and to seeking that essential characteristic.

What quality is common to the Sta Sophia and the windows in Chartres, Mexican sculpture, a Persian bowl, Chinese carpets, Giotto's frescos at Padua, and the masterpieces of Poussin, Piero della Francesca, and Cezanne? Only one answer seems possible—significant form. In each, lines and colors combined in a particular way, certain forms and relations of forms, stir our æsthetic emotions. These relations and combinations of lines and colors, the æsthetically moving forms, I call "significant form", and "significant form" is the one quality common to all works of visual art.

It would have been as logical for Clive Bell to select, as his one quality, the power of rousing his "æsthetic emotions"—whatever those special feelings may be. Roger Fry seems to know:

For the moment I must be dogmatic and declare that the æsthetic emotion is an emotion about form. In certain people purely formal relations of certain kinds arouse peculiarly profound emotions, or rather I ought to say the recognition by them of particular kinds of formal relations arouses these emotions.

If this is not arguing in a circle, it seems at least to be definition by label, as when one agrees that the common characteristic of all the causes of death is that they are lethal. Such a theory, moreover, leads to such judgments as this of Leonard Woolf:

I deny that the qualities which make the *Æneid*, or *King Lear*, or the *Iliad*, or *War and Peace*, or *Paradise Lost*, or *Mme Bovary*, or

Emma good stuff have anything to do with really good and up-lifting stories, interesting characters, and interesting scenes, though I agree that what the general public primarily wants from a book is a good story and a certain amount of uplift.

—this of Clive Bell:

To appreciate a work of art we need bring with us nothing from life, no knowledge of its ideas and affairs, no familiarity with its emotions.

—and this (lest you presume) of T. S. Eliot:

Very few know when there is expression of significant emotion, emotion which has its life in the poem and not in the history of the poet.

Nor has any Œdipus come forward to satisfy the many who, hearing the term "significant form", innocently wonder "significant of what?"

Among the conceptions of beauty as relation, the most popular has been that anything is beautiful which is an imitation of nature. This, of course, shifts the problem of beauty from art to nature, unless the beauty be held to reside in the fact of imitation. Aristotle spoke of the pleasure of recognition, but even before the development of the camera, Coleridge had declared simulations of nature, such as wax-work figures, disagreeable, and Dryden had said:

There may be too great a likeness; as the most skilful painters affirm, that there may be too near a resemblance in a picture: to take every lineament and feature, is not to make an excellent piece; but to take so much only as will make a beautiful resemblance of the whole; and, with an ingenious flattery of nature, to heighten the beauties of some part, and hide the deformities of the rest.

Dryden suggests an improving (Aristotle's "idealizing") imitation of nature; Coleridge would also have the artist refrain from copying, but because 'tis idle rivalry to match its perfection; the modern expressionist lays the same injunction, but with the remark: "Here it is, why bother trying to copy it!" The notion, indeed, that art holds a mirror up to nature is the frequent forerunner of divergent theories, each in that glass beholding his own form. Thus Hugo moves with his personal logic on:

But if it is an ordinary mirror, a smooth and polished surface, it will yield but a dull image of objects, with no relief—faithful but colorless . . . The drama, therefore, must be a concentrating mirror, which, instead of weakening, concentrates and condenses the colored rays, which makes of a mere gleam a light, and of a light a flame. Then only is the drama acknowledged by art.

Nietzsche more bluntly declares that "from an artistic point of view, nature is no model". While each in the mirror of art sees but himself, however, if the reader be sensitive and the work good, it may serve to make visible that in himself which without it he would never have seen.

In this division, beauty as relation, lie also the definitions that anything is beautiful which results from successful exploitation of a medium—though the word "successful" makes the definition fail; and that, as Irwin Edman points it: "Part of the beauty of a building is the sense it gives of its adaptation to its function, the nice adaptation of what is seen to the object it is intended to serve". Ruskin approaches this conception when, among his many searchings, he inquires "whether, if scorpion, it have poison enough, or if tiger, strength enough, or if dove, innocence enough, to sustain rightly its place in creation, and come up to the perfect idea of dove, tiger, or scorpion". Bergson, in his remark that

the more we are entangled in living the less truly we are able to see. We hardly see the object itself; we are content to know the class to which it belongs. We are content; but from time to time by happy chance men are born who are not bound to the treadmill of practical life. When they see a thing they look at it for itself.

—Bergson is supporting the definition that anything is beautiful which is the work of genius. First catch your genius.

The idea that anything is beautiful which reveals truth has been surveyed, and the various senses of truth or reality, the *Zeitgeist*, unity in variety, the ideal, the universal, need not further detain us; though Professor Helen H. Parkhurst rises in long rhapsody with the idea that beauty consists in the resolution of the great antinomies of the universe: unity in variety, the arhythmic in the rhythmical, "light and darkness, heat and cold, motion and rest, sound and silence, sleep and waking, life and death . . . The function of art, of all art, is to echo in its own terms the universal conflict." And indeed, as a relation, a harmony within the work, this concept holds the beauty of the classical mean.

The conception of beauty as that which leads to virtue has also had attention. Quite contrary to these, however, seems the notion that anything is beautiful which produces illusion. Konrad Lange thus extends Coleridge's prescription as the fundamental element in art: "the essence of æsthetic appreciation is conscious self-deception". There are two senses, perhaps one should say two qualities, of illusion in art. One carries the reader into the world of deliberate fantasy, over the housetops to Never-Never Land, or through the looking-glass to meet the White Queen. The other takes him into the world he more ordinarily ranges, and pictures that world with such intensity that for the time he forgets he is beholding only a selection from life. Herein lies a pitfall; while this ravishing of the senses, this sweeping away from all else in the overwhelming impression of the moment, when the works "make themselves be forgotten in what they represent", is the gift of the most serious art (as the pathetic fallacy may mark the highest soaring); so is it, on another plane, the easy boon to shopgirl and tired business man, to those who would forget their troubles at the play—as others do in drink, and which, is little matter. Art thus affords, possibly the artist, surely the reader, escape from reality*, release from the humdrum daily drudgery, from all the banality too often told in trite phrases: "art is the quickest way out of the Bronx". But this sort of illusion (which the cinema has taken it upon itself to supply) seems of distant relation to beauty.

A current "scientific" definition of beauty as revealing truth is embodied in such descriptions as that of W. T. Stace, who calls it

the fusion of an intellectual content, consisting of empirical non-perceptual concepts, with a perceptual field, in such manner that the intellectual concept and the perceptual field are indistinguishable from one another; and in such manner as to constitute a revelation of an aspect of reality.

By an "empirical non-perceptual concept" is intended such abstract ideas as order, evolution, perdurance; and the greater the intellectual element, the richer the work of art resulting from its organic fusion with a perceptual field. Although this description seems to prefer the abstruse to the simple, it aims more directly than most at a scale of beauty, it presses one principle by which critics may some day construct a callimeter.

The last definition considering beauty as relation is that of Benedetto Croce, which also has been considered. It is but fair, however, if one feels that something more than mere expression be essential to art, to record Croce's rejoinder that "no one has ever been able to indicate in what the something more exists . . . the limits of the expressions that are called art as opposed to those that are commonly considered 'not art' are empirical and impossible to define. If an epigram be art, why not a single word?" One may add, why not a

* See page 409.

comma? This *reductio ad absurdum,* however, seems a boomerang; for it serves to reëmphasize the need of more definite characterization.

Such a limitation is suggested by Leo Stein:

> Surgeons often speak of a beautiful operation, and engineers of a beautiful job, and if beautiful and æsthetic worth are to be taken as equivalent, their use of the term is accurate—[though his conjunction of a noun and an adjective is not!] The surgeon does not mean that the sight is beautiful, but he does mean that the operation is typical, a perfect expression of a felt interest, and therefore he has the right to call it beautiful.

But what a perfect expression of a felt interest many an urchin achieves by thumbing his nose! . . . We have already seen how the surgeon may look on his work as art.

"Beauty is no quality in things themselves", says Hume, "it exists merely in the mind that contemplates them". Whistler made an analogous remark to the woman in the art gallery who told him a picture was obscene. Intelligent persons are growing less prone to the fallacy of projecting the effect as a quality of the cause—speaking of wretched weather when the weather is tolerably void of feeling, though they are wretched; and the last group of definitions is content to consider beauty in terms of its effects. This is a looser (though not necessarily more vague) method of delimitation, for it insists on no single quality in the thing defined, admitting to the category whatever produces the specified effect.

The first of these definitions accepts anything as beautiful that causes pleasure. This admits perhaps the entire stock of the general country store, tobacco and bicycles and "sody-pop". Yet no less an authority than Ruskin it is who declares that "any object is beautiful which in some degree gives us pleasure", and Santayana who concurs: "Beauty is pleasure regarded as a quality of a thing". This interpretation is often held by those who point a close relationship between art and sex, as Haydon: "The beautiful has its origin altogether in woman" (forgetting the Greeks); the Freudians, less forgetful, equally emphasize the rôle of sex—or between art and play, as Grant Allen: "What play is to the active faculties, art and the æsthetic pleasures are to the passive". Psychologists, however, are beginning to differentiate between the "merely pleasant" in art, and that which is "æsthetically toned"; and pleasure is generally regarded as a by-product, the accompaniment of smooth functioning, rather than a limiting quintessential. The many who extend this definition to the idea that beauty is anything that rouses emotion, manifestly include such irrelevancies as an annoying child or blister, a revolver shot, and the course of a flirtation. Thus André Gide refuses Anatole France a place amid the highest because no "trembling" comes with reading him; and an English writer says that she recognizes great works very simply: they give her "goose-flesh" . . . It is as far as Croce's fallacy to leap from the thought that all beauty rouses emotion to the view that all that rouses emotion is beauty.

Many a follower of fashion is pinned by the comment that æsthetic pleasure often consists in the knowledge of what one should feel, rather than in feeling.

One of the most impressive definitions of beauty still current conceives of anything as beautiful that draws us into its being. Artists themselves frequently refer, in correspondence or in their formal works, to moments of absorption in nature, or in their product. Dickens wept when his favorite characters had to die. Flaubert tasted the poison he gave Madame Bovary; he seems, indeed, capable of more extended transfer:

This has been one of the rare days I have spent entirely in illusion. It is a delightful experience, no longer to be oneself but to live wholly in the world that one is creating. I have been man and woman today, at once lover and mistress. On horseback, through an autumn afternoon, under the yellowing leaves of the forest. I am the horse, the leaves, the wind, the spoken words, the red sun that makes them close their love-drenched eyes.

Such testimony, which many call "literature"—imaginative expansion for effect, figurative expression—is the basis of Lipp's doctrine of *Einfühling,* or empathy. Says Souriau: "We have only one way of imagining things from the inside, and that is putting ourselves inside them". Lotze asserts that we accomplish this feat: "We project ourselves into the forms of a tree, identifying our life with that of the slender shoots which swell and stretch forth, feeling in our souls the delight of the branches which drop and poise delicately in mid-air". Edman takes the blending for granted, and discriminates, declaring it "most notable and obvious in sculpture. We feel ourselves poised in movement and in rest with the discus thrower, and our own muscles grow tight with the tensions of some of the figures, tortured and muscular, of Michelangelo". Münsterberg brings it toward physiology: "If the energies we feel in the lines are external projections of our own energies, we understand the psychological reasons why certain combinations of lines please us and others do not. They ought to be such that they correspond to the natural energies of our own organism, and represent the harmony of our own muscular functions". And Vernon Lee sets it in the field of æsthetics: "When this attribution of our modes of life to visible shapes and this revival of past experience is such as to be favorable to our existence and in so far pleasurable, we welcome the form thus animated by ourselves as beautiful". While the objections of Ogden, Richards, and Wood to this definition are not especially convincing—they regard it as a vague return to the pleasure theory, and while other objections are with difficulty summoned*, it is unques-

* See page 373f.

tionably hard to repeat, with hopes of obedience, Shelley's imperative to the west wind.

Recognition of this difficulty has led some to limit the idea of empathy to events (works of art) involving a human conflict. Another modification of the theory is implicit in recent analyses of psychologists, who suggest three possible attitudes of the receptor of a work of art: as spectator, as participant, as "ecstatic". The first of these is a detached observation, regarding the work of art as any other phenomenon of life, refusing (or unable) to be caught in its seduction. Such an attitude may be critical, but will be without sympathetic understanding, without effort to see the work from within, through its own lenses. Here the pedant stalks. The participant identifies himself with one (or successively with several) of the personalities and forces of the work; his attitude is empathic. He is, of course, incapable of artistic evaluation, if not, indeed, led to false values by the greater ease with which he may sink himself into sentimentality. He will, furthermore, tend to weary of a work, seeking constantly new persons to become; though—since the identification obliterates all else—little more than the name need be changed. The novelist in *The Beggar on Horseback* is writing his sixteenth best seller by dictating the fifteenth. Beyond this attitude, however, lies a third, in a sort a blending of the other two. The receptor feels with the characters, is propelled by the forces, of the work; he enters into and shares its moods, taking the valid work with its intrinsic, self-set code—yet remains always himself, consciously understanding, enjoying, the work of art. His feelings then play upon what he enjoys: what is concordant stir within him, he attributes to it as beauty, which is thus revealed as love without desire.

This attitude may be more fully grasped after a consideration of the effect which the three English thinkers have been holding for their final definition. Worringer in Germany, indeed, suggests a dualism through the ages: man constantly seeking to intensify the forms and forces of life, to quicken their flow in him; and man ever desirous of withdrawing from the flux of life to contemplation. This objective regard the three call synæsthesis [18], and draw from old Chinese doctrine:

Having no leanings is called Chung: admitting of no change is called Yung. By Chung is denoted equilibrium; Yung is the fixed principle regulating everything under heaven. If both equilibrium and harmony exist everything will occupy its proper place and all things will be nourished and flourish.

The work of art produces harmony, in that it stimulates, at the same time, usually opposed impulses: keen thought with strong feeling, fear (as at a tragedy) yet calm. It produces equilibrium, in that these usually opposed impulses are stimulated in equal degree, are balanced so that there is no action or desire, but a general intensification of consciousness, of all the phases of man's being, exercising all man's faculties fully, and together. This theory involves, as corollary, the conception of relativity in art: to each man that is beautiful which affords him the greatest and most rounded stimulation of which he is capable; and doubtless, then, there are persons, to whom Sophocles must remain Greek, for whom *Abie's Irish Rose* and the newspaper comic strips are works of art. The value of a work of art, then, depends upon the level of intellectual and emotional complexity at which the stimulus works, or to which it raises the receptor [19].

Love being one of the "positive" emotions, that quicken all the aspects of one's being (save, proverbially, one's awareness of the faults of the beloved!) there may be something akin to this synæsthesis in the thoughts that link beauty with love. Certainly the symptoms of the contagion of love are similar to those of beauty's taking: that repeated transport Longinus knew—call it gusto, ecstasy; or with Chaucer know "the fresshe beautee sleeth me sodeynly". "Beauty", says Gilbert Murray, "is that which when seen is loved. As an element in experience, it makes the whole experience precious". Shelley derives poetic creation from love—though his idea is closer to empathy: "a going out of our own nature and an identification of ourselves with the beautiful which exists in thought, action, or person, not our own". Rebecca West suggests that "the bridge between love and art" is that art makes universal what love has kept personal: one loves for oneself, one beautifies for all. Love is an intense awareness, plus desire. In the presence of beauty, as Thomas Aquinas noted, desire is stilled. Perhaps one may say that beauty is love without desire, content to contemplate rather than eager to possess. It seems most satisfactory to explain beauty as a rounded stimulation produced in man by certain objects: if he covets these objects, what he feels is love; if he remains satisfied with knowing them, what he feels is beauty [20]. Beauty is thus, we may say, the passive voice of love; or, to apply the term to the external object,

> Beauty's the form love gives to things.

Sidney's Muse, who knew where to bid him turn, says also:

> But if (both for your love and skill) your name
> You seek to nurse at fullest breasts of fame,
> Stella behold, and then begin t'endite.

He, too, recognized a trinity: the object he beheld, the emotion he experienced, the work of art he produced. It appears to John Livingston Lowes as "the well, the vision, and the will. Without the vision the chaos of elements remains a chaos, and the Form sleeps forever in the vast chambers of unborn designs." Pater, foreshadowing the later analysis, and sensitive to love, writes of the fruit of a quickened, multiplied consciousness. Of this wisdom, the poetic passion, the desire of beauty, the love of art for art's sake, has most; for art comes to you professing frankly to give nothing but the highest quality to your moments as they pass, and simply for those moments' sake.

The first modern poet foreknew this trinity. Guido Guini-zelli woke the recognition that "Love and the gentle heart are one same thing", for Dante's uplifting to God who is truth, Virtue is love; the only true love is the love of truth; and—

> I am one who, when Love
> Inspires me, note, and in the way that he
> Dictates within, I give the outward form—

beauty's the form love gives to things.

* * * * * * * *

Although beauty is difficult to define, it is usually considered easy to recognize. As H. W. Garrod feels it,

Something is said, and all the intricate wards at once of the infinitely mysterious mechanism of our human nature, turn; all the parts of us meet decisively, yet softly, falling into place with that swift noiseless click which is the unresisting assent of the totality of what we are.

Even the scientific and psychological critics fall back upon an ultimate, individual judgment, a flash of recognition, an intuitive appreciation of beauty, that shares the qualities of faith rather than of knowledge. One knows a good book as one knows a good pudding: by taste. "The right reader of a good poem can tell the moment it strikes him that he has taken an immortal wound." Insertion of the adjective—the *right* reader—averts one controversy; but the assertion of the instantaneous firing of the spirit brings on another. For the human face which at once shows its character—the strong jaw, the stern eye, the friendly smile—in addition to being probably a mask, if an unwitting one, is likely to be a fixed

one. The truly expressive face, mobile, capable of revealing
the gamut of passions aplay within the breast, may on the
contrary seem expressionless in repose, seem, at first, without
"character". Similarly, it is suggested, the nudes of Manet
attract less immediately than *September Morn, Of Human
Bondage* than *If Winter Comes;* within the work that takes
the immediate eye is much of the sentimental or the commonplace. This notion is in itself not disturbing; for it may
be retorted that all beauty, all greatness, has a grain of the
universal commonplace, as all wisdom, being age-old, has a
core of platitude. Or it may be countered that beauty leaves,
at first glance, nothing to desire, yet much to discover. But
the point may be pressed deeper, following an implication
of such remarks as "Books wrote with labour deserve to be
so read"; and the suggestion be made that the fullest beauty
is at first hostile, cold, perhaps, on the surface, even repellent.
Its access is no easy climb; let only the worthy venture. So
they test the young prince in every fairy-tale. This attitude
is pleasantly expressed by the old Count in Norman Douglas'
South Wind, speaking of his *Locri Faun:*

You are aware of a struggle between your own mind and that of
the artist? I am glad. It is a test of beauty and vitality that a beholder refuses to acquiesce at first glance. There is a conflict to be
undergone. This thing thrusts itself upon us; it makes no concessions, does it? And yet one cannot but admire! You will seldom
encounter that sensation among the masterpieces of the Renaissance. They welcome you with open arms. That is because we
know what their creators were thinking about. They are quite
personal and familiar; they had as many moods, one suspects, as a
fashionable prima donna. They give pleasure. This *Faun* gives
pleasure and something more—a sense of disquieting intimacy.
While intruding upon our reserve with his solemn, stark, and almost hostile novelty, he makes at the same time a strange appeal—
he touches upon chords in our nature of which we ourselves are
barely cognizant. You must yield, Mr. Denis, to this stranger
who seems to know so much about you. When you have done so,

you will make a surprising discovery. You have gained a friend—
one of those who never change.

The remainder of the conversation, while tangential, is pertinent, as far as the remark that "Men have learnt to see
beauty here, there, and everywhere—a little beauty, mark
you, not much! They fail to see that in widening their capacity of appreciation they dilute its intensity. They have
watered their wine. There is more to drink. The draught is
poorer." Certainly it often seems that, for the artist, initial
difficulty adds to the later triumph:

> Oui, l'œuvre sort plus belle
> D'une forme au travail
> Rebelle.

In works where wit is predominant, at least, it is clear that
the pleasure rises partly from a struggle between author and
reader, in which the latter is forced to yield. But only the
strong—and loving—know it a joy to yield.

PERSONALITY IN ART

How did they all just come to be you?
God thought about me and so I grew.
GEORGE MACDONALD.

MUCH has been said, perhaps in envy, of the artist's expectation of a continuing life in the attention of countless ages of readers; Cabell is neither the latest nor the least to thrust shafts of irony at the classics, doled out to schoolboys and parsed by pedants. One is reminded of the cartoon in *Punch:* Shakespeare and Dante are looking at a half-dozen persons standing before the Florentine bust of Dante; Shakespeare asks who they are, and the other replies: "I know not. They are too few to be my commentators, and too many to be my readers." Some justification for such satiric attitude may be found in the extravagant claims of poets awooing:

> Not so (quod I) let baser things devize
> To dy in dust, but you shall live by fame:
> My verse your virtues rare shall eternize,
> And in the heavens write your glorious name. . . .
>
> So long as men can breathe or eyes can see,
> So long lives this, and this gives life to thee. . . .

(and the ages since have not even found her name); or, widening the boast:

> I might relate of thousands, and their names
> Eternize here on earth.

Thus three of our English great. Horace, however, had found a less personal justification for the poet's desire of immortality: it is in literature that there are preserved, with a certainty beyond marble, and a vividness more than the flesh, the great events and the personalities of time. A soldier in battle, even a general, or a journalist, watching the fight, loses the conflict in the cannon flash; this detail, then that, absorbs the spectator; his surroundings occupy the combatant. Literature, by selection and simplification, gives the sense of the whole; yet by effective choice keeps details sharp—showing at once the forest and the trees. To such argument Swift offers curt reply: "Whatever the poets pretend, it is plain they give immortality to none but themselves; it is Homer and Vergil we reverence and admire, not Achilles or Æneas".[21] Equally impersonal, though more concerned with the hopes of the individual artist, is Santayana's interpretation:

Fame, as a noble mind conceives and desires it, is not embodied in a monument, a biography, or the repetition of a strange name by strangers; it consists in the immortality of a man's work, his spirit, his efficacy, in the perpetual rejuvenation of his soul in the world. When Horace—no model of magnanimity—wrote his *exegi monumentum,* he was not thinking that the pleasure he would continue to give would remind people of his trivial personality, which indeed he never particularly celebrated, and which had much better lie buried with his bones . . . the deepest pleasure . . . very likely, flowed from the immortality, not of his monument, but of the subject and passion it commemorated; that tenderness, I mean, and that disillusion with mortal life which rendered his verse immortal. He had expressed, and in expressing appropriated, some recurring human moods, some mocking renunciations, and he knew that his spirit was immortal, being linked and identified with that portion of the truth.

Milton, both in his Latin prose and in his English verse, looked forward to marriage with Lyonors:

Of so much fame *in heaven* expect thy meed.*

Of more immediate concern than immortality are the problems of personality that our industrial world involves in

* See also Note 26.

ethical and even legal considerations. Originality, once scarcely more than a sign of an "unlearned" spirit, while writers "translated" or freely adapted into their own work all that they chose, has come to be deemed in itself praiseworthy; and plagiarism (mentioned, however, as early as Martial) is now in the forefront of the "literary crimes". Here, of course, financial concerns crop up. Did not Johnson declare that he who writes for anything except money, is a blockhead!

There are still, as through the ages, wide (and usually vehement) differences of opinion, in regard to the ethics of plagiarism. Commercially, there seems little question but that a man is entitled to the product and the profit of his labors—though even from this point of view, military service and socialism make other proposal. As literature, however, greater doubts arise. Such as believe, with T. S. Eliot, that literature is not an expression of but an escape from personality, will have little regard for property in art. As the genius, many have held, is in no sense self-made, his products belong to all men. E. M. Forster, commenting on the difference between science and literature, declares that information ought to be signed, that the public should know the source of statement-of-fact, that, indeed, "newspapers which are largely unsigned have gained by that device their undesirable influence over civilization"; and that, on the other hand, "literature wants not to be signed . . . while the author wrote he forgot his name; while we read him we forget both his name and our own". Art wells, he continues, from something beneath the surface personality—which may return, as the subject of gossip, after the enjoyment of the work. Gilbert Murray also attacks what he feels is a current over-emphasis on personality, on self-expression:

I might content myself with quoting the answer of an eminent French artist who was head of the Slade School, to a student who defended careless drawing on the ground that she wanted to express her personality. *"La personnalité de mademoiselle n'intéresse qu'à maman."* The truth seems to be, that whatever you do, you will inevitably reveal your personality, but that if your work is good, it will be an interesting personality, if not, not. Therefore you can safely concentrate on doing the work as well as possible, and let your personality look after itself.*

So Roosevelt differs with Franklin, asserting that character is a by-product, and that whoever seeks to develop his own character will succeed in producing a prig.

Kipling points to the antiquity of plagiarism as its justification:

> When 'Omer smote 'is bloomin' lyre,
> He'd 'eard men sing by land and sea;
> An' what he thought 'e might require,
> 'E went an' took—the same as me!

Seneca adduces no precedent to support his declaration that "whatever anyone has well said, is mine". By the time of the Puritans, æsthetic, if not ethical, progress had been made; Milton stated that "borrowing without beautifying is a plagiary". Dryden declared of Jonson that "he invades authors like a monarch, and what would be theft in other poets is only victory in him". The frequent opinion persists that an idea belongs to whoever has said it best. We have already noted Dryden's feeling that, though the metals may not be one's own, it is the workmanship that gives the price. Certainly few today would censure Shakespeare for his borrowings, whatever the courts may decide in regard to Eugene O'Neill.

For in literature about as fully as elsewhere, there's nothing new under the sun. "Horace Smith"—I draw from H. M. Paull, who acknowledges more obligations than he can name —"states that originality has been defined as 'unconscious or undetected imitation'. Emerson writes that a man is con-

---

* From *The Classical Tradition In Poetry*, copyright by the President and Fellows of Harvard College.

sidered original in proportion to the amount he steals from
Plato. Andrew Lang, in commenting on the schoolboy's definition of plagiarist as 'a writer of plays', suggests as an alternative definition 'any successful author'." Laurence
Sterne's vigorous attack on plagiarism is drawn directly from
Burton. These satiric approaches find their converse in the
tendency of critics to point out similarities of detail as instances of at least "unconscious borrowing"—so that Tennyson exclaimed "As if no one had heard the sea moan except
Horace!" But Georges Polti, in his discussion of the thirty-
six dramatic situations, and Kipling, more liberally (or more
carelessly content with a round number) referring to "the
entire stock of primeval plots and situations—those fifty
ultimate comedies and tragedies to which the Gods merci-
fully limit human action and suffering"—indicate the inevitability with which themes and plots recur.

More recently, with the growing sense of the ever-presence,
the contemporaneousness, of all art, there has been a more
serious practice of borrowings of which it is intended that
the reader, also, shall be conscious. At its simplest, this consists of a turn of phrase meant to recall its earlier employment; but more elaborate sought associations increase. Thus
Sturge Moore was astonished at the reproaches he received
for having incorporated passages from *Salammbo* in his writings; it was not until the second printing of *The Waste Land*
that T. S. Eliot—for less cultured readers, and belike with
mail of irony—pointed his many borrowings each its source;
and the long novel of James Joyce bids all who would comprehend it, know Homer's *Odyssey* . . . In the fact that such
men borrow, and in what they take, there is as valid material
as in "original" work, for those who consider that the style is
the man himself, who feel that art is valuable chiefly as the
expression of personality, who echo Johnson's words:
"Language most shows a man: speak, that I may see thee".

IMAGINATION'S RÔLE

Be mindful, when invention fails,
To scratch your head, and bite your nails.
                                    JONATHAN SWIFT.

THERE has been considerable emphasis on the part played by imagination in the arts. The poet's inspiration has, of course, been trumpeted, but—being a possession by the Muses—has been generally regarded as a mystery beyond analysis. Thus Emerson says:

The universal nature, too strong for the petty nature of the bard, sits on his neck and writes through his hand; so that when he seems to vent a mere caprice and wild romance, the issue is an exact allegory. Hence Plato said that poets utter great and wise things which they do not themselves understand.

In our own time, we are told by Laura Riding and Robert Graves, among others, that the poet must hold his personality apart from, and his will submissive to, that which writes through him. Certain mathematicians, it is true, have made attempts to snare this, as other immaterials, in an equation. We have been told that genius consists of two-fifths inspiration, and three-fifths pure fudge—in which connection it should be noted that Americans are the world's greatest consumers of candy. Further analysis has assured us that inspiration is nine-tenths perspiration. That it is "an infinite capacity for taking pains" brings us to the higher calculus—even if the last word be made singular. A variant of this formula presents genius as the combination of a fixed and tireless attention with a prompt and perpetual penetration. Some friend of P. T. Barnum it may be, who first observed

that every genius is twenty-five percent charlatan, and it is
the charlatan in him that takes the public. Swift held to a
different point of view, in his remark that "when a true
genius appears in the world, you may know him by this
sign, that all the dunces are in confederacy against him".
This takes for granted one's ability to recognize dunces; but
that is really not very hard, as one quickly learns which persons disagree with one. . . . But most of those who have
accepted the doctrine of inspiration rest content with the
belief that the poet is born. One may, however, add the reflection that genius begins beautiful works, but toil completes them—and balance this with the recognition that
genius sets out to discover an ocean-road to India, and lights
upon a new world.

Imagination has called for fuller discussion. Not only is
it a quality more readily identified and more generally
possessed, but the first allusions to this aspect of man's functioning are embodied in Plato's attack upon poetry as falsification and as emotional lure; the ages, therefore, have been
turned toward it, to defend. The first counterblasts, indeed,
turned Plato's words of the divine madness, inspiration,
against his other argument, and continued by pointing out
the lengthy and ennobling training the poet must undergo.
Modern psychology gives those who take this position new
terms for the old theorizing: "One may suspect", says such
a classicist as Gilbert Murray, "that the poet is really in a
state of what is loosely called 'double consciousness' "—
illustrating with the anecdote of the Othello who at the
height of a passionate scene warned Desdemona of a defective trapdoor in the stage. Murray speaks of the lover, who
"spends a large part of his time consciously, and far more
subconsciously, thinking about the beloved". But whether
the combined ecstasy and labor of classical tradition be supported by "subconscious thinking" and other concepts of

venturesome psychological schools, or be ignored, that the imagination plays a great part in the artist's activity is taken for granted in utterances of every sort, from the Crocean identification of intuition and art, to the Shelleyan cry that "Imagination is as the immortal God should assume flesh for the redemption of mortal passion".

Rebecca West, indeed, builds upon this assumption to distinguish two types of memory, the one mechanical, the other truly imaginative. One, she avers, stays still in the present and lets past occurrences flow forth; whereupon the extraordinary, the striking, only, will come forward to give their flavor to what in consequence seem tragic years or "the good old days". Or, with the lyric poets, and with novelists of late—George Moore and, as the title of his book shows, Marcel Proust—one may deliberately seek remembrance, wandering at will (and therefore under control, under critical control) through times gone by. In this way, Rebecca West feels, the artist may project himself into his past, as into imagined, experiences.

Just how does one project oneself into one's past, or imagined, experiences? What do we recall when we remember? What do we behold when we imagine? In bold challenge to the general conception, Alain builds upon an analysis of the imagination a *System of the Fine Arts* that is salutary in returning emphasis upon the work.

Pascal calls imagination the mistress of error; Montaigne refers to "those that think they see what they see not". Schopenhauer declares that the essence of genius lies in the energy and validity of its perception. The popular use of the term imagination unquestionably stresses the illusion that lies at the basis of all fancy. Modern psychology (various schools concurring) makes us aware how a passionate expectation proves the wisdom of the bidding Seek, and ye shall find; how, out of flickering impressions upon an ex-

pectant mind, a false judgment rises, a vision without object
—yet made real in, "proved by", the bodily tumult that is
the emotion's cause and sequent sign. The momentary image
vanishes, the feeling lingers to show it has been "real". So,
on coming out of darkness, one deems intense a glimmering
light. Or, at night, one hears a thief's footfall in every house-
sound (or is it a mouse?). Thus, while perception seeks the
actual through the elimination of the moment and the mood,
imagination accepts the immediate testimony, feeling and
impression intertwined. Hence, as Descartes views it, imagination judges of the presence, the position, and the nature
of objects after the order of human feelings; and naught remains of the false image save our own roused and quivering
bodies.

It may be claimed that the artist, in planning or in conceiving his work, consciously journeys among these illusions,
granting there the obverse of the willing suspension of disbelief we are later to yield to his products. Many, indeed, feel
with Velona Pilcher that "a miracle of mimicry is not worth
an ounce of imagination"; yet others as vehemently declare
that in the great artists imagination is replaced (if ever it be
else) by fulness of observation, minuteness and aptness in
noting things seen, and breadth of association. Of the great
living French poet Alain states: Paul Valéry "never imagines,
he always perceives". For Alain declares bluntly that all
such wandering is idle reverie, that "there are no images
when no present objects are perceived", and that there is no
art—and no artist—until the object is present in the work
begun:

We may maintain that no conception is work, and no reverie is
work. And this is the moment to warn every artist that he wastes
his time if he seek among the various possibilities for the most
beautiful, for no possibility is beautiful; the actual alone has
beauty. Make, then, and judge as you go. Such is the first condition of all art, as the relation of the words artist and artisan

well shows; but ordered reflection on the nature of the imagination leads still more surely to this important idea, that all meditation without a real object is of necessity sterile. Think your work, of course; but one thinks only of what is; therefore, make your work.

So also, in life, the work often dictates its sequel or its own progression: the ambitions of Napoleon sprang from the events.[22]

Many have pictured the great masterpieces they might create, if but their conception flashed in the instant to being; they have lamented the hardness of their materials, the difficulty of "unnecessary but unavoidable" technique; they have longed for a power that could carve as they dreamed to dictate. Such rubbers of the lamp Croce calls artists; Alain, idlers; and among artists he who has "too great a facility" is doomed.

Happy the man with a hard stone to work. . . . He who easily imagines novels will write few good ones. A madman is not in the least an artist, though he believes he sees many things we others do not. And his error lies in wishing to order his actions upon these vain images, whereas it seems that the artist, quite the contrary, orders his images upon what he makes, I mean upon the object that comes to being beneath his hands, or upon a balanced song, or a measured oration. The natural movement of a man who wants to imagine a cottage is to build one; and there is no other way of making it appear; as with the song, than to sing.

The movement of creation allows no facile play. While a tongue is in its formative stage, the necessity of choosing the proper word, of creating the language, checks the fancy, confines it, makes it circumspect; and, since every work of art is a new language, facility and art are incompatible; rather, an artist should labor with a native ease and an acquired difficulty. More than the dome of the Sistine chapel bids us believe (as we have already said in the original) that

Fairer the work wells
From a form that
Rebels.

The work of art, according to Alain's conception, does not
stimulate the imagination of the receptor; rather it frees
him from imagination, giving a firm support to his will and
to his gathering thoughts, acting for him as an anchor, as a
definite and unchangeable object. The vague confusion of
reverie, the sterile agitation of boredom, find reassurance
and repose with the resistant, unvarying form of the work of
art. Alain continues:

Every artist is perceiving and acting, always artisan in this.
Attentive rather to the object than to his own passions; one might
almost say impassioned against the passions, I mean impatient
especially of idle reverie; this trait is common to artists, and
makes them seem hard to get along with. Besides, the great number of works naïvely attempted after an idea or the image one
thinks one has of it, and failing because of this, explain why the
potent artist, who rarely talks, is too often judged by the ambi-
tious and errant artist, who talks a great deal. . . . The meditation of the artist is thus rather observation than reverie; still better, observation of what he has done as source and rule of what he
has to do. In short, the supreme law of human invention is that
one invents only while at work. . . . For works that are born and
die without stopping, like the oration, the dance, the song, the
first object is the first movement, which adorns itself with what
follows, yet which also announces what best will follow, so that
artists in these genres are perhaps less free than others, although
in music the opposite seems plainly the case. . . . It remains to
tell wherein the artist differs from the artisan. Every time the
idea precedes and orders the execution, it's industry. A good verse
is not first projected, then made; it appears, beautiful, before the
poet; and the beautiful statue reveals its beauty to the sculptor,
in measure as he brings it forth; and the portrait takes its being
under the brush. Music here gives the best evidence; for in it
there is no difference between conceiving and creating; if I think
it, I must sing it. This naturally does not preclude one's entertaining the notion of singing to celebrate a hero or a wedding, the

woods, the harvests, or the sea; but such a notion is common to the mediocre and the true musician, as the plot of Don Juan is common to Moliere and others, as Æsop is the model of many writers of fables, as an artist's model is at every call. Genius is made known only in the work, painted, written, sung. So the rules of its beauty appear but in the work, and there are held, so that they can never, can in no way, serve in the making of another work. . . . The art in which the resistance of the material makes itself most strongly felt, is architecture. Now this is not the latest comer, nor the pupil; it is the master, and the father, of almost all. On the contrary, the freest art, that of prose, is also the youngest, the most groping, the most treacherous of all.

Those who believe that art is a product of, and is properly considered by, the intelligence, concur in the opinion that one should turn from the play of the imagination to concentrate upon the work of art. On the other hand, such books as Max Nordau's *Degeneration,* as Jeannette Marks' *Genius and Disaster,* prolong in other pitch the olden cry, that

> The lunatic, the lover, and the poet
> Are of imagination all compact.

Other phraseology is employed by Agnes Mure Mackenzie:

What makes a man an artist in the first place is the innate possession of a "complex derived instinctive disposition" to react strongly to the emotional significance of objects perceived, by means of a particular activity—the attempt to separate the emotionally charged experience from himself, and give it an existence of its own apart from his.

The phrase she quotes from McDougall's *Outline of Psychology* too closely for comfort joins "derived" and "instinctive", but seems to intend little more than what others mean by imaginative power.

Imagination, it must be evident, is another of the long list of terms in philosophy and æsthetics that have different but too often undifferentiated meanings. When Mallarmé says that "the spirit of Gautier, the pure poet, now watches over the garden of poetry, from which he banishes the dream, the enemy of his charge"; when Roger Fry adds "Nothing is more contrary to the essential æsthetic faculty than the dream"; they are considering an aspect of imagination that lures from constructive thought. When Professor Whitehead states that "fools act on imagination without knowledge; pedants act on knowledge without imagination", he seems to mean association of ideas, sense of relationships. When Baudelaire emphasizes: "I have often said that the poet is supremely and preëminently intelligent, and that the imagination is the most scientific of the faculties, because it alone understands the universal analogy between things"— thus reiterating Aristotle's emphasis on the "gift of metaphor" as the basis of the poet's power [23]; and when Schopenhauer affirms that "the imagination is required in order to complete, arrange, give the finishing touches to, retain, and repeat at pleasure all those significant pictures of life, according as the aims of a profoundly penetrating knowledge and of the significant work whereby they are to be communicated may demand. Upon this rests the high value of the imagination, which is an indispensable tool of genius"—they are so employing the term as to make it include memory and association, (it's a poor sort of memory that only works backward), so conceiving of the imagination as to render it equivalent to the fullest and most fertile play of thought.

CHAPTER VII

POETRY

Should a tyrant rise and say
"Give up wine!" I'd do it;
"Love no women!" I'd obey,
Though my heart should rue it.
"Dash thy lyre!" suppose he saith,
Naught should bring me to it;
"Yield thy lyre or die!" My breath,
Dying, should thrill through it!

GOLIARD SONG.

WHAT IS POETRY?

The Dog-star rages! nay 'tis past a doubt
All Bedlam, or Parnassus, is let out.

ALEXANDER POPE.

THE many definitions of poetry in the *New English Dictionary* range from "the body of work" produced by the poet, to "imaginative or creative literature in general"—with Ruskin's extension of the term to include all means of expression (e.g. painting) used for a noble end. Carl Sandburg, in what he seems to intend as a poem, entitled *Poetry Considered,* numbers a variety of statements, each beginning with the same two words, from "1—Poetry is a projection across silence of cadences arranged to break that silence with definite intentions of echoes, syllables, wave lengths" to "38—Poetry is the capture of a picture, a song, or a flair, in a deliberate prism of words". If only to indicate how richly varied the concept poetry is, some other—mainly emotive—efforts to imprison its essence may be presented here.

SHAKESPEARE:
As imagination bodies forth
The forms of things unknown, the poet's pen
Turns them to shapes, and gives to airy nothings
A local habitation and a name.

M.N.D. I, 1

WORDSWORTH: Poetry is the breath and finer spirit of all knowledge; it is the impassioned expression which is in the countenance of all Science . . . the spontaneous overflow of powerful emotion, recollected in tranquillity . . . truth carried alive into the heart by passion.

Pref. to Lyrical Ballads

ISAAC NEWTON: Poetry is ingenious fiddle-faddle.

COLERIDGE: Prose is words in their best order; poetry, the best words in the best order.

Pref. T.T.B.

Milton refers to poetry as being "simple, sensuous, and passionate".

KEATS: I think poetry should surprise by a fine excess, and not by singularity; it should strike the reader as a wording of his own highest thoughts, and appear almost as a remembrance. [Similarly, Lowell remarks that whenever, in his own creation, he hit upon what seemed a good line, he wondered where he had heard that line before.] Second, its touches of beauty should never be half-way, thereby making the reader breathless instead of content. The rise, the progress, the setting of imagery, should, like the sun, come natural to him, shine over him, and set soberly although in magnificence, leaving him in the luxury of twilight. But it is easier to think what poetry should be than to write it. And this leads me to another axiom: that, if poetry come not as naturally as the leaves to a tree, it had better not come at all.

J. W. MACKAIL: The essence of poetry is not so much that it is rhythmical (which all elevated language is) or that it is metrical (which not all poetry is) as that it is *patterned* language. That is its specific quality as a fine art. [Patterned language, he explains, is composition with some sort of a "repeat".]

JOUBERT: Poetry is the waking dream of a wise man.

Edith Sichel calls poetry "prose written with a diamond".

ROBERT FROST: Poetry: words that have become deeds.

The living poem is something that is felt first and thought out afterwards. It begins with a lump in the throat, a home-sickness or a love-sickness. A complete poem is one where an emotion has found its thought and the thought has found the words. . . . It is absurd to think that the only way to tell if a poem is lasting is to wait and see if it lasts. The right reader of a good poem can tell the moment it strikes him that he has taken an immortal wound—that he will never get over it. That is to say, permanence in poetry, as in love, is perceived instantaneously. It hasn't to await the best of time. The proof of a poem is not that we have never forgotten it, but that we know at sight we never could forget it.[24]

GOETHE: To make a beautiful, enlivened whole: that is the business of the poet.

WALTER DE LA MARE: Every poem says much in little. It packs into the fewest possible words—by means of their sound, their sense, and their companionship—a wide or rare experience.

WALTER SAVAGE LANDOR: Poetry, like wine, requires a gentle and regular and long fermentation. What is it if it can buoy up no wisdom, no reflection; if we can throw into it none of our experience; if no repository is to be found in it for the gems we have collected, at the price sometimes of our fortunes, of our health, and of our peace?

Lascelles Abercrombie defines it as "the expression of imaginative experience, valued simply as such and significant simply as such, in the communicable state given by language which employs every available and appropriate device."

BYRON: Poetry is the lava of imagination, whose eruption prevents the earthquake.

E. MERRILL ROOT: Whatever philosophy has been logically developed in prose has been intuitively surpassed in poetry. Prose is, at best, life only red hot; poetry is life white hot.

ARTHUR DAVISON FICKE: The aim of poetry is to capture those rare moments of the poet's experience when, for good or evil, the consciousness of life sweeps through him like a flame; the moments when he becomes passionately aware of the crises of his life's secret drama, and sees a pattern taking shape in the void, and words of utterance come singing to his lips.

CHRISTOPHER MORLEY:

Bivalves

The pearl
Is a disease of the oyster.
A poem
Is a disease of the spirit
Caused by the irritation
Of a granule of truth
Fallen into that soft gray bivalve
We call the mind.

RUSKIN: A good, stout, self-commanding, magnificent animality is the make for poets.

ROBERT GRAVES: Poetry is not a science, it is an act of faith.

MASEFIELD (echoing Wordsworth): Art is a strong excitement in perfect control.

ARCHIBALD MACLEISH: A poem should not mean, but be. [Mr. Macleish would probably, if pressed, grant that a poem does have meaning, but that it "means" itself, the inter-organization of its component parts, the full significance of which can be conveyed in no other terms than the poem.]

CLEMENT WOOD: Poetry is the singing incarnation of man's stretch toward two intangible goals of reality, beauty and truth: two that are one: two that are all. [We may hearken the silent protest of the third member of the trinity.]

LUCIA TRENT: Poetry is the most eloquent manifestation of man's age-long adventuring in search of spiritual fulfilment.

ALBERT MORDELL: We like to think of the poet as one who belongs to the minority, as a non-conformist, as a champion of liberty, as a sponsor for advanced ideas. We want him to be uttering and singing not the commonplaces of today but the truths of tomorrow.

WILLIAM BUTLER YEATS: We make, out of the quarrel with others, rhetoric; out of the quarrel with ourselves, poetry. [*Facit indignatio prosam.*]

JOHN STUART MILL: Oratory is heard; poetry, overheard.

ROBERT BRIDGES:—the very seal of his poetic birthright, the highest gift of all in poetry, that which sets poetry above the other arts, I mean the power of concentrating all the far-reaching resources of language on one point, so that a single and apparently effortless expression rejoices the æsthetic imagination at the moment when it is most expectant and exacting, and at the same time astonishes the intellect with a new aspect of truth.

RALPH CHEYNEY (applying Nietzsche): Chaos gives birth to a dancing star only if we breathe into it that visible, audible, fragrance of passion which is poetry.

Irwin Edman, attempting analysis, declares that poetry is a hybrid art, being part music and part communication— "the half-way house of song and story."

Edith Sichel approaches the question negatively also, by seeking to determine what is the matter with bad poetry—the lack of what quality makes it bad. Her answer is, reality:

Want of reality always means a want of true feeling; it means also a want of precision: of precision and experience and expression. Good poetry is neither vague nor sentimental; bad poetry is both. And what is sentimentality but the professional language of

emotion without emotion to inspire it? The blur of trite images
and generalities in which bad lyrics indulge means no less than the
lack of that grasp, that realization of details compelled by the
sincere love of a subject.

She has, however, achieved a better definition of sentimentality than of poetry ... A line of thought we may later follow
leads from the declaration that when a poem is bad, either
the communication is defective, or the experience communicated is not worth while.*

John Livingston Lowes also approaches the subject cautiously. He reminds us that Coleridge changed his line "The
furrow followed free" to "The furrow streamed off free",
then in defiance of truth restored the original reading. While
truth may be stranger than fiction, fiction may be realler than
truth. Reality is to the artist, as Keats observed, but "a
starting-post towards all the two-and-thirty Palaces". Thus,
Lowes continues, the poet may be likened to "Saul, the son
of Kish, who started out to find his father's asses—and found
a kingdom". And poetry is the presentation of truth, through
illusion, and tinged with emotion.

EDWIN ARLINGTON ROBINSON: Poetry has two outstanding
characteristics. One is that it is, after all, undefinable. The other
is that it is eventually unmistakable. [Which might be left as
final word, were we not driven to observe that "eventually" re-
opens the whole problem.]

* See page 446.

VERSE, POETRY, AND PROSE

Piping hot, smoking hot,
What I've got
You have not,
Hot grey pease, hot, hot, hot,
Hot grey pease hot.
There is more music in this song, on a cold frosty night,
than ever the Sirens were possessed of, who captivated
Ulysses; and the effects stick closer to the ribs.
HUGGLEFORD, On Hunger (Mother Goose Melody).

A MORE commodious definition of poetry than a sentence permits, might be developed through an essay; yet the fervor of many whose words we have just read must be supplemented by study, before distinctions of value are drawn. It becomes clear that the word poetry has been widely employed in two senses, to both of which the word prose has served as complement.

The double use is recognized by Wordsworth, who regrets the confusion he fosters:

I have used the word poetry (though against my own judgment) as opposed to the word prose, and synonymous with metrical composition. But much confusion has been introduced into criticism by this contradistinction of poetry and prose, instead of the more philosophical one of poetry and matter-of-fact, or science. The only strict antithesis to prose is meter; nor is this, in truth, a strict antithesis; because lines and passages of meter so naturally occur in writing prose that it would be scarcely possible to avoid them, even if it were advisable.

In his last remark, Wordsworth is influenced by his theory that the language of poetry should approximate that of ordinary life; it is commonly considered that metrical prose is merely bad prose. The opposition he urges between poetry and science is that of De Quincey's literature of knowledge and literature of power. Coleridge adds that

> the proper and immediate object of science is the acquirement, or communication, of truth; the proper and immediate object of poetry is the communication of pleasure.

James Burnham makes a vigorous attack upon this distinction, advancing the charge that pleasure and truth are of different categories and cannot be set in opposition any more than, say, apples and beds. Yet it seems valid to mark the different aspects of man's inquiring activity—religion, philosophy, science, art, etc.—as tending toward different satisfactions; and Mr. Burnham praises the distinction drawn by Louis Grudin, who beats through a forest of newfangled phrases to the same clearing: that, in prose, words are used as signs of other things, its criterion being the truth or falsity of the reference; while, in poetry, words are a part of what they signify, its criterion being the beauty or the banality of the association.

This interpretation of poetry, from the point of view of its spirit, at once sets aside the formal conception: prose and verse then overlap as were scientists to contrast flying and non-flying creatures, and startle to discover bird, mammal, insect, fish, in both divisions. For between Shelley and the mnemonic device whereby one recalls which months have how many days, there are few points of spiritual contact; and *Hudibras* is closer to Mr. Dooley than to *The Blessed Damosel*. Thus William Rose Benét is led to the emphatic statement that "the thing called poetry has nothing whatever to do with the construction of what we call verse as opposed to prose". A current phrasing of De Quincey's demarcation tells that prose is presentation; poetry, representation. "Representation" has been accepted by some as the meaning of Aristotle's *mimesis,* imitation; for Empedocles is held a physicist, not a poet, though he composed in verse, and the prose Socratic dialogues are poetry. It is this conception which the *New English Dictionary* gathers, with instances in English as early as Chaucer and Caxton, into the phrase "imaginative or creative literature in general".

Despite this wide application which the ages have justified by making, there is a strong feeling that the formal distinction, which regards poetry as mainly metrical (at least, patterned) composition, as opposed to the freer prose, either marks or produces a subtler difference, in spirit. The neoclassicists, following Horace instead of Aristotle, considered meter, if not essential to poetry (their bow to the Greek), at least its invariable accompaniment, an "essential accident"; the general understanding unquestionably intends meter when the word poetry is used. As a matter of fact, the formal distinction itself has little to rest upon: what is the difference in form between poetry and prose? The word pattern has been used, but manifestly a novel is patterned by its plot, as any work is patterned by its structure. John McClure suggests that

poetry, as a form of utterance distinct from prose, is simply music in words—an attempt to create beauty in rhythm and tone. Its sole distinguishing characteristic is its harmonization of syllables in rhythm. There is no such thing as a poetic idea. Whatever claims they may make to the contrary, poets have no monopoly on imagination, sentiment, or tropes. These belong equally to prose, and they characterize any good creative writing . . . It is not an intellectual quality, and we need no more attempt to explain it than we need attempt to explain the charm of music, which is also a charm of sound.

No one today can take this point of view, however, without also considering the "charm" of sight, the various typographical effects—of capital and lower-case letters, of italics and other type-faces, of irregularly spaced and placed lines, of words cut in two at a line-end—with which (for however brief a vogue, as the middle ages knew) the modern poet may seek to strengthen his appeal.

Professor Parkhurst sets much the same distinction into analogy: "The difference between prose and poetry is the difference between the speaking voice and the singing—two things qualitatively distinct, and yet incapable of exact description". She must admit at once, however, the wide range of "impassioned declamation" between her classes; and she seeks to bolster her tonal criterion with a prosaic reliance on the sentence, as opposed to poetry's dependence on "foot or line". Which permits us to draw no line—save at Professor Parkhurst's distinction!

A more systematic study of the subject has been made by Professor William M. Patterson, who, with the help of a number of students tested by various passages of what are accepted as poetry, music, and prose, has reached imposing conclusions. He bases these upon the natural time-intervals felt by sensitive persons he calls "timers". We are all, in varying degree, time-bound, as the patterns into which we form clock-ticking (at will tick-tock or with the emphasis reversed) and train-wheel rolling sufficiently indicate; and some speculators have gone so far as to suggest that the stress-unit in poetry matches the beat of the human pulse, and the verse-unit the length (of course more variable) of a human breath. Professor Patterson goes to music again, for his terminology, and he declares that

language is regarded as rhythmically prose so long as between the accented syllables and the under-unit series of subjective time, syncopation and substitution predominate over coincidence, between intervals. When coincidence predominates, language is rhythmically verse.

This test, apparently, is to be applied line by line, for free verse is reduced to a "jumping back and forth from one side of the fence to the other", and gives to the timer who reads it "the disquieting experience of attempting to dance up the side of a mountain". Such speculations, perhaps, it is that have led others to the conclusion that not merely prose and poetry, but prose and verse—the formal aspects—are inseparable; Joel Elias Spingarn says:

> The fact is, there is no distinction between prose and verse. Out of the infinite varieties of rhythm in human speech, it is possible, for convenience' sake, to separate the more regular from the more irregular, and to call the one verse and the other prose: to say where one ends and the other begins is impossible.

There, if the distinction were purely formal, the matter might be permitted to rest, and each work be called—poetry, free verse, prose-poem, polyphonic prose—just what its author labeled it. But there rise insistent voices to declare that between poetry as mainly metrical expression and prose as freer composition, other qualities, subtler yet more important than form—or indeed the very mental set of the reader—create a significant distinction. Ezra Pound, for example, finds the boundary in meaning:

> Great literature is simply language charged with meaning to the utmost possible degree . . . The language of prose is much less highly charged; that is perhaps the only availing distinction between prose and poetry. Prose permits greater factual presentation, explicitness, but a much greater amount of language is needed. The total charge in certain nineteenth century prose works possibly surpasses the total charge found in individual poems of the period; but that merely indicates that the author has been able to get his effect cumulatively, by a greater heaping up of factual data; (imagined fact, if you will, but nevertheless expressed in factual manner).

A differentiation more frequently pressed between the two forms is based on the idea that good prose is marked by a nice adaptation of the language, the medium, to what it has to say; whereas in poetry, the medium is part of what it has to say. In other words, in prose one may begin with an idea, a motive, a theme, and throughout the work continue its development; in poetry, whatever one begins with (and some maintain that one begins with the first phrasing) one can continue to develop—not the idea, the emotion, the theme— but only the poem itself. All structures of prose hold first by the thought, by the tale they carry onward, the character they bring to life; thereafter we may appreciate the language, the form, which could rise to our attention at the moment only as distractions; every structure of poetry is simultaneously meaning and form; we must grasp both together, as one, to hold it at all. Prose can be summarized, explained; the only explanation of a poem is the poem.

The diction of the poet (and the orator) is balanced in the ear, danced in the mind for its accordances and resolving discords; words to them are things in themselves, objects to work with, bricks in the building. [The orator perhaps does not fully develop his ideas in advance of the speech; their warmth comes from the fire of their immediate creation, their instant fusion with the words; the orator convinces not only his audience, but himself, as he proceeds.] The objects of the prose writer are ideas, events; his unit in building is the phrase or the sentence [25]; and words must take their places in the structure of his thought as naturally as syllables in the constructions of the poet. In ordinary speech, it has been said, words serve to recall things; but when speech is truly poetic, the things always serve to recall the words.

The sustaining element in prose is thus the idea, whereas poetry is upheld by the element of time. Prose, in order to maintain the sense of unity, to keep the whole always in mind, lingers, returns; it may move from events back to emotions and ultimate causes: poetry flows on. In oratory and in poetry, meant—even when printed—for the ear, the past is past, irrevocable, disposed of (and, in oratory, judged); in prose it is held for analysis. In prose tales, which follow the order of events, all has happened, everything is past, whence arises a certain calm, a position outside of the world, as with the Olympians, for no one now can experience these effects. Wherefrom spring hopefulness, reassurance, strength; "to the simplicity of the tale responds a majesty in the reader"—as the Biblical narrative most effectively holds the spirit. In narrative poetry, on the other hand, it is less the idea than the feeling that carries us; we are caught into the sense of time; the past is past, but the future is still future, and we are drawn in its coursing. Wherefrom spring a sense of eternal movement, of change, of a destiny that bears us beyond our will, as the regular rhythm of the narrative subtly carries us on. "Poetic contemplation is naturally religious, for on the one hand are always calm and resignation, and on the other the rhythm that draws us, one might say, to accept the order; and the poet is a god, who presents instead of proving".

Before proceeding to the analysis of the methods whereby poetry makes these accomplishments seem natural, brief pause must be made to remind ourselves that, whether or not most poetry is verse, surely much verse is not poetry. Samuel Butler of *Erewhon* declares that "the preface of *Pilgrim's Progress* is verse, but it is not poetry. The body of the work is poetry, but it is not verse." Accepting the formal concept of the term, however, as the basis of further discussion, we are confronted with a large body of mere verse, which, Robert Graves assures us, may be easily set aside, because "Verse makes a flat pattern on the paper, Poetry stands out in relief".

It may be said that, while single works in poetry and prose may display contrary features, the great body of poetry is, in theme, more often emotional and personal; and in diction, more frequently concise, figurative, and euphonious. In form, a poem may possess rhythm, meter, and rhyme: if it have all three, it is verse; if but rhythm and meter, blank verse; if rhythm alone, free verse. Thus there is no outstanding formal distinction between free verse and prose; and between verse and poetry the lines of demarcation lie in the field of the spirit. The rhythms of free verse are often more fluid than the more broken surges and falls of prose; but they are individual, and therefore often disagreeable (and unrecognizable) to those who expect regularity in verse. To some extent, of course, the arrangement on the page assists in determining the rhythm, as it helps indicate the points of greater and less attention, and attention itself is a wavelike, therefore rhythmic process.

Here again we pause at a point as fundamentally personal as the sense of beauty. Each will interpret in his own being's way the emotive words we have read in characterization of poetry—of which we may last present those of the "ineffectual angel": "poetry strips the veil of familiarity from the world, and lays bare the naked and sleeping beauty which is the spirit of all its forms . . . the perfect and consummate surface and bloom of all things . . . the record of the best and happiest moments of the best and happiest minds." The contradiction involved in the first two of these statements, and the philosophical problems opened by the third, should serve as warning against the ready acceptance of any effort to drape the concept poetry in verbal garb, which, the more attractive in itself, the more holds us from examination of what lies beneath.

THE AGES OF POETRY

*When people have nothing better to say, they say "Youth!
Youth!"*

ANTON CHEKOV.

IT WAS Peacock who suggested that poetry moves, in recurrent cycle, through four periods or ages. The first of these, the Iron Age, is the primitive period, when rude bards in rough numbers sang the valor of their lord. When fighting and feasting were the chief occupations of conquering tribes, it was fitting at the victor's board to celebrate the triumph. This is the period before the epics, of the ancient bards, of the medieval gleemen and troubadours. The second, or Golden Age, is that in which there arises the great traditional, national poetry, telling the tales of the heroes of the Iron Age. This is the epoch of Homer—of *Beowulf*, we might fancy, but Peacock names Ariosto, and Shakespeare, and Milton. Follows this the Silver Age, the period of civilization and polite society. Now are recast the themes of the Golden Age, with an increasing emphasis on form that presses toward sterility, through Vergil and his imitators, through Dryden and Pope and theirs. Whereupon arises a new generation, the Bronze Age, that seeks (but vainly seeks) to recapture the prime simplicity—the Nonnic period, the Romantic revival, trying to return to the unspoiled source of inspiration.

This pretty picture underwent even further simplification, in the fancies of his contemporaries whom Peacock lashed. Overlooking his first age of long preparation, they found their beauty already full-blown in the primitive. *Le monde naît, Homère chante.* "The first poets of all nations", declared Wordsworth, "wrote from passion excited by real

254

events"; all succeeding poets erred in studying the effects of the earlier writers, instead of composing directly from the event. What might have been dismissed as the vagary of an enthusiastic group of rebels is, however, given substance and coherent development by Macaulay, who charges that "as civilization advances, poetry almost necessarily declines". He points out that in the sciences progress is slow but gradual, and achievement cumulative: ages were spent in collecting the materials, and others in separating and combining them, in finding the most logical systems. Music, sculpture, painting—still more, poetry, follow no such gradual course; the arts flourish, rise early to great heights, and as suddenly decline. Nations, like individuals, first perceive, then abstract. The language of early peoples tends to be poetical; that of enlightened society, philosophical. As we develop, we create better theories, and poorer poems. We are more skilled in the analysis of human nature, in the detection of hidden motives (Macaulay might have been previsioning psychanalysis, and the development of the novel); but poetry does not dissect, it presents. Ontogeny being a summary of philogeny, we find that (as the Greek rhapsodist, Plato tells us, could scarce recite Homer without falling into convulsions) the effects of art, its potent illusion, its power over the emotions, are strongest in childhood; and in a sense the poet, in order to create, must become a child. This conception may be linked with various current theories—Heaven lies about us in our infancy—of those who connect poetry with religion, or of those who dismiss it as play.

But the scholar, trudging patiently behind, affirms that the beauty of the primitive is a twi-horned myth. For in the first place, the oldest extant books, the Homeric epics, the Hebrew *Genesis* and *Judges*, show marked conventions, the growth of a tradition of style, and knowledge of earlier literature. Gilbert Murray reports that one of the earliest poems, unearthed in Babylonia, contains a lament that all reasonable subjects for literature are already exhausted. As far back as we can trace their work, poets were acutely aware, and eagerly studious, of what had been done before them. And in the second place, the complicated forms and fine variations in the art of existing "primitive" peoples, which excite naïve admiration at their subtlety, seem to be the consequence of nothing more than ignorance, than untrained powers of perception and association. Recorders of primitive music, for example, seeking a scale for the quarter-tones and sliding notes of the natives, meet with approving cries when they strike tones of our developed scale—toward which the primitive singers, with untrained ears, were apparently groping (though it should be noted that the thirteen-note scale is arbitrary; that Hans Barth is playing compositions on a quarter-tone piano, Julian Carrillo on a harp-zither that divides the octave into ninety-seven parts; and that conductors like Leopold Stokowski, dancers like Ruth St. Denis, and many composers and critics, hail the approaching day when the musician will have as great variety of sound as the painter of color. Here, however, we move far from the quest of the primitive). Around such early works, as around the grotesques of primitive art, long tradition has again drawn the robe of its sanctification, and imitation has grown to ritual, devotion to dexterity. Milton, holding out a hand for guidance to

> Blind Thamyris and blind Mæonides,
> And Tiresias and Phineus; prophets old

makes one of that endless chain which—despite the taunt to the evolutionists—leads us towards the light.

THE THEMES OF POETRY

For so to interpose a little ease,
Let our frail thoughts dally with false surmise.
JOHN MILTON.

IN PROSE, it has been stated, the idea sustains the work; it is no novel thought that, in poetry, the subject-matter is not the particular story the writer may have to tell, or emotion to outpour, but that the matter of the poem is the medium itself, the language, the form. This conception was advanced by the Italians of the Renaissance. It was so far accepted in England that in 1727 Chamber's *Encyclopædia* said of poetry: "Its matter, long and short syllables, and feet composed thereof, with words furnished by grammar; its form, the arrangement of all these things in just and agreeable verse". The returning emphasis on the object, on beauty born in the work, is based on a similar understanding; Paul Valéry says, speaking of La Fontaine: "One must not wonder at the great simplicity of these heroes: the chief characters in a poem are always the sweetness and the vigor of the verse".

Others, still intent on an impetus outside the "story", but holding less to the concrete materials of which the poet builds, find the basis of his work in emotion. The feeling in poetry, as in prose the thought, is to them the core of the creation. Love, and the heightened perception through love we know as beauty: beauty or passion starts the poet on his course; intertwining they keep him on his way. "In the *Ode On a Grecian Urn*", says Henry Wells, "beauty is the host and passion the guest. In the *Ode To a Nightingale,* beauty is the guest and passion the host. One poem leaves us calm in the delight of uncontaminated loveliness, the other, as Keats himself insists, only too keenly aware that beauty may for a time assuage, but never can kill pain."

Followers of Poe, Baudelaire, and Mallarmé have come to speak of a "pure poetry". In its beginnings, this seems to have sprung with the symbolist expression: as opposed to the romantics, who flaunted their feelings, these poets maintained a surface objectivity, allowing nature's objects and events, merely through their presentation in the poem, to convey the human emotion: similarly from the point of view of form they sought the less obvious rhythmic movements, the subtle undertones of harmony, the inner music. The two aspects have in the half-century grown apart: Paul Valéry and George Moore stress the formal element, the surface objectivity, and draw poetry toward music and mathematics; the spiritual implications are emphasized by Henri Bremond, who calls its appeal a

welcoming magic, as the mystics say, that invites us to a repose wherein we have but to let ourselves go—but actively—with one greater and better than ourselves. Prose, a lively and leaping phosphorescence, that draws us far from ourselves. Poetry, a recalling of us inward, a confused weight, said Wordsworth; a holy warmth, said Keats: "an awful warmth about my heart like a load of immortality." *Amor-Pondus*. Where does this weight seek to precipitate us, if not toward those august retreats where there awaits, whereto there summons us, a more than human presence? If we must believe Walter Pater, "all the arts aspire to rejoin music". No:—they all aspire, but each by the intermediary magic of its kind—words; notes; colors; lines—they all aspire to rejoin prayer.

The difference between these two attitudes is very great, if one considers their conclusions in mathematics and religion; yet these seekers have but walked in different directions on one quest, behind the immediate sense impression harkening for the music of the spheres.*

* See page 423f.

One effect of the recent stir of æsthetic self-consciousness has been the (perhaps temporary) discarding of the theory of imitation, or representation. It seems clear, to those who today give the matter thought, that poetry is not a verbal reproduction of experience, but a verbal transformation of experience—that all art, in fact, is transformation of experience, according to the personality (intelligence, sensitivity, temperament, mood, æsthetic values) and the skill of the artist, in terms of the particular art.

The general reader is likely to desire a classification of poetry by the various fields of object or event dealt with through the words; and the rhetorical ages afford no dearth of such types. They may be grouped in three large (and loose) divisions: the narrative, which includes the epic and the dramatic; the personal, which covers epigram, elegy, and lyric; and the contemplative, which—for those who see no contradiction between teaching and poetry—may embrace the didactic, as well as the pastoral and the idyll.

To state that the subjects of narrative poetry are almost always chosen from the past may seem a truism, for no events can be related until they have occurred; but some less obvious import the statement bears. For the period chosen is usually remote in time or place, so that the glamour of distance, the mystery of the unknown, permit heroic stature, so that the poet is free to elaborate or to invent, so that men may be set upon their own legs—without the accustomed, almost unnoticed, props of civilization—to stand or fall. The virtues that appeal are those of the heroic ages. Gilbert Murray points out that the only great concept Christianity has contributed to imaginative literature is that of the martyr—and such calm defiance of implacable fiendish foes is the favorite story of Norse legends, is the tale of Prometheus, is familiar in the East.

Nor is this all, or it would need no telling, for prose narratives may also find material in the past. Indeed, though they frequently dwell upon the present, and occasionally venture into the future, all that they tell is presented as though it has happened. The author is spectator. In poetic narrative the author is participant; he moves with his epic heroes; so that past, present, future—caught always in the poem's regular flow of time—take their real meaning, and the reader is aware of a changing world, instead of a world that has moved beyond recall.

The personal types of poetry deal more frequently with the instant time; but in these the presentation, contrary to first appearances, is more objective. The poet, concerned with his own states of mind, his own emotions, sets them forth; they become the object; he is thus able to contemplate them and to present them in calm. Probably the romantic youth who cries "I fall upon the thorns of life! I bleed!" is staunching his wound with the words. Wordsworth approached recognition of this, in his famous characterization of poetry as the "spontaneous overflow of powerful emotion, recollected in tranquillity"; T. S. Eliot implied it when he called poetry an "escape from emotion": the creation of the poem is often the resolution of the poet's conflict. Subtly here, too, the rhythm and the feeling accord; the insistence of the rhythm, the "hardness of the material", helps in the passion's control; and the reader is also calm despite the deep feeling.

Philosophical poetry springs from a mood of contemplation, and the measure of detachment already existent permits greater flexibility in the verse itself, in the form but more fundamentally in the spirit. Descriptive poetry, carrying the bearer ever on, gives each image enough development to afford a hold for the memory, without permitting the attention to fix upon and dissolve it, as Orpheus was condemned never to see Eurydice, for having looked on her. Like the other types, the contemplative carries us on, stopping for no question or denial, satisfied to assume and to present, and not concerned with proving or with probing. As it has been said that time is the chief character of every tragedy, so it may be felt that the passing of all things is the theme of every poem.[26]

THE FORM OF POETRY

> As with the old Chinese ginger jars, so in poetry: not only is the syrup delightful, but even the pot may be interesting.
>
> WALTER DE LA MARE.

AFTER this gallop about the pastures of Pegasus—more exhilarating, at least, than the plodding of pedants to survey—there comes a sense of security at the concrete wall of form [27]. Rhythm, which the natural stress upon certain syllables in the words of our language brings, however choppy, into all verbal composition, is a basic quality in both poetry and prose; its effects are furthered and heightened by the concentration and repetition of meter, which is the chief formal element in poetry. After it stands rhyme.

Rhythm is as the growing vine upon the trellis-work of meter. Its flow is continuous yet infinitely varied; leaves lift in profusion along its twining way; everywhere its flowers are expected yet unpredictable. Rooted in the poet's words, which give it being and course, it is the diction's easily perceptible yet elusive product. The march of the syllables, however, is ordered upon the length of the phrase, itself dependent—as is even the tone of voice—upon the movement of the thought and mood.

The effects of meter, which are many and mutable, are due to its rousing an expectancy in us, which it shall ultimately satisfy. Before that awaited return, however, we may be held through a greatly varied series of postponements, seeming betrayals, half-proffers, disappointments, surprisals—until the necessary fulfillment of the promise brings the turn. In such a form as the eighteen line stanza of Spenser's *Epithalamion,* for instance, the regularity with which the sixth and eleventh lines are shortened, and the last line is lengthened, grows in the mind; then, as the poem develops, the stanza takes on one more line, and shortens the seventeenth as well. This is, of course, a complexity resulting after a long tradition of such poems.

It has been remarked that impassioned speech tends to be metrical; indeed, that all impassioned activity tends to assume a regular rhythm. It may in truth be said that all continuous movement is likely to fall into a rhythm, a sing-song, an alternation of effort and repose, a largely subjective cradling and crooning—the intent or effect of which is to destroy any emotion, to render the action more mechanical, and thus postpone the feeling, the saturation point, the fatigue. Thus meter in poetry may be felt by its regularity to lull the passions, to induce a gentle calm; too regular a meter has, to be sure, often brought on the peace of somnolence; yet, properly modulated (with duration, intensity, and pitch all brought to serve), the verse may, as Yeats describes it, "lull the mind into a waking trance". Coleridge says that "as a medicated atmosphere, or as wine during animated conversation, [two lost arts in America!] they act powerfully, though themselves unnoticed." By the simplest of metrical forms we may become patterned; successive waves of expectation roll through us to the shore.

This waking trance, this soothing relaxation, in which the music cradles us gently into the poem's mood, is of further value to the poet, in that it lulls our critical spirit as well. An increased suggestibility, a greater sensitivity to the induced impressions—the dropping of a mental barrier—opens our mind to images, to notions, we else might question. To one not thus rapt into his work, the directions for reading his verse that Lindsay gives seem faintly ludicrous; they are hostile indeed to Swinburne who resist his sensuous spell. It was perhaps in exaggerate recognition of this effect of

* Impones metanerent .

poetry that Beaumarchais remarked: "What's not worth saying, you can sing."

The hypnoidal effect of meter serves one mood of the poet; quite another is that in which he may use his varying lines to convey the suggestion of motion. Here, naturally, the choice of words plays concordant part; yet much may manifestly be due to the meter alone. The outstanding example of movement in meter is Browning's *How They Brought The Good News From Ghent To Aix;* only a martinet will keep schoolboys from stamping out the hoof-beats in its lines:

I sprang to the stirrup, and Joris, and he;
I galloped, Dirck galloped, we galloped all three;
"Good Speed!" cried the watch, as the gate-bolts undrew,
"Speed!" echoed the wall to us galloping through;
Behind shut the postern, the lights sank to rest,
And into the midnight we galloped abreast.

How different the movement in the lines:

And down the long and silent street,
The dawn, with silver-sandalled feet,
Crept like a frightened girl.

How poised, here, with the thought:

Still with unhurrying chase
And unperturbèd pace,
Deliberate speed, majestic instancy,
Came on the following feet;

or in:

And singing still dost soar, and soaring ever singest.

gathering momentum in:

Him the Almighty Power
Hurled headlong flaming from the ethereal sky
With hideous ruin and combustion, down—

seeming to urge each entreaty in:

> Arise now, lift up thy light; give ear to us, put forth thine
>   hand;
> Reach toward us thy torch of deliverance—

lifting the head with the contrast in:

> Give me a lover old with grief,
> Lonely, and wise.
> Perhaps I could lift sadness
> From his eyes.

It is this element of poetry which leads one school of elocution to declare that verse should be read precisely as prose:
the rhythm will then not be deliberately thrust forward, but
will play over the stream of the words with the wind of the
poet's spirit.

Rhyme adds one more note of expectancy, and the greatest,
to our awakened desire for a return. We are willing to wait,
once the promise is made, to a long stanza's end, and through
the next, for a recurrent refrain. An excellent instance of
expectancy and delay has been noted by Gilbert Murray,
where Shelley—

> Thy brother Death came and cried:
> "Wouldst thou me?"
> Thy sweet child Sleep, the filmy-eyed,
> Murmured like a noon-tide bee:
> "Shall I nestle at thy side?
> Wouldst thou me?" and I replied,
> "No, not thee!"—

Shelley matches the final sound of the second line but without
the shortening, and holds us three lines longer—with a tricky
repetition—for the full return.

The part played by rhyme in aiding the memory needs no
emphasis, the nursery and the school use the mnemonic device; but to the efforts of the Elizabethan classicists to belittle the beauty of rhyme, to our contemporary classicists'
remark that Greek and Latin needed not the device, because

their meters are clear, but modern tongues require it to mark line-ends, the reply need be no proud but avoidant mention of blank verse: it has been fitly made by Oscar Wilde:

that exquisite echo which in the music's hollow hill creates and answers its own voice; rhyme, which in the hands of a real artist becomes not merely a material element of metrical beauty, but a spiritual element of thought and passion also, waking a new mood, it may be, or stirring a fresh train of ideas, or opening by mere sweetness and suggestion of sound some golden door at which the imagination itself had knocked in vain; rhyme, which can turn man's utterance into the speech of the gods; rhyme, the one chord we have added to the Greek lyre.

In blundering about for a rhyme, in truth, one makes more than one discovery, and is often repaid for what one seeks without finding by what one finds without seeking.

The fact that verse has for some centuries been much more frequently received through the medium of the eye than of the ear is of less disadvantage than many seem to believe; and the efforts of some poets (as Lindsay, as Kreymborg) to revive recital, and to write verse for reading aloud, result in a tendency toward obvious rhythms, naïve repetitions, and other characteristics of primitive verse. For the inner ear may equally demand rich and harmonious varieties of sound; at the same time, the eye more lengthily holds an expectant rhyme, and aids the other senses to follow subtler and more intricate rhythms; while thought comes with a new power into the poetry, which can rise beyond simple emotional or narrative presentations, can attain philosophy; and the art that was an evocation of mood or a story's framing becomes a deep stirring of the full powers of man.[28]

THE DICTION OF POETRY

On a poet's lips I slept.

PERCY BYSSHE SHELLEY.

IN THE beginning was the word. Often to the poet it seems beginning, middle, and end. Much more frequent than the Byronic careless rapture (in which he was indeed unlike the bird!) is the search of *le mot juste*—the one inevitable word that alone of all symbols must come to fill the waiting place. Poets, for want of a single word, have obeyed the Horatian injunction. Wordsworth seems to scorn such a practice, in his theory that the poet's language should be that of daily life; but his own diction is more in accord with the ideas of Dante and most other poets; though not to the measure of the remark that the poet's is to ordinary speech as the statue to ordinary man. "Words", said Maupassant, "have a soul. The majority of readers and even of writers require of them nothing more than a sense. But it is necessary, just the same, to discover and bring out this soul, which is revealed in their contact with other words, and which illuminates and transfigures certain books with ineffable splendor." While Maupassant probably had prose in mind as well, his attitude is more frequently stressed in regard to poetry alone, the prosaic point of view being nearer that of Alice's Duchess: "Take care of the sense, and the sounds will take care of themselves." The poet has rather known the answer of Galileo: What pains in polishing a lens! . . . . But how clear, and how far you can see!

That the disagreement is no new one we learn from Aristophanes, who makes Euripides exclaim "Oh, let us at least use the language of men!" Aristotle declares that the virtue of poetical diction is to be clear and not mean. The clearest is that which is made up of the usual words for things, but it is mean, as is shown in the poetry of Cleophon and Sthenelus. To be impressive and avoid commonness, diction must use unfamiliar terms: by which I mean unusual words, metaphors, lengthened forms, and everything out of the ordinary—though a style consisting entirely of such will result in riddles or barbarism.

There is really no controversy latent in practice: all poetry involves selection and arrangement, all poets have chosen and ordered as they deemed the immediate work required; only from each poem may the question of propriety be answered. Argument is usually sterile, unless it be, really, analysis. Landor divides poetry into the diaphanous, which is simple and clear, and the prismatic, which is ornamented with all the devices of diction. Each is valid as it is appropriate.

Wordsworth's notion, however, that the language of poetry had become divorced from reality, because poets copied one another instead of life, found excuse if not justification in the practice of his predecessors. The eighteenth century seemed to prefer the abstract term to the concrete, the general class to the specific object. Thus Johnson elaborated:

Turn on the prudent ant thy heedless eyes,
Observe her labours, sluggard, and be wise.
No stern command, no monitory voice,
Prescribes her duties, nor directs her choice;
Yet, timely provident, she hastes away
To snatch the blessings of a plenteous day;
When fruitful summer loads the teeming plain
She crops the harvest and she stores the grain.
How long shall sloth usurp thy useless hours,
Unnerve thy vigor, and enchain thy powers?
While artful shades thy downy couch enclose,
And soft solicitation courts repose,
Amidst the drowsy charms of dull delight

Year chases year with unremitted flight,
Till want now following, fraudulent and slow,
Shall spring to seize thee, like an ambushed foe.

A century earlier, the same passage had been differently set down:

Go to the ant, thou sluggard, consider her ways, and be wise: which having no guide, overseer, or ruler, provideth her meat in the summer, and gathereth her food in the harvest. How long wilt thou sleep, O sluggard? When wilt thou arise out of thy sleep? Yet a little sleep, a little slumber, a little folding of the hands to sleep. So shall thy poverty come as one that travaileth, and thy want as an armed man.

In discussing his own choice of words, J. M. Synge says "When I was writing *The Shadow of the Glen* some years ago, I got more aid than any learning could have given me from a chink in the floor of the old Wicklow house where I was staying, that let me hear what was being said by the servant girls in the kitchen." The prospects for literature, in a world where even the servant girls no longer talk spontaneous poetry, alarm F. L. Lucas:

We say that we are "well-off", and not one of us remembers that this is in origin the nautical metaphor of some sailor who had seen the breakers white and threatening on a lee-shore. Today the phrase is but an empty shell that has ceased even to murmur of the sea. "Let us burn our boats", cries the popular orator, "and launch out in the open sea." And how are we to breathe any of the beauty of poetry into the dramatic speech that represents a society where men do not even speak, like Monsieur Jourdain, prose?

(or even write, like Mr. F. L. Lucas, it?) To take seriously the lament for metaphors that become common coin of daily use is to bewail the constant enrichment of the language, through such continual minting—though protest may well be made against the quality of current coinage of figures. Nor is the mixing of metaphors in our speech as frequently ludicrous as Mr. Lucas would have us believe it . . . Those who feel that life and poetry are on divergent ways are called dead dreamers of an olden time—probably as unpoetic, on the whole, as ours,—by the many who seek their beauty and poetry in life as they find it today, endeavoring to give the world around them, and man's relations in that world, appropriate expression.

Words in poetry made a three-fold appeal, of sound, sense, and suggestion. They are, first, a logical symbol—though perhaps we are gripped even sooner by their emotional summoning; they may grow through associations with other ideas and feelings; and they may support these by the sound effect. For the sound may be atmospheric and fortify the sense, as in onomatopoetic words: *buzz, hiss, murmur;* or it may be emotional, and build upon the feeling: *ghoul, dastard, sly.*[29] Beauty in a word, said Theophrastus in his lost treatise, is that which appeals to the ear or the eye, or has noble associations of its own. Some words, intrinsically or in certain contexts, may have a sound, indeed, that stirs in such a way as to conflict with the sense. This is most obvious in proper names—an athlete christened Percival can continue only by the aid of a nickname; but the frequency of the term *golden,* as contrasted with that of *yellow,* may have auditory as well as monetary (or visual) cause. The sound of *peace,* at this moment of writing, is to me gratingly and hissingly discordant with the sense, fit for such use as Patrick Henry's; but such considerations are nice and individual; noting their existence, each can determine only his own particular responses.

The emotive use of words has already been discussed, but their power of suggestion has been extended, in poetry, by many associations. The use of so-called poetic words, for example, ensures a freedom from thoughts of one's neighbors or one's dinner, and links the work with the great poems of the past—which makes such use the greater peril. Archaisms seem poetic because they have lost the lustre of instant meaning, and strike entirely through form; they may be new evocatory symbols of a glamorous time—or empty husks of long-consumed emotion. John Drinkwater distinguishes several difficulties the modern poet must face, because of earlier linkings.

The fresh simplicity of a Chaucer, he avers, has become almost impossible. The early poet could cry

> Ther sprang the violet all new

and it was beauty. Even Shakespeare had to move in greater complexity:

> daffodils
> That come before the swallow dares, and take
> The winds of March with beauty.

The poet of today must seem not to be merely copying, must maintain his own freshness, in original phrasing, while at the same time avoiding inflation . . . Yet any period may have its Burns, its Housman, or its Frost.

Many words have definite verbal linkings, firmly set; so that to most who know English the albatross, in literature, brings thought of the cross-bow; a country churchyard, of mute inglorious Miltons it may hold. Shakespeare wrote

> not poppy nor mandragora
> Nor all the drowsy syrups of this world;

Keats after him dared speak of autumn "drowsed with the fume of poppies"; he will be a bold, or an ignorant, writer who next combines these terms—unless, of course, like T. S. Eliot, he seek deliberately to evoke the earlier times.

Journalism too, has had its way with the language. "Whole tracts of English have been turned over to this business of conveying useless information to people who are no whit the better for receiving it, or of giving an appearance of independent profundity to rough and ready mass opinion." This onslaught on our diction has had several results. It has created so many clichés that even in newspaper offices lists of prohibited trite phrases are compiled. Many writers have been led deliberately to seek the unusual, as though avoidance of the ordinary were in itself a merit. Some words, frequently employed in prose, have developed a vagueness of overtone that makes them dangerous: *expensive* as contrasted with *costly; gorgeous, valorous, conceited,* as opposed to *magnificent, brave, vain; exquisite; brilliant; sublime.* The necessity of fitting words into headline space has its effects (not always ill) upon the language, as in the increasing use of *wed* instead of *marry.* The desire to avoid the trite produces—especially among the reporters of sports—a far seeking of figures, and augments the flood of slang.

Further changes in the connotations of words rise from many causes. Man naturally desires to think well of himself; he tends to magnify his powers, all deeds that touch him, and to belittle all else. From this spring the associations of *beast, swine, dog,* and the other animals given objectionable human traits that they may then be brought into comparison with humans; hence, too, the excitement that exaggerates man's tales into *sensational* or *phenomenal* occurrences (which every occurrence must be), and has made *very*—since each of self-knowledge suspects his neighbor's presentation— almost a weakening term. The tendency to avoid even mention of what would make one socially uncomfortable, of what the code of the time deems dishonorable or shameful (relic of the tribal taboo) produces the many curious variants of *pregnant,* and the parent-words (not baby-words) for the excretory acts. Ignorance, and consequent fear—again magnified,—lead to other associations; the magic power once felt to reside in a name (so that early priests hid from even their own peoples the true name of their god) still associates the adjective *nameless* with the most hideous of dreads or sins. The desire of children to master the sounds of the language, which leads, as the Gnat tried to teach Alice, to puns and other plays on words:—

"When I use a word", Humpty-Dumpty said, in a rather scornful tone, "it means just what I choose it to mean—neither more nor less."

"The question is", said Alice, "whether you *can* make words mean so many things."

"The question is", said Humpty-Dumpty, "which is to be master—that's all. . . . They've a temper, some of them—particularly verbs: they're the proudest."

the love of play of word and idea (which has given us such words as *sophomore* and *dunce*) combines with the dislike of sameness, the desire for novelty, choosing new fashions "just for a change", to keep the language in a state of flux. A century ago, the dictionaries defined the noun *pluck* as "the liver and lights of an animal", ignoring then its usual sense today; while those who now seek a more vigorous term than the commonplace *pluck* go once more back into the viscera for the exclamation "He's got guts, that guy!" The poet, while treading cautiously among all these snares, yet boldly makes his words do triple duty and (like Humpty-Dumpty) "pays them extra" by giving them new beauty in their settings.

Aristotle divides into six sorts the words a poet may use: the terms of current speech; foreign words, from other dialects or tongues, such as *braes* or *blasé;* metaphorical expressions, like *lion-hearted;* periphrasis, roundabout allusion, as to the Stagirite, or to the Bard of Avon; new-minted coins of language—*chortle, runcible;* and forms created as variants of existing words, *margent, damosel, yestre'en.* To these, in the modern tongues (though even Homer knew them) might be added archaisms, restorations of forgotten or moribund terms, such as *feateously, cymar*. Further sorts suggest themselves: new forms from familiar stems, *impurpurate, wassailous;* reclaimed uses of transformed words: "wide air's *depending* pall"; and words drawn from science or other specialized fields, as *gules,* as *phonograph* and *dynamo*.

Still another possibility of choice is open to the poet in English, because of the compound origin of the tongue. The development of the language has been such that the structural words and those closest to childhood, to the hearth and the soil, are Saxon. The use of Saxon terms, therefore, gives a sense of earthiness, of the elemental, fundamental moods and matters, in contradistinction to the intellectual tone given by a greater proportion of words of Latin or Norman-French extraction. Failure to recognize that these "secondary" words with us are—in cognate forms—primary with the French (for *home* and *death* carry emotions, as well as the denotations of domicile and mortality) gives emphasis to the common English charge that French poetry is intellectual rather than emotional. "Remuneration", says Shakespeare's clown; "Oh, that's the Latin word for three farthings." Saxon words, furthermore, often convey something of the original image through their several meanings; "he has a *way* with him"; "it's always *fair* weather"; "play *fair*"; "a good *deal*"— whereas only the scholar traces the original of *fact* or *occasion*. This retention of the image is still more striking in compounds: compare Saxon *schoolmaster* with classic *pedagogue; uprightness* and *integrity;* observe the *ne'er-do-well* and the *Jack-of-all-trades* beside the *factotum;* note that *sycophant* contains, for the learned, an essay in political economy, *pastime* holds its story for all who read. As early as the Elizabethans this quality was recognized; Gascoigne in 1575 declared:

the most auncient English wordes are of one sillable, so that the more monasyllables that you vse the truer Englishman you shall seeme, and the lesse you shall smell of the Inkehorne: Also woordes of many syllables do cloye a verse and make it vnpleasant, whereas woordes of one syllable will more easily fall to be shorte or long as occasion requireth. . . .

Out of this triviality (going back to the image), there rise, also, for the author's choosing sets of words; sometimes Norman and Saxon—*cordial, hearty;* at others, Norman and Latin—*lawful, legal;* even by all three roads—*kingly, royal, regal; brave, valiant, valorous;* with denotations the dictionaries may be hard put to it to distinguish, but with gathered associations that make for the poet's unhesitant choice. In general, the possibilities of the tongue are indicated by the scientist A. N. Whitehead:

Latin and Greek are inflected languages. This means that they express an unanalyzed complex of ideas by the mere modification of a word; whereas in English, for example, we use the prepositions and auxiliary verbs to drag into the open the whole bundle of ideas involved.*

By judicious choice of words the poet, then, may bring into relief any aspect of an idea or feeling.

The diction of poetry, I have said, is more frequently concise, figurative, and euphonious. It is well-sounding because of the harmony between word and meaning, because of the music in the fellowship of the line. It is concise because of the many associations each word comet-like leaves as a glowing trail upon the mind, and because it is figurative, building its meaning through images, through tropes ("turnings"). "The greatest thing by far", says Aristotle of the poet's need, "is to be master of metaphor. It is the one thing that cannot be learnt from others, and it is a sign of genius, for to make good metaphors is to see similarity in things dissimilar." Helen H. Parkhurst goes so far as to define all art as metaphor.

A figure of speech, which is the use of a term in other than

* See page 309.

its common application—as when a lamppost is employed as a yard-stick to measure a tall man—may serve to add vigor, or clearness, and beauty to an idea. This is recognized by others than the artist, whence the pungent use of slang. The objections to slang are of two orders. Spiritually, there is usually a snarl, or a sneer, contumely or condescension, slipping along on the smooth lips of slang. Intellectually, the cant term is on every tongue for every purpose; pleased surprise expels the same oath as anger; the forcefulness of the expression is lost in the many mouthings, and one flat phrase pursues another down the ways of oblivion. But the metaphor that pierces to a hidden identity beneath the varicolored surfaces of things, and at once bares it and robes it in beauty, carries alms to put in the wallet of the years, stay-money to envious and calumniating time.

Of the various figures at the service of the poet, little need here be said. Puttenham's list of over a hundred may attract those who delight in classifications. One large group consists of such devices as hyperbole, metonymy, synecdoche, and the other selective figures, which focus attention upon one aspect of an object and thereby represent the whole. As a great grin might be a cartoonist's picture of Roosevelt, or an enormous paunch his portrait of Capitalism, so these figures by selection and isolation tend to magnify the part or quality they present: even in so simple a shift as "He's fond of the bottle" or "Glorious Rome hath lost her crown", one may sense the slight distortion.

More frequent and more effective is the union of two pictures, the intensification through a second image, achieved in metaphor and simile. It is worth pointing out that metaphor is not, as too many schoolbooks tell, step-child to simile, an implied comparison, "without like or as"; rather, as Demetrius observes, "a simile is an expanded metaphor". The figure is an older and sturdier growth than simile, frequent with primitive peoples and children as well as poets, being the brave and direct *identification* of unlike things because of a common feature: the hero *has* the wild stag's foot, the lion's heart; the lover bids his beloved, not to play make-believe, not to juggle *als ob;* but

> Drink to me only with thine eyes;

the bride pacing into the hall may, in pallid simile, seem "red as a rose", but such weak comparisons are spurned in the sonnet

> My mistress' eyes are nothing like the sun

by the poet whose metaphors, in the world of man's thought,

> The multitudinous seas incarnadine,

who says to the one he woos:

> Thou art the grave where buried love doth live,
> Hung with the trophies of my lovers gone,
> Who all their parts of me to thee did give:
> —That due of many now is thine alone:
> Their images I loved I view in thee,
> And thou, all they, hast all the all of me.

Of late, indeed, the pressure of past poetry, and the tension and sense of speed of our own age, have caused poets less frequently to employ the simile, and more often the metaphor. This figure, indeed, has taken a sharper and more brilliant—if more brittle—quality; at the cost of more frequent obscurity it has dared a more single binding. "The wild stag's foot" suggests the hero's grace as well as his speed, his daring, too, of hazardous attainment; "the lion's heart"* brings majesty to mind, fortitude, calm, decision. "Those are pearls that were his eyes": shape, and dull lustre, and the fate of foundered things. At the reader's best, the metaphor by several points of similarity reënforces the linked feeling; at his worst, he grasps any one of the common char-

* Bithae used to describe Sohrab.

acteristics, and is content. Since Mallarmé, however, poets have searched farther, for metaphors whereof the bound images have but one trait in common:[*]

> Rend open the heat,
> Tear it to tatters (H.D.);

firs topped with "an emerald turkey-foot" (Marianne Moore); "the moment's spurious diamond" (Joseph Auslander); "Pyrrhus you call him. Pyrrhus because he purrs"—this at its most trifling; though E. A. Robinson (see Note 2) is guilty with more than the cat. Baudelaire has been credited with the first quest of these unique correspondencies, but they are to be found in Anglo-Saxon riddles: "the windless wave of the wild bull's spear" is mead from a drinking horn; and Dante, blinded by the first brilliance of the apostles Peter and James, cries out

> Wherefore I lift mine eyes unto the hills
> Which erst had bowed them with excessive weight.

The characteristic of these "radical" metaphors, at the root of the novelty of the new verse, consists in their mention of only one term of the identity. Hugo speaks of

> The fleece of the sinister sheep of the sea.

Valéry is content with

> This tranquil roof where pigeons peck,

leaving us to discern that he speaks of sea and dipping sails. We may have grown familiar with the device, in Browning. At times, indeed, the one symbol may draw several ideas, each by a single thread, into its woof. Hart Crane tells us that in his lines

> And wrecks passed without sound of bells,
> The calyx of death's bounty giving back
> A scattered chapter, livid hieroglyph

* Even in Homer this is to be found – e.g. old men compared to cicadas (speech

the calyx stands for the vortex made by the sinking vessel, which in turn, ironically, brings to mind a cornucopia, as the whirlpool sends up its wreckage. Here we approach, however, such complexity as makes the new vocabulary of James Joyce a guessing-game for the reader.*

A figure may be based on either symbolic or emotive reference, on a similarity in thought, or in the desired emotion. The second summoning is the more frequent, in both slang and poetry: for one man whose appearance resembles that of a pinhead, a dozen draw the appellation for the feeling it conveys. Failure to recognize such use may lead the literal-minded to deem irrelevant an emotionally apt figure. While the images brought to mind are usually precise, and center what might otherwise be a vague conception on a definite, particular object; there may be times when the opposite end is desirable, when the image should carry the mind from a too close dwelling upon the original thought. "Wealth", for example, that may suggest prosaic millionaires and fluctuant stock-markets, may, on the other hand, be "of Ormuz and of Ind" and carry a glamour outside reality; or be

> beyond
> The dreams of misers crouching at the hearth
> And every spark a treasure

and light a new avenue of fancy.

These figures, through the summoning of objects to the mind, and the stirring of incipient impulses and movements, make the subject come, as it were, to life in the receptor, and give it a vividness a tale without figures could not find.

The fable, the allegory, the parable, are of course but extended metaphors; frequently an entire poem (*The Faerie Queene*) is substituted story.

* See Note 47.

Because I built my nest so high
Must I despair
If a fierce wind, with bitter cry,
Passes the lower branches by,
And mine makes bare?

I shall but build, and build my best,
Till, safety won,
I hang aloft my new-made nest
High as of old, and see it rest
As near the sun.

Only those who believe the photographer will look for the bird.

THE GREAT CONTROVERSIES

"Wot's wot?" repeated one of the buccaneers in a deep
growl. "Ah, he'd be a lucky one as knowed that!"
R. L. STEVENSON.

OF THE several moot points that have pressed upon
prosodists, the most frequent, and perhaps the most futile,
has been the claim of quantity to rule the line, as against the
familiar accent. Since the Elizabethans there have, indeed,
been continuing experiments in classical forms; Tennyson
has essayed alcaics, Swinburne, Robert Bridges, and many
more have made efforts which somehow are usually looked
upon as "experiments in Greek meters", rather than as
poems. In these, moreover, it may be generally observed that
the normal English accent falls where the classical meter
demands a long syllable; and those who comment on the
two aspects of emphasis have recently been seeking to reconcile them. Elizabeth Barrett Browning suggested that accent
is but one way of establishing quantitative differences within
the line, because every stress involves a holding or a pause.
Herbert Read speaks of rhythm as establishing harmony
between quantity and accent, which lengthily through the
ages have disputed the line. Robert Graves, indeed, attempts
to keep the two separate; he links the orderliness of classical
verse with the ordained regularity of the feudal system,
whereas the ruggedness of accentual verse stirs with the
upward urge of the people "threatening the classic scheme
from below. The rare poets who have contrived to reconcile
the two principles have always had, like Skelton and Shakespeare, one foot firmly planted in the aristocratic set, and the
other equally firmly in the crowd." Mr. Graves, we note, has

sought rather far for his first poet, and probably the devil could quote Shakespeare. The classicist Gilbert Murray feels that the element of quantity grows important as we grow careful in our speech. But Dionysius of Halicarnassus discussed the obvious inequality of various classical long syllables, and short ones; A. J. Ellis has calculated forty-five degrees of stress in English verse; and J. Schipper has found, in Chaucer, sixty-four forms of the decasyllabic line. Nor is it possible to estimate the rhythmic quality of the line apart from its meaning, which often dictates otherwise unrecorded variations in the flow. The controversy is dismissed, these days, with the general recognition that the Greek terms, iambic pentameter, trochaic tetrameter, and the rest, are the more systematic and complete; and that some variation—of intensity, duration, pitch, whatever the moment affords— always occurs, to give more importance to certain elements in the line, to make the reader there hold his attention more closely. That this centering may be produced by means wholly non-metrical is made cleverly manifest when W. S. Gilbert, in *Patience*, stresses four different words in four uses of the line "He was a little boy".

Another controversy, long since laid in the museum of dead importancies, yet interesting because of contemporary parallel, is the quarrel of rhyme and blank verse. Tumbling on its way in the disregarded drama, the unrhymed pentameter moved with the plays through popularity to esteem. Dryden lamented that it was vain "to strive against the people's inclination, won over as they have been by Shakespeare, Jonson, Beaumont and Fletcher"; but he was even thus grudgingly tolerant of the form only in drama, and said of Milton that "rhyme was not his talent, he has neither the ease of doing it nor the graces of it". Byron, one of the last to regret the intrusion of blank verse, protested that no one who could rhyme, except Milton, deemed the other mode worthy of use. Milton himself looked upon rhyme as "no necessary adjunct or true ornament of poem or good verse, in longer works especially, but the invention of a barbarous age, to set off wretched matter and lame meter; graced indeed since by the use of some famous modern poets, carried away by custom, but much to their own vexation, hindrance, and constraint to express many things otherwise, and for the most part worse, than else they would have expressed them". Johnson declared that English poetry, being unmusical, may, perhaps, "subsist without rhyme, but it will not often please"; and Voltaire, translating Shakespeare into rhymed hexameters, gave high sanction to the notion, general among rhymesters, that blank verse may be composed as spontaneously as a letter, and costs but the trouble of dictating.

Echoes of this outcry have recently been heard, against the many offerings in free verse, which have been called anything from "chopped prose" to typographical juggling. "Vers libre", says G. K. Chesterton, "is no more a revolution in poetry than sleeping in a ditch is a revolution in architecture". And those teachers of verse technique who astonish classes by composing—on the blackboard, before their very eyes—regular, consecutive blank verse lines on any suggested subject, have a way of remarking that free verse written by eight-year-olds has been widely hailed. There is no doubt that one who is facile can easily compose in blank verse or in free verse; in his day, says Demetrius, "indeed, many people talk in iambics without knowing it"; rhyme itself, to be sure, presents little more of a problem; yet the bee and the wasp suck the same flowers: the only thing hard to write, in any of these forms, is poetry.

There is a notion, somewheres prevalent, that the poet is a long-haired idler, who at times languidly indites an immortal line; those who have framed such a picture—which it must be confessed some poets have helped to paint—need not be told of the active lives many poets lead in the industrial world, often spared but the night hours for creation; they may, more simply, take Elinor Wylie's suggestion and try to type out—with additions and emendations if they desire—*Prometheus Unbound* or *Paradise Lost*. Lamartine said "I never think; my thoughts think for me"; but Poe bears with a bludgeon upon such sophistical nonchalance:

Most writers—poets in especial—prefer having it understood that they compose by a species of fine frenzy—and ecstatic intuition—and would positively shudder at letting the public take a peep behind the scenes, at the elaborate and vacillating crudities of thought—at the true purpose seized only at the last moment—at the innumerable glimpses of idea that arrived not at the maturity of full view—at the fully matured fancies discarded in despair as unmanageable—at the cautious selections and rejections—at the painful erasures and interpolations—in a word, at the wheels and pinions—the tackle for scene-shifting—the stepladders and demon-traps—the cock's feathers, the red paint, and the black patches which in ninety-nine cases out of the hundred constitute the properties of the literary histrio.

Earlier emphasis on the labor of the poet is laid by Dryden:

Mere poets and mere musicians are as sottish as mere drunkards are, who live in a continual mist, without seeing or judging anything clearly. A man should be learned in several sciences, and should have a reasonable, philosophical, and in some measure a mathematical head, to be a complete and excellent poet; and besides this, should have experience in all sorts of humors and manners of men, should be thoroughly skilled in conversation, and should have a great knowledge of mankind in general.

But surely such remarks are not needed, to show that the poet's journey is no painless, pansied stroll.

The last of the great controversies, and the only one still flourishing, is that of sound and sense. This opposition, long smouldering, took new fire from the effort of the symbolists to turn poetry into music—from Flaubert's regret, overemphasized by his followers, that he could not construct a

novel entirely of form, and his judgment that a beautiful
poem without meaning (a concept beyond the comprehension
of opponents of the school) is preferable to a less beautiful
poem with meaning. Of two poets in two tongues, whose work
shows predominant concern for form, it has been said:
"Swinburne is wild where Baudelaire is grave; and where
Baudelaire compresses some perverse and morbid image into
a single unforgettable line, Swinburne beats it into a froth
of many musical lovely words, until we forget the deep sea
in the shining foam". Thought is put at times so far in the
background that the efforts of some contemporary experimental writers, such as Gertrude Stein, who uses combinations of syllables that happen to have meaning in English,
and Hugo Blümner, who uses combinations mainly without
significance in any tongue, may be described as structures in
sound.[30] There is explanation if not justification of the stress
laid on sound, these days when *clamor omnia vincit*.

Building a classification on such a distinction, Ezra Pound
states that poetry is charged with meaning, energized, in one
or more of three manners. In *Melopœia,* beyond the meaning,
is some musical property which directs the bearing or trend
of that meaning. *Phanopœia* casts images upon the visual
imagination. Mr. Pound neglects the other senses, of which
especially the kinetic finds frequent poetic appeal (but for
which, possibly, no neatly coined titles occurred); his third
class is *Logopœia,* "the dance of the intellect among words,
that is to say, it employs words not only for their direct
meaning, but it takes count in a special way of habits of
usage, of the context we expect to find with the word, its
usual concomitants, of its known acceptances, and of ironic
play. It holds the æsthetic content that is peculiarly the domain of verbal manifestation and cannot possibly be con-
tained in plastic or in music." Thus indeed every poet
unawares has been composing *Logopœia!* All writing, Mr.

Pound continues, is built of these elements, *architectonics* being the process of inter-ordering them so that they have meaning only through the organism, in the companionship of the whole.

Build with words the poet may, as the prose writer with ideas; sound, sense, suggestion, and companionship his guides at once and goal; and pleasing in its beauty the structure that he rears: beyond all controversial passion and partisan zeal, underlying all manifestoes of all schools—each in turn rebel and rule—lies the feeling, crooned into the nursling at the breast, dancing through children in their common play, bright in the songs of soldiers and of slaves, loud in the rhythms of revelry and of toil, and lifting to the sun of the most cloudless mind, that closest of man's expressions to his heart, most deeply penetrant to his responding spirit, is that fluid essence of life's moods which we call poetry.

CHAPTER VIII

DRAMA

No, 'tis not so deep as a well, nor so wide as a church-door; but 'tis enough, 'twill serve.

WILLIAM SHAKESPEARE.

DRAMA AND THE THEATRE

Soon as the actor, thus bedizened, stands
In public view, clap go ten thousand hands.
"What said he?" Naught. "Then what's the attraction?"
Why,
Yon woollen mantle with the violet dye.
ALEXANDER POPE.

IN THE consideration of drama, one is confronted with a question that requires instant facing. There has been argued by theorists and stage-men, lengthily through the vicissitudes of the theatre, the point pressed by the men of "the profession" that a printed play is as a libretto or scenario of the drama, and by the tribe of "undramatic critics" that a good play is literature, and has valid existence, in the book. Both forces have argued so potently that, while *theatrical* has come to imply the meretricious, an equal measure of opprobrium attaches to *closet-drama*.

The first blast in favor of the drama as literature was blown by Aristotle, who admits that the setting "has an emotional attraction of its own—but of all the parts is the least artistic and connected least with the art of poetry. For the power of tragedy, we may be sure, is felt even apart from representation and actors." Remembering that the entrance of the dread chorus in Æschylus' *Eumenides* produced faintings and premature deliveries in the theatre, the Greek critic protested: "Terror and pity can be induced by spectacular means, but it is much better to produce them through the writing." That a play takes new power from adequate production none will gainsay. Many a playwright has regretted the limitations of the printed page (were not the first printed plays rushed into type only to prevent piracy?); and the practice has recently developed of setting down stage directions in more chatty style, to stimulate the imagination of the reader, attuned to the novel: the printed plays of Barrie are full of confidential asides not in the dialogue; Eugene O'Neill gives descriptions no scenic artist can reproduce, such as (speaking of the two great trees in *Desire Under the Elms*) "They are like exhausted women resting their sagging breasts and hands and hair on its roof, and when it rains their tears trickle down monotonously and rot on the shingles"—it does not rain during the action of the play; or he offers philosophical speculations, such as the final remark "And now, perhaps, the Hairy Ape at last belongs".

Voltaire declared that "without actors a play is without life; it is you who give it its soul; tragedy is intended to be acted even more than to be read". Despite Lamb's dictum on Shakespeare (which, however we endure the scenes in *King Lear* he shudders for, would be supported today in regard to *Titus Andronicus*, which keeps the ravished Lavinia long onstage with tongue excised and hands hacked off, and makes the spectators behold the proffer of Titus' hand as forfeit, only to have it return on a platter with the heads of Titus' sons)—few will dissent from Voltaire's opinion; the question at issue is whether in the reading, or only in the performance, one can truly experience drama. Experience and—since critics insist—judge; for odd opinions rise according to the point of view, as when three professors remote from the metropolis (Lewisohn, then of Ohio, Chandler of Cincinnati, Henderson of North Carolina) write books that lengthily consider the essay-dramas of Shaw but remain inattentive to the then unpublished plays of Barrie; as when H. D. Traill declares (losing track of number through the comma-maze):

Of every drama, as we moderns understand the term, it may, I
hold, be affirmed that, though some of them may, and do, contain
great literature, they are, to the extent to which they are literary,
undramatic, and, to the extent to which they are dramatic, un-
literary.

—or as when this view is flatly challenged: "To tell an interesting or amusing story through the medium of dialogues
which appear to be the natural speech of human beings—
that *is* literature." W. A. Darlington observes that "whenever a literary man publishes a play that is finely written, the
academic critics hail it as a dramatic masterpiece. If it is then
tried in the theatre and proves a dramatic failure, its non-
success is regarded by the academic critics as a reflection,
not on their judgment, but on the theatre and everything
connected with it". The long popularity enjoyed by such
pieces as *Abie's Irish Rose* warns us against the opposite
error of judging the value of a drama exclusively from the
degree of its stage success. Some valid works of art in
dramatic form, Tennyson's *The Princess,* Shelley's *The
Cenci,* perhaps, though this has been effectively performed,
his and Browning's and Swinburne's renderings of Greek
tragedies, and Hardy's *The Dynasts,* for examples, were not
intended for the stage; the question concerns not these, but
only such plays as, because or in spite of (or without regard
to) their fate in the theatre, have made more lengthy claim
upon the years.

When the drama, after the Renaissance, became object of
critical consideration, Aristotle was the guide; of the Italians,
of Corneille, of Dryden who declared that to be read "I am
sure, is the more lasting and the nobler design". In truth
eighteenth century comment seems often a *reductio ad
absurdum* of the Greek, as when Voltaire (a foolish consistency is the hobgoblin of little minds) exclaimed "What
has the stage decoration to do with the merit of a poem? If

the success depends on what strikes the eyes, we might as well have moving pictures!" As well, indeed! Yet as early was the bold challenge flung: "It is not true, what Aristotle says", affirmed Castelvetro; stating first that few can fancy in the reading what all can see in the staging and, secondly, that reading gives a different delight: the peculiar pleasure of the drama springs only from the performance. The Elizabethans, free of Aristotle, felt this, as Marston, in his preface to *The Malcontent,* and Webster, in his to *The Devil's Law-Case,* attest; but it is surprising to note that Rymer's attacks on Shakespeare are against poetry, for dramaturgy. Diderot most fully develops the doctrine of the drama as theatre-material, attributing the decline of the French drama to its obeying Greek rules without the Greek conditions: "for works of this kind we need authors, actors, a theatre, and perhaps a whole people". Simplify the drama and beautify the stage. This argument Lessing attacks, adducing Shakespeare and the lack of decoration on the Elizabethan stage, as proof that the play's the thing and in itself all-sufficient. Yet Shakespeare more than remedied the deficiency by coloring his plays with many lyrical and descriptive passages, throughout *The Tempest,* in Portia's garden—How sweet the moonlight sleeps along this bank—Juliet's balcony, and elsewhere, checking the play of the dramatist for the display of the scenic artist. And Lessing himself queries: "Wherefore the hard work of the dramatic form? Why build a theatre, disguise men and women, torture their memories, invite the whole town to assemble at one place, if I intend to produce nothing more with my work and its presentation than some of the emotions that would be produced by any good story that every one could read by his chimney-corner at home?"

A subtler consideration leads A. W. Schlegel to the same conclusion. To him. drama differs from the novel in that it

presents a conflict without explanation by the author; and
the only way in which it can be made clear without such interference, is by the reproduction, before the receptor, of the
persons involved in the conflict, acting out its events in something like their natural surroundings. Grillparzer continues
this line of thought, declaring even that whatever is truly
dramatic is also soundly theatrical. The definition of the
drama given by Francisque Sarcey centers upon the audience;
and for the past century the view has increasingly prevailed
that the printed play alone is poor prop to judgment of the
drama. C. E. Montague declares that the dramatist often
"has to do what is sometimes called in the trade 'getting out
of the way of the acting'. As a rule, when a scene acts well, it
is not that the actors express over again in pantomime just
what the author expresses in his words; that would give an
effect of over-acting; but it is just as likely in such cases
that the author has over-written as that the actors are over-
acting. What the more skillful dramatist consciously does is
to divide the opportunities between his actors and himself.
Of all the things that he would set down on paper if he were
writing a piece of dialogue simply to be read, as in a novel, he
will leave a large proportion out, in order that the actor may
have these significancies to convey in his own way." And
Granville Barker tells that he has "seen a performance of
Chekov's *The Cherry Orchard* in Moscow, and to read the
play afterwards was like reading the libretto of an opera—
missing the music. Great credit to the actors; no discredit
to Chekov. For—and this is what the *undramatic* writer fails
to understand—with the dramatist the words on paper are
but the seeds of the play."

Against all these critics Joel Elias Spingarn emphatically
stands.

Unfortunately the demoralization which forty years ago Flaubert foresaw in all this *arcane théâtral*, all this pedantry of

"dramatic technique", or "dramaturgic skill", of *"scènes à faire"*, of the conditions of the theatre, the influence of the audience, and the conformation of the stage, this demoralization, I say, has overwhelmed the criticism of the drama. What the unities, decorum, *liaison des scènes*, and kindred petty limitations and restrictions were to dramatic theory in the seventeenth and eighteenth centuries, these things are to criticism in the nineteenth and twentieth. They constitute the new pedantry, against which all æsthetic criticism as well as all creative literature must wage a battle for life.

Regarding the theatre, therefore, not as a place of amusement (although in that too it has of course its justification as much as golf or cricket), not as a business undertaking (in which case we should have to consider the box office receipts as the test of a play's excellence), not as an instrument of public morality (since our concern is not with ethics or political science), but regarding it solely as the home or the cradle of a great art, what do we find its relations to dramatic criticism? Merely this, that for æsthetic criticism, the theatre simply does not exist. For criticism, a theatre means only the appearance at any one time or in any one country, as Croce puts it, of a "series of artistic souls". All external conditions, as he points out, are only dead material which has no æsthetic significance outside of the poet's soul; and only in the poet's art should we seek to find them.

Some have gone so far, in countering this argument, as to suggest that the play itself is no more than a set of directions, to take life from the art of the scenic designer, the director, and the players; and in Russia particularly some plays have been written as loosely as the commedia dell' arte. Those who have seen and read such a drama as O'Neill's *The Emperor Jones* will probably recognize that the effect of the audible drum-beat is different not in degree but in kind from the effect of the printed note that it occurs; as the rhythm of *Porgy* surges only on the stage. Without going to such an extreme, it may be pointed out that, as a "sonnet" of twenty-one lines (save for early variations) is a contradiction in terms, so is a play (save for closet-drama) unthinkable save

as something to be played; every art has not merely its conventions, (universal or local, lasting or temporary), but its
materials, inextricably bound with its development and very
being; and the theatre has been a persisting convention of
the drama, the stage and its appurtenances have always been
materials of the dramatist's art.

THE ORIGIN OF THE DRAMA

What little town by river or seashore,
Or mountain-built with peaceful citadel,
Is emptied of its folk this pious morn?
JOHN KEATS.

ALTHOUGH neither space nor the scope of this work permits a history of the drama, the subsequent development and form of the art are in many ways so dependent upon its origin as to make necessary some consideration of that source. It should be hardly necessary, today, to remind the reader of the growth of tragedy and comedy out of the ancient ritual, the religious ceremonies or—more accurately—the magic invocations, by which early peoples sought to summon the New Year, the spring rebirth, the annual resurrection. There is the hero, the Year-Son, who marries Earth (as there were Ouranos and Gaia), who as he grows aged and winter-hoar, is (with his wife's assistance) slain by his own child (as Kronos, who killed Ouranos, in turn is destroyed by Zeus). Nor were these patricides and incests the habits merely of created gods; priests and kings (often both were one) among our earliest kind were similarly slain, in battle or in sacrifice, that young blood might redeem the tribe; and the queen died with her mate or joined the destroyer. Out of the *comos,* or love-feast, rose comedy; out of the wintry death rose tragedy —holding the whispered spring of resurrection. The priest of the temple of Diana at Aricia (who impelled Frazer's grand tour of *The Golden Bough*), the scapegoat annually thorn-crowned as "King of the Jews": the sympathetic magic of expiation by transference lapsed into milder sacrifice to the god; the dance of the magic formula or celebration grew into the drama.

The many traces in Greek drama of its religious origin—as the reluctance of the Greeks to present violence onstage, the holding of the chorus inviolate and the theatre as sanctuary—naturally faded as generations made their source more remote. The debt of the drama to religion, however, was renewed in the Middle Ages; the story of the Christ parallels the olden movement. The origin of *Hamlet* in a nature myth, a year-drama, is convincingly traced by Gilbert Murray, and its inconsistencies, long troubling to critics, seem drawn from the dual rôle of the king-slayer as the life-spirit and the scapegoat. As Œdipus is the saviour of Thebes and the polluter of Thebes, as Orestes is at once redeemer and matricide, so Hamlet (and before him Claudius) is avenger yet sinner. The tragic conflict is in the essence of the tragic tale, the native burden of the tragic hero. In hunting Hamlet's mother, Gertrude, through many forms back to earth, to the Earth-Wife, the Earth-Mother—to Gerutha of the Sagas, wife of Horvendil, Teutonic god of the dawn and the spring—is found the explanation of her various affiances, of her devotion to her husband and to his slayer, and of the attitude toward her son that permits psychanalytical performers today to read an "Œdipus complex" into her impulses. Not to dwell too long on the one play, observe that in *Lear*, *Macbeth*, *Julius Cæsar*, in *Ghosts*, in *Desire Under the Elms*, in many more that come to mind, destruction flares from one close to the victim—with often the promise of ultimate peace, after the tumult and disaster of the storm.

For comedy ends in the church; tragedy, in the churchyard. Though the Greeks were not insistent on the ceremony, throughout the history of the theatre, (despite O'Neill's declaration that *Anna Christie* has not a happy ending), the comedy culminates in the love-revelry, the tragedy terminates in the death-dealing. As Gilbert Murray emphasizes:

The poets and dramatists have not deliberately wished to end upon the note of rejoicing for love or of weeping for death. Thousands of them have tried hard to escape from so hackneyed an ending, and to prove themselves "original". But the tradition is too strong for them. There is one general joy greater than other joys, one universal fear darker than other fears; and the poet who throws himself on the stream of his song is borne almost inevitably toward the one or the other. Aristotle speaks of the Homeric epos as the fountainhead of tragedy; Longinus distinguishes the *Odyssey* from the *Iliad* as a "comedy of character". Both judgments are easily explicable. The last line of the *Iliad* tells us: "So wrought they the burial of Hector tamer of horses". And the last line of the *Odyssey*, according to Aristarchus— though in our present version there are many lines after it— runs: "So came these two to the rite of the ancient Marriage- Bed".*

Out of the rising of the mummy from its bier, the wan Nile to its fertile floods; out of the slaying of the Year- Father by the Year-Son, each in turn smiled upon by the Earth-Mother; out of the leaping dance at the birth of Dionysos, the noble bull, whose hide is later stuffed and driven with the plough; out of the song of the scapegoat (the word *tragedy* means *goat-song*) who dies to save the people; out of the similar sacrifice of Jesus, and the saintly martyrdoms— but more deeply out of the medieval as the ancient fears and prayers, and subsequent rejoicings when the sun returned and all the earth was green anew:—remained on the one hand fear, and superstitious fervor, and religious faith and exaltation; and sprang on the other song, and dance, and the conflict of man's mightiest fears and joys and passions in the drama.

* From *The Classical Tradition In Poetry*, copyright by the President and Fellows of Harvard College.

THE DEFINITION OF TRAGEDY

Fierce warres, and faithfull loves, shall moralize my song.
EDMUND SPENSER.

"TRAGEDY, then, is an imitation of some action that is serious, entire, of some magnitude, by language embellished and rendered pleasurable by different means in the different parts, presented not through narration but in action, effecting through pity and terror the purgation of these passions."

In such words Aristotle offered the first of the ever unsatisfactory definitions of tragic drama. Out of them rose the smoke-clouded genii of the three unities; of the hatred of the common—interpreting *serious* and *of some magnitude* as demanding noble birth and high estate; of the final disaster: all the bogies with which critics have harassed practicing playwrights. With the revival of drama these misconceptions grew; Chaucer declares that

> Tragedy is to seyn a certeyn storie
> As olde bokes maken us memorie,
> Of him that stood in great prosperitie
> And is y-fallen out of heigh degree
> Into miserie, and endeth wrecchedly.

Thus, by the sort of etymology that derived *drama* from *dream,* we are told that a tragedy is so named because of the goat's shaggy abundance before, and wretched baldness behind. Puttenham, whose volume is a sound echo of contemporary thought, says that "tragedy deals with the doleful falls of unfortunate and afflicted princes, for the purpose of reminding men of the mutability of fortune and of God's just punishment of a wicked life". The pagan sense of destiny is here replaced by the Christian idea of moral punishment; but the notion of fatality, or inevitability, has crept back into our conception of tragedy, freeing us from any need of taking sides, permitting us often to feel, in good drama, that "every character is in the right".

The vicissitudes of Aristotle's definition, and of the Aristotelian prestige, have been traced in several volumes. In 1439 an Italian scholar said "To defend Aristotle and the truth seems to be one and the same thing". Filelfo was speaking of the Greek as a philosopher; a century later, this aspect of his thought was more suspect, and a French scholar, Peter Ramus, successfully defended the thesis that "the utterances of Aristotle, one and all, are false and vain imaginations". Within the quarter-century the Council of Trent placed his philosophy on one plane with the Roman Catholic dogma; but his authority in that field was increasingly disputed. As he waned as a philosopher, however, Aristotle grew as an æsthetic dictator; the words of Sidney elaborate the Elizabethan accord (and protest—as Shelley later warned— against the mingling of tragic and comic moods):

Our tragedies and comedies (not without cause cried out against) observing rules neither of honest civilitie nor of skilful poetry, excepting Gorbuduc (again I say, of those that I have seen) which notwithstanding, as it is full of stately speeches and well-sounding phrases, climbing to the high of Seneca his style, and as full of notable moralitie, which it doth most delightfully teach, and so obtayne the very end of poetry; yet in troth it is very defectious in the circumstances: which greeveth me, because it might not remain as an exact model of all tragedies. For it is faulty both in place and time, the two necessary companions of all corporall actions. For where the stage should always represent but one place, and the uttermost time presupposed in it should be, both by Aristotle's precept and common reason, but one day: there is both many dayes, and many places, inartificially imagined. But if it be so in Gorboduck, how much more in al the rest? where you shall have Asia of the one side, and Affrick of the other, and so many underkingdoms; that the player, when he commeth in, must ever begin with telling where he is; or else, the tale will not be conceived. Now ye shall have three Ladies walke to gather flowers, and then we must beleeve the stage to be a garden. By and by, we heare news of shipwracke in the same place, and then wee are to blame, if we accept it not for a Rock. Upon the back of that, comes out a hideous monster, with fire and smoke, and then the miserable beholders are bound to take it for a cave. While in the meantime, two armies flye in, represented with foure swords and bucklers, and then what harde heart will not receive it for a pitched field.

Now, of time they are much more liberall. For ordinary it is that two young Princes fall in love: after many traverces, she is got with childe, delivered of a fair boy; he is lost, groweth a man, falls in love, and is ready to get another child, and all this in two hours' space: which how absurd it is in sense, even sense may imagine, and art hath taught, and all ancient examples justified: and at this day, the ordinary Players in Italie will not erre in. Yet wil some bring in an example of *Eunuchus* in Terence, that containeth matter of two daies, yet far short of twenty yearres. True it is, and so was it to be played in two daies, and so fitted to the time it set forth. And though Plautus hath in one place done amisse, let us hit with him, and not misse with him.

But they wil say, how then shall we set forth a story, which containeth both many places and many times? And doe they not knowe, that a tragedy is tied to the laws of Poesie, and not of Historie? not bound to follow the storie, but having liberty, either to faine a quite newe matter, or to frame the history to the most tragicall conveniencie. Again, many things may be told which cannot be shewed, if they know the difference between reporting and representing. As for example, I may speake (though I am here) of Peru, and in speech digresse from that to the description of Calicut: but in action I cannot represent it without Pacelots horse: and so was the manner the Auncients tooke, by some Nuncius to recount thinges done in former time, or other place.

But beside these grosse absurdities, how all theyr Playes be neither right tragedies nor right comedies: mingling Kings and Clownes, not because the matter so carrieth it: but thrust in Clownes by head and shoulders to play a part in majesticall matters, with neither decencie nor discretion. So as neither the admiration and commiseration, nor the right sportfulness, is by their mungrell Tragy-comedie obtained. I know Apuleius did somewhat so, but that is a thing recounted with space of time, not represented in one moment: and I knowe, the Aunciens have one or two examples of Tragy-comedies, as Plautus hath *Amphitrio*. But if we mark them well, we shall find that they never, or very daintily, match Horn-pypes and Funeralls. So falleth it out, that, having indeed no right comedy, in that comical part of our tragedy we have nothing but scurrility, unwoorthy of any chast ears: or some extreame show of doltishness, indeed fit to lift up a loude laughter and nothing els: where the whole tract of a Comedy should be full of delight, as the tragedy shoulde be still maintained in a well-raised admiration.

From the practice of Shakespeare it must not be assumed that he was ignorant of the Greek precepts—to which tavern discussion must have made him hail-fellow. Rather, the earlier examples in his native tongue—rewriting which formed probably his first dramatic discipline—gave him courage to ignore, and with popular approval, the rules Ben Jonson followed. In *Henry V*, Shakespeare alludes to the unity of time, and mentions "th' abuse of distance"; Polonius makes matter of Plautus and Seneca; the last play, *The Tempest*, observes the unities.

While Aristotle was ignored on the one hand and misunderstood, with strict obedience, on the other, the process of questioning and comprehending was begun. Even Lessing considered the criticism of the Greek "infallible as the elements of Euclid"—how time crumbles all our standards!—but he aided in the return toward understanding, as is revealed in his comment on the unities:

The French, on the contrary, who found no charms in pure unity of action, who had been spoilt by the wild intrigues of the Spanish school, before they had learnt to know Greek simplicity, regarded the unity of time and place not as consequences of unity of action, but as circumstances absolutely needful to the representation of an action, to which they must therefore adapt their more

complicated and richer actions with all the severity required in
the use of the chorus, which, however, they had totally abolished.
When they found, however, how difficult, nay at times impossible,
this was, they made a truce with the tyrannical rules against
which they had not the courage to rebel. Instead of a single place
they introduced an uncertain place, under which they could
imagine now this now that spot; enough if the places were not
too far apart and none required special scenery, so that the scenery
could fit the one about as well as the other. Instead of the unity
of a day, they substituted unity of duration, and a certain period
during which no one spoke of sunrise or sunset, or went to bed,
or at least did not go to bed more than once, however much might
occur in this space, was allowed to pass as a day.

Coleridge also recognized that the secondary unities, of
time and place, were in the Greek drama mere consequences
of the chorus, "who could go no farther from their dwellings,
nor remain absent longer than it was customary to do from
mere curiosity"—though even the Greeks did hurry the
action. Practice, and the need of justifying what was so manifestly enjoyed, led to increasing attack on Aristotle, until
today F. L. Lucas is emboldened to state that nothing remains of the famous formula but the "bare tautology: Serious
drama is a serious representation by speech and action of
some phase of human life".

THE ESSENCE OF TRAGEDY

Love bade me welcome; yet my soul drew back,
Guilty of dust and sin.

GEORGE HERBERT.

ONE does not rest content to know that tragedy is "to seyn a certeyn storie"; nor is a listing of its usual themes—love, strife, death, and that which is beyond death—respite from the search of man for surety. So many crowding things are turbulent through life, that it sometimes seems we keep our footing only by assigning groups of objects each a label, which may serve as something to clutch when we stumble, a restful hold, a satisfying substitute for thought.

Two aspects of early drama, sprung from the magic representation and the overflow of rejoicing at its success, William Archer calls imitation and passion. To the lyric exaltation of the olden plays (for Greek tragedy with its poetry and music and high cothurni and colored masks is beyond modern remolding) have succeeded but the opera and the ballet; from their direct presentation has grown the realistic drama of today.

Imitation was always, so to speak, the indispensable substratum of drama; but it was everywhere overlaid in early years by what I have called passion, expressing itself in the rhythmic movement and lyric utterance. Slowly, very slowly, has imitation come into its own, and the stage learnt to hold a plain, unexaggerating, undistorting mirror up to nature . . . That something has been lost in the process nobody would deny. The impassioned tragedy and luxuriant comedy of the past gave infinite pleasure in their day and offered a field for the manifestation of superb genius. But the change is wrongly described and deplored as a process of degeneration. On the contrary, it may rather be called a process

304

of purification—the liberation of pure drama, of faithful and consistent imitation of life, from a number of conventional and heterogeneous adjuncts.*

These last words seem paltry characterization of such plays as *Peter Pan, The Sunken Bell, Peer Gynt,* to mention but modern instances; yet Mr. Archer damns them more roundly still with his word to the critics: "Here, then, we have, I think, some approach to a rational principle of appreciation: we can record as good, as in harmony with an inevitable tendency, any abandonment of exaggerative, in favor of soberly imitative, methods." †

Most critics, instead of dividing drama into sorts, and ranking these, have first sought some one underlying and essential characteristic of all drama. Brunetière, pointing out that most plays present a struggle between human wills, suggests the term *conflict* as emphialling the essence of all plays. The exception proves the rule (the word *prove,* be it recalled, meaning *test*) and Archer too brings forward stones to break Brunetière's bottle; he seeks to pour all drama into the term *crisis.* Clayton Hamilton admits the value of both suggestions, but, asking what conflict or crisis lurks in *The Pigeon, The Madras House, The Work-House Ward,* names, as his carry-all, *contrast.* Often in the drama and indeed in history, opposing forces have ranged beneath the standards of two great figures: Cæsar and Pompey, Pitt and Fox, Disraeli and Gladstone, Richard II and Bolingbroke; or, in a lighter vein, Valentine and Proteus, Hermia and Helena have been contrasted. As *contrast,* however, while it does cover some cases otherwise not included, seems too pallid to characterize the frequent fierce struggle of men and passions in plays; while words are being bandied about, let me adduce one equally inclusive yet more suggestive of *action,* and say, some *opposition* is the basis of all drama.

* From *Playmaking,* copyright, 1912, by Dodd, Mead and Company, Inc.
† See the opinion of Gilbert Murray, page 405.

For, whatever opposed natures or wills may be initially presented, it is through action that they are revealed or grow. Action, says Aristotle, is fundamental in a play; in this all else takes root and finds its sustenance.

Here again one treads fearing mines or serpents; for the great popularity of melodramas, filled apparently with nothing but action, on the one hand; and on the other, the frequency of two-legged ideas and the recent growth of essays-in-dialogue, discussion dramas, have been developments and have stirred distinctions not foreseen by Aristotle. The comedies and the tragedies of the Greeks made his remark seem natural: plot is emphasized because through it the characters live and the story progresses, moving inexorably through unwaiting, though unhurried, time.

Direct disagreement with Aristotle came, as naturally, from the English, who had before them Shakespeare's men and women. Dryden states definitely: "The story is the least part"; Vanbrugh: "I believe I could show that the chief entertainment as well as the moral lies more in the Character and the Diction than in the Business and the Event". Wordsworth, indeed, observed:

> Action is transitory—a step, a blow,
> The motion of a muscle—this way or that—
> 'Tis done, and in the after vacancy
> We wonder at ourselves like men betrayed:
> Suffering is permanent, obscure, and dark,
> And shares the nature of infinity.

Those who consider the authority of Aristotle still worth preserving take either of two lines of defense: they reinterpret the Greek to fit modern requirements; or they pack modern methods so as to fit them into the Greek box. Thus Gilbert Murray states that Aristotle's term *praxis* meant to the Greek action as determined by being, whereas character is being as revealed or as forged by action. The plays of

Shakespeare to him show the opposite of what they told the Augustans, for the subject of *Romeo and Juliet* is not a series of characters, but *The Tragic History of Romeo and Juliet;* and the tragedies display figures held in situations that—however melodramatic, artificially arranged—are the impelling force of the dramas. In all cases, Professor Murray concludes, the story is the essential thing, though it might "be about a human character, as it might be about a passion or a vendetta or the development of a railroad".

It is a fine distinction indeed that permits one to aver, in a story "about a human character", that the story is more fundamental, or more important, than the character. Less verbal juggling is required for the assertion that Aristotle really meant what Goethe calls the *motive,* what has been termed the *significant situation;* or to point out that with the progress of the drama from outer to inner conflict, action and passion, plot and character, grow more inseparable, more recognizable as really one.

With sound but subtle logic, Alain approaches the question quite differently. Characters in tragedy are, to him, models rather than copies; they take their reality from the flow of the action. The pressure of time (which, incidentally, especially in prose drama, is made manifest in the performance—another reason that plays cannot be felt satisfactorily in the mere reading) works upon these beings, forcing them to its course. It is Hamlet's failure to heed that pressure which brings his tragedy; when Macbeth dreams and hesitates, time casts the king into his closing hands. Everything moves, but moves to a destined end, an end determined by the beginning, by the passions involved in the opening situation. "It is good that the sword of Cassius point to the setting stars, on one of the most remarkable nights of history. And always the march of the hours must be felt, the external necessity that drives the passions on, and ripens them sooner than they would. That onward movement of time, which, without heeding our desires or our fears, attains their goals, is doubtless what gives a tragedy its sustaining force. But the dramatic poet should pass by those movements of a capricious spirit, which have, and expect, no consequences. What is of moment is that the passions link themselves along the chain of time. It may be said that passion is the substance, and time the form, of every tragedy." "Let me remind you", says A. N. Whitehead, "that the essence of dramatic tragedy is not unhappiness. It resides in the solemnity of the remorseless working of things". This conception is similar to that which Valéry and others entertain of poetry, and indicates that those who consider the work from the point of view of its creator are likely to emphasize, more than the subject chosen —which may indeed be common to genius and clod—the movement the artist infuses into the materials of his art.

THE GROWTH OF TRAGEDY

> "In *our* country", said Alice, still panting a little, "you'd generally get to somewhere else, if you ran very fast for a long time as we've been doing."
>
> "A slow sort of country!" said the Duchess. "Now *here*, you see, it takes all the running *you* can do, to keep in the same place."
>
> LEWIS CARROLL.

FROM many angles of vision, the picture of tragedy through the ages shows a shifting of emphasis. Its increasing realism has already been mentioned; this quality is manifest not only in theme, but in dialogue, in acting, in scenic presentation. With recurrent revolts toward suggestive simplicity or toward symbolism, from the Greeks to the Augustans in Rome, from Shakespeare to the English Augustans, from amphitheatre and platform to picture-stage, more and more the theatre has been presenting "a slice of life". The Pulitzer Prize for the American drama most representative of the best in American life was won in 1929 by a play that is entitled merely *Street Scene*.

But with this change have come many more. All literature, in a sense, parallels the movement of languages, from synthetical to analytical presentation—from *morituri* to *who are about to die;* from *potuero* to *I shall have been able*. Most philologists speak as though the second method has supplanted the first—probably because they do not stress the obvious fact that without synthesis there can be no communication. What has happened, in both language and that special use of it we call literature, is that a method of synthetical presentation has been developed that permits, within the whole, a greater conspicuity of the parts. It is perhaps as a result of such increased power of analysis that there has also been a gradual increase in the intellectual element in drama. The mysticism of Æschylus was succeeded by the ruthless logic of Euripides; the will of Corneille by the theories of Voltaire; the passion of Marlowe by the humours of Jonson; the fervor of Ford by the wit of Sheridan; the tension of Ibsen by the talk of Shaw, by the living based on philosophy of James Joyce, and by the intellectualized symbolic satire of e. e. cummings.

In longer progression, the tragic conflict has moved from external compulsions to the impelling of internal forces. (Grouping, for single characterization, in the phrase *Greek tragedy*, work as diverse as that of Æschylus and of Euripides, permits of course only the loosest of generalization. *The Devil's Dictionary* would probably define the generalization as a "convenient falsehood" that has led astray more persons than have been lost in the maze of its opposite, the concrete particular. The *Electra* of Sophocles, for example, moves to a final calm; Euripides' handling of the same theme stirs unanswerable questions, reaches toward the mood of the modern *Anathema* that beats upon the bolted doors of truth. The artificial calm with which Euripides, by fiat of the gods, brings some of his plays to their close, is an ironic employment of the conventions of the day, as far from Æschylus as is Maeterlinck from Shaw. Making this wide reservation, we may then say that) Greek tragedy, despite its messengers, depends largely on action; its development runs through the gradual revelation of a state that has resulted from earlier events—perhaps presented in other parts of the trilogy, but always known to the audience. We do not wait to see what, under such circumstances, this or that sort of person will do: under such circumstances one thing only is to be done. The sole distinguishing feature, so far as will is concerned, among the many defiant Greek figures, is the outward circumstance.

The morality play, by setting the action upon such figures as Everyman, Humanum Genus, and the vices and virtues, moves toward an inner conflict. In Shakespeare outer and inner tragedy stir side by side: the external tumult, of murder, torture, copious bloodshed, contrasted with the poignant stillness of the inner strain, as emotion battles with temperament or ethical code. Spanish tragedy rests almost wholly on the opposition of love and duty. From tragedy of blood and outer greatness, plays have progressed to tragedy of soul and inner nobility. The Greek gives the action, through which we see how strong humans behave; the Elizabethan of course action, but emotion (therefore character) as well; Ibsen probes beyond, as in *Hedda Gabler,* for motive; and Maeterlinck, whose *The Blind* shadows forth all humanity endlessly groping through darkness, seeks farther still, for universal spirit.

A distinction F. L. Lucas seeks to draw suggests another angle of approach. He names two types, the tragedy of circumstance:

> As Flies to wanton Boyes, are we to th' Gods
> They kill us for their sport

—and the tragedy of recoil:

> The Gods are just, and of our pleasant vices
> Make instruments to plague us

wherein, as Hegel puts it, "the character which is dramatic plucks for himself the fruit of his own deeds". In Greek tragedy we find a moral destiny greater than the gods, a *moira,* that has placed a sin upon an unwitting man, or of another's crime has set on him the vengeance—at its most powerful has laid a sin upon an unwitting man, noble though in some respect at fault: a sin so great its very revelation is the catastrophe. And always is this caught into physical final symbol: the chorus moans, Œdipus blinds himself. With

Shakespeare the disaster springs more definitely from the evil or the weakness of the protagonist, from his indecision, or his ill-decision. Conscience more definitely makes victims of them all. In Ibsen, again, the disaster springs from an outer doom, an impossibility of adjustment (at that early stage of the industrial era) between the well-meaning but ineffectual idealist and the pragmatic, practical, smug hypocrisy of the day. Again as in the Greeks but not in Shakespeare, there is the final symbolic gesture, a floating crutch, a slammed door, a maniac's cry. Shakespeare's tragedies, on the other hand, end with a promise of peace: the death of the lovers closes the Montague-Capulet feud; the killing of Hamlet, of Macbeth, means calm in the kingdom: whereas with blinded Œdipus and crazed Oswald, the tragedy has but begun. More than in Shakespeare, too, is the end bound inevitably with the beginning; the Greek plays move to a close determined by conditions in the characters' lives before their start; Oswald Alving's end is his father's framing—while Hamlet is to die, just how he comes to his death is matter of chance. With Clytemnestra, with Doctor Stockman, while the implacable hand of fate is visible to us, the victim moves unwitting on; the moment of tragic height is that in which the protagonist becomes conscious of the trap his deeds, or others' for which he must atone, have set for him. Œdipus and Gregers Werle are equally horror-stricken at their handiwork. In the Greeks, social laws drive through external coursings; the Elizabethans present more personal conflict, wrought internally as well; in Ibsen social laws again press upon the needs or the desires, though of weaker individuals.

But the moral emphasis has shifted, to make these weaker beings as strong protagonists as the undaunted heroes of Greek tragedy. Instead of finding the tragedy in the violation of the rules, we see it in their very existence. It is not the

individual, but society, the code, which is at question
Anathema, by Andreyev, for example, presents the tragedy
of a speculative society, of which social and industrial injus-
tice are ingrained assumptions, that seeks for the meaning
of existence. It is a self-questioning, self-torturing spirit,
wondering what value lies in life, behind the veils of religion,
the shams of philosophy, the lures of love and power. It is
the tragedy of the man that turns from the practical problems
beneath his eyes and hands—which are blinded and bound
by ignorance and fear—to beat his despair against the turrets
of the world. The tragedies of today, with these new implications, interweave the old oppositions, within and without, of
personal desires and social ends; with the aid of psychanalysis, O'Neill has given expression to the tragedy implicit
in starved lives, showing us the drama that would be, if such
persons had power to feel and to do. James Joyce has revived
a neglected note in tragedy. Mr. Lucas declares that "the
deepest tragedy is not when men are struck down by the blow
of chance or fate like Job, or Maurya in *Riders to the Sea;*
nor yet when they are destroyed by their enemies like
Polyxena or Henry VI; but when their destruction is the
work of those that wish them well or of their own unwitting
hands". But in *Exiles* the disaster springs neither from
ignorance nor from evil; it is foreseen by both spectators and
victim—foreseen and avoidable. Although the play is too
wholly intellectual in its appeal for wide popularity, its hero,
more than the demi-gods, like the martyrs, goes open-eyed
to his end for the sake of his ideals. Nor is his punishment
in one stroke final; it stretches from the drama's end through
lengthening years. So does the opposition of tragic forces
shift—with no chronological progression yet with increasing
emphasis—from clash of arms and bloody death to clash of
wills, to strain of irreconcilable motives in a single mind, and
long dwelling in the dungeon of the spirit.

THE POWER OF TRAGEDY

Kissing sometimes these purple ports of death.
WILLIAM DRUMMOND OF HAWTHORNDEN.

THE hold which tragedy takes upon the mind, which has made many declare it the greatest of the arts, and Aristotle to feel that in discussing it fully he is providing a key to the other literary forms, is open to no easy capture in words. All works of art release in one outpouring what their creator has accumulated with long, laborious care, as a medieval soldier toiled lengthily to fill and heat the pot of oil one touch whole-emptied on the besiegers' heads. The arts of the theatre, the personality of the players, the immediate acting out and bodying forth of the events, the insistent pressure of time, all add to the power of the playwright, in measure beyond the command of other writers increasing the forcefulness of his appeal. Yet, as with the other arts, aught more than ephemeral in that appeal will probably be due, not to any adventitious support the conventions and materials of the drama allow, nor merely to an exciting story or an unusual character, but to the feeling somehow conveyed that the play is more than a unique story about a particular set of persons, that it reaches out to include the audience, and all mankind, in its movement. Time and the unrolling of events carry us ever toward the end all tragedies foreshadow and attain; the appetites, the ambitions and ideals, the shortcomings, ob-stacles, and frustrations we ourselves have known, are what we wish to see working in the drama.

The two principle means of suggesting this universality need separate consideration; the most obvious manner of im-plying it is through the hero of the tragedy. When a man of

"high fame and flourishing prosperity" sinks to ruin, more
lives and fortunes than his own are like to fall. The fate of
the king not merely symbolizes, but frequently determines,
the fate of his people. The comparative failure of such plays
as *A Woman Killed With Kindness* and *Arden of Faversham*,
which deal with persons of low rank and common stature,
may be attributed to their finding no other way to achieve the
universal, especially before a public accustomed to watching
the downfall of princes . . . though indeed another reason for
presenting persons of "high estate" lies in the fact that
leisure, freedom from economic concerns, permits the development, and increases the importance, of the passions, with
which most stories deal.

With the rise of personality in the Renaissance, brave
hearts became, more than coronets, the standard of worth.
Man's struggle against the many forces in the world about
was then the means of suggesting some greater than individual import; power, wealth, and knowledge as their source,
seemed to all bold attainable yet to but few accorded; the
tragedy that comes from reaching too far, clutching more
than any man may hold, found instant echo in the universe.
And Marlowe makes the victims of overmuch desire, a
peasant risen to a king's estate, a Jewish money-lender too
enamoured of his jewels, and a German country doctor who
prized experience more than his soul.

In Shakespeare especially, though frequently in all drama,
a kinship between the elements and the events helps to extend the impulsions of the audience beyond the present story.
When nature meets the mood of the coming deeds—Lear wandering through the storm upon the heath; the ominous night
before the Ides of March—it seems clear no common, individual disaster is impending. Other forms of external symbolism are also frequent in tragedy and through the figure
point wider application of the tale. *The Wild Duck, The Sea*

Gull, The Sunken Bell, carry their symbol in their names; the mask in O'Neill's *All God's Chillun Got Wings,* the Priapus in Toller's *The German Hobbleman,* give extended import and increased power to the dramas.

Other devices have found repeated use. The subplot—not in ancient tragedy, but common since—by showing the main theme or a contrasted development on another plane manifests that here is no isolated instance. Before Shakespeare in the moralities, and again after him, the hero himself may be made a symbol, the embodiment of a faith or an ideal, the representative of a movement or a class. Several of the plays of Ibsen and of Galsworthy employ this device. The ancient sense of fate has already been referred to; this has its modern counterpart, in the forces of the environment, as in Kaiser's *From Morn to Midnight,* Sholom Asch's *The God of Vengeance,* Sophie Treadwell's *Machinal;* or in the power of heredity, which both Ibsen's *Ghosts* and Dreiser's *The Hand of the Potter* emphasize. Subtler elements of suggestion add to the implication of larger burdens, as when the hero embodies the power and dignity of his kind, making us murmur "What a piece of work is man!"; or when the vastness of the universe is borne upon us through the undercurrents of the drama, its lyric lifting, its poetic utterance, its onward surge of time.

THE SUPERNATURAL

Yet who of late, for cleanliness,
Finds sixpence in her shoe?
                                    BISHOP CORBET.
Pyrzqxgl.
                                    L. FRANK BAUM.

ONE of the most popular means, throughout all drama, of reaching to wider implications than the story shows, has been the introduction of some aspect of the supernatural. This has, over all other methods, the great advantage of suggesting a life beyond the human, beyond this world, where the hero may rise in greater glory to deserved heights. But always a sense of awe, of mysterious powers no man can match —can even dare to name, comes with the supernatural. The extent to which this other-worldly element has been introduced varies from vague atmospheric suggestion, as of some of Maeterlinck's dramas, to the bringing of the gods upon the·stage. The manifestations may be grouped in three main divisions.

The first approach of the supernatural is when other-worldly beings come upon earth to mingle with mortals. The Greeks gave their gods access to the stage, so extensively that the practice grew as artificial, with the "god from the machine", as W. S. Gilbert's effecting the surrender of the victorious pirates to "Queen Victoria's name". The medieval drama, in passion plays still performed, and in moralities (Hugo von Hofmannsthal's version of *Everyman* is a recent revival), presented the person of Christ the son, and at least the audible voice of the omnipotent Father. Other supernatural beings, demi-gods and heroes, witches and especially ghosts, have in all ages haunted the theatre; the hope that "the ghost walks" has become universal. The apparitions in Shakespeare are usually prepared for by prior discussion; and Hamlet's father will speak only to the Prince, as Banquo's spirit appears but to Macbeth. In the blood and thunder plays, however, they rush on in battalions; again, Gilbert makes burlesque use of the custom, when the ancestors step down in *Ruddigore*.

More recent plays have not foregone the advantages of the supernatural come to earth. Grillparzer's *The Ancestress*, Strindberg's *Spook Sonata*, Ansky's *The Dybbuk* (in one recent season successful in three languages, in New York), not to mention the host of melodramas, such as Bram Stoker's vampire-play *Dracula*, all bring embodied spirits into the action. Other dramas—Belasco's *The Return of Peter Grimm*, Charles Rann Kennedy's *The Servant in the House* —leave a loophole for those who insist on explanation, and make their supernatural mood rest—rather lightly—on realistic ground.

Those playwrights are bolder who carry their mortal beings into the supernatural world. Here they are much freer, as none living can correct them; yet here, too, they have but triple choice. The dramatist may present the next world that he expects to find. So Dunsany, opening the glittering gate, sees only "the great big bloomin' stars". And Shaw, in *Man and Superman,* pictures hell as the place where everyone gets what he desires—the one thing barred, intensity. The dramatist may show the next world the audience expects, as when Sutton Vane, in *Outward Bound* carrying several characters across a river they discover is the Styx, leads them to the heaven and hell of rewards and punishments. In *The Green Pastures* God turns out to be "just like the Reverend Mr. Dubois". When his concern is with a single figure, however, the playwright may portray the afterworld the character expects, as when Molnar sets Liliom before a

police magistrate god. A variation of this occurs in Elmer
Rice's *The Adding Machine:* working in the office is "hell on
earth" to Mr. Zero; picking flowers in the woods with the
fair maid beside him would be "just heaven"; in the great
hereafter he is accorded these experiences, magnified. The
possibilities of this journey to the next world, not neglected
by Homer and Dante (both surer of their find) are but recently, like the Egyptian tombs, being again explored.

The playwright may, finally, employ the forces of the
unknown by setting his play within a dream. Not even the
recent study of dreams prevents the employment of this
device as a gloss over shoddy: *The Wonderful Visit,* a combined effort of St. John Ervine and H. G. Wells, tells us in
its last minute that the angel's coming is all no more than
a dream; by that time we have either forgotten the supernatural condition, or dismissed it in a general rejection of
the play. But the dream, or the delirium of illness, may be
validly employed—more frequently in comedy—to carry the
effect. A sound serious instance is in Pierre Loving's *The
Stick-Up,* where a dream—that they are "holding up" a
comet—occurs to three train robbers; waking to discover the
comet is the rising sun, the leader cries to his comforted men:
"What's your religion, Kid! What's your wild hunger to
touch things, Pete, alongside the dream I dreamed!" Effective
but lighter suggestion is aided by the dream device in *The
Beggar on Horseback,* where it permits the wild extravagance
of the body of the play, with its mock-tragic culmination, and
the happy ending when they wake; and through delirious
fancy in Barrie's *A Kiss for Cinderella,* Eleanor Gates' *The
Poor Little Rich Girl*—which titles tell their tales, and Ossip
Dymov's *The Bronx Express,* in which the creatures of the
subway advertisements come to life.

The derivation of *drama* from *dream,* in truth, marks an
appropriate viewpoint. In America, audiences most fre-

quently desire to have the illusion of life, the sense of reality, sweep over them; on the Continent, the more usual attitude of the playgoer is one of conscious makebelieve. "In short", says Joubert, "for a performance to be beautiful, one must believe one is imagining what one sees and hears; all must appear as a beautiful dream."

In speaking of the supernatural, one seems within reach of the long arm of coincidence, and the finger of fate. Not merely in melodrama does the birthmark identify the rightful heir; it is chance, or that pressing finger, which drops the handkerchief Iago's way, which brings Duncan opportunely to the castle of Macbeth, which holds Friar John from reaching Romeo. Prophecy, also, is a potent means of inspiring awe and sense of mightier powers; though the most dramatic form of foretelling is rare. It is easy to make a statement of future fact, knowing beforehand that on the Ides of March Cæsar will fall, that the man "not born of woman" will come with Birnam Wood to Dunsinane. It is more difficult to announce a fact already accomplished, the gradual revelation of which, as to Œdipus, shall be the drama's movement. But the rare prophecy that makes itself come true—as when Macbeth is hailed as Scotland's king—that, once spoken, so works upon the natures of those that hear as to make its fulfilment inevitable, most deeply impresses us with the mystery of life, and shows us in another's story how dark the swirling forces round ourselves.

DRAMATIC IRONY

The wound of peace is surety,
Surety secure.

WILLIAM SHAKESPEARE.

SUSPENSE is often considered the firmest anchor by which
the receptor's interest is held to the progress of a story: and
it is true that, by making them share in the character's expectancy, anxiety even, the playwright takes strong hold
upon his audience. This absorption in the event, however,
may be so personal to the beholder or, in his mind, to the
person in the play, as to fall short of—even to destroy—extended implications, wider significancies; its power is therefore likely to lessen with renewed contact, and a test of art
is that it repeat its thrill.

The still more ephemeral element of surprise has had its
advocates, and its examples, in drama. Lope de Vega, most
prolific of playwrights, advised: "Keep your secret to the
end. The audiences will turn their faces to the door and their
backs to the stage when there is no more to learn." Manifestly, surprise lasts no longer than the first performance,
despite the desires of melodramatists: the author of *Cheating
Cheaters* protested that it was unfair of the newspaper reviewers to betray his plot; and occasionally, in program note,
audiences have been requested not to tell their friends the
play's ending. Shakespeare once makes effective use of surprise in tragedy, when Othello takes the "turban'd Turke"
by the throat; but in general it is not so pleasantly moving to
be fooled as to watch others being fooled. As Trollope remarks: "The author and the reader should move along in
full confidence with each other. Let the personages of the

drama undergo for us a complete Comedy of Errors among themselves, but let the spectator never mistake the Syracusan for the Ephesian." Lessing elaborates the point:

For one instance where it is useful to conceal from the spectators an important event until it has taken place, there are ten and more where interest demands the very contrary. By means of secrecy a poet effects a short surprise, but in what enduring disquietude could he have maintained us if he had made no secret about it! Whoever is struck down in a moment, I can pity only for a moment. But how if I expect the blow, how if I see the storm brewing and threatening for some time about my head and his? For my part none of the personages needs know the other if only the spectator knows them all. Nay, I would even maintain that the subject which requires such secrecy is a thankless subject, that the plot in which we have to make recourse to it is not so good as that in which we could have done without it. It will never give occasion for anything great. We shall be obliged to occupy ourselves with preparations that are either too dark or too clear, the whole piece becomes a collection of little artificial tricks by means of which we effect nothing more than a short surprise. If on the other hand everything that concerns the personages is known, I see in this knowledge the source of the most violent emotions. Because they acquaint me with the secret intentions of the speaker, and this confidence fills me at once with hope and fear. If the condition of the personages is unknown, the spectator cannot interest himself in the action more vividly than do the personages themselves. But the interest would be doubled for the spectator if light is thrown on the matter, and he feels that action and speech would be quite otherwise if the characters understood one another. . . . Only then shall I scarcely be able to await what is to become of them, when I am able to compare what they really are with what they do or wish to do.

Upon such an understanding (though Lessing's words are description rather than analysis) may be based a more effective surprise and suspense, which hold the character in their grip, yet leave the informed spectator free to watch the power of these impulses. The beholder thus, in a sense, shares in and moves with—instead of merely being moved by—the

greater forces that direct the world, and has gained the sense
of universality through becoming part of the superhuman.
He watches the persons of the play carried on ways unknown
to them he has foreseen; he may sympathize with, enter into,
their emotions; but he himself, forewarned, is free. Thus,
if a sleeper be awakened by someone stumbling in the next
room, he is surprised. When he grasps the revolver from beneath his pillow, and awaits a second footfall, he is in
suspense. If the audience has no more knowledge than the
householder, it may share his feelings. If it has had fore-
knowledge of the marauder's approach, it can without being
startled follow the feeling of the awakened man. But if the
audience knows that this intruder, who in a moment will face
that revolver in the hand of a frightened man, is that man's
own son, unwittingly stolen into the home from which he
had once been driven, expectancy is keyed to a higher pitch,
and all are most fully drawn in the current of the drama.
When Lady Windermere threatens, before the curtain falls,
that if the questionable woman her husband has invited comes
to their ball, she will strike the guest across the face with her
fan—Brander Matthews declared "You couldn't have pried
me out of my seat with a crowbar"; but Brander Matthews,
and those equally tense around him, knew that the woman
threatened with Lady Windermere's blow was Lady Windermere's mother. This is dramatic irony.

In almost any play, or any story,—save those written
deliberately to mystify—the mood set in the opening tells
what the end will be. Even in the mystery story, it is not
what will happen—how often has Sherlock Holmes failed?—
but by what particular events that end will be attained, that,
until the first full beholding, we may not know. Making this
discovery along with the person of the play puts us on his
plane, brings us to his level, to the individual concern; how
slight that interest beside the Olympian power of knowing

what is to come, of foreseeing the events themselves, and watching the struggle of the victim as he becomes aware! — the courage of his stand, in that dark hour when the light strikes him blind, affirming our brave humanity.

Four types of dramatic irony are distinguished by F. L. Lucas: of word, and of deed; within each, that in which the speaker or doer is unconscious, and that in which he is aware, of an import of which the victim always is unwitting. But there seems a less mechanical grouping. There are some situations in which the irony rises from the fact that the person prepares his own doom. Often in fairy tales the villain is asked to devise a punishment, only to discover it is for himself; King David once was told: "Thou art the man!"; the curse laid by Œdipus falls heavy on his head. So Nora's action, trying to save her husband, is what ultimately tumbles her "doll's house" about her ears, and wakes her to maturity. Or the person talking may be another than the victim, and speak in terms that fall innocently upon the doomed man's mind, until he is blasted by the reality. So do the fears of Mrs. Alving leave Oswald undisturbed, until the light once breaks upon his brain—and leaves him crying forever for the sun. Finally, the oncoming events may be known to no one of the persons involved in the action, as the audience alone know who lie hidden behind the screen—the literal screen of *The School For Scandal* and Labiche's *The Italian-Straw Hat* (Gilbert's *The Wedding March*), or the soon-to-be-folded screen of time: as Othello comes radiant from Desdemona to hear Iago's tale, as the triumphal homecoming of Agamemnon is to an unseen tomb. The Greeks, indeed, always foreknew their drama's endings; in tragic irony they contemplated the characters' fixed doom, and felt how all men move—and let them meet it bravely!—to an end whose time is dark yet certain as the night. In truth, so risen is man at the fatal moment, so erect in the drama against the final blow, that for the victim after he is aware, as for the audience, it may be said the tragedy lies not in the catastrophe, but in the waiting. It is the flow of time that it is hard to bear; the end brings peace, and sometimes hope of resurrection.

THE EFFECT OF TRAGEDY

My pen's the spout
Where the rain-water of mine eyes runs out
In pity of that name, whose fate we see
Thus copied out in grief's hydrography.
                              JOHN CLEVELAND.

THE final phrase of Aristotle's definition of tragedy has led to more roundabout than sound consideration of the effect of serious drama. It has seemed necessary to critics to reconcile Aristotle and the truth—with the result that one or the other has invariably had to yield. Aristotle says clearly that tragedy effects, *through pity and terror, the purgation of these passions.* Yet some critics alter the *these* to *such;* and others, unable else to fit it to what they deem the facts, generalize to *the* passions. This appeasement is pictured at the end of *Samson Agonistes:* "Calm of mind, all passion spent"; but it seems hardly fitting to characterize the effect of tragedy as a state of mind more easily produced by an evening next door the theatre (as Dekker would say) at the brothel.

Some have suggested that Aristotle means the ridding of the soul of emotions harmful in life, yet universal; here at the play one exhausts these baser feelings, and goes forth cleansed. Yet is pity an emotion to be purged? And if so to the sterner Greek, does the nature of tragedy change with our softening ethical code? It has been otherwise claimed that tragedy rids us of self-pity—for we put ourselves in the protagonist's place—and of terror for our own being, in that the story, on the level of an exterior object, leaves us with an easy sense of safety. Drawing this thought to its logical conclusion, some have said that the pleasure of tragedy is derived (a refinement on the crowds at the hangings in old England or the lynchings and murder-trials of young America) from the spectacle of others' enduring pain from which we are exempt—and in the drama we need not feel sorry for them, as we might for our neighbor.

Certainly Prometheus would resent our pity, as he defied the gods' more potent wrath. And what converse would Othello have, majestic in his death, or firm Cordelia, with the spirit that sheds tears over little Eva on her way to heaven? Shakespeare seems sometimes to lean to pity (as at other times to comedy) for relief: after the wild awfulness of Lear upon the heath, Cordelia bends over her father; after Hamlet's philosophical contemplation of life, mad Ophelia sings. Edith Hamilton, indeed, quoting Professor Dixon's apothegm: "The spirit of inquiry meets the spirit of poetry and tragedy is born", declares that Ibsen's plays are not tragedies because they rouse only pathos; they lack the pain "charged with exaltation"; they but simmer with small souls. But she herself soon shifts the emphasis from the size of the victim's soul to the amount of poetry in the author's; the tragedy may reside in our sense that life must make souls small. But grandeur there will be; and most frequently in the hero. Pity wells in us for "a woman of no importance", perhaps, for the lesser figures of the "problem plays" on the level of life; the statues of tragedy, in their nobility triumphing over death—man ever climbing the tree of the knowledge of good and evil, to beat upon the doors of heaven and wrest more knowledge, more power, from the omniscient, omnipotent gods—fill us rather with a sense of heroic grandeur, with the knowledge that, despite the inevitable hour of death, life so lived is warrant for man's being. Beyond the quickening of all his powers that is the gift of every art, tragedy gives man a pride and an assurance, a song to sing against despair.

THE TRAGIC HERO

So lykewys the fall of a heigh and lofty Tree maketh
greater noyse than that which is low and little.

WILLIAM PAINTER.

WHAT manner of man is this, whose fate and inner spirit
example us for our travail?

He is like to be what is called a manly man, stern, unflinching; the few women who are chief figures in tragedy—
Electra, Medea, Lady Macbeth—drive from them the softer,
feminine emotions. He is, however, deeply influenced, for
good or ill, by a woman, as Portia inspirits Brutus, as the
failure of Ophelia contributes to Hamlet's ruin—other examples are more obvious; otherwise he stands alone. Comedy
crowds the stage: Rosalind, Celia, Orlando, Jacques, Touchstone; in tragedy one or two figures loom beyond the rest.
Mr. Lucas declares that throughout tragedy (as Shaw says
throughout Shakespeare) women have taken the initiative.
Certainly their portraits, from Clytemnestra through Lady
Macbeth to Hedda Gabler and Nina Leeds, have been more
fully and more subtly drawn; yet (at least until the feminist
movement of recent years) these women have most frequently been companions to the towering men, through
whom, perhaps, they worked, but in whom the tragic power
centered, and lurked the tragic flaw.

When Orestes, when Brutus, when Hamlet kills, we feel
that the death is deserved, yet the slaying is a sin. The tragic
hero, says Aristotle, is "a person neither eminently virtuous
and just, nor yet involved in crime through deliberate vice and
villainy, but because mankind is frail". The development of
the drama necessitates wide extension of this remark. Hebbel

declares that the tragic hero is the last defender of an old order, or the first proponent of a new: the doom, inherent in the lack of harmony between the man and his time. This sufficiently describes Galsworthy's *Old English* on the one hand, and Joyce's *Exiles* on the other; but it is far from all-inclusive. Probably no single characterization can enclose all types of tragic hero.

In many, if not most, tragedies, the opposition is within the hero himself, (possibly out of the old magic duality in which the protagonist was at once the enemy who must die and the god who was to save—a cause of the confusion that has made Judas, ordained to his rôle for the redemption of man, the object of the centuries' hatred). The "error" of the hero may be unconscious, as in *Œdipus Rex,* in Otway's *The Orphan,* in the many incestuous marriages that marked the Restoration drama. It may be conscious; the result of deliberate action, as with Medea and Macbeth; the outcome of thoughtless folly, as in Antony and Lear. The disaster may spring from the vastness of the forces opposed to the hero's desire—be he strong as the leaders in Marlowe, or weak as Galsworthy's Pigeon, as Sam Pickens in Michael Gold's *Hoboken Blues.* The hero may be torn between two opposed ideals, as in the conflict of love and duty that makes the Spanish drama, as in Dryden's *All For Love;* or he may be drawn by circumstances into evil ways, as in Schiller's *The Robbers,* as the good-bad man of the eighteenth century, further sentimentalized in pictures of Jimmie Valentine and Robin Hood. Finally, though not in Shakespeare or the Greeks, there may be tragedies without embodiment in a hero; it is *justice* that is slain in Galsworthy's play; Hauptmann, Toller, Lawson, have written dramas in which society, or masses of men, must bear the brunt of the tragic action.

THE GROWTH OF A PLAY

That one action worked through in one place and one day
Hold the theatre filled till the end of the play.

NICOLAS B. D. BOILEAU.

THE lyrical element of Greek drama, drawn from religion and dance, while it still occasionally sweeps through a play like *Riders to the Sea,* has grown less prominent through the years. Blank verse, "the language of ordinary life rarefied and exalted", has largely given way to prose; though in comedy the moods of Aristophanes, Shakespeare, and Moliere remain in the verse of Gilbert and of Rostand, as well as occasionally gleaming in the stanzas of musical comedy. Mr. Lucas has conducted a lengthy analysis to show that, in various ways, "modern tragic dramatists have succeeded in keeping a poetry of phrase and rhythm without lapsing into the unreality of verse". The Greek chorus cavorts in musical comedy and struts in grand opera; and its functions—supplying the lyric intervals, acting as a bridge from play to audience—are, in some degree, carried on by the lyrical episodes and songs of the Elizabethans, by the recurrent confidant, and by the crowds of such plays as Toller's *"Mass-Man"* and Buechner's *Danton's Death.* The episodes of the Greek drama, which had become fixed at five, determined the number of acts for the obedient ages; Ibsen cut the number to four; current favor has settled upon three, though of recent plays some have been much longer, and others have built through episodes again, instead of acts.

A play, says Aristotle, must have a beginning. For the Greeks this usually was a point in the story which today would open the last act. Nor did the problems of exposition

330

concern them, for the entire story was known to the
audience in advance, and repeated in prologue lest some
detail have been forgotten. The exposition in Shakespeare is
often crude; characters are given information they already
possess, for the sake of the less fortunate audience: "What's
the new news at the new court?"; or as in the catechistic questioning of Ariel by Prospero. This practice, degenerating into
the opening conversation of butler and maid, is satirized in
Sheridan's *The Critic;* and methods of conveying information
improved until in Ibsen the necessary knowledge of prior
fact is pressed item by item through the play, involved in the
tense action. Contemporary plays, however, show a tendency
to return to the direct method of clearing such matters out
of the way at once: in *Strange Interlude,* for example, the
characters muse aloud at the start, remembering things
gone by.

Through its "middle", a play must, say the ages that
revered Aristotle, observe the unities of time, place, and
action. There is no doubt that a rapid flow of time swells the
tragic surge; and in Shakespeare the passing of time is frequently pointed, though the passage of actual days and years
is usually ignored. Yet the drama has, on occasion, employed
the "epic unity" of a lifetime for its scope. Some, indeed,
have so little regarded the movement of time as to outvie
Joshua and build their play backward, as Clayton Hamilton
once suggested, as was approved in Elmer Rice' *On Trial.*
Actually, such plays merely take a backward leap, to
approach the climax, through the forward movement of time,
with redoubled power. The unity of place, wholly disregarded,
(save for Jonson and an occasional chorus-word) on the comparatively bare Elizabethan stage, has—for reasons, one
imagines, bound as closely to the box-office as to the dramatic art—to a large extent returned; though the closing-in
of the end upon the beginning makes a single scene natural.

The more frequent use of a revolving stage, on the other hand, promotes swifter transport. Unity of action—"a thing whose presence or absence makes no difference to a whole is not part of that whole"—exists in every work of art; Falstaff plays no rôle in the history of Henry IV, but in the play *Henry IV* is as essential as the enthronèd king. All the episodes of a good drama, however irrelevant first glance may show them, move in the single current of its art.

A play, too, must be "of a certain magnitude": large enough to permit the details to stand out, yet of such compass that the receptor may view the whole. "One must take space to spread one's wings. If incoherence is monstrous, too close a cohesion destroys all majesty. The thoughts in a book should follow one another, like the stars in the sky, orderly, harmonious, but at ease, and apart, not touching, not intermixing, yet not without sequence, accordant though distinct. They should revolve without tight bondage, so that they can subsist independently, like unstrung pearls." We may appreciate, severally, the Prince Hamlet, his speeches, his fellows, and the play that bears his name.

Principally, a play must have an end. Freytag, thinking of the five-act play, divides its form into exposition, rising action, climax, falling action, and denouement. The climax was then defined as "the turning point", the "point of highest interest", or in other figurative fashion. This habit of thought has betrayed many a present-day writer on the drama; thus Professor Baker, whose workshops at Harvard and at Yale University have sent forth many successful playwrights, says: "Climax is whatever in action, speech, pantomime, or thought (whether conveyed or suggested) will produce in the audience the strongest emotion of the scene, act, or play." Such a definition ignores the many plays at which spectators grow increasingly bored, so that the strongest emotion felt toward the play rose at the beginning—save for the still stronger feeling that bids one reach for one's hat and leave the playhouse. To be properly inclusive, a definition in such terms must state that "climax is whatever . . . ought to produce" or "is intended to produce, the strongest emotion". At once the absurdity of such "defining" is apparent. The drama today, in three-act form, has simply lopped off the last two elements of Freytag's five-act division, setting the climax (which the Greeks called catastrophe) in its proper place at the close. For the climax is the decisive moment of the dramatic conflict, the point at which the opposition is effaced; after which (as Odysseus knew) nothing is left but to clear the bloodstained floor. The Greeks needed time for the slow departure of the chorus; today a more rapid departure of the audience makes clear its attitude toward any "falling action" after the climax. *The Madras House* ends mid-sentence, with the printed note: "She doesn't finish, for really there is no end to the subject"; but most dramas today run through an action that moves to a climactic close, and when they reach it bring the curtain down.

As the play grows, it bears with it the persons whose characters are revealed, or determined, by its sweep, who are given life by its movement and their action. These persons, however, may be made manifest from several viewpoints. They are, in many plays, mere creations of the author, each embodying that aspect of life, that phase of the drama's intent, which the playwright assigns them. More often, in good drama, each person comes to life in his own right, bodied forth as an individual, rounded and ripening, judging and feeling and acting as such a character must or might. In some tragedies (as in Shakespeare's), the individuals may be pointed, as it were, instead of rounded: not seen fully as complete individuals, but achieving life and even gigantic stature through the sweep of the situation and the passions— tremendous in power though limited in range—that are in them roused. In still another mode, called monodrama, each person is viewed through the eyes, not of the author, but of a character within the play, whose personality and point of view—and fortune—selects the incidents and the other characters and colors them. A program note to Arthur Richman's *Ambush* states that the play grows through the eyes of the rather ineffectual clerk who is its leading figure; more eccentric development of the form, in expressionistic style, occurs in Meinhard and Bernauer's *Johannes Kreisler* and in Kaiser's *From Morn to Midnight*. In any of these ways, characters may be projected that satisfy the needs of the action, that we accept as living when they stir with their passions, and out of their travail speak.

The dialogue of drama, the form in which the characters speak, is now almost universally prose, though some critics find "poetry" in the diction still, and others prophesy the evolution of new verse forms. The greater flexibility of prose, the already fixed associations of blank verse, and the present decline of free verse, in which some dramatic efforts have been made, make it seem likely that, for some time at least, prose will continue to dominate in drama. The danger of prophecy, however, is shown in the recent return, and even expansion, of that frequent interruption of dialogue, the soliloquy.

For the most part, with the coming of the "well-made" play, the actors have been expected (and told by printed stage-direction) to indicate by act and attitude what the soliloquy once conveyed; of late, along with other direct methods—such as the bare exposition at the start—there has been new use of the convention of the soliloquy. There are perhaps (again that number first confronts us) three ways in which the soliloquy has been utilized. The first—to dismiss an apparently dead form—is the old aside, wherein the as yet unacknowledged villain (be he Orlando's Oliver or

Miss Ivory's Mr. Inkwell) leers his identity to the audience. Almost equally abandoned is the soliloquy that has for its purpose the conveying of essential information; though *Strange Interlude* and Zoe Akin's *The Furies* both open with this device. What seems a more valid use of the soliloquy, alike in *Hamlet* and in *The Hairy Ape,* is that in which the character muses aloud, reflecting on the events pressing upon him, and the decisions he must face. This hearing of thought has been attempted in various other ways: first in the drama, perhaps, by the dim companions of Alice Gerstenberg's one-act play, *Overtones,* who speak, after every utterance of the persons, the feeling their words disguise; it has been further developed by mask put on and off, for dissembling and frank words, in O'Neill's *The Great God Brown;* by setting the action within the brain, as in the present writer's brief *Echo* (which, incidentally, shows the critical spirit at work during the creative process). In O'Neill's *Dynamo* the soliloquy rises to a fuller growth, virtually replacing ordinary dialogue. For, as most of O'Neill's plays give inarticulate and clodden beings the power to feel, to think, to speak and act: Here is what would happen if they were sensitive enough to respond, to rebel, in this situation—so in *Dynamo* does he carry his characters' speculations and feelings through audible thought, with scarcely more than their decisions breaking into communication, into dialogue. In this device, which seems at first most artificial, there is an approach (to the mode of the novel, but also) to life, and in one more way drama comes closer to realistic portrayal, to "imitation" of the deeds of man.

* * * * * * * *

The critic Sarcey, we are told, used to visit the theatre when a new play was produced, stay for one act, go home and construct the remainder of the play, and return to watch the next performance and check the playwright's development by his own. Something of this construction the critic of today can frame, in the ten minute entr'acte—if social preoccupations do not preclude such entertainment. As a test for serious drama, Archer proposes three questions:

Does it present a reasonably faithful imitation of what may be called the visible and audible surfaces of life, without intrusions or gross caricature, or shiftings from one plane of convention to another?

Is the story developed, and are the characters presented, in such a way as to make the best use of the mechanism of the theatre, and to beget in the audience, in high intensity, those emotions of growing interest, suspense, anticipation, sudden and vivid realization, which it is the peculiar privilege of drama to produce?

Does the play say something and mean something? Has it a practical bearing either upon thought or conduct? In seeing or reading it, have we not merely enjoyed a pastime, but undergone an experience? Are we, in a word, intellectually the richer or morally the better for it? I think that Aristotle, in saying that tragedy ought to purge our emotions, was formulating something very like this last demand.*

And here, by way of another wrung interpretation, we have come back to the man who first gave considerate attention to tragedy, the art form that most widely and most deeply has held mankind in its spell, as through the ages it has shown time sweeping to their doomed end the passions of man.

* From *Playmaking*, copyright, 1912, by Dodd, Mead and Company, Inc.

COMEDY

> Every one is as God made him, and oftentimes a great deal worse.
>
> MIGUEL DE CERVANTES.

IN *The Merry Wives of Windsor*, Falstaff is the butt of many pranks, and we watch amused; in *Henry IV*, he is cast off by Prince Hal become king, and we pity him. This difference in our attitude springs not merely from a sense that in the one play the fat knight is a manikin, and in the other, a man. A deeper cause contributes: in watching comedy we grant not so much a willing suspension of disbelief as a suspension of sympathy. Most comic situations, manifestly in Restoration drama, but equally in other times, would cease to be comic if thought of as real: it is not necessary to count the ineptitudes, the deceptions, the adulteries, at which we laugh: consider only the conventional happy ending: does not comedy end with the marriage "because that's where the tragedy begins"? What deeply stirs us in *Othello* amuses in *The Way of the World*. As a result of the loosening of the cords of sympathy, there is, despite the pious defenders of the stage, no moral uplift, no purging of folly and vice, likely to come from comedy. We change what wrings us to wrath or tears; *Oliver Twist* and *Uncle Tom's Cabin* effect reforms, not *Tristram Shandy, Gargantua, Huckleberry Finn*. If *Don Quixote* laughed Spain's chivalry away, it was because only the shriveled leaves were left to be blown in the gusts of laughter. If, as one may think, poetry presents the triumph of faith, tragedy shows its failure, comedy, its folly.

Yet there is hope while there is comedy, for it is at ourselves we really laugh. "It's been said that misers don't go to the theatre; but, then, there are no misers as comedy shows

what of the effect of satire?

337

them, rather movements, impulses, flashes of avarice in us all. Likewise the amorous folly, that wants its love with precautions and constraint, is in us all and develops as much as we yield to it, especially as we seek to cover it with cloak of reason. *L'Ecole des Femmes* is not to teach an Arnolphe; a fool of that sort is no more likely than all those valets forever atiptoe behind the door . . . Comedy cures us better, without sense of shame; for the force of the spectacle keeps us from thoughts of our neighbor. So the laughter's not spoiled by our thinking that we are laughing at others, or that they are laughing at us". Some disagree with these last words of Alain, and think man more gleefully beholds comedy through feeling himself free while recognizing his neighbor in the butt.

In either event, one laughs with the herd. Comedy is almost always conservative; men may think alone, they laugh in unison. On the other hand, the wit smiles with those who are smiling; the comedian, in the midst of the laughter he has roused, stays solemn alone. The height of importance, without any importance, is the basis of the ridiculous, we are told; but the easily overcome appearance, in the comic, refuses to yield, and the more its empty shell is recognized, the more deliberately and seriously it is polished and adorned. The comic calls for gravity, as the pathetic for moderation. Who would make others weep must not yield to lamentation; who would win laughter must not recognize its cause. The spectators, however, laugh as one, at what seems laughable to all: comedy presents the one as the butt of the many. It may be objected that satire is often radical; surely Shaw is not yet accepted by the majority. The obvious response to this is that Shaw *is* accepted by the majority—of his readers; the audience at *The New Playwrights' Theatre* was radical before the play. Satire does not convince; it merely flays, or (which is more ominous, for the attacked escape by absence), it flatters. Yet if those at whom the shafts of comedy are leveled be the majority in life, it is superficial to declare that they are but a small percentage of the spectators. What is less immediately apparent is that the original objection is also superficial. A successful drama wraps its audience in its intrinsic mood. And comedy and tragedy are alike in that, *within the play,* because of the ethos of the people involved, the majority is a mass force against the victim. The tragic hero has violated a fundamental law; the comic butt has set at naught a conventional code. Each must feel the chastening power of society, the call to conformation.

The sympathy that is withdrawn when we watch a comedy remains, however, in tragic mood, to turn us against the mob. The opposition in comic drama is usually external, an un-divided one against the many; in tragedy, an inner opposition centers our sympathy upon the hero. Thus, even in the tragedy of the Greeks and of Shakespeare, there is an implicit ques-tioning of the moral codes of the day; in Ibsen and his suc-cessors it flames forth; until the tragedy lies, as we have said, not in the violation of the rules, but in their existence. Andreyev's *Anathema* identifies Prometheus—Lucifer, the lightbearer—with man, eternally vainly daring to seek the forbidden knowledge that shall make him master of the secrets of earth, following the road of the star-hitched farmer, the star-finding poet, and the star-probing scientist, to the star-strewn portals of God.

[margin note: only in Euripedes. Certainly not in Aes. & Sophocles]

Comedy stands on earth, in the herd-ways, laughing. In the exuberance of Aristophanes and of Shakespeare, as in *Pantagruel* and *Tristram Shandy,* it laughs with the bubbling spontaneity of childhood, fresh and innocent, whatever its theme. In the controlled expression of Moliere ("common sense incarnate", he has been called), and in most comedy since [31], the laughter springs from the (fear or the) derision of manhood, sophisticate and "superior", whatever its theme.

Beyond its measure of appreciation of dexterity, the pleasure experienced from comedy lies in the sense of well-being, or of being thought well, of running with the herd, the majority, the successful—who, as democracy (itself, some say, no paltry comedy) assures us, must be right. Tragedy affirms: this is what happens to man; comedy suggests: this is what man is like, or would like to be. Tragedy sees life as eternal questing; comedy assumes that its problem has been (or never will be) solved. Comedy succeeds because we are all "the man who knew Coolidge"; tragedy, because we are all the man who stood alone against a hill.

* * * * * * *

The opposition in comedy, for the reasons presented, is usually of one, or of a pair, of eccentrics, and a world of supposedly normal folk. The old father recurring in Terence, and since; the hypocrite; the fop; the beau; long-winded Polonius; wrong-worded Mrs. Malaprop; Beatrice and Benedick; Kate the Shrew and the shrew-tamer; the many warriors in the eternal strife of love (that has led Meredith to say tragedy is masculine; comedy, bi-sexual); all develop in character the incongruities also evident in the action. It is this suggestion of balanced forces beyond the individual, and the enlisting of the spectator on the "superior" side— making him one with an idea or an ideal—that give "high" comedy its universality. It is usually too cynical, at least too unemotional, for the employment of the supernatural, save as destiny pulls the strings to which the figures dance. Confusions, the result of chance, such as in long separations of twins, further suggest the dependence of life on what no man may know. The follies and foibles of comedy, also, centered though they may be in types of a period, are such as characterize human nature in every age. Even the most eccentric figures, whose very names—Snout, Bottom, Dogberry, Toby Belch, Sir Andrew Aguecheek—mark them out, represent a quality universal. The subplot, repeating the main motif, is much more common in comedy than in tragedy; a Restoration version of *The Tempest* provides Miranda, who had never seen a young man, with a sister beloved of a youth who had never before seen a maid. Symbolism, in comedy, is likely to be verbal or wrought through scenic or acting devices; it appeals as often to the eye as to the ear: Bottom become the ass; Jourdain putting on his nightcap to dance the minuet—for comedy, if it goes behind the manners and the deeds, seeks less the specific weakness than the general folly of which it is a kind. The nature of the chosen weaknesses depends, in some measure, upon the sensibility of the age: Shylock, with his long knife whetting for the pound of flesh, was played as a buffoon until Pope's day. A current French version, (Gemier's) of *The Merchant of Venice* changes Tubal's alternate play upon Shylock's love of money and his lust for revenge, to make the taunts come from a Christian, and the comfort come from the Jew. Every art form in its development, probably, as the cinema now shows, moves from a puerile delight in the custard-coated face to more intellectual forms of comedy; the ontogenetic insensitivity of the child being satisfied in the perennial circus clown.

From the tumbling frolics of village square and sawdust ring, to the suave gestures of drawing-room wits and intimate playhouses, comedy has ranged. Based upon horse-play, or word-play, as much of it is, it would seem to dwell more easily with prose; we speak of comic verse, seldom of comic poetry. On the other hand, being based in greater proportion on intellect, comedy less often achieves an intensity comparable to the emotional heights of tragedy. Yet in the Athens of Pericles, and in the England of Elizabeth, gorgeous tragedy strode with uproarious comedy romping at its side.

The distinction between wit and humor may be, for the

moment, postponed; but it needs now be pointed out that the emphasis on intellect is laid in one type of comedy only; it is an easy step from the sublime to the ridiculous because both build mainly on emotion. As tragedy is poetry at its deepest earnest, comedy is poetry in unlimited jest. Thus Coleridge sets apart the comedies of Aristophanes and of Shakespeare: a riotous abandonment of all concentric aim; the whole work a great jest, with hordes of littler jests borne in its sack—events, characters, appearances, manners, thoughts, allusions, words. As Sophocles is monarchic in form, Aristophanes is anarchic. As tragedy moves to one inevitable end, comedy moves to every end—and no end.

The true comic successors of Aristophanes and Shakespeare are Sterne, and Lewis Carroll, are W. S. Gilbert and the writers of the modern revue; all light drama else has followed the way of the "new comedy" of Menander and Moliere (which indeed holds some of Shakespeare in its current). In this, the boisterous irrelevancies are whittled down to fit an insistent plot, the unforeseen flashes of fancy becomes set sparkles of wit, and the exuberant grin of good humor thins to a superior smile. At the close of their plot, the Merry Wives (and their husbands) invite the discomfited Falstaff home to dine; Moliere might have made him the type and symbol of senile lust. What many readers call the finest English comedy—Congreve's *The Way of the World*—failed when first produced, as it has little story, and much grace of brilliant wit; Farquhar's comedies of situation play more successfully. Later, the intellectual comedy of Oscar Wilde became popular; and even the lighter plays of Bernard Shaw bear a heavy mental charge . . . The comedy of wit sharpens the intellect, it leads to recognition, to knowledge; the comedy of humor adds the grace of understanding. Here the moralist may rise to defend the drama, reminding us that to understand all is to pardon all.

THE CAUSES OF LAUGHTER

> Nature hath fram'd strange fellows in her time;
> Some that will evermore peep through their eyes,
> And laugh, like parrots, at a bagpiper;
> And other of such vinegar aspect
> That they'll not show their teeth in way of smile,
> Though Nestor swear the jest be laughable.
>
> WILLIAM SHAKESPEARE.

"COMEDY", says Dr. Johnson, "has been particularly unpropitious to define." The difficulty, which has led such men as Ribot, Croce, G. Stanley Hall, to declare humor indefinable, springs probably from the effort to include under one explanation what has several possible causes. Physiologically, laughter has been explained as a discharge of surplus energy, the most immediate escape-valve our system has devised for expectant, then unused, forces. This basic hypothesis, enunciated by Herbert Spencer, fits the variants of all three theories the centuries have supplied.

Plato is perhaps the originator of the *derision* theory, the idea that the pleasure experienced in laughing is an enjoyment of other folks' discomfiture. He is followed by Hobbes, Meredith, Bergson—the last (as of course many others) adding the moral tone: "In laughter we always find an unavowed intention to humiliate, and consequently to correct, our neighbor, if not in his will, at least in his deed." He continues: "Laughter is incompatible with emotion. Depict some fault, however trifling, in such a way as to arouse sympathy, fear, or pity—the mischief is done: it is impossible to laugh." This laughter sustains the sense of superiority.

Aristotle follows with the equally widely known *disappointment* theory, laughter as the result of a deceived expectation.

343

Cicero blends the two theories by saying that we laugh at ourselves for having made the mistake, but most keep the notion pure. Thus Kant declares laughter rises "from the sudden transformation of a strained expectation into nothing." In this connection it is pointed out that the comic effect is greater when it begins with an impulse of fear, the alarm increasing the strained attention. Napoleon, talking of the Queen of Russia, describes a literal lessening:

> She received me in tragic fashion, like Chimène: "Justice, Sire! Justice! Magdeburg!" This she continued in a way most embarrassing to me. Finally, to make her change her style, I required her to take a seat. This is the best way of cutting short a tragic scene, for as soon as you are seated it all becomes comedy.

Interesting, in connection with the description of a sense of humor as the discerning of the incongruous, is Professor Parkhurst's recognition that "humor is the direct antithesis of poetry: for poetical insight is nothing but the sudden perception of the congruous. This congruity and incongruity alike are of feeling-tone rather than of idea . . . The most perfect metaphor seems to arise from the juxtaposition of two ideas having for ordinary perception no similarity whatsoever. The most perfect joke seems to result from the sudden breaking asunder of two ideas which had appeared to be practically identical." To reach her conclusion, Professor Parkhurst has identified poetry and metaphor; but G. K. Chesterton, in *The Defendant,* makes an analogous linking of nonsense and faith, the two extremes of the non-rational, "the two symbolic assertions of the truth that to draw out the soul of things with a syllogism is as impossible as to draw out Leviathan with a hook". Similarly, Cabell says that "wonder is the gateway to the palace of art."

The third theory describes laughter as the outcome of abundance, of freedom. Hobbes calls it "a sudden glory". According to Hegel:

Inseparable from the comic is an infinite geniality and confidence, capable of rising superior to its own contradiction, and experiencing therein no taint of bitterness nor sense of misfortune. It is the happy frame of mind, a hale condition of soul, which, fully aware of itself, can endure the dissolution of its aims.

"It is," says Carlyle, "a sort of inverse sublimity, exalting, as it were, into our affections what is below us."

Humor is thus regarded by some as the sense of proportion, freeing man both from pessimism and from vanity, by keeping him smaller than what he does, and greater than what befalls him. Lucien Fabre regards laughter as associated with the instinct of self-preservation, an assertion of assurance; it thus may spring, however, after any type of false-alarm. Darwin links this laughter—for it must by now be evident that there are several types, differently sprung—with the eager play of childhood, with general high spirits; he calls it "meaningless laughter". Freud, of course, states that naught man does lacks significance, and that suppressed tendencies find escape in humor. Lessing, with his notion that the ridiculous requires a contrast and a blending, perhaps approaches the recognition that laughter may be produced in a variety of ways. It may be of more profit, as it is more pertinent, to note some of these, as used in comedy.

Emptying the Aristophanic sack we have imagined, we note that laughter can be produced, first, by objects or events. It may seem difficult, at times, to dissociate the object from the diction: if the humor disappears when the language is changed, it is purely verbal. Thus, objecting that a surface innocence in a certain woman hides sophistication, one may retort, to "She's a child of nature": "No, she's a child of Nietzsche!":—here the pun hangs on enunciation. But Cicero's remark that the farmer who ploughed the family burial field was "cultivating his father's memory" would help amaze Candide; equally unspoiled by translation is the response of the Frenchman who, boasting that he could jest on any subject and offered "The King!" replied at once: "The King is not a subject!" (Even here, however, one may be betrayed by the similarity of cognate tongues.) Events may entertain us when there is a change: for the better, as when in *Volpone* the gadfly replaces the fox; for the worse, as when Bottom is transmogrified. The unexpected—in a play by Labiche a frightened man takes by the throat the marauder who has roused him from sleep, and cries "Be careful, I have a pair of pistols in my pockets!" "Is it possible!" responds the intruder, and with his free hands takes them out and subdues his host; the impossible—as when the servant of three masters sits on a chair painted on the backdrop; the incongruous—as when the lumpkins perform at Theseus' court—are other means of exciting laughter through situation.

Character may in many ways lead to laughter, as is manifest in the great variety of comic types, automata in the grip of a vice or folly. There may be manikins of the word: Lady Agatha's "Yes, mamma", at Lady Windermere's ball; "There's nothing derogatory" in Sean O'Casey's *The Plough and the Stars*. Often the incongruity is of manners—of different social levels as in Shaw's *Pygmalion;* or of inability to escape one's usual mode. The lawyer, the doctor, the teacher, may be recognized out of hours. In $2 \times 2 = 5$, the politician must often, in social gatherings, be checked in his tendency to begin a stump speech; in *The Beggar on Horseback* the business man plays golf with a telephone attached to him, and his wife, even when she walks, is fixed to her rocking-chair. There may be incongruity of appearance; a tall woman and a short man, the Mikado and his page; Malvolio's costume; bodily deformity grows less often the subject of laughter, what causes mirth in Bardolph's case being pathos in Cyrano's.

Thought and language also may play their part in producing laughter. Puns of all sorts are too common to need exampling; garrulity—if, like Dogberry's, properly squelched —may be briefly entertaining; Mrs. Malaprop has ancestors in Dame Quickly and Sancho Panza—who protests, indeed, "I was never brought up at school or varsity, to know when I murder a hard word"—and a numberless train of descendants, as befits such a lady; Touchstone by verbal device proves the damnation of Audrey. The subtler varieties of this intellectual exercise can be observed in Oscar Wilde, as their more exuberant flowering waves in the breezy music of Arthur Seymour Sullivan. In proportion as comedy is intellectual, it shifts its emphasis from situation and character to thought and word. In e.e. cumming's *him,* the development is a spur to intelligent delight; in the plays of Bernard Shaw, the pleasure is largely derived from the embattled onslaught of ideas.

THE TYPES OF DRAMA

All forms that perish other forms supply.

ALEXANDER POPE.

IN THIS shifting of emphasis from situation to idea, and
that more noticeable movement from the remote to the
familiar, it is possible to draw out certain types, and to distinguish them by label. The exaggeration of a single element
of action, the basic situation, or the vertebral plot, which
carries all else in its movement, produces farce, comedy's
caldron. If it be feelings that are similarly exaggerated,
enchaining characters, dictating deeds, the result is melodrama, buffo tragedy. Comedy has been classified in various
ways. Professor Erskine divides it into romantic, realistic,
and fantastic; Bonamy Dobree, into critical, by which he
means satiric, free, which points no moral, and great, the
mongrel tragi-comedy. An historical survey of the English
drama distinguishes the romantic comedy of Shakespeare;
the comedy of humours, which tends toward realism, in Ben
Jonson; the restoration comedy of manners, the artificial
comedy wherein Lady Betty Modish, Lord Plausible, Lord
Froth, Sir Harry Wildair, and all the genteel company, bow
through their refined adulteries—though some part from this
the more cynical genteel comedy of Queen Anne's days, and
the comedy of intrigue of the Georges. This, in turn, moves to
the sentimental comedy, the mixture of serious and amusing
elements that aims at once to win the smile and start the tear.
Lack of copyright laws made for rapid flow of dramatic currents across the English Channel in the nineteenth century,
and this type of play, increasingly "well-made", grew into
the more serious social drama and problem play, in which

the appeal is emotional rather than intellectual, but the characters are life-size, lacking the awful loom of the tragic, and the action more closely drawn from daily life than either the arranged situations of comedy or the driven deeds of tragedy. For in the end, as in the beginning, tragedy is by all recognized as the richest mode of the drama, and by many regarded as the highest form of art.

the appeal is emotional rather than intellectual, but the characters are life-size, lacking the awful loom of the tragic, and the action more closely drawn from daily life than either the arranged situations of comedy or the driven-deeds of tragedy. For in the end, as in the beginning, tragedy is by all recognized as the richest mode of the drama, and by many regarded as the highest form of art.

CHAPTER IX

PROSE

On the Monday Jack went once more, and hired himself to a cattle-keeper, who gave him a donkey for his trouble. Although Jack was very strong, he found some difficulty in hoisting the donkey on to his shoulders, but at last he accomplished it, and began walking slowly home with his prize. Now it happened that in the course of his journey there lived a rich man with his only daughter, a beautiful girl, but, unfortunately, deaf and dumb; she had never laughed in her life, and the doctors said she would never recover until somebody made her laugh. This young lady happened to be looking out of the window when Jack was passing with the donkey on his shoulders, its legs sticking up in the air, and the sight was so comical that she burst into a great fit of laughter, and at once recovered her speech and hearing. Her father was overjoyed, and fulfilled his promise by marrying her to Jack, who was thus made a fine gentleman. They lived in a large house, and Jack's mother lived with them in great happiness until she died.

(EUROPEAN FOLK-LORE.)

TOWARD THE NOVEL

> "Good words, friend," said the Bee, having now pruned
> himself, and being disposed to droll; "I'll give you my
> hand and word to come near your kennel no more; I was
> never in such a confounded pickle since I was born."
>
> JONATHAN SWIFT.

IN THE attempt to define poetry, much was perforce said
of its complement, prose. Such opinion as preserves any
radiant bearing on the subject is likely to present the idea
that in poetry "the thought is the word and the word is the
thought", the words being "made-to-measure", the word
become deed; whereas in prose the idea develops through
the use of "ready-made" words. The mind must be centered
upon and held alive in the idea: words that permit one to slip
into a groove of habit replacing thought; or words that, *per
contra*, draw attention to themselves, alike defeat the purpose. The flow of the narrative is then checked; analysis is
borne to dreaming instead of judgment. Almost in spite of
oneself, one seeks a rhythm to lull one along. Hence common
words are the basis of prose—though they must be distinguished from commonplaces. "For what marks the commonplace is not the common thought; but habit and the
mechanical play of the imagination, supplanting the idea."

It's through familiar words [says Joubert] that the style bites
into the reader. It's through them that great thoughts gain currency and are taken in good faith, as gold and silver of a known
stamp. They inspire confidence in him who uses them to make his
ideas plain; for such a use of the common parlance marks a man
who knows life and keeps close to it. Such words, furthermore,
make the style frank. They announce that the writer has long
been nourished on this thought or feeling, that he has made it so
intimate a part of himself that the most ordinary words suffice him
to express the ideas, become his own through long conception.
What he says, finally, is more likely to seem true; for no other

diction is as clear as what we term familiar, and clarity is so fundamental a characteristic of truth as often to be taken for truth itself.

It would be laboring the obvious to classify prose according to its subjects, as science, history [32], biography, and the like, though many writings in these divisions have literary distinction, and the recent development of "fictionized biography", history gone gossip, in which the writer "permits the subject, nay invites the subject, to control the biography", represents an interlocking of modes. In all prose, whether dissertation or essay or novel, it is the event (object or idea or act) from which the feeling springs, to which the feeling clings, so that, while it may progress, it does not, like poetry, take us into its time, but keeps us still contemplative of the whole. Prose carries its chambered structure on its back. It may be *analytical*, weaving and interweaving parts and whole, separating the known from the conjectured, assigning causes, tracing motives and results; it may be (as in maxims, "characters", essays) *confidential*, making the reader a friend who may be burdened with less solemn things, opinions, suppositions, moods, who may be taken by the arm and lectured, dreamed with, or laughed with, for the stroll; it may, intertwined with these, or bare, be simply *narrative*, without explaining or judging, fluid with the facts.

All of these ideas will probably be contradicted in the subsequent discussion, for Monsieur Jourdain is not alone: prose, especially prose fiction, is the last, apparently the freest, surely the least organized and most disputed, of literary forms. The *New English Dictionary* defines a novel as "a fictitious prose tale or narrative of considerable length, in which characters and actions professing to represent those of real life are portrayed in a plot". The French lay the emphasis otherwise, calling it "a fictitious prose story in which the author seeks to rouse interest by portraying emo-

tions or manners, or by the strangeness of the adventures".
From the dictionary definitions, however, the conception of
the novel has so extended that French and English critics
(e.g. Abel Chevalley and E. M. Forster) alike are content to
describe a novel as "a fiction in prose of a certain extent".
Paul Valéry declares that "neither rhythm, nor symmetry,
nor figures, nor forms, nor even a determined composition,
is imposed upon it. One law only—but on pain of death: it is
essential (and it suffices) that the flow carry us toward and
even make us seek an end, which is the illusion of having
profoundly or violently lived an adventure, or else of having
come thoroughly to know invented individuals." Mr. Forster
emphasizes that "principles and systems may suit other
forms of art, but they cannot be applicable here, or if applied
their results must be subject to re-examination". Virginia
Woolf goes farther: "There is not a critic alive who will say
that a novel is a work of art and that as such he will judge
it". And "to me", says Richard Aldington, "the excuse for a
novel is that one can do any damn thing one pleases".

Yet Mr. Forster has ventured partially to delimit the
form. The novel, he declares, is "bounded by two chains of
mountains, neither of which rises very abruptly—the opposing ranges of Poetry and History—and bounded on the third
side by a sea—a sea that we shall encounter when we come
to *Moby Dick*." The white whale, of course, draws the captain to drown in the sea of metaphysics. The fourth side,
which Mr. Forster leaves uncharted, is bordered by the slough
of journalism. Fielding claimed the right to set his own
stakes; while he regarded the novel as a "comic epic poem in
prose", he declared: "I am, in reality, the founder of a new
province of writing, so I am at liberty to make what laws I
please therein".

Other distinctions have been labored, by which such works
as *The Satyricon, The Tale of Genji, The Thousand-and-One*

Nights, the medieval fabliaux, the renaissance picaresque tales—all books indeed prior to Richardson's *Pamela*—may be marked off from the novel. The most instructive of these is perhaps that between the romance and the novel: in Congreve's words:

Romances are generally composed of the constant loves and invincible courages of heroes, heroines, Kings and Queens, Mortals of the first rank, and so forth; where lofty language, miraculous contingencies, and impossible performances elevate and surprise the reader into a giddy delight, which leaves him flat upon the ground whenever he gives off, and vexes him to think how he has suffered himself to be pleased and transported, concerned and afflicted at the several passages which he has read, viz. these knights success to their damosels misfortunes, and such like, when he is forced to be very well convinced 'tis all a lye. Novels are of a more familiar nature; come near us, and represent to us intrigues in practice, delight us with accidents and odd events, but not such as are wholly unusual or unprecedented, such which not being so distant from our belief, bring also the pleasure nearer us. Romances give more of wonder, novels of delight.

While our more accustomed age attains neither the giddy delight nor the after-vexation, the two types of fiction are still rivals for popular favor.

Despite Arnold Bennett's flat denial, most critics concur in the opinion that in the novel, as in the drama, the essential element is the story—the action—the play of events: the play's the thing wherewith to catch the conscience of the king: character is revealed or determined by the event. In romance this need not be true, for romance is the kingdom of free will; there, the hero fights the mechanisms of life, and chooses his path—even when it leads to destruction. Romance is action giving consistence to the dream. But the novel, born of late centuries, bears in its being the genes of determinism.

The opposition involved in a story requires the existence of two forces, striving toward a common goal, or one desirous of preventing the other in the attainment of an end. The presupposition of a reader introduces two further elements: sympathy with (not, of course, sympathy for) one force, which may be embodied in an outstanding figure, thus the hero; and the early establishment of the mood of the story, humorous, satiric, austere, what the author wills. The presentation of these matters is technically known as the foreshadowing; that the story take not place in a vacuum, the atmosphere—time, place, and environing conditions—is usually also made known. Some press a distinction between mere story, the succession of events in the order of time, and plot, a succession of events emphasizing causality. This, while it turns the attention from curiosity about the future to intelligent concern with the full flow of time, is but another way of characterizing the events of the conflict, which may be presented in either of two general schemes. There may be a number of climaxes, each prepared for ere its predecessor is passed, and each involving the chief figure in greater difficulties, until the episodic series come somehow to a halt. *Robinson Crusoe*, Dickens, Alger (the dime Dickens), use this development. The events of the story, on the other hand, as in most of the greater novels, may move in a single sweep of accumulating forces to the decisive moment. Some critics, indeed, protest that such a scheme may serve the drama, but is less valid when applied in the novel, in which the author's ability to probe beneath the action, to talk about his persons' motives, or to reveal them in "subconscious" flow, shifts the emphasis from action to character. Actually, however, only the locale is shifted: what we behold, now within the individual, is still the struggle of contending powers. Plays of Eugene O'Neill, granting actuality to needs and impulses life would suppress, have carried these "unconscious" tendencies (by the magic carpet of *als ob*) onto the stage, and indicated that, though its effect may be in spiritual change instead of action, the desire is equivalent to the deed.

ON TRUTH IN FICTION

> Moone: All that I have to say, is to tell you, that the
> Lanthorne is the Moone; I, the man in the Moone; this
> thorne bush, my thorne bush; and this dog, my dog.
>
> WILLIAM SHAKESPEARE.
>
> This may seem to be a truism, but it is nevertheless true.
> W. P. KER.

THE test of the novelist, says E. M. Forster, is his power "to bounce the reader into accepting what he says". This power of a rough road over the occupants of an automobile has impressed Mr. Forster; he insists: "The novelist must bounce us; that is imperative." But the categorical imperative should not swallow its tale; the important phase of the remark lies in the "accepting what he says". For willing suspension of disbelief is too passive a term to characterize the active credence some novelists desire for their works.

The statement has often been made that every man has in his own life the material of a novel; it has also been declared that all an author writes is his autograph—at most, his biograph. Quite other than this is the declaration, or implication, or allowed rumor, that the characters or events of a novel are based upon life. There unquestionably is a glamour, for many readers, rising from the thought that wealthy or prominent citizens (whose names are bruited), or recent "scandalous" or otherwise exciting occurrences, are being recounted in the current story. Although such a feeling interferes with the consideration of the work as art, it adds to the delight of the publisher; the popularity of such works as Dreiser's *An American Tragedy* and Upton Sinclair's *Boston* (which uses the actual names of its real figures) was increased by the facts that the former "follows the court records at times verbatim" and the latter deals with the world-stirring Sacco-Vanzetti case. Rarely, the notoriety of actual events may harm a work, as when the proper audience was turned from Sophie Treadwell's *Machinal* by its linking with the notorious Snyder-Gray murder.[33] Such a withdrawal of the desired audience from a work is, however, so little likely that we hear of Defoe's bribing a criminal, condemned for heinous offense to be drawn and quartered, to make scaffold confession and repentance, and loudly entrust the full story of his appalling and monstrous crimes, as a warning to all the public, to honest Mr. Defoe! Time, however, soon eases such concerns.

Aristotle saw clearly, when he said that "probable impossibilities are better than improbable possibilities"; modern science seconds him, in that its statistical improbabilities are far less likely than the old "impossibles", some of which have even come true. "Why is a puppet show more convincing than the Comédie Française?" queries Mr. Keith in *South Wind*—and answers: "Because it is still further removed from reality. There is so much make-believe that you cease to struggle." Too close a quest of truth-seeming may indeed mire the author in facts, as many think James Joyce and his followers are muddied over. (Joyce, you remember, declares that when a man hides aught of himself, it is inevitably the divine that he does off.) Yet casually the clown walks through a door his hand has traced in air, and Alice crawls at last through the key-hole: there is no question of falsity when truthfulness is not sought. Truth in fiction is often precisely what no one would say.

For of the four degrees of truth in literature, art lies in the extremes. The best sellers of yesterday displayed the improbable, as their successors parade the probable; the best books of any day soar with the daring of the impossible, or trace the slow course of the inevitable. From the fairy-tale through Rabelais to *Alice In Wonderland, that which cannot be* as lastingly holds us as, from Greek tragedy through Ibsen to the Russian novelists, *that which must be* maintains its endless grip. Beyond the falsifications of the middle ways, the stories that are inevitable, or are impossible, stand forever true.

Truth in fiction, then, is not truth in fact. As often in æsthetic theory, the problem rises from a confusion in terms: *truth* in art means simply fitness, consistency. That is true in art which accords with the mood, the event, the character— which (like perhaps the Hairy Ape at last) "belongs". To the work of art may be applied the honest adage:

> To thine own self be true,
> And it must follow as the night the day,
> Thou can'st not then be false to any man.

"In form", says Valéry, "the novel approaches the dream; both can be defined in terms of this singular propriety, that all their irrelevancies belong!" Schiller, indeed, goes so far as to attribute "devotion to the real" to human weakness, need of support; and to declare that "indifference to reality and interest in semblance represent a true progress for humanity and a decisive step toward culture". Without accepting this extreme view, one may recognize that an "emotional belief", a sharing of the mood, rather than an insistence on factuality, is the only belief relevant to a work of art.

It may be noted, in passing, that the miracles of fairyland occur on the material plane; on the moral and spiritual plane —affections, characters—there reigns a fixity of law even greater than in life: Prince Charming, changed into a bird, flies to his love and sings to her. Enchanters may transport victims or friends, but cannot change their transports: love (if there only) endures forever after. In the fable, as old as the fairy-tale, the despotism of reality appears, instead of the merit-ruled republic of romance. The cheese drops; the hare is bested; the fox cannot reach the grapes; the laws of thermo-dynamics resume domain. Thus it is that in the fairy-tale the spirit rules, and love and virtue triumph; in the fable, might makes right, and cunning is better than kindness. On the one hand, faith moves the mountains; on the other, persuasion is better than force: heaven stooping to virtue, and the best policy reaping its reward. Each appropriate to the story's mood. And each, in its aspect, true.

Stevenson remarked that when in his reading he came upon a passage notoriously untrue, he always suspected that it was a direct transcript from life. Unique as the actual event may be, however, it is less its own strangeness than the ineptitude of the author that makes it artistically untrue. By a deft disposal of emphasis minor inconsistencies may be slipped by, as the O an instructor (no Giotto!) curves upon a blackboard is allowed to pass for a circle by a class in search of some general truth. As early as Aristophanes, his translator Frere points out, it was demonstrated that almost anything is credible, if properly conveyed. In *The Birds*, while Peisthetairus, visitor from human-land, is lengthily advising the building of a great bird city, a messenger comes breathlessly in with word that the metropolis he has suggested is complete. Peisthetairus is as astonished as we; yet he accepts the news as fact, and is even piqued that he, the inspirer, has been given no opportunity to superintend the work. In the demeanor and words of the messenger, moreover, and at once of the chorus, we may subtly surmise that Peisthetairus has in the moment lost prestige. Finally, the messenger, far from expecting disbelief, boasts of the fact that no outside aid forwarded the swift labor of the birds. By the time the hearer's mind has followed this devious path, taken by the sound psychology of each step, he has forgotten any prior incredulity: the place is matter of fact. In like fashion, the circumstantial method of Defoe accumulates unsorted details until there are no questions to ask and therefore no doubts to rise.

The interweaving of episodes or sub-plots gives greater solidity to a story, and helps make it seem real. A second action, involved about the first, draws the mind by more movement from lingering inspection, and seems by added length and stir to grant fuller existence.

The impossible need not, however, be hid in a bushel of chaffer; however bold the initial assumption of a story, it may take itself for granted, provided the subsequent happenings be consistent. In this connection it must be remembered that two Mrs. Partingtons are more potent than one. An improbable event is an intrusion into the order we know; on two impossibilities we erect another world.

A NOTE ON CHILDREN

It is a mean and scandalous practice in authors to put notes to things that deserve no notice.

GROTIUS.

IT IS apparent to all who have considered the history of fiction, and the question of permanence in literature, that, while the popularity of *Gulliver's Travels* and *Robinson Crusoe,* the liking for Scott and Dickens, have not diminished, the level of interest has changed: what was concern for the slow perusal of our fathers has become entertainment for the running through of our children.

This shifting of attention has not been universal, nor unaccompanied by perhaps illuminating vicissitudes. *Pilgrim's Progress,* for instance, has encountered in the new generation of boy readers a sudden indifference; whereas twenty years ago Pilgrim's was one of the essential grand tours of childhood, along with those of Sindbad and Robinson and Gulliver, today scarce five of a hundred lads [34] have followed him to the Celestial City. Thackeray, on the other hand, has never, in any way comparable to that of Bunyan and Dickens, won to a general popularity among children. Tom Jones and his boon fellows—by some that are aware of them—are too carefully hidden from childhood's eyes to justify more than a guess as to how they would be welcomed. The appeal of a Sterne, a Trollope, a Peacock, is to a special taste that draws to these novelists each his group in every generation, but for the development or recognition of which maturity seems requisite. Yet most of the books read by adults in any generation are read—if at all—by the children of the next.

In the case of *Gulliver's Travels,* the sloughing of the

political aspect is well known; but what other volume (unless the nursery rhymes be really medieval satire!) has undergone such cleansing? The abuses depicted in Dickens' lengthy tales of boyhood are as vivid to the lad of today as to the man of the Eighteen-Fifties; thoughtless and cruel, loving and kind, elders are as numerous and as important in a boy's life now as when it fell to Oliver's lot to ask for more to eat, as when Nicholas tried teaching in Dotheboys Hall. The change is to be sought in the readers, not in the books.

Books of this sort probably come, in the course of a child's reading, two stages beyond the fairy-tale, directly after Horatio Alger, Oliver Optic, or their current equivalents, and those unending (because constantly reprinted) series that carry Nick Carter and the Harkaways and the Merriwells on their unceasingly triumphant and glorious careers. Boys rapt in the delight of these stories properly refuse to credit their parents' dismissal of them as trash, nor accept their teacher's word that *Tom Sawyer* and *Treasure Island* are better books because they are written by good writers. The crux of the matter is in their truthfulness, in the sense of consistency that resides in the characters. The natural boy is a pagan. So is Huckleberry Finn; he is interested and absorbed in every minute for itself. But the dime-novel boys (like most adults) are puritans; Alger's young heroes work joyfully to remove the family mortgage; Tom Sawyer looked more truly into his fellows. Stealing apples from the neighbor's trees, or the corner barrel, or slipping two-for-a-nickel through a subway stile, is a boyish lark—until the heavy hand of adult morality wakes the lad to other standards. Fresh from the fairy-tale and Santa Claus, but unknowing of the world, the young reader is fascinated by the wide vistas and the strange true deeds of Henty's paired heroes or the Motor-Boat boys; until, suddenly, perhaps, this world in turn spins on its axis to his own twirling: he knows it for a toy, and he discards it. Thereafter he is ready for the books his fathers knew.

Universal education, if the phrase were even as fully realized in its second as in its first term, might in some measure account for the earlier interest in these stories; as schooling goes, the forced reading of a book in class is too frequent cause of a turning from the classics to the paper-bound volumes "teacher" destroys at sight; and the extension of the ability to read without an accompanying elevation of understanding and taste produces the public that gulps down best-sellers, "true-story" magazines, and the "tabloids". Motion pictures and tabloid sensations are, however, phenomena too recent for the change to be among the charges laid to their swift shifting. Yet the tendencies they foster, of which indeed the tabloid is effect as well as cause, are those wherein today's child is overtaking yesterday's man. The rate of life's stir is increasing; without any greater consciousness of his goal man is rushing more rapidly through time. The recent developments in the study of radiant energy, the new accomplishments in physical speed, are the accompaniment if not the cause of a nervous acceleration, of an urge to be getting on, of a fever for movement. Even the poet cries:

> I want to take the next train out,
> No matter where it's going.

The hectic succession of events that seems, to all who cannot win calmer detachment, to characterize our life, the haphazard rush of things upon us, brings early home to us the external facts of existence, makes us, almost as infants, aware, sophisticate as children, as youths, blasé.

In 1795 over two million of *The Cheap Repository Tracts* were sold in England to adult readers. In ten years these had surfeited, and there appeared frequent advertisements of "moral tales for children". *The Way Of All Flesh* pictures a lad reared on such nutriment. The individual decline of *Pilgrim's Progress*, though partly attributable, no doubt, to the non-English heritage of most of our city children, I incline to consider rather an outcome of this sophistication and an accompanying disregard for the moral and ethical symbols of the past; in this fall is involved the general wane of religion. *Pilgrim's Progress* presupposes the Sunday School. More universal, however, and of earlier growth, is the extension of the interest of the child from the kingdom of faëry to the realm of fact. Attention to action naturally precedes curiosity as to causes, springs earlier than concern with character; and we need not wonder that Scott and Dickens are read before Thackeray and Meredith.[35] The apprehension of an embracing philosophy of life behind a story is a still more difficult achievement, its expectation of which bars a book perhaps forever from wide circulation. But facts are no sooner found than made note of, and he who runs may read.

The complexity of life today, which has engendered an age of specialization, of intensive training that absorbs most of man's energy in one main pursuit, calls for the earlier acquisition of that general view which will enable one to choose one's single field. While most persons are, unfortunately, drawn or driven to their life-activity by less reasoned impulses, they nonetheless run more rapidly than their fathers along the lines of social contact; the problems of love and labor are sooner seen. Sex education, manual training, and other developments of recent years, but more fundamentally the forced intimacy of crowded cities and the increased intensity of life during the industrial revolution, have made themes and details that once were the revealed observations of genius, part of the ordinary equipment of the child.

The result of this process has been to convert the child

into a half-baked man. Education, the function of which is to fit the individual to express himself most fully, in harmony with his age and his environment, has become too exclusively an attempt at preparation for the present adult world. Facts and figures, ethical codes, attitudes perhaps desirable in the adult, are thrust upon the children; the recent vogue of long trousers for eight-year-olds aptly presents the mental dressing of the rising generation. Instead of attaining a fully rounded child development, the children of our time rise to the level of an underdeveloped man. And their reading, whether it be *Dead-Eye Dick* or Dickens, is that of an underdeveloped mentality. Only, in the latter case, knowledge has increased beyond understanding.

The child and the man enjoy equally the impossible and the inevitable. *Alice In Wonderland, The Thousand-and-One Nights,* are read by perhaps as many adults as children; Dunsany has his wonderland for the mature. The retribution that comes upon the wicked one of the fairy tale is to the child as inevitably rooted in character and misdeeds as is to the adult the consequence of the violation of natural or human law in tragedy. But the underdeveloped, of whatever age, relish the improbable and the probable, dreaming it actual of themselves. The post-adolescent underdeveloped intelligence and taste runs to sentimental stories of temptations resisted and trials sustained, with wealth and happiness dripping honey at the close; pre-adolescents of this type take their tales with less love and more adventure, but equally freighted with cargo of triumph for the ultimate port. The adult whose mental growth has not kept pace with his body neglects the last generations, the last season's, best sellers for his own. There is enough memory of the pagan in every boy to make such natural children as Tom Sawyer and Huck Finn choicest reading; but the restrictions and regulations by which his elders keep him properly quiet and in his place, and the intricate course of preparation through which he is to become fit for a grown-up world, draw the child from his natural expansion into an early (however unwitting or unwilling) adoption of adult standards, and lead him to such books as the penny dreadfuls, where man's moral codes animate the boy heroes, or to the more eventful stories among the books his fathers read. What then, shall we expect of a generation whose fathers have abandoned Dickens and Scott for "wild-west" magazines of blatant shades, whose mothers have never heard of Miss Mitford and Jane Austen, but grow round-eyed at the "true-stories" of the passionate press?

THE PERSONS OF THE TALE

Worth makes the man, and want of it the fellow.
The rest is all but leather or prunello.

ALEXANDER POPE.

"THE foundation of good fiction", says Arnold Bennett, "is character creating and nothing else." Stevenson, directing his stories to children, was fully aware that what they most want is the tale; yet to the adult there is, unquestionably, considerable pleasure to be drawn from the contemplation of the persons in fiction.

There are many ways among which a novelist may choose, for the effective introduction of his characters. Frequently—as in *Pamela, Nicholas Nickleby, Of Human Bondage*—the story begins with a death, which forces a readjustment in the life of the main figure, toward whom, incidentally, our sympathy is at once drawn. The arrival of a stranger, or the return of one long absent, also often helps introduce a story's chief character.

As to these persons, much has been said, of which the remarks of Clayton Hamilton may be taken as recording the general view—which he approaches wrongly:

Every great character of fiction must exhibit an intimate combination of typical and individual traits. It is through being typical that the character is true; it is through being individual that the character is convincing.

It were invidious to harp upon the confusions in the second sentence, or to stress the further comment, following a discussion of Benjamin Franklin as an epitome of his age, that "men so representative are rare in actual life; and the chief business of fiction is therefore to supply them". For Mr.

Hamilton proceeds to mention characters "typical but not individual", the figures of the morality plays and of allegory. Bunyan's Christian, he curiously observes, "is one man and one man only, and we could never in our thought confuse him with any other character in or out of fiction". Yet perhaps the most important fact we observe in regard to the moralities is the manner in which they moved toward the people's daily life, toward the particular: how picture Gluttony, save as the town's fat boy; how Drunkenness, save as the village sot? On the other hand, Christian—and Gargantua, and Jurgen, and all allegorical figures—are individual, not in the sense that they are uniquely complex, like rounded, living humans; but in that they are uniquely simple, a quality come to life—not particular at all, but universal, universal in a single aspect. Barkis, who is always willin', Micawber, forever waiting for something to turn up, are perhaps instances of individuals not made universal. Mr. Hamilton repeats:

A great fictitious character must be at once generic and specific; it must be an individualized representation of the typical qualities of a class. It is only figures of this sort that are finally worth while in fiction—more worth the reader's while than the average actual man.

Here we need not object to being asked always to look at representatives of a class, nor do more than observe that if the last remark of Mr. Hamilton be true, it destroys the value of his first unless his meaning is that live persons are too complex for us to see through them as we see beneath the simplified creations of the artist. We may merely point out that Barkis and Micawber, his examples, are minor characters; that with every lengthily developed figure a good writer achieves the synthesis, the shadowing forth of the universal seen likewise in the drama; that if any individual be truly shown, his fundamental, universal tendencies and impulses appear.

Various degrees of importance, the Micawbers remind us, may be assigned his characters by the author. Often he presents a chief figure who thinks for the reader, in whose place the reader may stand, to follow, to be moved by, to reflect upon, the events of the story. This person, however, may not appear in the tale though he pervade it; for the author himself may be both creator and guide. There will probably be several other persons, seen by this first one, viewed as individuals of whom he must have regard, rounded beings acting as their natures dictate. Beyond this group may appear still others, more casually entering the story's flow, and borne for their moment like straws upon its stream; automata, or sketches, that busy themselves briefly, but fill the world wherein the others dwell. Professor Ker compares Shakespeare's histories, especially the *Henry IV*, to the great novels, in which we feel that "many other things are happening at the same time, and many things in the intervals, which are not told, but which might be as lively as what we are allowed to see"—as a lamp lights the object for which it is held, and a score of others unattended round. Some authors, indeed, write in their notebooks the full biography of) *Balzac* every person, however insignificant, they may employ; what is no more than a bent figure trundling a barrow, giving shape to another's musing, in one book of *La Comédie Humaine,* may in another of Balzac's novels become the central figure.

However important, a character may be presented as static or dynamic. It may, that is, be changeless in a changing scene, where the events disclose its constant nature, steadfast as Milton's Lucifer;* or it may not be thus *flat*—to use a frequent but hardly appropriate word, for many go through numerous experiences fundamentally unchanged, but by their attitudes

* *Add. but Lucifer develops in sorrow and suffering.*

and responses roundly revealed—but instead be altered by strain of circumstance, like the figures of Shakespeare, like Silas Marner "dying, and being born again" when life applies or lightens its cold pressure. In either case, what the reader demands of the character may be briefly stated: that, in the reading, it shall seem to live.

ON LIVING THE PART

Get with child a mandrake root.

JOHN DONNE.

MANY readers not merely want the character to live, but want to live the character. The delight of those who merge their identity with that of the main force in the work before them is so great, indeed, that they have raised it as a test of beauty. The doctrine of empathy is one that from some aspects challenges the fundamental viewpoint of the critic, and calls for more extended consideration than could be granted it among the many definitions of the beautiful. Noticeably in America, life and art have drawn together; a generation shocked into insensitivity seeks to rouse itself by greater shocks. Literature is in large measure written to stir the emotions, without regard to the intellect; plays and novels seek to effect a transfer of the receptor's identity into the moving figure. Music is mainly to dance to; we hear the modern cacophonies, "the jingle of jazz to jangle the jungle of nerves". The spread of the feeling may be illustrated by an advertisement widespread: under the pictures of semi-nude actresses the call: "Take it from these well-known stars, tantalizing scents waft screen possibilities to the un-seen audiences and compel them to live through the romances being enacted before their eyes". And the tendency to become that which we desire grows to a theory of art. Here, too, we may revert to the drama, and draw upon the testimony of those collaborators with the playwright, the players, who solve the problem in their every performance.

Since drama, by stepping out of the church, drew away from life and turned to "play", two theories as to the actor's art have held the stage. To present Diderot's dogma in the words of Coquelin, champion of the intellectual approach: "To move others, one should be unmoved". Equally emphatic and more recently iterate, George Arliss insists that the good actor must live his part. Bergson, speaking for the receptor of novel or play, declares he must be no longer a spectator but an actor.

The easiest way to settle the dispute is to deny the difference. Man acts as an organism, the scientist declares; all parts of his being respond in unison; separation is possible only in the enthusiasms of fanatics or the speculations of pedagogues. It is possibly in recognition of this false dichotomy that George M. Cohan, when asked his point of view, was first "inclined to agree with George Arliss", then paraphrased Coquelin: "To move others, one should appear not to be unmoved". Dudley Digges, hanging by his toes to laugh at his fellows who sit the see-saw, swings back to conclude: "I understand that the most frequent method is to discard all such notions and theories and to rely simply on genius. This unquestionably produces the greatest acting provided you smoke Lucky Strikes."

Yet the logican who defies anyone to sunder top and bottom knows that the extremes, though inseparable, are distinct. Now intellect and now emotion, bound always by the walking-beam of will, takes for the moment upper hand. In many situations and events—surely in so special a mode of conduct as play-acting—it should be possible to determine which has exercised the greater measure of control. When we hear that Helen Hayes "bordered on hysteria" at every performance of *Coquette*, may we not reasonably assume that it is emotion which seems to overcome her? When—contrariwise—E. H. Sothern (père), accidentally stumbling at his first entrance on his first night as Lord Dundreary, and hearing the spectators shriek with delight, repeats the trip nightly, may we not equally adjudge the intellect is his guide?

The theorist may reason that the approach varies with the nature of the player and the play. "For instance", says so sensitive an actress as Lynn Fontanne, "there are some that have wells of emotion in them so near the surface that all they have to do is say 'Mother', and they burst into tears. And there are others who have to hypnotize themselves into a state of complete accord with the part they are playing before they can emote successfully. And there are others who can give such a perfect imitation of grief, sorrow, and love, that it doesn't matter whether they are feeling or not." For herself, the same actress declares, the method "depends very much upon how much the author has done for me"; yet in its ideal state, she continues, "it's pretty much a combination of the two. By that I mean the ability to keep the temperature of your head at zero while your heart is at ninety-nine in the shade."

The last remark, despite the qualification, seems an acceptance of the intellectual approach. And often, in comedy at least, it does seem both impossible and undesirable for the player to lose himself in the part. In the commedia dell' arte, certainly, where the actor was given a framework on which to build the play with impromptu lines, a constant alertness, an instant wit, were essential. The technique of comedy today (*a fortiori* of the musical variety) is so finely developed that—even ignoring the diminution of feeling due to mechanization, in this as in all activity—the performer must often be conscious of timing, of cues, of distances and distortions, to the utter loss of any sense of identity with the character.

Tragedy, the theorist may maintain, is surer field for the emotions. Here, with deeper if not nobler impulses to action, with more serious subjects, and usually more unified persons, the actor, having a part nearer human moods to present, may well share the feelings experienced by the character he "becomes". It is undeniable that the actor feels. He may present a conception that is the result of study, of an intellectual grasp of the rôle assumed; he may move by more "intuitive" flashing into the spirit of the part; he may employ almost external devices to induce the appropriate stir: did not Edmund Kean stalk about, back-stage, working himself into a passion for Othello's angry moments—always the magic idea of association proves sound psychology, and the representation of the emotion causes it to be.

James-Lange theory but not so sound.

The actor feels; but does he live his part, or does he hold his mind aloof, ever the watcher as well, ever the critic? Despite Arliss and the host of emotional actresses, what answer can be found for Louis Calhern's query: "How can one 'live' a death scene when the doctor gives him medicines and his wife moans on definite, exact, word-cues?"* Ann Harding as cogently protests:

> The theory of living the part won't stand any sort of test: how in heaven's name are you going to live Hamlet eight times a week? How about Camille? Do the exponents of that doctrine *actually die* twice on Wednesdays and Saturdays?—or do they seem to die? . . . It has been my lot in this business to weep and sob every evening of my life for five years. I should imagine that even a practiced pessimist in the best of training would find that a trifle wearing, and for a person of my cheerful disposition such an existence would be suicidal—if "lived". It becomes trying now and then even on sheer technique.

The type of performer commonly called emotional, who seems to live the part, is often observed to weaken as the play runs on, to give a more ragged, sometimes a more haggard, presentation with the season's waning. The public hears with sympathy of the strain to which such an actress is subjected, and throngs to behold the passion torn to shreds. Probably such a player is least gifted with emotion. The scientist, who earlier objected that man acts as an organism, reminds us now that man reaches toward the world with triune grasp; that while they may never be exactly aligned, intellect, emotion, and will keep marching pace; that the most fully developed being has wide understanding, deep feeling, and solid will: he may, in moments of great stress, be outwardly calm, collected. The poorly developed man, however, with narrow comprehension and shallow feelings, also lacks weight of will, has little control; when they surge, his emotions (phylogenetically first and most frequent) though puny seem in their despotism things of stupendous power. The little reason of the little man plays equally the tyrant. But on the stage, merely living the part does not suffice: its implications must be conveyed to the audience.* To accomplish this requires control, manifest in the intelligence functioning as will.

The consensus of opinion seems to be that, if Coquelin is honest, Arliss at least is wise. All art stands within a frame. The footlights of set purpose leave the audience in the dark. In the succinct words of Ann Harding: "our public want to feel that they are observing *life*, and they feel that they have been duped if we admit that we are 'only acting'. It embarrasses them to be so stirred and taken out of themselves by someone who isn't caught in the same ecstasy. . . . You need your wits about you on the stage—and moreover, the dear public are not interested in watching you feel: they want to feel themselves."

* * * * * * *

That the public "want to feel themselves" is less frequently denied, nor the success doubted, whether the pronoun be object or pleonasm. While one may hesitate to admit that one lives the part of the chief figure in, shall I say, Gray's poem *On a Favourite Cat, Drowned In a Tub of Gold Fishes*, one can scarcely deny that most readers coalesce with the hero or the heroine of the work of fiction they are absorbed in, that the motion pictures owe much of their success to the

*May it not be always? thru a slight exaggeration of the natural or subtle?

vicarious experience they afford, that wild-west stories enrich the dull lives of city clerks with (alas, ephemeral) adventures, and that subway-crushed salesgirls escape to the arms of Eros and the voluptuous ease of sinful luxury as they drain the chapters of each age's new Elinor Glyn. The successful use of literature as escape involves the identification of the reader with the man so fortune-blessed (and virtuous and brave) as to win the heroine, or with the woman so virtuous (and brave and "fortune"-blessed) as to deserve the hero.

It may be no more worthy an impulse than a desire to feel superior to such a quest, that leads one to suggest that this frequent attitude may nonetheless be inappropriate, irrelevant to the work of art, and to maintain that the public should not live the part.

When Francesca da Rimini and Paolo "melt into an ancient tale" and move in its telling to the fateful kiss, their embrace is imposed upon them; not these two join their lips, but the olden lovers. Does not Francesca murmur Launcelot's name? Here is the perfect instance. Less romantic, but no less rapt in the tale, is the naïve playgoer (mimicked at recent revivals of Dion Boucicault's *The Octoroon, After Dark, or Neither Maid, Wife, Nor Widow*, Augustin Daly's *Under the Gaslight*, and other thrillers of a cruder day), is the simple fellow—Jacob Riis once was guilty—who hisses the villain, and mayhap shouts a word to warn the hero. In polite restraint, many a playgoer of today has curbed that impulse. Art, however, is commonly thought to induce not action but balanced contemplation.

Hiss the villain, we have said. But in a work of art, who wears that name? Is not every character in the right? Monodrama may perhaps receive proper response when the spectator "becomes" the man whose vision determines the play. But most dramas, and other works of art, seek to portray several

figures fully, in the round; and any character so revealed
bears its own justification. When a man's actions are understood, down to the basic impulses all men share and the
driving forces no man controls, tolerance replaces condemnation, sympathy comes in judgment's stead. The moral value
of art, as we have seen, lies along this path. Notice, however, what the idea involves. If the only way of imagining
things "from the inside" is "putting ourselves inside them",
the man who would come into full contact with the work of
art must identify himself, not merely with the chief figure,
but with every figure there presented. He must be not only
the hesitant Hamlet, but Polonius the bore, the sly Rosen-
crantz, Ophelia, Hamlet's mother, the murderous king. He
must in an insult's hurling be Antonio to thrust and Shylock
to submit. He must be at once the blow and the cheek that
bears it. Easy identification with the hero is the weakling's
ruse; the person truly taking to himself a work of art must
every moment live each person there concerned.[36]

The ludicrous nature of this shuttle-cock identification
seems to discredit the doctrine of empathy; for one cannot
continue such jumpabout tactics, yet one must view the entire
story with a comprehension greater than that of any single
character within it. From this point of view, we see the man
who is "so absorbed a cannon couldn't shake him" as sunk
in a single-phased surrender, rather than as fully responding
to the work of art. The truly appreciative, while his emotions
range with the work's sending, "keeps the temperature of his
head at zero"; he is alert for every subtlety of portraiture,
every shifting of emphasis, every technical turn. He will
recognize the feelings of every character, but he will feel
what is appropriate to the situation and action as a whole.[37]

It has often been remarked that when a man is listening
most attentively he may seem most distrait. Those who laugh
at the "hypersensitive" musical critic that requests a person

behind him to stop chewing gum, fail to recognize that the most delicate receptivity, the most sensitive response, is the most easily disturbed. It is easy for the adolescent (of whatever age) to founder in emotion, for the pedantic to lose himself in the colder delights of the intellect. Somewhere thousands are still sobbing at *Abie's Irish Rose*; a professor I heard a score of years ago is doubtless still making modest mention of the praise he received for counting the times Vergil used the interchangeable *ut* and *uti* (as one might count Milton's use of *though* and *although*). Yet, as the man of weightiest affairs seems always unhurried, so the man most intensely receptive may appear detached. Deep feeling and wide comprehension are, in truth, natural concomitants; their force, exerted simultaneously in grasping a work of art, holds still (though ready) the walking-beam of the will—and leaves the most interested apparently aloof. . . . And as no position in æsthetics is free from the pretender, the man incapable of concentration may rejoice—if he ever attain the knowledge—that the outward aspect of the appreciative is even as his own.

ON FORM IN FICTION

He thought he saw a rattlesnake
That questioned him in Greek:
He looked again, and found it was
The Middle of Next Week.
"The one thing I regret," he said,
"Is that it cannot speak."

LEWIS CARROLL.

THE quarrel in regard to the novel, says Wilbur Cross, "is primarily over the question of technique." Thus plot, character, and form, has each its champion. While the story, and the persons involved in it, however, are more or less definite elements, susceptible to summary or analysis, form, the most tangible element in terminology, proves the most elusive in fact. The word, remember, is borrowed from the field of the visual arts; and analogy—especially when one forgetfully thinks he is talking literally—digs pitfalls as it proceeds. Thus Percy Lubbock states that "the best form is that which makes the best of its subject—there is no other definition of the meaning of form in fiction"; disregarding the tautology, note that for "form" you may substitute "style" or "diction" or "novel" or many a thing more; and also, that you are still completely in the dark as to what the best form is. When Mr. Lubbock suggests analysis to discover whether the author has used the form "by which the most is made of the story to be told", he would hoist sail on never-charted seas, with ignorance as captain and presumption mate: for his only way of learning the story is in the writer's chosen form, and to tell the author another form would be better is to bid him make a different work of art. But behind all this lurks an *a priori* judgment, for we are assured that "the most was never made of any story except by a choice and disciplined method". Whereto Parson Sterne and Doctor Rabelais have made reply.

The wiser attitude in regard to form in fiction seems that which begins with no assumptions, and allows all forms, feeling that each work of art contains its own laws, yet holds them so fast they cannot be extracted for other application. Out of the grace and ease of the writer's development, in his work upon the resistant material of his art and of his theme, the form grows; and the trace of that ease and grace, in the finished work, is what we call the style. "Works of the spirit", says Alain, "lead to form, or to style, only insofar as they resemble manual labors; for our human condition is such, through the fashioning of our body, that action alone will clear away the passions and free the heart and thought. . . . What turns upon another object is flat; what turns upon the author's wisdom is pedantic; but when the work is respondent to itself, and guides the author as well, then it has style."

Some books develop their theme in such a manner as to display a definite plot-pattern, which may be seized upon as a recognizable element of the beauty. Such an isolable structure often forms the framework of the book; as in Schnitzler's *Reigen* (*Hands Round*) passion moves through linked couples until the first two reunite at the end; in France's *Thaïs* and James' *The Ambassadors,* the "hourglass design" is notable, two lives crossing while one moves toward fulfilment and the other toward defeat. Alice through the looking-glass queens her pawn. Occasionally no such pattern is discernible, though almost always at least sausage-string coherence may be posited of a novel. Sometimes the movement of the plot, of the characters' changing, traces—as in Tolstoi's *War and Peace,* as in Melville's *Moby Dick*—a design over a basic mood or theme. In the present writer's *From Whose Bourne,* the title indicates that country within his mind each person creates with consciousness and dwells in all his days; the story is developed with streamings of consciousness, with changes in the narrator's perceptive point, and with some two hundred notes (from a word to a dozen pages) presenting off-shoots of the actions or thoughts; and the "double hourglass" plot centers on a man whose material success brings increasing complacency and spiritual flatulence, and a woman whose material descent leads her to spiritual heights. . . . More, or less, apparent, plot structure forms the most pervasive single element of style.

In connection with prose style the question of rhythm recurs. A disciple recently hunted through the plays of Bernard Shaw, finding many passages that formed consecutive lines of blank verse, and thinking that he was thereby proving the playwright essentially a poet. But "any professional writer of prose", C. E. Montague remarks, "soon comes to feel that when he flops into two lines of blank verse running, it shows he is tired and ought to knock off work for the day. Anything sentimental in a prose writer's thought [Dickens flashes to mind] any weak, half-pressure state of his imagination, pushes him toward unconscious versification. . . . And where prose is best of all, as in parts of Goldsmith and Swift, and in Shakespeare's prose letters, it heads off any approach of formal meter with a wary persistence that cannot be accidental." [38]

The basic movement of rhythm, expectancy with varied return, is more legitimately sought in prose fiction. Recurrent symbols are, of course, as frequent as the Homeric epithet; but mere repetition is less potent than a renewal with a difference, as Silas Marner's lost gold grows into Eppie's curls. These variant returns, however, even when managed as subtly as by Proust, cannot produce the tidal effect of verse rhythm; they are spaced far apart, irregularly, like oases where the reader may drink of a mood, ever more deeply as the journey goes; they deserve the name rhythm only in wide figurative extension; but they may unquestionably be an important factor of style.

× Note extreme frequency of blank verse in the emotive descriptions of Ruskin.

Of diction in the novel little need be said, as there may be the widest ranging. The comparative length of the form, indeed, permits a dalliance, an occasional triviality (as when the ladies doff their cloaks for the party at the Red House in *Silas Marner*) that the more time-bound drama and poetry seldom admit. In his lingering the prose writer may even follow the meadow path into a plucking of the flowers of diction for their beauty's sake. C. E. Montague points out a "little recipe for vivacity . . . calling half-dead words back to life, reviving by dexterous use the original metaphors now petrified . . . a lively writer calls a shower bath 'a light aspersion', or says of boating renewed after a frost 'Again the stream suspects the keel' and behold! the educated mind of you is pleasantly tickled"—and you have been carried far off the story's course. Such verbal devices are more likely to be employed in the essay, therefore, than in the novel, of which the usual word has been described, remember, as a syllable of the idea. Yet the artist weighs even his letters, as, before the scientific critics of today, Stevenson showed, tracing the theme and variations of the sounds KANDLSR through *Kubla Khan*, and after study of many passages concluding that the most beautiful consonantal chord is PVF.* We are reminded that good novels "play for the reader" with good prose—however well the art conceal the art: "your easy reading", Sheridan exclaimed, "is damned hard writing!"

One of the most difficult elements of novel writing is the essential description, without which the story is likely to seem bare as a summary, yet which in descriptive passages too often seems barren and cold. It has been suggested that if the reader keep the mood and the action in view while reading the descriptions, they will repay him by giving background and body to the tale's movement. Many authors, how-

* For the poet's emphasis on sound, see pages 263 and 270, and Notes 47 and 48.

ever, prefer more direct efforts to build the two elements together. In the case of description of character the problem is simple, for by a man's acts shall ye know him; and even his appearance can be casually mentioned in the course of his movements. But descriptions of places are less readily woven into the fabric of the story; so that they may often be easily isolated, and some readers boast that they have "learned to skip"—a process that possibly adds to their enjoyment, but also sets it upon another plane than the keen consciousness and wakened thrill of response to the unified work of art.

The difficulty of writing description is inherent in the fact that a scene is usually caught by the eyes as a whole; in life (and in painting) the general sweep takes us, thereafter we may dwell among details; whereas in literature the details must be presented singly, in a sequence that however ordered is nonetheless artificial, and gradually the several aspects and items grow into a single wide impression. Description must in the reading grow bit by bit, so that it acquires an external movement similar to the flow of events; unless such a flow be naturally imparted, it will prove false and disappointing. For this reason—rather than to preserve Professor Erskine's "decorum"—poets avoid detailing their beloved's bodily charms, and wrap the maid from sight in fluid tropes. For this reason, too, as the most obvious blending, a scene is often visioned through the eyes of one walking or riding through it, so that the human motion bears the description on. Variations of this device are naturally sought; Doone Valley, for example, first entered by John Ridd as he fishes, is first fully described in the formulation of plans for an attack upon the stronghold, considering every barrier and every avenue of approach. Some writers, trusting in their genius, present the description by itself, and so have done; however it be offered, the characters must not be temporarily lost amid the trees, nor the forest hewn for the relentless movement of the tale.

THE FORMAL EMPHASIS

> For pray, gentlemen, was ever anything so modern as the spider in his air, his turns, and his paradoxes? He spins and spits wholly from himself, and scorns to own any obligation or assistance from without.
>
> JONATHAN SWIFT.

> St. Nicholas brought three children alive out of a pot when they had already been boiled down into soup; which may be said to mark the extreme assertion of form against formlessness.
>
> LATER MIRACLES.

"ALL depends on *how* it is presented, nothing on *what*." These words of Roger Fry indicate an emphasis he presses by averring he is as deeply moved by Rembrandt's painting of a carcass hanging at a butcher's shop as by his portrait of his mistress, or his picture of the Crucifixion. Whenever the moral aspect of art has not advanced its claim, the prime importance of the element of form has been asserted or assumed. Aristotle, as most of those whose views of art have been bound to views of conduct, emphasized the subject matter of the work of art. Even among the Greeks, however, the intimate bond of theme and treatment was recognized. Demetrius felt that, important as the subject may be, the presentation is more potent.

The man who listens to a great subject is promptly beguiled into thinking that the discourse itself is great. "Beguiled", I say: for we must consider not so much the things narrated as the method of their narration, since great topics may be told in a manner that is mean.

Quintilian observed that Aristotle's definition of rhetoric stresses invention and neglects expression; he noticed as well the opposite tendency to overemphasize the formal elements in art, and himself (as likewise Dionysius) considered subject and treatment interfused. Joubert—to leap the centuries —declares that true taste distinguishes virtues and vices of substance from faults and excellences of form—yet adds that, in every work of genius and taste, form is the essential, and substance but accessory.

Several meanings of the word *form* must be marked off. Form may mean merely the general "kind" of the work, as epic, drama, novel; it may, by a narrowing from this sense, signify the particular pattern or frame, as a sonnet, a farce. On the other hand, form may designate the outline or scheme of the idea—the contents, the matter, of the preceding sense —while the matter, in this meaning of the term, is the language which fills the form. This too may be turned about, for the word form has been employed to mean the words of the author and their handling. Among the confusions resulting from these several senses, spreads the insistence that the form of a work of art can be nothing but the work of art: thought become word, word become work.

Whichever conception of form one may employ—and some shift as ease disposes them—emphasis on form as the basic element in art persists. The fundamental reason for this perhaps lies in the needs of communication. In order to be properly received, art must find expression that, while varied and infinitely variable, will be recognizable in that a given symbol will produce a relatively uniform response; the symbols, furthermore, must be physically within the artist's control. In truth, the meaning may often, in human development, have come after the symbol, as with the pyramids, grown into significance from early protective stone-piles. Language, we have been told, is the beginning of idea. And every art is a language.

Other causes, increasing the emphasis on form, lead also to a constant quest of novelty in art. In all his doings, as

Aristides learned, man must have change, even if the new order be stork for his log; in art, which seems least bound to the other concerns of life, this fever for novelty can be most, and most harmlessly, indulged. Ideas change slowly, but—in the extent to which they are employed in art—can be quickly consumed. Philosophy, science, ethics, move gradually through the ages; the associations of the images—the ideas— in a work of art can be encompassed, digested, used up. "What never grow less or evaporate", Roger Fry insists, "are the feelings dependent on the purely formal elements." In philosophy, science, and ethics, furthermore, we are seeking truth, usefulness, and goodness; in art we are seeking we know not what, but pleasure is our touchstone; since monotony, even the continuance of one delight, soon palls, constant variation is essential; and since the ideas in art cannot so swiftly change, the quest of novelty follows ever the avenues of form. It is, furthermore, a tendency of all periods of uncertainty or revolt (as which generation is not?) to look about them—back, abroad, within—for more successful or appropriate means of self-expression. The subjects, they draw from life around them and from their inner conflicts and exaltations: the current conditions set a frame for the recurrent themes, for nature, for love, life, and death; their quest follows ever the avenues of form.

It may be objected that through all these changing periods the great works of art have retained their strong appeal. Without raising the question, however, as to how many theatre-goers really prefer Shakespeare to the season's farce-hit, how many readers prefer Dante to E. A. Robinson or Edgar Guest, Homer to Cabell or S. S. Van Dine, it may be suggested that the lasting works endure through being big enough to embrace all attitudes or, perhaps one should say, supple enough to bend with every breeze. To Aristophanes, Homer was a moralist; to the eighteenth century, he was a model of decorum; to the nineteenth, a prize of primitive simplicity. The seven ages of Spenser in English literary taste have been described; and every great writer of older days has been admired, sometimes for irreconcilable reasons, through the special lenses of each succeeding generation.

The pursuit of novelty, then, is no newfangle singularity. The cry "What's the latest?" was heard in the *Odyssey*. Longinus refers to the quest as "an orgy in which the present generation revels". Voltaire praises the seventeenth century for using "kinds unknown to antiquity"; Marivaux had rather "be humbly seated in the last row of the little troop of original authors, than proudly placed in the front rank of the vast herd of literary apes". John Webster declares that "most of the people that come to the playhouse resemble those ignorant asses who, visiting stationers' shops, their use is to inquire not for good books, but for new books!" There is no lack of authors to supply them. Even Wordsworth succumbed to the writer's impulse to novelty; he tells us he "abstained from the use of many expressions, in themselves proper and beautiful, but which have been foolishly repeated by bad poets until feelings of disgust are connected with them"—as though the most tarnished words would not shine with one fit use! Readers and many reviewers find it simpler to take sides (according to their inclination) and to praise or condemn whatever is novel and condemn or praise whatever is traditional, than to seek the good in whatsoever guise: a new form is a lifted banner to fire under, or at; but authors themselves may be the dupes of their form. Some expressionistic dramatists are so extreme in their technique as to be unaware of the saccharine sentimentality of their mood. The "revolutionary" form of James Joyce often fails to hide banality—especially in those who are followers of fashion; the only protection of some modern versifiers is their comparative impenetrability. And language offers a compromise to those who at once fear, and feel a need of, novelty: they polish their phrases.

The industrial age, hurrying many processes along, has further increased the demand for novelty of form. This is an era of advertisement, of self-assertion; merit may be modest, but novelty wins attention and acclaim. More subtly the period poisons the judgment: as in automobiles and safety-razors the latest model is (*ipso facto*) the best, and the old is the old-fashioned, the discarded; so with each season the new books flower and the old books, gone from memory and the shelves, may, like drooped bouquets from the last night's feast, be sent to lighten the hours of patients in hospital wards. A few, thanks to more thoughtful readers somehow extant, or to a publisher's hope, are gathered into one and another of the "modern libraries" wherein they are enshrined (if not entombed) as contemporary classics; but the exaggerated fervor of the first reception in most cases is counterbalanced by swift oblivion.

At the onsurge of the industrial revolution—

> The world is too much with us; late and soon,
> Getting and spending, we lay waste our powers—

Wordsworth in more than his poetry protested against the excessive stimulation and consequent insensitivity of man; social critics of today unite in characterizing society as fungoid with ennui. Constant shock—of machines and war and endless exaggerate words in "sensational" news, and cinema and sex and speed, and "easy" money and "speak-easy" thoughts, and war and machines—has dulled the senses, has laid a "savage torpor" on the mind, that novelty, incessant, violent shock of further novelty, alone can stir.

Those that have somehow avoided or withstood the Scylla of these shocks, have not always escaped the Charybdis of instant objection to all novelty in art. The scientists of today, themselves sufficiently recovered to sit up and look dazedly around, admit that most great inventions or discoveries seem, at first, compact of folly. "No possibility is beautiful", says Alain, "the actual alone has beauty"; yet it must be noted that whatever is, was apparently inevitable. Having happened it is, of course, irrevocable, and our tendency is therefore to feel (as with wars) that it was unavoidable even before it came. Yet, as Proust observes,

every event is like a mould of a particular shape, and, whatever it be, it imposes, upon the series of incidents which it has interrupted and seems to have concluded, a pattern which we believe to be the only one possible because we do not know the others that might have been substituted for it.

Thus any form finds justification in the quality of its being. Art is in flux, in a state (if the word may be used) of continuous change, nor ever is the next step likely to be foretold. Experiment is therefore inevitable and essential; most of it will probably miss the way; yet all of it may serve, exploring the various fields of expression, setting here a lone light in a desert, leaving there the warning of many sun-bleached bones, so that the way may be ultimately clear for farther journeying, into the provinces of beauty, through the forms of art. And as the subject matter of works of art becomes puerile through long acquaintance, or incomprehensible as the tongue of oblivion laps up the words and ways that gave them life, they bulk even as the loom of a temple of which the shrine is desolate and the feelings that gave it rise long dimmed. The arch remains. Archeologist and historian may seek to recapture their meaning, to reconstruct the civilization of their birth; the lover of beauty will be content to contemplate their form.

THE TELLING EFFECT

I saw the man that saw this wondrous sight.

NURSERY RHYME.

THE success of a story—as every kindergartner and traveling salesman knows—depends on the way it is told; and there are as many right ways of telling a tale as there are good stories. Into some books, however, the authors delight to enter, for a friendly chat with the reader, speculating as to the characters' thoughts and motives, analyzing their attitudes and acts; while from others the writers hold themselves sternly aloof, allowing the tale to flow unhindered by their conscious checking. The intimate, easy-going way was especially frequent when serial publication was the rule, when an author might have several stories running at a time, nor know their endings; his fancy might easily carry him into pleasant divagations, or even an interpolate essay on the superstitions of the countryside or the relation between Yorkshire housewifery and masculine morals, while the printer's devil stood importunate at the door. The letter form of *Pamela* prevented Richardson from giving sign to those who beleaguered him along the street, but Thackeray omitted Amelia and Dobbin for a few chapters at a correspondent's request.

The objective manner is, of course, but relatively aloof, the writer's nature and disposition coloring his book beneath his consciousness, beyond his control; but in several ways the author may make semblance of keeping himself out of his tale. He may, as it were, dramatize the story, presenting action and counteraction, remark and rejoinder, allowing the events to marshal themselves for the fray, as does Henry

James in *The Awkward Age*. More frequently, he assumes
the rôle of an interested bystander or of one who has been
listener; he then tells no more than he has seen or heard,
leaving aught else, moral implications, character analysis,
wider application, for the reader to draw from the events.
Galsworthy, at his best, can present the physical plane so as
to make the outer, apparently casual incidents and the conversations reveal the deeper thoughts and emotions they
"intend" (in life) to hide. The telling of a story with little
moral comment or psychological explanation Gilbert Murray
deems a mark of early life and simple societies; perhaps it
marks also the desire of the most complex. Professor Murray,
indeed, admires that "this characteristic of the Heroic Age
lingers on as a deliberate point of style in fifth-century
Athens"; it is similarly current twenty-five centuries after.

Conrad and Kipling—

> The captain told the cook,
> The cook told the crew,
> The crew told me, so
> The story must be true—

work often on the theory that hearsay is the best evidence [39];
Maupassant provides a listener who (like the Wedding Guest
in *The Ancient Mariner*) may by his responses play chorus
and indicate the appropriate attitudes for the reader. Often,
too, the story comes from the mouth of the most important
character—of whom we must then beware: John Ridd is not
so simple as he protests (remember Antony's "I am no orator,
as Brutus is"), nor Jim Hawkins—the astute reader learns
in Silver's tavern—so clever as he thinks. The presentation
of a story by a hostile character, as in Browning's *My Last
Duchess*, may lead to a fuller sympathetic understanding of
the main figure. The narrator appears within the story—thus
"keeping the author out"!—in many other guises; a recent
effective device is that of Beatrice Seymour in *Unveiled*, in

which a friend of two lovers long dead is telling their story to their children, wondering whether her understanding of this event is accurate, what the effect of this revelation will be —and always, incidentally, enlightening the reader. When events occur that one character cannot know, an easy shift, as in *Treasure Island*, passes the yarn to another spinner; a minor figure may for a moment take upper hand, as when attorney Stryver writes two chapter-heads in *A Tale of Two Cities*; in these and other ways the author may endeavor to keep himself and his notions out of the reader's mind, which is left free for full absorption in the story.

The rôle of the innocent bystander is open to subjective treatment as well, for the author may wonder as to what he has seen; but the most frequent attitude of the writer, whether he holds aloof or walks within the tale, is that of the Olympian, who is as understanding of his characters' hidden motives and "unconscious" thoughts as he is aware of their words and open deeds. This assumption of omniscience is common from Fielding to Joyce; if expressed or potential fulness of knowledge about them be not, indeed, what sets the men in fiction off from men in life. Henry James has varied this complete revelation by raising one character as a pseudo-Olympian, in whose keen mind words and actions are assorted and true motives assigned. The power of perception assumed by a novelist may, of course, vary within the work; some critics object to such a mingling of points of view, but others consider that it brings the novel closer to life, wherein we know one person quite well (at any rate, best), and others in varying degrees of intimacy, guesswork, and ignorant unconcern. As with the author's chatting with the reader about his characters (though Forster declares such a procedure sacrifices illusion and nobility), the sole criterion must be the success of the individual instance. In the realm of the hidden depths of character, psychology has given the

Olympian a farther vision and a new recording scheme; and in recent fiction there has flowed unendingly the "stream of consciousness" indicated by William James, wherein the main current is broken by insistent flotsam, now bobbing gaily along, now sifting gradually to the deeps, now with a splash plunging; wherein the continuing thought is constantly disturbed—as were Donne's prayers—by "a memory of yesterday's pleasures, a fear of tomorrow's dangers, a straw under my knee, a noise in mine eare, a light in mine eye, an anything a nothing, a fancy, a Chimera in my braine". Though *Ulysses* observes the unities of time and place, the prime unity of action (in the sense of closely knit plot) less frequently binds these novelists, for in the interior monologue there is like to be little forcing or clash of wills, but a flow that accepts and includes whatever may come. Chekov has said: "When one has written a story I believe one ought to strike out both the beginning and the end. That is where authors are most inclined to lie"; and indeed many stories today move from no formal beginning to no definite end.

The novel thus returns, at a different height of the helix, to an earlier formlessness; and Wilbur Cross declares that fiction is ever renewing itself, that "in the past lie strewn everywhere intimations of all the methods practiced by contemporary novelists". To present these in the various fashions of the many books on the novel would be as repetitious, and as profitless, as to study humanity in classes according to the color of the skin, again according to the texture of the hair, again according to geographical distribution, again, and again. (When each knows his race is the chosen people.) Grant Overton, to take an instance, traces the novel from an "infinite" phase wherein man's quest of "the thing it has moved him most to believe in" is embodied, to a "finite" fiction, which "perfected itself in the novel of character". From the two faults of this finite fiction, sentimentality and moralizing, writers sought escape by the diverging avenues of fantasy and prophecy. Among the prophets Mr. Forster names Dostoievsky, Emily Brontë, D. H. Lawrence, and Melville; but Grant Overton, accepting the first and last of these in the seer's rôle, deems the other two bound closer to realism. A quite different point of view may be adduced, in the observation that the novel (like the drama) has moved from a robust, hearty, physical sweep to a more frequent inner concern; that the flow of events, once unimpeded by the simple psychology, is now often stopped for complex analyses, in franker terms; that a new sense of form has come (again as in the drama) from France—but is not always heeded; that from the same soil a farther seeking of reality has entered the novel; and that new conceptions of morality and of woman's place in the scheme of things have considerably altered our outlook. It has been suggested that, in these and other ways, the novelist's themes are being destroyed: science has annihilated the supernatural; power and wealth have swept away royalty and aristocracy; the new, practical woman is brushing aside the old, romantic love: on the contrary, not only are new themes phœnix of the old, but the very changes and conflicts, the dying ways, lift hydra-heads of stories. Incidentally, the old themes remain valid. "Patterns of conduct that governed our ancestors cease to fit us", says Elmer Davis; therefore the literature sprung of these "ceases to have any but historic interest". The very work he analyzes for his proof—Euripides' *Electra*—suffices, if you will read it, to refute him. For, as I have stressed in discussing the drama, it is not merely its own virtues that a period admires, but always the grand heroic code. We may know— what Mr. Davis seems to think disastrous—that Rider Haggard's imaginary kingdoms cannot be in mid-Africa; but what reader ever asked the latitude and longitude of Eutopia or Erewhon—ay, or of Graustark? And while Stendhal's

"crystallization", the identification of the woman one desires
with all the aspirations of mankind toward the good, the
true, the beautiful—a centering manifest in the life of Baudelaire—may be gone as far as the troubadour *domnei* (ceremonial worship of his lady) from the sophisticate mind
of the modern young man, it seems hard to believe that on
this account most of the novels considered great up to 1914
will have been dismissed as worthless by 1934. Many of them,
doubtless,—for social conditions and ethical concepts, always
as steadily changing, and imperceptibly, as the hour hand,
have recently seemed to move with the minute-hand of time's
great dial—will lapse from adult to adolescent reading. The
scene and the objects—the seen things—alter, but the
thoughts and emotions and prior impulsions, love, and the
movement through life toward death, unceasingly hold man's
course upon their way, unendingly draw his interest to their
driving. Speaking of the physical plane, Hugh Walpole
declares that all great novels imply three distances: the
immediate setting, as the New York money market today; a
widening background of similar marts, the Bourse, the Rialto,
of other countries, and other times; and against all this the
contrasting aspects of the world, art, science, the slums, the
bourgeoisie;—so, too, on the psychological plane, one sees
the character as an individual, with his eccentric, his particular, responses; within these, the attitudes and actions
typical of all of his class, gentleman, lawyer, Scotchman,
what may be; and beyond, the tendencies, impulses, and
affections common to all mankind.

THE SHORT STORY

Still ending, and beginning still.

WILLIAM COWPER.

"THE short story is a story that is short." Despite the many efforts to distinguish a so-called "short-story" from the more leisurely tale, the swifter anecdote, and various other brief narrative forms, more and more writers are coming to feel that brevity is the soul of it. H. G. Wells, indeed, allows it more expansion, defining the short story as "fiction that can be read in less than an hour". No pattern—the surprise ending of Stockton and O. Henry, the involved narrator of Maupassant, the aloof reporter of Conrad—no single mould has formed its Protean shape; no special rule confines its mood or theme—save only this. Brevity is the sole of it.

Much of what has been said of the novel is therefore of equal applicability to the short story. Of all art, however, one expects a unified impression; here the limitation of the short story's extent cuts sharply. For of all the aspects of the novel—story; character portrayal, development, and analysis; background of local color [40]; mood; interplay and succeeding contrast of emotions—each short story is likely to isolate and present but one. In an adventure story every moment adds to the stir of the turbulent events; in a humorous tale the happenings justify themselves only by their comic effect; a presentation of character (as by Barrie or Katherine Mansfield) may scarcely have "story" at all; every word of *The Masque of the Red Death*, of *The Fall of the House of Usher*, moves in the single mood.

The commercial opportunities afforded by the many magazines of short stories have established certain patterns of

398

popular taste. The formula of the detective story, as first applied by Poe, has been little varied. A literary agent offers clients a pattern—swift opening, so many words and a climax, so many words and a reversal, so many words—that promotes the sale of their products:

Every five speeches there should be an identification of the person; what he is doing, what he is thinking, what his mood is. For example: Jim tapped the cigarette on his thumb-nail, thoughtfully wondering what in the world she wanted to do that for. The three mediums are there put together.

Correspondence schools advertise a similar claim. A man who sells stories to the magazine with the world's largest circulation has advised the aspirant always to remember that a story deals with a likeable fellow who is on the way to a goal of which the writer approves, and is checked in his progress by some person or obstacle the writer disapproves. And one remembers that equally valid Americal formula, which emphasizes a religious background, an aristocratic tone, brevity, and a dash of spice—according to which the prize short story consists of the sentence: "Good God, Duchess, take your hand off my knee!" Fundamentally, none of these pat patterns, none of the descriptions or definitions—not Sherwood Anderson's defi: "Plot is story-poison"—improves or even alters Poe's characterization, that a short story is a narrative short enough to be read at a single sitting, written to make a single impression on the reader, excluding all that does not forward that impression, complete and final in itself.

There is no need here to trace the short story from the bare Egyptian tales of perhaps sixty centuries ago, down the long trail:—Pandora's box, ninth century B.C.; the book of Esther, second century B.C.; Æsop's Fables, four hundred years later; the Gesta Romanorum; The Arabian Nights; the medieval fabliaux; Boccaccio and the Italian novelle; the Canterbury Tales; the Spectator sketches; the tales of

Irving, the apologues of Hawthorne; the short stories of Poe.
And beyond this recognition of the form:—the quest of the
inevitable, in word and in result of action, in Maupassant;
the capture of "human interest" from journalism in Kipling
and O. Henry; the abandonment of plot in Barrie; the endless variety of subject, of action, person, emotion, setting, and
mood, today.

The short story is as close in its relation to the novel as the
one-act play to the full length drama, exhibiting in petto
the characteristics of the larger movement, different in degree
but not in kind, and—with the one additional convention of
its brevity—manifesting the same freedom in its growth to
the same ends. Prose fiction, we are constantly reminded, is
the freest of all art forms: "the novelist is the ape of God".
He may be Caliban,[41] but he may prove Pygmalion. One of
these rôles must every artist play.

CHAPTER X

SCHOOLS AND SCHEMES

"I took only the regular course."

"What was that?" inquired Alice.

"Reeling and Writhing, of course, to begin with," the Mock Turtle replied; "and the different branches of Arithmetic—Ambition, Distraction, Uglification, and Derision . . . " counting off the subjects on his flappers . . . "Mystery, ancient and modern."

LEWIS CARROLL.

WITH PRAYER TO ARIADNE

Faithful and simple and of plain belief
She is, with her fair garland bright like gold.
GUIDO CAVALCANTI.

UNTIL the nineteenth century the classical spirit dominated literature. The dissidents, that is to say, made no attempt to fortify their practice with walls of critical justification. The romantics and the realists among the Greeks and the Romans fell mainly outside the great periods; and all were alike *the classics* to the renaissance, which based its own romanticism upon a reverence for the ancients. Anyone appreciative of literature, therefore, is fronted with so great a body of works of art embraced within the term classical, that to deny its prime validity were to try to outface the sun. The nineteenth century romanticists themselves, though they felt the frigidity of the neo-classicists, could do no more, in attacking the term, than seek to wrest it from their precedessors: "a work that is good all through", said Goethe, "will surely be classic". Opposition between classicism and romanticism has been drawn; as in the declaration that the one emphasizes the outer form; the other, the spirit within—intellect vs. emotions; as in Pascal's remark that the classics are based on imitation of nature (but "no one knows what the natural model is, that one must imitate"); as in the older Goethe's comparison of classicism and health, romanticism and disease; as in the statement that classicism maintains an ideal of objectivity, and is social, whereas romance is unmistakably subjective, and individual. More frequently, however, classicism is withdrawn from the maze of dark distinctions, and left to characterize all that is felt to be valid and vital. Pater, in one mood, says that

the classic comes to us out of the cool and quiet of other times, as the measure of what a long experience has shown will at least never displease us;

in more positive tone he declares that "at its best, romantic literature in every period attains classical quality, giving true measure of the very limited value of those well-worn critical distinctions". Bulwer-Lytton gives further measure of the term's inclusiveness: "In science read, by preference, the newest works; in literature, the oldest. The classic literature is always modern." When Valéry characterizes the classical author as "a writer who bears within himself a critic, whom he intimately associates with all his work", he is extending the term to include almost every artist. And Ramon Fernandez, though referring classicism to the judgment and will, romanticism to feeling and faith, continues: "A healthy and really alive classicism always, or almost always, presupposes a romantic movement. It is really no paradox to say that romanticism is, in its essence, a classic achievement." Some thinkers, on the other hand, attribute a general decline of the French people, in finance and politics as well as literature, to the imposition of an alien (Anglo-Germanic) romanticism upon a native classical spirit. Herbert Read, for example, in an appreciation of Julien Benda, declares:

The classicist is also a realist, and the war has left behind a generation of realists who have not yet made themselves felt. When realism and classicism at last join forces, the eclipse of romanticism and sentimentalism will be complete.

We may overlook the linking that in the second sentence, here, begs an important question, as well as the contradiction the two sentences involve; and hold only the recognition that, in virtually all these views, the classical is the ideal.

The two literary attitudes more frequently opposed are realism and romanticsm, felt as tendencies in the author's work which, in their fulness, are the extremes of which classicism is the mean. The Greeks, Gilbert Murray declares, were saved from romanticism because when their emotion rose above a certain degree of intensity, it turned from art to religion. But from them have sprung, he continues, the divergent schools.

Ancient comedy and tragedy tried to re-create the highest or intensest moments of experience: that has developed or decayed into Romanticism. The new comedy, the genre sérieux, tried to represent external life with utmost illusion of naturalness, so that, if nothing was ecstatically sublime, everything was convincing. That has developed or—again let me admit the possibility—decayed, into Realism.*

These opposed attitudes have usually appeared together: Greene, Nash, Deloney, among the Elizabethans; Balzac and Zola, beside Hugo and Dumas. Mankind is ever curious; from the infant watching the railroad train and the boy breaking open a watch, to the psychologist tapping the monkey's brain, everyone likes "to see the wheels go round". We always rejoice in voyages of discovery, ever seeking the unknown, the wonderful, the remote. At first this remoteness depends upon physical distance; but space with its conquest holds less of mystery, and man comes to seek the remote within the familiar. The nineteenth century contains, it seems to me, an epitome of this questing. The Gothic romance, the tale of far-off ages and climes, came from Orinoko and the farther isles swiftly nearer home. Realism awoke attention to the everyday, familiar actions and ways, making conscious again—with a sense of novelty —what had grown through long habit mechanical. Into the closets then naturalism searched, the "notebook psychology", as Nietzsche called it, "constant spying on reality, and every evening bearing home a handful of fresh curios". It dug through the subcellars to find newness near at hand, revealing the unfamiliar by showing that which in life was of preference ignored. Farther down it was impossible to go without reaching the infernal regions, and diabolism had its brief day, with Villiers de l'Isle Adam's *Cruel Tales,* Borel's *Immoral Tales*, Barbey d'Aurevilly's *Diabolic Tales*, and the horror-love of Hoffman and of Poe. Actually, such a deepening of the quest marks a transfer from the physical plane to the psychic; naturalism became supernaturalism. "In matters of art", said Heine, "I am a supernaturalist"; and Baudelaire approved, explaining: "In certain almost supernatural states of the soul, the very depth of life is revealed in the ordinary spectacle one might behold, which becomes its symbol". Here, then, symbolism is born.[42] The realistic observation and the romantic individuality thus blend in the "scientific" search for precise expression and sharp-edged form for unique and personal—often obscure and mystical—feelings. But the quest within the individual was relentlessly pursued. The novel, slower than poetry or the drama (Ibsen, Chekov, Maeterlinck, O'Neill) to build with symbolism, though there are *Vathek* and *Caleb Williams* and *Frankenstein,* and Poe, and Hawthorne, and *Moby Dick,* and *Dorian Gray,* moved nonetheless toward an endeavor to capture the whole of the "psyche", in search of which writers went back to the primitive, then beyond the primitive to the earliest hunting-grounds of the intellect, to da-da-ism; and on into the unconscious, where we are told our truest selves abide, with superrealism. From the mind to the spirit the search continued; that eternal essence which is in all things, beyond the primary reality of the senses, beyond the secondary reality of mathematics and physics, is the goal of the unanimists. Says Jules Romains:

> The air I breathe is fresh with spirit-savour.
> Men are ideas that a mind sends forth.
> From them to me all flows, yet is internal;
> Cheek to cheek we lie across the distance,
> Space in communion binds us in one thought.

And Richard Beer-Hofmann in most of his work presents men who through crises grow aware of their relation to all life; it is the death of George, for instance (in the book of that name) that gives impetus to the complacent Paul and brings him to seek wisdom in submission to universal law:

> His life did not fade away as a solitary tone in the void but, harmonizing with a vast solemn melody preordained since the birth of time, it swept on to the accompaniment of universal eternal laws. Nothing unjust could happen to him, pain was not expulsion nor did death mean severance from the all. As an inevitable part of a universal whole, every deed was perhaps a sacrament, pain perhaps an honor, and death perhaps a mission.

Following the figures of symbolism, without asking for their soul, came imagism (and the cleansing laughter of "spectrism", the free verse hoax). Still intent upon translating the essence of life into symbol, expressionism won a wide vogue, especially in the theatre, which, indeed, for a time threatened to sweep his predominance from the playwright in a surge of "productionism". Writers having been made self-conscious, many a man has issued a manifesto and set up a school, often with himself as master and sole disciple. *The Little Review* printed on its cover the names of a dozen groups to whose expressions it gave print; Baudelaire spoke of the "consumptive school" and the "lunatic school": neo-paganism, vorticism, ultraism*— though not yet non-plus-ultraism!—and other mock-serious or sincere developments of individual tastes and tendencies, all variously season the mixture the years to come shall taste, now boiling in the great caldron of modern art.

* See page 432f.

REALISM AND ROMANCE

Ah Love! could you and I with Him conspire
To grasp this sorry Scheme of things entire,
  Would we not shatter it to bits—and then
Remould it nearer to the Heart's Desire!
                                OMAR KHAYYAM.

THE opposition between realism and romance has been drawn through many windings, and seems as determined a dualism as tweedledum and tweedledee—or, possibly, Cain and Abel. Which is which, of course, depends upon the tendency of the particular commentator.

"The Romantic", says T. E. Hulme, "is one who does not believe in the fall of man"—but, one can picture Cabell's adding, finds it convenient to believe in the resurrection. For Cabell, scoffing at Wilson Follett's failure to adduce Jane Austen in support of his dictum that "first-class art has never reproduced its own contemporary background", himself defines realism as "the fallacy that our mileposts are as worthy of consideration as our goal; and that the especial post we are now passing reveals an eternal verity." This challenge he puts into the mouth of one John Charteris, leaving himself free to contradict; nor is it easy to separate the thought from the chaffer of one who, like the medieval psilosophers, tries to see how long he can dangle an idea from the point of a pen; but Cabell's novels as well as his essays point the theory that romance is the "demiurgic" force that leads man toward the ideal. For it is only in fiction—is it not?—that we find practiced the virtues and living the heroes we would have and be; persuaded, however, by ubiquitous vanity and blinkered by universal dulness we move (as Oscar Wilde remarked) toward the realization of those impossible goals set in our books we may through the desiring yet attain.

Through the purging and the smelting we are sustained by an instinctive knowledge that we are being made into something better. For this we know, quite incommunicably, and yet as surely as we know that we will to have it thus.

And it is this will that stirs in us to have the creatures of earth and the affairs of earth, not as they are but "as they ought to be", which we call romance. But when we note how visibly it sways all life we perceive that we are talking about God.

Neither the urbane cynicism of Cabell, nor his quoted definition, conforms to the most common distinction, which tells us that the romanticist shows men as they would like to be; that "as they ought to be" is the revelation of the more sober classicist; while the realist portrays men as they are; and the naturalist, through partial portraiture or misapplied emphasis, as worse than they are. To this it may be at once objected that every picture of life is partial, through the artist's conscious selection, and through his unconscious limitations; that both the realist's and the romanticist's worlds are imaginary; that if the muddled incompetents of Cabell's romances are what man wishes to be, then realism and romance are less twain than twin. In truth, Carlyle remarked that "Romance for grown persons is Reality"; and to some, life is so much stranger, more intense, more intoxicating [43] than fiction, that literature of any sort seems pallid beside the human comedy.

This view of romanticism narrows to its expressions the notion of art as escape; much has been made of this conception, especially by the disciples of Freud. Thus, placing romantic books on the same basis as dream "wish-fulfilments", both for the author and for the reader identified with the hero, Albert Mordell declares that "when Shakespeare grew weary of London life, he drew a picture of life in the forest of Arden in his *As You Like It,* such as he would have liked to have enjoyed"—the only objection to which pretty theory being that, for all we know, Shakespeare might at the time have been enjoying the spring among the willows of the Avon. Baudelaire recognizes this view of romanticism, when he avers that its products are draped in rich colors out of longings born in gray Northern skies; whereas the South is naturalistic, for there Nature leaves nothing for mankind to desire. But Baudelaire was not well acquainted with the literature of the South, and he overlooked the fact that even in Eden man found something to desire. According to this escape theory, the romanticist is likely to construct Utopias, in which little allowance will be made for the animal side of man, as Plato with the *Republic,* as Shaw among the ancients of *Back To Methuselah.* It should be observed, in this regard, that there are several sorts of escape possible to the reader, that is, several things from which he may desire to flee. From his immediate environment, most obviously: from its banal monotony into a wonder-world; or from its despair to the calm of art, as with Pater. And from the emotions, as the burlesque show or Wagner may "purge" one, by emptying one (without social harm) of lust, as the mystery play releases fear; as the laughter at the butt of slap-stick farce leaves us better natured. Only no one has yet established that such effects result.

Yet those who speak glibly of art as affording escape from life overlook the likelihood that men turn to it not to avoid but to encounter life. If questioned and articulate, such a reader would probably respond that he has never *really* lived, never, that is, had opportunity to exercise to the full all his impulses and energies. The "average reader's" conception of living, without wide canvass of experience, colored by the distant view of wealth and power, is far from the actuality others may see; but it possesses an abundant vitality, a clash of strong wills in proud endeavor, that most men vainly desire. . . . This view produces no more than a shifting of emphasis: the reader seeks to escape his present drab existence; but it has not been stressd that what he seeks is no withdrawing dream-world, but "real life", life as by the standards of his desire it should be. Hence the popularity of "true-stories" and "real life tales"; hence the influence of the movies on lads who run away to live their own lives; hence, partly, the effect of the sensational press on our civilization.

The theory of escape is involved in the recognition of romanticism as a growth through three stages—in any one of which an author's work may lie. The first comes with the overwhelming realization that the answer to life's problems is beyond the reach of the intellect, that the control of his destiny, his days, is beyond the individual's power. This is the period of the *Weltschmerz*, of Werther, of Brand: "the school of the drowned-in-tears". After the pain has lessened, when one considers life again, it seems that reality must be evil. Here Epicurus, Schopenhauer, Byron, Melville stand. Possibly God is not omnipotent, not omnibenevolent; perhaps there are only mechanical forces driving us on material ways; perhaps man is driftwood on the chancy currents of void. The pressure of such thoughts moves in the novels of Hardy. Others, in the spell of this vision, turn from life in a light-minded melancholy, hedonism over an abyss. Pater has preached this turning; Schnitzler has dallied along its bypaths, where many have whispered "I have been faithful to you, Cynara, in my fashion". The strongest, however, find their way through this dark journeying to a recognition that while a cold and cruel struggle for existence, a trial-and-error survival of the fittest (and devil take the hindmost), may characterize the outer world, there is an inner world where justice and love may reign, where man may seek his goal and come to triumph of the spirit. Thus Hawthorne sees sin and its penance leading to resurrection of the spirit in this life; and Dostoievsky feels that through suffering man finds love and thus achieves godhead. In more airily expressed confidence in the teeth of doubt, denying validity to all things, even frustration, by smiling at them: —what is man that his fate be deemed important?—Anatole France and Cabell imply the victory of spirit over matter.

Gertrude Stein says that "Romanticism is then when everything being alike everything is naturally simply different, and Romanticism".

Many further characteristics have been suggested as marking realism off from romance; most of them seem of limited application. Thus we are told that one stresses character, the other action; but Dickens has an abundance of action in his "realism", and Leatherstocking is but one of many clearly drawn characters in romance. What indeed, as Henry James observes, is character but the determination of incident; what incident, but the illustration of character? Both abound in the better books of either type.

Realism—another distinction is suggested by Bliss Perry: "is that which does not shrink from the commonplace and the unpleasant in its effort to depict things as they are". But the romanticist Cooper has much that is commonplace; the realist Jane Austen avoids the unpleasant; the romanticists Poe and Huysmans seem often to seek it out. These definitions, indeed, not only increase the confusion as to the meaning of the terms, but make the possibilities of application to authors often interchangeable.

A more positive statement is made by Clayton Hamilton, who affirms that "the difference between the methods is merely this:—the realist induces his theme from his details, and the romanticist deduces his details from his theme."

All men, he avers, are either inductive or deductive, and the type of fiction they write is inclined from that bent. This analogy comes from Ultima Thule: all fiction gathers different details to form its single impression; induction gathers *like* particulars to deduce a general rule. Deduction . . . Mr. Hamilton himself says that the "technical devices of argument lead even the novel with a purpose to fail of that purpose". Some psychologists agree with Mr. Hamilton's classification, insofar as he means that certain men achieve their creative synthesis through gradual development, whereas others sense the whole in an immediate vision and then apply the details. The two types are called by Ribot the reflective and the intuitive; but as most creation is regarded as a blending of the two processes, the distinction is of little present service. Perhaps a more general sorting of mankind is attained by Jung's division, of introvert and extravert; again, however, the applicability of the distinction is minimized by the subclasses that must at once be made, and nullified by the fact that either group may yield romantic or realist.

The earlier implication that romance is idealistic has also been pressed. But on the one hand, it may be asked what ideals are prominent, say in *Treasure Island,* or in the many romances that pander to popular taste; on the other hand, it may be urged that realistic literature, its observation of life promoting understanding hence sympathy, is even more accordant with man's ideals.

PAGAN AND PURITAN

Let both grow together until the harvest.

THE BIBLE.

THE terms realist and romantic, indeed, have come to have the convenience of labels, the validity of which few question. Yet one must always beware of the convenient word; too often it insinuates welcome sound into the place reserved for meaning; it allows the argument to flow undammed by a floundering for expression or a search for idea. The label may be either a substitute for thought, a mask that hides vacuity, or a disguise for thought, a mask under which every man imagines a different face.

Radical, liberal, conservative, reactionary, are terms occasionally applied in the fields of art, though clear enough to require but mention here. Only it should be noted that they sometimes overlap. Particularly in regard to the preservation of the intact form of a work of art, may the radical be conservative. Alain speaks of a cherished book as a breviary; Pater declares, of works that have been deemed great, that their forms "become now a weighty tradition as to the way in which things should or should not be done, are like a music, to which the intercourse of life proceeds—such a music as no one who had once caught its harmonies would willingly jar". "My friend Erskine", comments Professor Meiklejohn, "said to me: 'Keep the best of the past; be sure of that'. And I said 'Yes, and the best of the past is change, and change is life; life that does not change is death'." But John Erskine seems not to agree, protesting: "The immature in the world of art, as elsewhere, try to rearrange the universe, not knowing that it has been here for

some time and is set in its ways." Being set, then, seems to
him a virtue, despite Tennyson's warning lest one good order
should corrupt the world. (Though indeed Erskine's later
books seem more eager to upset!) There is also Falkland's
view: "When it is not necessary to change, it is necessary
not to change." But this pursuit is unending as fruitless.

A writer is sometimes, on the evidence of his work, referred to as an optimist or a pessimist. As applied to literature, what meaning have these terms? How may they be
assigned? It seems self-evident (defying *The Devil's Dictionary!*) that he who is an optimist in the sense that "God's
in His Heaven, all's right with the world" simply is no
longer an artist. Such a one may achieve the heights of
Pollyanna; but no one who is blind to the tremendous burden
of lust and greed out of fear that weighs upon mankind,
has the sensitivity art demands. Optimism and pessimism
alike recognize the suffering of today; they differ only in
their expectations for tomorrow. Hopeful of ultimate good,
the optimist is likely—one may think—to strive for its less
distant accomplishment: the satires, the utopias of art, are
products of his attitude. Yet Hardy has been called a melio-
rist. The pessimist, on the other hand, convinced of the
vanity of life, may find no value in writing and not write,
or may seek escape from the futile world to dally with fair
creatures of romance.

This ·superficial observation overlooks the fact that any
work of art is likely to be much more immediately determined. Not by the artist's degree of faith in a remote
redemption, but by a more personal and closer feeling: a
sense of isolation; its converse, a need of love; hatred;
scorn; joy in the deft fashioning; a masochistic pleasure in
the pain of creation; a deliberate scheme to win more of
life's comforts—who dare say what urge impelled the
writer? dare speak of the ultimate value of life as revealed

in art? Possibly, too, the thought that a genuine pessimist would commit suicide must check our vagrant fancies. The urge to self-perpetuation (which goes by many names un-caring) possesses man more fully than some may suspect; if one feels no ultimate value in the world, there is no value in creation, therefore—it might seem—no will to create. Nonetheless, the American writer who is most ruthless in his rending of the yashmaks of illusion weaves himself a new veil of the shreds, finding it advisable to follow the greater Frenchman who bids us recognize the illusions, yet accept them. For, after gathering the force of insuperable logic to demonstrate that all the values of life are devices spun by romance, the arch-God of illusion, for the com-fortable deception of man, Cabell turns upon this reasoned apodeixis with the bland (or despairing) cry: "Behold the miracle! still I believe life to be a personal reaction between myself and Omnipotence: I believe that what I do is some-how of importance"—adding that spawn of our wish is the knowledge we are being made into better stuff. While he may declare, however, that this acceptance of illusion is deliberate, the artist is impelled by incomprehensible forces deeper than faith itself, forces urging, perhaps, toward ages to come, indifferent alike to hope and its denial, moving man to that which he is to be. His obedience to this im-pulsion the artist justifies with such verbal subtleties as he can frame.

In the effort to show that the terms optimist and pessimist bear little significance to art, it was suggested that the hope-ful man might be spurred by his faith to view the world about him in realistic study, the hopeless to entertain him-self in romantic flight. For a penultimate query, what are these two faces of the coin of art, realism and romance? It is already obvious that no artist shows life as it is, that the worlds of both groups of writers are alike imaginary.

Yet the writer who thinks he withdraws from life to a wholly imaginative world is guilty of a false abstraction; with the possible, though at bottom doubtful, exceptions of da-da-ism and the tours de force of nonsense, no one accepts in literature that which he cannot in one way or another connect with what he thinks of as reality. Every writer, despite any claim advanced as to escape from reality, is tied to the principle that however far a bird may fly, it takes its tail along.

Perhaps another than the current distinction establishes a more valid difference. The realist portrays the individuals about him, distinct and possibly human personalities; he shows them involved in actions that are daily recognizable—and insofar as he succeeds in fully bodying forth the individual, he will have embodied a symbol of the universal. His Babbitt, his Sister Carrie, his Sidney Carton, satisfy in some measure man's delight in the generalization: the individual makes clear mankind. The romanticist in opposite journeying avoids everyday haunts and the folk who by ordinary frequent them; he fares with strange fellows through unfound lands; his figures may be but living attributes, feelings or ideals personified—and insofar as he succeeds in carrying his readers along, he will have captured in universal symbol the designs and the desires of the individual. His Aladdin, his Don Quixote, his Jim Hawkins, contain, for every man, that man himself. Man may view life through either end of the telescope of his fancy: the two aspects of his vision—distinct yet inseparable—are realism and romance.

The two terms are swept suavely aside by Henry Wells, who suggests a contrast between the materialists, close to the world of action, objectively minded, socially inclined, lovers of common sense, and the spiritualists, close to the world of dreams, subjectively minded, individual, "living in a universe no longer anthropocentric and so scorning common sense", and he adds: "Literary critics have often, it seems, grasped for this distinction with the use of the words realistic and romantic". In spite of Mr. Wells' telling the critics what they have been seeking, Walter Lippman finds his opposition, at least for America, between the village, which likes Longfellow, Holmes, Riley, Whittier; and the city, which prefers Whitman, Henry James, Huneker, Cabell. But such a contrast would probably be more accurately presented in the past tense: advertising, *The Saturday Evening Post*, radio, motion pictures, have largely broken the barriers; those planes on which "true stories" and the newspaper syndicated "comics" thrive, cut alike through urban and rural sections.

Several other possible attitudes of the literary artist have been mentioned with increasing frequency since psychanalysis widened the field of search. These may be conveniently presented by suggesting that every writer takes toward life, with varied change of ground, the post of an observer or the position of a doer. To one man life is a shifting he may watch; to another it is a combat in which he must engage. Worringer, remember, makes this duality the basis of his theory of beauty.

Within each of these groups there is a sharp division. To some observers, life is a stream that flows outside their ivory tower; as comfortably as may be they sit within, spectators of the ever-changing waters. They may be slightly amused by the spectacle, relieved of the gathering weight of boredom. They may be mischievous, like "the playboy on the curbstone of the world, throwing pebbles as life plods or races by". They may be scornful, indignant, contemptuous, bitter. They may enjoy the cakes of condescension, the sweet luxury of the flavoring, in famous (or you may make the preposition also prefix!) formula, of irony and pity.

They will always be unreal. For such spectators establish a false separation of subject and object. Let a performer in a three-ring circus continue his feats and at the same time watch the entire show. No man may view the whole of which he is a part. To see life steadily and see it whole is the unattainable end of the artist that, if attained, would destroy art by identifying it with life. The other type of observer is the seeker, the man who does not act because he does not know how to act, who studies life and records his observations, in the hope of finding a way now unknown to an equally unknown destination. In his ultimate hopes this type of observer is equally beyond the possibilities allowed by the current logic: he tries vainly to comprehend a whole of which he is a prisoned part. Yet he may be pictured as below the lofty tower, immersed in the stream of life, neither breasting nor crossing the current, but floating while his head is atilt to watch the banks, to judge depth and speed by the ripples, to catch a glimpse of those who swim nearby.

Those who swim the stream fall into two great groups we may denominate the puritan and the pagan. We can study the pagan close at hand, for every boy is a natural pagan. "Solon, Solon, you Greeks are all children", said the Egyptian priest; nor did the Hebrews often play; while the Romans (as frequently ourselves) made a serious business of their games. The pagan attitude toward life is of those who believe (or without consideration live according to the idea) that life is intended to be enjoyed, that every moment is new and therefore not to be judged by predetermined standards, that what you want to do is what you ought to do. The pagan seeks the savours, not the saviours, of life. The puritan is with us also, for in some degree maturity makes puritans of us all. The process of adjusting oneself to society demands the limiting of individual desires because of social needs, enforces the acceptance of outside standards. Many of these concepts are beaten (by parent or circumstance) into the boy, and become what is known as the conscience. The development of a conscience is what transforms the pagan into the puritan. The puritan may take what he desires from the goods of another, but he knows he is "doing wrong"; he is likely to send some kind of conscience money—spiritual or material; in endowing libraries or establishing censorship societies—to atone: the pagan, if he thinks of it, will think it a natural act. Conscience, the voice of the standards of the past, is thus the first mark of the puritan; the second is his regard for the future. Either in the next world or in this, the puritan expects, seeks, his reward—or punishment. For himself, or even unto the third and fourth generation. His acts are not the unpremeditated expression of a desire, but the calculated development of a plan. The puritan does not merely live, he lives for . . . something. Life has to him an ultimate purpose that probably no one can understand, but towards which everyone must urge. The puritan, indeed, is concerned not only with his own prospects; he feels himself as well his neighbors' keeper. To the pagan, life is immediate, the present all that matters; to the puritan, life is a process toward something "beyond life".[44]

Behind all these classifications, all the confusion of successive terms, one contrast may be intended. Puritan, seeker, realist, optimist: all seem to have sufficient concern in and hope for the future to make life's combat worthy of their weapons. To the extent to which they feel certain that life moves toward good they are deep in error (yet who knows that they are wrong?) for what man hath gained omniscience that he may speak surely? Insofar as they foresee a possibility of good, and work with its attainment as their goal, what logic can accuse them of greater sin than failure to see all? To them the trouble with the world is the unanswered "Why?" Pagan, spectator, romanticist, pessimist: all appear

unconcerned with the ultimate goals of life and seek to find
what nourishment they may in the present. Insofar as they
declare that life is futile, purposeless, unending evil, they
exceed their command of truth (yet who knows that their
words are lies?) for no man can withdraw from the world
to be its judge, nor speak without bias of personal implications concerning that which includes himself. Full understanding is prerequisite to—and then replaces—judgment.
To the extent to which they withhold from a struggle toward
unknown ends, what logic can accuse them of greater sin
than failure to see all? To them the trouble with the world
is the anxious "Whither?"

The pagan plays, the puritan plods. Which produces the
greater art? Shaw is an ardent puritan, Anatole France a fair
pagan. The two spirits, carried through the ages, come to
western civilization by respective ways of the Greek and the
Hebrew; the stern puritans of the old testament have carried
the day in the north (where probably Nordic roundheads
awaited their creed), and in England and especially America
the puritan rules. Southern Europe has kept freer of the
puritan advance; Christianity tempers the pagan impulses
of France and Italy and Spain, but despite Inquisitions and
Dreyfus Cases and other outbursts (which are indeed pagan
weapons in puritan hands), the pagan spirit has never been
more thoroughly subdued than in America today. [This may
be in large measure sprung from the greater dominance of
women in this land.] It may be pointed out that the puritan
comes after the naïve pagan in the history of mankind, but
it seems possible that after the self-concerned puritan the
cycle—or circle—moves onward toward the pagan again,
this time the highly trained, sophisticated, deeply feeling and
delighting pagan. The puritan is unquestionably the more
efficient in the present world; is he therefore a better being?
a greater artist? Art is, many puritans claim, a sport, a by-

product of life on its journey, a non-essential; is not therefore the pagan more naturally the artist? Or does life, twisting art to its purpose, render it puritan? The artist may be concerned or not, but his product to be considered art must yield an imaginative glimpse of the world, must light some phase of living, must feed our sympathetic understanding, must approach the puritan.

The sweep of our thought gathers the inertia of its momentum and bears us to farther speculation. In the progression of wordly affairs, the woman's natural bent is to the practical, to the ordering of life for its continuance, to the future; even after she learned to associate an act with its distant consequence woman has continued to undergo the pains of childbirth. Men erect their monuments of present pride; immediate victory, ever-present display, ever-triumph, is their desire. It is true that out of woman's forward-looking much instant pleasure grows, as out of man's unrealized desire may rise enforced delay and planning; essentially and by virtue of their physiological beings the male thinks of the present, the female considers the future. (Psychologists, when they used to list characteristics by sex, were careful to remind the reader that this by no means limits their possession to that sex; the assignment indicates, rather, a general tendency and is, like all generalizations, but a convenient falsehood.) Pagan literature, then, romance, is masculine; puritan literature, realism, is feminine.[45] And the two impulses of all creative work may be seen as the two impulses of all life, the opposing schools representing the eternal duellists in the unending struggle of life, endlessly imaginatively recorded in works of art.

THROUGH SYMBOLISM

Baa-baa, black wool, have you any sheep?
Yes sir, a pack-full, creep, mouse, creep.
Four-and-twenty little maids hanging out the pie,
Out jumped the honey-pot, Guy Fawkes, Guy!
Cross-latch, cross-latch, sit and spin the fire,
When the pie was opened the bird was in the brier!
WILLIAM BRIGHTY RANDS.

IF REALISM and romance be the infra-red and the ultra-violet of the classical light, naturalism would seem, to the eyes of some critics, to be the ultimate darkness. Though it appears an extension of the realistic attitude, naturalism has been critically associated with the other approach to art. It has been called "romanticism drawn to the dregs"; and Zola defending it declared, as we have seen, that it is the ordered, scientific development of "the initial, troubled period" that is romanticism. In its "antipathetic interpretation of life" these hostile critics discern even an unwitting humor, as Brunetière has discussed the "unconscious vaudevillian" in Huysmans: the trivial details presented exaggerating to burlesque "the banal ferocity of the real". In truth, naturalism is but the bludgeon of embattled realists.

As an historical development, the Romantic Period was in large measure a revolt of the individual against the social theories and mechanistic philosophy that bound him. Within the same years, however, science was also shifting its emphasis; the new era was one in which physics, which deals with general forces, was temporarily overcast by biology, which makes the individual the basis of its system. In it, however, that individual's being and growth are no less predetermined; he becomes, indeed, the prime puppet, the basic toy of elements and forces that moving in him move him. The naturalist, therefore, studies the individual—be it mantis or man—in its environment, as reacting inevitably and automatically as the stimulus dictates. "Two persons, a plank, and a passion", says Galsworthy, "is the charming province of the romantic or poetic dramatist . . . To deal austerely and naturalistically with the life of one's day is to find the human being so involved in his environment that he cannot be dissociated".

The only defense that the older romantics could find against this deadly attack rose in such remarks as Hugo's that "art is as natural as nature" (which was deftly turned so as to protect the most sordid presentations of romance's archenemies, in Anatole France's phrase: "Everything is in nature, and therefore natural"). The protests against the "photographic" copies of life increased, until many came to feel that presentations of the sort were informative, often interesting, but surely not art. Thus Matthew Arnold says of *Anna Karenina* that what it lost in art it gained in reality.

While naturalism was coming into being, however, its antidote was also being born. Baudelaire, not content with denying art to mere "slices of life", pointed out that line and color are actually not in nature, but in our perception, that nature is "a challenge to our slumbering faculties", not for our imitation, but as a field from which our imagination may take flight. The imagination, he insisted, moves in accord with the intelligence; together, experiencing through the senses, they seek the universal harmonies beyond. His sonnet *Correspondences* is the battle-flag of symbolism.[46]

> Nature is a temple whose living spires
> Send mingled words at times upon the air;
> Man journeys through a wood of symbols there
> That kindle as he goes with friendly fires.
> As long-drawn echoes in a far-off bond

> Blend in a deep and shadowed unity,
> Vast as the night and as vast clarity,
> Color and sound and fragrance correspond. . . .

That all things answer each to each is inevitable, he says, they "having always been expressed through such reciprocal analogies from the day when God declared the world a complex and indivisible whole".[47]

Within the object, the essence; behind the deed, the spirit. For, in the first place, the infinite, the universal, the spirit—all essences—can be expressed, can be sought, only in symbols; and, in the second, many persons are at one with Teufelsdröckh, who saw, "in the highest sensible phenomena, so far as Sense went, only fresh or faded raiment, yet ever, under this, a celestial essence thereby rendered visible". Every man has an individual approach to the deeper forces of life, by virtue of which the natural objects he beholds are images, are symbols, to him, of this inner universal welling. It is manifest, therefore, that the metaphors of the symbolist, packed as they are with meaning to himself, may be quite personal, approaching if not crossing the limits of the communicable. A precise picture, indeed, may be too definite to permit the mind to travel from its details to any essence; music, by virtue of its freedom from the concrete image, is hailed by many as closest to the capture of man's spirit. Nor do these artists seek so much to suggest to others what they themselves have felt, as to create for others motifs of suggestion. It has been felt, on the other hand, that complete capture of the externals is the surest way of making the spirit visible: Encolpius (in *The Satyricon*), visiting an art gallery, sees a work of Apelles "so correctly finisht to the life, you'd have sworn it an Image of the Soul too". (Friar Lubin offered the middle ages a formula whereby any meaning could be read into any words.) There is no measurable relationship between the clearness and exactness of an image presented as a symbol, and the understanding grasp of its essence a receptor will achieve. Indeed, the particular image awakened in the receptor may be held immaterial, if the various evocations—the stormcloud summoned to one's mind, the troubled paternal brow, to another's—are emotional, spiritual, essential equivalents. And it must be recognized that what is called obscurity may rise as well from the packed presence of meaning as from its absence; indeed, a passage called lucid may employ well-known words in a familiar order, be so accepted without thinking—and have no food for thought.

André Fontainas, it is true, defines the symbolist position thus:

The task of the artist is this: with full understanding, long study, and unflinching surety of his craft, to choose from the details and the whole of the object those aspects the balanced blending of which will correspond to the total effect desired, the expression sought; and will reconstruct for the eyes, the heart, and the brain, a synthesis and a harmony that will most naturally hold the highest philosophical implications.

But the inevitably individual growth of the symbols—tropes that incline to no visible sun—has, with the persistence of symbolism as perhaps the chief influence upon recent poetry, turned attention rather to the other great element in its expression: that harmony which the symbolists feel beyond the visible aspects of nature, they strive also to achieve as the ineffable current of the rhythm of their verse. "Poetry touches on music", says Baudelaire, "by a prosody whose roots plunge deeper into the human soul than any classical theory indicates."[*] Two generations later, Valéry declares "What has been baptized symbolism is, very simply, the determination of several groups of poets (otherwise enemies) to recapture their endowment from music. We are nourished on music, and our literary heads dream only of winning from language almost the same effects as pure sounds produce on

[*] See Note 23.

the nervous system."[48] Thus the two aspects—body and soul —of symbolism are sundered: the quest of sound associations and musical effects leads to the languageless syllabic sound poetry of Blümner and to such writing as that of Gertrude Stein; while the search of the endlessly unifying essence of all things continues in the spiritual themes of Maeterlinck, in the unanimism of Jules Romains, in the present increase of the religious element in German drama. Here, too, is the wedge that has split the notion of "pure poetry", which finds, all agree, its essence in an inner music, but which Valéry draws from mathematics, and his fellow-academician Bremond draws to prayer.

Most of the other important literary attitudes of recent years are also spun out of symbolism. In poetry the most fruitful of these has been Imagism, under the banner of which such poets as Amy Lowell, Richard Aldington, H.D. (Hilda Dolittle), and D. H. Lawrence have produced their work. The relationship is clearly shown in the Imagist manifesto, drawn up by F. S. Flint and Ezra Pound, in 1915:

1. An image is that which presents an intellectual and emotional complex in an instant of time. The instantaneous presentation of such an image gives the sense of liberation from limits of time and space and that sense of sudden growth which we experience in the presence of great art. It is better to produce one image in a lifetime than to produce voluminous works.

2. Treat the thing, that is, the image, directly, whether it is subjective or objective. Go in fear of abstractions, that is, use concrete images having the hardness as of cut-stone.

3. Use absolutely no word that does not contribute to the presentation. Use either no ornament or good ornament. Do not mop up the decorative images of one or two poets that you happen to admire.

4. Study Sappho, Catullus, Villon, Dante, Heine, and Gautier (sometimes), and Chaucer, especially.

5. Do not attempt philosophical or descriptive poetry.

6. Compose in sequence of the musical phrase, not in sequence of the metronome.

7. Study cadences, the finest that you can discover, preferably in a foreign language so that the meaning of words may be less likely to divert your attention from the movement. [No key is given for the determination of cadences in a strange tongue.] Saxon charms, Hebridean folk-songs, Dante, and the lyrics of Goethe and Shakespeare (apart from their meaning), are especially recommended.

8. Study the possibilities of verse-forms as the musician studies musical construction. The same laws govern, and you are bound by no others. In other words, the recognized metrical standards in English do not hold.

In a sense, indeed, Imagism may seem a revolt against the obscurities of the parent school; it seeks, says Amy Lowell, to "render particulars exactly and not deal in vague generalities, however magnificent and sonorous". While emphasizing the musical aspect of symbolism, in other words, it concerns itself less with an ultimate vision or underlying essence than with the immediate image. As a result, while it avoids the vagueness of mysticism, its frequent flitting—what Louis Untermeyer calls its "acrobatic leaping"—from object to object, its succession of juxtaposed pictures, sometimes forms a more material maze. Yet a poem may, as the first article of the manifesto proclaims, content itself with a single figure, such as another poet might offer amid a large development— as Ezra Pound's

In a Station of the Metro

The apparition of these faces in the crowd;
Petals on a wet, black bough.

The impulse toward the spirit behind this movement, though no longer explicit and avowed, still leads its expression into the quieter tones, the nuances of suggestion. A bolder front is reared by that *"reductio ad absurdum* of romanticism" which Tristan Tzara and Francis Picabia invented in 1916, and which they called (*ma-ma* being an emotional cry) after the first wakening expression of the intelligence. Da-da denies all values save the immediate intuition, inspiration, of the individual, who is therefore sole judge of his product—and, one may sometimes feel, alone in his enjoyment. "If you know what da-da means, you are not a da-da-ist!" Although Gide declared that "everything was done when the name was invented: all else is anti-climax", this seemingly preposterous, eccentric school represents a stage through which many of the important post-war writers of Europe have passed.[49]

[handwritten margin note: actually they found the word in a Czech dictionary.]

The da-da-ists apparently follow the method of dissociation of ideas, an even more active expression of which is the work of the superrealists (or as their leader says they might, following Beaudelaire and Gerard de Nerval, have called themselves, the supernaturalists), who have gone, at the pointing of symbolism, into the unconscious where, Freud teaches, the protective cloaks of consciousness are doffed, and true humanity revealed. Superrealism is defined, in André Breton's manifesto, as "a pure psychic automatism by which one sets about expressing, verbally or in writing, or in any other way, the true functioning of thought. The dictation of the thought, in the complete absence of any control exercised by the reason, beyond all concern for morality or æsthetics." Instructions are given for writing superrealistically: start with whatever comes to mind, write rapidly until hesitation shows that reason is intervening, then begin once more, ensuring automatic activity by having the next word begin with a letter chosen in advance.

> ". . . everything that begins with an M."
> "Why with an M?" said Alice.
> "Why not?" said the March Hare.
> Alice was silent.

This sounds weird, and so do some of the products [50]; but in its most intelligent aspect superrealism claims the best moments of all great writers, and identifies itself with that mysterious and compelling force we still call inspiration. We have been told on excellent authority that Coleridge walked the road to Xanadu entirely in the realm of the unconscious—and brought back *Kubla Khan*.

An earlier and more fruitful development of symbolism, especially, as we have known it in English, in the drama, is the activity called expressionism. This is related to Croce's theory of expression as art only to the extent that both are manifestations of the modern mind. Impressionism, a mode in the art of painting, seeks to present on canvas the impression, or something that will reproduce the impression, an object has made upon the artist. The work of art is a natural prolongation of the feeling. In truth, impressionism manifests itself in all the arts as a movement toward music; and "program music" is the return of that art upon itself in terms of poetry and painting. For music never has given, perhaps never can give, more than the feeling, the impression, wakened by an event: Debussy's *Garden in the Rain* presents no specific garden, but at most suggests the mood appropriate to such a place and season. Music has always been an abstract art, in this sense; the movement of the other arts, from the immediate object or event to the mood it has evoked in the artist, is called impressionism.[51] Expressionism, like all symbolism, seeks to go behind the immediate object or event, and capture its essence in a symbol. "A copy of the universe", says Rebecca West, "is not what is required of art: one of the damned thing is ample." The expressionist, as Kasimir Edschmid tells, moves on from that point: "The world is here, it would be absurd to reproduce it. The chief task of art is to penetrate the world before our eyes, to seek out its intrinsic essence, and create it anew." When an ordinary mortal, for example, is overwhelmed with bad news, the essence of his feeling, of the situation, may be an immediate and startling consciousness that the world spins on, regardless of the fates of the midges that infest its surface: in *The Adding Machine,* when Mr. Zero, after twenty-five years of faithful service, is surprised with word that he is discharged, the part of the stage on which he stands begins to revolve at a dizzying pace. The program of expressionism, as set down by Otto zur Linde in 1911, reveals its symbolist origin: it calls upon the artist to deduce the universe from his own ego. Being equally subjective in its endeavor to attain the impersonal essence, it may be even more obscure, for it presses more boldly along the external ways it takes, often to the point, says Pfister, "of unrecognizability or of suppression of all external reality"—in quest of the inner truth.

It is, however, impossible to consider expressionism apart from the period that gave it being: the desire of a new order is manifest in its themes, especially that of conflict between father and son, which occurs in the first expressionist drama, Sorge's *The Beggar,* written in 1912, and in many more [52]; this need of building anew is recognizable also in the syntax and the diction: the language to be disintegrated and recreated (as later with the proponents of the "revolution of the word"); and the disjunctive speed of modern life, the desire for compression, is reflected in the "headline" or "telegram" style of the dialogue, which may, as in Carl Sternheim and Georg Kaiser—as excessively in August Schramm's *Forces*—consist largely of monosyllabic exclamations that gestures and action must enlarge.

An expressionist anthology, *The Twilight of Man (Menscheitsdämmerung)* was issued in Berlin in 1920; the influence of the movement on dramatic forms, especially in combination with monodrama, has been widespread, and widely noted. The superrealists for some time issued a monthly magazine, and among those who have subscribed to their doctrine are young writers—Aragon, Delteil, Eluard, Soupault, Vitrac—internationally known. Da-da, for its time, ran through every field of literature. Although these attitudes developed more fully and more freely among continental authors than in English, they have had no little effect upon the younger writers in our tongue. They are, furthermore, signs of the persistence of the quest of the symbolists, which, indeed, many will advance as the eternal goal of the artist: the revealing of an ultimate and spiritual unity within the immediate and manifest variety of the event that, through this revelation and binding harmony, becomes the work of art.

* * * * * * * *

Underlying all these movements seem to flow two withdrawals, in opposite directions, from the discerned or imagined evils of preceding works. In rebellion against the rules of neo-classicism, though in a sense with "the classic" as their mean, romanticism and realism had similarly moved to their extremes. Despite contrary characteristics often overemphasized, these two spirits are alike in their rebellion against form, in their "return to nature", and in their focussing attention on the individual. To the romanticist, nature was an ideal background to be recovered, to be caught with an intimate, personal rapture; form was forever unique with the always peculiar event; and the individual was all-important, his emotions eternally significant for the recording, his one desire to be himself, self-expressing, self-revealing, free. To Shelley, his bleeding on the thorns of life is fit theme for a great poem; Alfred de Musset records his weeping, his crying upon all spirits for aid; confession becomes the literary vogue. The realist, equally impatient of, perhaps alarmed by, the neo-classical discipline, sought freedom—like the medieval friar, like the French eighteenth-century libertines

—through the opposite channel of complete material submission: to him, nature is the realm of absolute, mechanical law; form, the infinitely varied surface of the universe whereon grim forces drive; and the individual of interest (as I have said) as the prime puppet, the laboratory unit, God's guinea-pig (though deity is supplanted by drift) in the midst of experiments too complicated for human measure or control.

Through the centuries, the classical attitude has seen in art a resolution of the antinomies of the philosopher: the one and the many, the body and the spirit, the world and I. But from the inner unity to the surface variety emphasis has constantly swayed. The period that was marked by the romantic and the realist rebellions had laid stress upon externals, upon the manifest crowding incidents of life, upon physical details and human portraiture, upon the unending variety of particular events—if upon universals, universal laws of form. From these, by the swift road of diabolism there was return to the inner unity of the spirit; through the flesh men sought the soul; the instant event was seen as the manifestation of an essence, of an underlying harmonious tenor of all things. The recent recurrence of the stress upon this aspect of the classical conception came to be known as symbolism. Symbolism declares that art must seize things "in their vital principle"[53]; not examining this but uniting with it, becoming aware of its trajectory (as Bergson puts it) by "fusing yourself into the point that describes it and taking its movement"; this being accomplished not intellectually but rather by a withdrawal from the intelligence to intuition, to a "state of pure love". Yet, as in classicism, the one and the many are harmonized; symbolism linking the object, as its sign, with the essence.

So today, in a sense with symbolism as their mean, are two recoilings, this time from the emphasis on the individual. In both we find the responding strain to the triune stress of the romanticist and the realist: a renewed quest of a more objective form, set by considerations outside the personal; an effort to divorce the human from the natural, the animal; and a desire to pull the individual down from his pedestal, and to set the one subservient to the whole. The Shelleys of today are self-conscious, self-critical; ironic and cynical toward themselves, and all others, rather than expose themselves to others' irony and cynicism—if indeed they are not biophysicists instead of poets. But in close contrast to romanticism stirs a broad, unchristened tide by a few called ultraism; while in loud and sharp attack upon realism rears the mace-armed giant that has named itself the new humanism.

Ultraism (by criss-cross from the earlier pair) seeks to escape the individual by moving toward the denial of the human. As a phase of symbolism, it seeks beneath every particular for the universal; but it tends, as in expressionism, to renounce the deed for the spirit. Individuals lapse to types: *Mr. Zero*, "a Man, a Woman," "the earth-Mother", the great god Brown whose name is Man: events are lost in essences. The futurist manifesto declares: "The movement we wish to project upon the canvas will no longer be a fixed moment of the universal dynamics; it will be simply the dynamic feeling itself". Some paintings of Picasso and others, some poems, have sought to break completely from the recognizable particular, to achieve the absolute abstraction; but few have ventured quite that far toward the *reductio* of all extremes. More make us recognize that it is not inability that produces the distortions of persons and objects in present-day paintings, and their many aberrations from former modes, nor incompetence that has made the "new" poetry, the "new" novel, the "new" theatre, so strikingly different from the old; they demand that we grow aware of a

movement toward a more objective, more emotionless world
(Debussy after Wagner; after Baudelaire, Mallarmé) whose
creators beat upon the human to strip it of its personality,
leaving only the all-human, which, being everyman's, is particularly no man's. Reality is wrenched to style, substance
polished away to form.[54] On this dehumanizing quest, many,
from Mallarmé to T. S. Eliot, insist that neither in creating
nor in contemplating works of art is emotion relevant—remember Eliot's characterization of the poet as catalytic agent.
Thus the ultraist, as far as he dares, would fend all human
quality from art.

As a restorative after many turbulent years, the voice of
humanism has again been raised, crying, as in the cinque-
cento, that the proper study of mankind is man. Just as the
one term nature, however, was used by Dryden, by Hugo,
by Zola, in diverse, even contradictory, connotations, so the
"new humanism" becomes the shibboleth of every sect. A
book with that title, by Leon Samson (following, it is true,
the tendency away from the individual) is devoted to a strong
attack upon private property. The Rev. Charles Francis
Potter has founded the *First Humanist Church* in New York
City, and has given his disciples the testament of that faith.
In its aspects as a point of view widely proclaimed and here
relevant, humanism removes man from nature by positing
three levels of existence, natural (animal), human, and
divine, and crying out upon both naturalism, which subjects
man to the laws that govern things, and humanitarianism,
which by aiming at (an unattainable) perfection would
make men gods. Here on the central plane man marches,
limited but endowed beyond things natural in that he has
free will [55] to choose his way, and standards (the will
triumphing over emotion and intellect, centered upon the
"higher immediacy" akin to the divine purpose, as opposed
to the "lower immediacy" of the individual desire) to point

his direction. This formulation of Irving Babbitt becomes with some of his disciples (as gathered in essays collected by Norman Foerster) a plea for the past—"we must seek aid in more venerable traditions, carefully winnowed, which have won the unchanging respect of the ages"—and a discarding of the methods and the results of science, an anti-intellectualism, that leads Henry Seidel Canby, who deems himself a more tolerant humanist, to protest that from their scheme

out goes everything which directly or indirectly, in any way whatsoever, implies or includes the fraction of an idea that there is more to be learned of the mystery of the universe than has been vouchsafed to us already in those laws unwritten in the heavens, the suggestion that by experiment with matter any true knowledge may be had of intellectual man, and the hope that by extensions of feeling man and man, in a nature which interpenetrates them, can come closer to understanding . . . They condemn and rightly the bestiality of mass civilization without admitting that the instruments of precision which made our mass prosperity possible may conceivably be of use in the reaction against its excesses.

The bland dualism of higher and lower "immediacy" seems hardly a touchstone amid the complex and subtle interrelations we are but beginning to recognize, and deliberately counters the current doctrine of continuity; but the humanists are outspoken in this braving: their central assumption, says Mr. Foerster, is that of

a dualism of man and nature, as opposed to the monism assumed by naturalism . . . In the motion picture of reality that science offers there are no values, but only quantitative measurements of force, mass, etc. Yet values are in fact the main concern of man, the perennial object of his ardent striving. . . . Humanism assumes the freedom of the will to conform to a standard of values.

Whence this standard is to be drawn presents now no simpler problem, for the humanists turn at this juncture either to religion or to intuition—an "inner check, co-existent and co-

operative with nature, but outside and essentially irreconcilable to it"; and neither criterion contents their monistic foes;
but both their alternatives, positing a standard, require the
imposition of restraints, and imply something inter-personal,
all-human, that controls the individual, that absorbs the one
into the whole.

Two great French writers of today may be instanced, to
give these thoughts direction. Valéry appears as the poet of
polish, the intellectual dealer in ideas: "I can think only with
disgust", he says, "of all the ideas and all the feelings engendered or roused in man but by his ills, but by his fears,
his hopes, his terrors; and not freely by his pure observations
of things and in himself." Gide is concerned in his novels
only with acts and thoughts that do rise from the viscera,
with the extension and intensity of feeling, with the problems
of morality in the modern world.

Whether by the one extreme of superrealism we strike
for inspiration to the unconscious and therefore to the fundamental, universal impulses that are greater than individual
efforts at their modification—with ultraism escaping from
ourselves to the essence of man-ness, from aught specific to
the pervasive generic; or by the other extreme of humanism
we accept religious or "intuitive" (divinely given, for the
humanist rejects the evolutionary concept of conscience)
checks upon the individual in the interest of mankind,* and
so we transcend the personal: these surging movements
sound a cautioning call, that the machine is not the single
source of power, that no person, and no age, can exist without
those that have come before; and that the aim of the
classicist, to "imitate" the unity and variety of nature, must
not in a surface representation lose sight of the goal of the
symbolist, within the substantive variety to light the tran-
scendent unity, to disclose within the individual that extension to the universal for which man in many fields searches,

* in practice of the new humanists, in the interests of those who
may check their acquisitiveness, having acquired almost
everything material.

and comes perhaps nearest to finding in the work of art.

The central problem of the Greek thinkers lay in the reconciliation of the one and the many, the dichotomies of life and death, matter and essence, particular and universal, the antinomies of the finite and the infinite, freedom and necessity, beginning and endlessness. As an imitation of life, every work of art therefore knits into one concordant pattern many aspects of being, interweaves unity and variety. Emphasis may be laid on either element of this duality; but through the ages it has been fused in art.

And through the ages shifting emphasis has created the rival schools. In the truly classical, work "good all through", the one and the many are balanced, the diverse manifestations of the natural world and the single spirit within, the noumenon of all phenomena. But now the one essence, now the many events, grow important in the artist's eyes, and further schools are born.

Realism and romanticism mark the two offshoots of emphasis on the variety, on the individual manifestation. The romantic sees the individual driving; the realist sees the individual drawn. Such contrasted (yet complementary) emphases upon the particular seem to rise when the classical sense of an underlying spirit, which the individual event but symbolizes, has been warped to a proclamation of universals in the form of types and laws, each work being labeled "after its kind" and held to conformity. Remember the contrasted comments of Reynolds and Blake. It is such an aspect, the neo-classical, that in England marked the epoch of nature methodized, the age of politeness and good sense—

Content to dwell in decencies forever,—

of decorum ubiquitous. It is such a development that in France set forth the era of the precious, the days of refinement and good taste,

When even "I hate you!" was tenderly breathed,—

of propriety everywhere. (In like wise, the humanists brought medieval allegory from spirit to flesh, abandoning the heights of theology in flights of rhetoric.)

But upon the heels of the romantic and realist rebellion against so vapid an assertion of the classical unity, a more vital urge toward the spirit makes itself felt. From Shelley and Zola the world of art turned to Baudelaire, who sees the body as the pathway to the soul. Within the event writers probe for its meaning, its essence; and in the school of symbolism the classical duality is once more approached. As swift, however, is the double recoil. Ultraism seeks to find the essence of things by doffing the individual, by stripping the core of an experience of its external wrappings. An analysis of Joyce's *Work In Progress* declares that "to uncover the essential identity of everything human under the variety of external phenomena is the basic point". And what ultraism seeks by means of the non-personal, humanism strives after through the super-personal, that inner check which is no man's because it is all men's, humanity's. The editor of the most challenging of the experimental magazines states:

In the essay which *transition* is publishing in this issue, an epochal step forward has been made. Not only does the unconscious contain the repressed elements of the personal life of the creator, says Dr. Jung, but it is also the vessel containing ingredients that relate him to the collective life of humanity.

Thus, by an epochal forward movement, our most radical art flames toward the fusion of the one and the many that is the classical goal. From this, as we view them, four great lines of rebellion stream: two that emphasize the object, the individual, two that emphasize the essence, the universal; in each of these groups, one stresses natural phenomena or laws, one elevates human beings or mankind. When events order, realism shows the victims, romanticism the heroes. When the essence reigns, humanism sets anthropomorphic (therefore moral) standards, ultraism seeks the bare genera of things. The romantic and the humanist, concerned with man, tend (despite Keats) to link the beautiful with the good; the ultraist and the realist, intent on things, bind rather the beautiful with the true: whatever the alliance of those who give theory voice, the work of art creates the trinity. For always these are turbulent stormings, with spindrift wake of beauty, it may be, but clouded from the concordant calm, the harmonious sun, of the eternal classical mean in works of art. And—faint echo of the fourfold sense the middle ages sought, weaving the classics into allegory— the symbolist strives, says Mallarmé, to make every term "a plastic image, the expression of a thought, the stir of a feeling, and the symbol of a philosophy": object and essence, the view and the vision.

WRITERS AND READERS

And I shall shortly be with them that rest.
JOHN MILTON.

HAVING classified works of art in various ways, it seems but fair to subject their creators, and their receptors, to a similar categorizing. A division at once suggests itself between the man that has a story to tell, and takes the words for its telling, and the man that quickens to the feel of words, the use of the language, the challenge of expression, and finds a tale to clothe with his delight. Close to this distinction is that suggested by T. S. Eliot's picture of Donne as "constantly finding an object which shall be adequate to his feelings", while Lancelot Andrewes "is wholly absorbed in the object and therefore responds with the adequate emotion".

The ages of poetry suggested by Peacock form the basis of another natural division of writers. There are, first, the inventors of a process or a mode, the men, usually lost in the mists of prehistory, who blazed the trails. The bards before Homer; the troubadours; shall we say Æsop, and Richardson, and Dujardin? There follow these the masters, of the golden ages, who often invent—every work of art is an invention—but who also assimilate and coördinate the earlier inventions, bending and blending them into appropriate service. The diluters come next, lowering the intensity of the masters as they copy the modes but cannot infuse the spirit. After these—here Ezra Pound suggests a divergent grouping —may be placed the minor writers, Wyatt, Donne, De Quincey, Hunt, who present acceptably the style of a period; then the belles-lettrists, who bring a particular mode to a very high development: Longus, Prevost, Pater; finally—

Gongora, Macpherson—the starters of crazes. "The point is", Pound concludes, "that if a man knows the facts about the first two categories, he can evaluate almost any unfamiliar book at first sight. I mean he can form a just estimate of its worth, and see how and where it belongs in this schema." Unfortunately for such "evaluators", the first two categories are filled less with works of art than with disputation; also, "knowing the facts" suggests ability to prophesy how these groups themselves will alter: but what contemporary shall say whether a new work (such as *Ulysses*) is a valid invention or the impetus to a craze?

It is easier to consider writers in respect to the type of reader to whom their work appeals, though it should be observed that this "appeal" may not be deliberate. However implicit in all art the hope of communication may be, and however, once his work is done, the artist may desire recognition, during the actual process of creation the urge to expression, the concerns of the craft, the intensity of the need to find form, to give voice to the inner turbulence, move in the artist to a personal satisfaction. But with the work, the reader has then to do. Between Poe and Whitman, the two well-springs of modern poetry, the contrast is vivid; they may be named aristocrat and democrat. The aristocrat, if he considers his readers at all, assumes in them a culture, a depth of sensitivity, a width of reading, a breadth of understanding, that will respond to delicate suggestion, subtle allusion, complex musical rhythm, deft play of verbal and sensuous device, and, on occasion, profundity of thought. Yet these writers, at their best, are profound in clear terms, and not in terms obscure. "Thus difficult things become easy in their turn; and they grow charming as they go deep, and into these sombre caverns, entered but of late, is brought the pure and ancient clarity of ages less informed but more luminous than our own." Baudelaire, Browning, Meredith, T. S. Eliot, find readers of this aristocracy. On the other hand are those whose work, of deliberate policy or because of the author's nature, appeals more widely. Tolstoi, we have said, maintained that the simple and pious peasant is the judge of art; Milton hoped his work would "fit audience find, though few"; Baudelaire compared the public, relative to genius, to a watch that's running down; of his poems he declared "This book is not written for my mistresses, my daughters, or my sisters, nor for the wives, the daughters, or the sisters of my neighbors". It has been suggested that the aristocrat, in reader and writer, is readiest to face harsh reality, to find material for art, or for enjoyment, in sordid incident or banal surroundings. The democrat, like the nouveau riche, rather avoids reference to such things, or sugars them with sentimentality. When the "democrat" rises in cultural or literary level, he often bears with him a vague uneasiness as to his background and his breeding. "It is notorious", says the dramatic critic of *The New York Times,* "that the vulgarest people have the deepest sense of the proprieties and that the most cultivated, like the well-born lady in *The Spoils of Peynton,* plume themselves on their hearty digestions. 'I'm quite coarse, thank God!' she said." There is food for present thought in the adage that a gentleman is equally at home with a beggar and a king, sets townsman and tramp alike at ease. Similarly, during the world war, complaint about "K. P." seemed to come most bitterly from those who were equally burdened with manual work outside the army; others more frequently could take it as a lark, as "part of the game". To the aristocrat, life is somewhat of a game, in which his play must, as the English put it, be "cricket".

Another development of this attitude is in Joubert's remark

that those who are simple by nature and estate have little liking for simplicity in the arts, it holds too little surprise: "hence the great and the noble have better literary taste".

"Tam o'Shanter or *The Jolly Beggars"*, says E. E. Kellett, "will be preferred to *The Cotter's Saturday Night,* and *Don Juan* to *Childe Harold,* only by critics with some touch of the man of the world in them." One of the early literary dictators of democratic America, Joseph Dennie, was emphatic in his pronouncement: "So far from courting the mob, our editors should treat the herd of swine and their feeders with the most ineffable contempt, and be satisfied with the general applause of scholars and gentlemen, men of honour and cavaliers". In 1838, James Fenimore Cooper was more analytical:

The tendency of democracies is, in all things, to mediocrity, since the tastes, knowledge, and principles of the majority form the tribunal of appeal. This circumstance, while it certainly serves to elevate the average qualities of a nation, renders the introduction of a high standard difficult. Thus do we find in literature, the arts, architecture, and in all acquired knowledge, a tendency in America to gravitate toward a common center in this as in other things; lending a value and estimation to mediocrity that are not elsewhere given.

A defense of such mediocrity, on the other hand, is urged by James Douglas:

Let us not despise the primers of poetry. They may lead the people into the promised land by way of the wilderness. I believe that every lover of poetry goes through an evolution in taste. It is a long way from Longfellow to the great poets, but it is at least a way. In his verse there is a weak dilution of poetry, but even diluted poetry is good for poetic babies. . . . I submit that the tenth-rate poets are useful as sign-posts of the poetic highway. They point the way to the pilgrims. The lover of Longfellow may hew his way to the high bards who make the high songs. An attempt to murder Longfellow is like an attempt to murder the alphabet.

Some may more cynically suggest such poets have committed suicide.

The drama, of all the literary arts, most inevitably depends on popular appeal; hence some critics have tended to consider it the most pandering of the arts. This attitude is put into the mouth of one of the characters of Henry James; Mr. Nash in *The Tragic Muse* speaks of

the essentially brutal nature of the modern audience . . . the *omnium gatherum* of the population of a big commercial city at the hour of the day when their taste is at its lowest, flocking out of hideous hotels and restaurants, gorged with food, stultified with buying and selling and with all the other sordid preoccupations of the age, squeezed together in a sweltering mass, disappointed in their seats, timing the author, timing the actor, wishing to get their money back on the spot—all before eleven o'clock. Fancy putting anything exquisite before such a tribunal as that! There's not even a question of it. The dramatist wouldn't if he could, and in nine cases out of ten couldn't if he would. He has to make the basest concessions. One of his principal canons is that he must enable his spectators to catch the suburban trains, which stop at 11.30. What would you think of any other artist—the painter or the novelist—whose governing forces should be the dinner and the suburban trains? . . . What can you do with a character, with an idea, with a feeling, between dinner and the suburban trains?

The answer, of course, is: the greater the marvel that it has been done! The conscious exaggeration of James' presentation, however—and the efforts of others to keep the great drama of the Greeks, and Elizabethan, and French classical, drama, out of the argument, by indicating that the audience for these was drawn from the aristocracy (though still other critics suggest the contemporary success of Shakespeare as compared to Jonson as proof that the instinct of the crowd is sound)—serve but to emphasize that there are several levels of receptor for whom one may write. There is a persisting tendency to elevate the general taste as final judge, and therefore standard, of art, counterbalancing the ever advanced claim that the cultured alone can truly esteem a work. Thus, in our day, Art Young bends up from his drawings to drawl: "I suspect there are people who would not read *Paradise Lost* because Milton got only three pounds for it"; and Edwin Muir affirms that "in the modern world, the power most solidly obnoxious to the artist is not the public but the intelligentsia". It has already been suggested, however, that almost every man is a "highbrow" to some other less fortunate or less aggressive soul; and, aspiration being by no means an uncommon trait, many a person seeks to rise by pretending to like, trying to like—and ultimately liking—what those just above, his chosen mentors, have admired. Thus the vogue works its way like rainwater down the receptive strata; and often when a storm has long left the topsoil dry, deep-rooted and far-sprung of it new glorious plants will rise.*

The earlier statement that, when a work is bad, either the communication is defective or the matter communicated is of no worth, must, then, be modified by the recognition that one man's Robert W. Service is another man's e. e. cummings. The present state of the drama suggests a somewhat different division from others that have been made; for on our stage we may behold plays of yesterday, plays of today, and plays of tomorrow—plays, that is, which appeal (whatever his physical age) to the mental and moral child, adolescent, and adult.

The plays of yesterday are likely to be the season's successes, for they strike to the raw-boned, crude emotions that maturity may supplement and subdue, but not destroy. An intelligent playgoer can, in proper mood, be entertained by such plays as *The Whip* or *Abie's Irish Rose,* which are the normal diet for childish minds, for those who think with

* See page 27f., also Note 10.

their feelings. The child sees no grays; to him everything is black or white. But this state of affairs does not disturb the child; he likes his villains black; he would not understand and would detest a half-hearted criminal; he enjoys hissing at least as much as he does cheering. The adolescent sees the world as black and white, but is greatly troubled at the spectacle. He feels the urge of the reformer; he would make all blacks white, would have his villains repentant—and forgiven. It is the adolescent, the youth (of whatever physical age) that leads all revolutions. The mature man has discovered that there are no such things in character (or in nature) as pure light and absolute darkness; what seems so is but one or another shade of gray. "Never hit anyone in cold blood", says Bernard Shaw, knowing that maturity keeps cool. The child also, though otherwise, is obedient of this injunction; but the adolescent, even though he may be sincere in the remark "This hurts me more than it does you", believes in punishment for the offender's good.[56]

Plays of today, when well constructed, are often commercial successes, though rarely with the long runs of the plays of yesterday. The child insists on the happy ending, the youth desires it, the adult wants what fits the theme. But the child and the man are alike impatient of the moral. The youth wants to better the world; the child hasn't begun to think of such a task; the adult has given it up. Childhood makes waking dreams of its ultimate personal grandeur; youth spreads its dreams into a structure that shall shelter the world; age draws its dreams into a hut that may keep it warm. Maturity has no time for such dreaming, being too busy with life. (Hence, in truth, the artist must always, in his adult mind, be able to recapture the adolescent or the child—which indeed snares most of us too often.) Whatever the child or the mature man finds in his way, he seeks without qualms to destroy. Youth either tries to win it over, or finds pious phrases to justify the destruction (phrases the cynical adult may fashion to delude others, not himself): of god, of liberty. The child fights because he hates, the adult when he cannot secure what he desires in any easier way, the youth to make the world safe for democracy. In the theatre, beyond the plays that appeal to the childhood of our intelligence and will, there is a great body of dramas, from O. Henry's *Alias Jimmy Valentine* to O'Neill's *Anna Christie,* that play upon the impulses and powers of youth.

Maturity of mind and will are rare in life; naturally, they are no more prominent in the drama. There are various attitudes toward the world possible to the adult: none of them includes the imposing of moral judgments. The most obviously mature plays, therefore, are tragedies; and the intellectual temper of an age may be measured in terms of what it has considered tragic. To Shakespeare, for instance, tragedy always involves the violation of a social law, of loyalty to family or to king. The dramatists of the industrial era in every land draw their tragedy from the pressure of the forces of life, the mechanizing influences of a capitalistic order, upon the impulses of the individual. Whether it be in Galsworthy's *Justice,* a well-made play of the old type, or in Kaiser's *From Morn to Midnight,* an ingenious drama of the new, the implacable forces of society that swirl around money, the need of it, the fierceness with which we clutch it, the fever and display with which we spend it, the urging power it bestows, the hatred with which we attack those who would seize it, are vividly shown. Other aspects of the conflict imposed upon individuals in the world today are studied in countless dramas. Social condemnation or approval, moral judgments, of course appear in these plays; but they are those of the period and the people pictured, not necessarily those of the playwright. The dramatist records, he does not embrace, them.[57] The hero dies not because the author wants virtue (or vice) to triumph, or because he thinks the audience may—indeed, we are usually in sympathy with the victim: but because some dominant force in the life around the main figure inevitably moves him to that end.

Another attitude possible to the mature is the complete avoidance of moral issues, of social problems. The adult who, because of temperament or economic stress, is a direct participant in life, will strive to analyze the forces that urge in society and in the individual, and will, if he be a dramatist, throw them in opposition on the stage, in problem play or tragedy. But some more favored ones are financially free from concern, or temperamentally (as, at moments, all may be) less players than spectators of the human comedy: Anatole France, for his stay in the ivory tower; Oscar Wilde, as in *The Importance of Being Earnest*, when he was not muddled—and muddied—with morality. Manifestly, these persons move in the domain of high comedy. Recent work by Hungarian playwrights displays both types of mature mind: Molnar in *The Goat Song* symbolizes the fundamental conflict between the individual and the conventional, and in *The Glass Slipper* portrays a single aspect of that duel in more realistic fray; and Lothar in *The Werewolf*, Sil-Vara in *Caprice*, scintillate along the surface of life, with no concern—at least no regard—for the terrors of its deeps.

High comedy, and such comic opera as that of Gilbert and Sullivan, which pays attention to the forces of society only to mock them, to turn them into topsy-turvy burlesque, are the lighter aspect of the stir of the mature mind that in more sober mood turns to the problem play and the tragedy. The term "problem play" is widely inclusive; it really marks a growing toward maturity, and villainous villains and stalwart heroes may stalk in it; moral judgments, and the final adjustment of happy ending, may leer; in its best manifestations it moves impartially toward the close implicit in its opening conditions. It may not then be a play of wholly adult appeal; few plays, indeed, are, and, like Joyce's *Exiles,* they then seem cold; for the greatest writers, knowing of self-knowledge (or bound by the fact) that the child and the adolescent walk within the man, make three-fold appeal. They then have attained the serious play of tomorrow, the tragedy, wherein the conflicts inherent in life, in the existence of the one and the many—society and the individual—are bravely traced, wherever their urgings may send, and the noblest child of the drama is born. Aristotle felt that he who knew tragedy knew the other arts; its basic problem—of the one and the many: unity in variety—is that which is resolved in each success of every artist; and through its levels the various types of receptor may be discerned. In all of these, a basic intuitive response to a work flashes—or fails—for reasons beyond our present ken: we can say no more than that wide, sympathetic reading, and considerate thought, increase the sensitivity, and the rounded stimulation, and the delight, of the mature mind contemplative of the work of art.

NOTES

When found, make a note of.

CHARLES DICKENS.

NOTES

(1) There are more practical, i.e. monetary, ways in which an author may profit by criticism. In these days of the book-of-the-month organizations, the brief description of the chosen book, backed by the critical authority of the selection committee, may mean a sale of seventy-five thousand copies. Many individual journalists have large followings; and booksellers have compiled statistics as to the number of sales that follow a recommendation by this or that reviewer, or even a casual mention in Soandso's gossip column. A century ago, the articles in the great reviews stimulated considerable reading, and even hostile reviews—as in the case of Wilson's notorious damning of Wordsworth, as with the reception of *Don Juan*—might serve to launch a book or an author on the sea of public attention.

(2) Arnold wisely wrote, in a letter to his mother: "I would far rather have it said how delightful and interesting a man was Joubert than how brilliant my article is. . . . One can only get oneself really accepted by men by making oneself forgotten in the people and doctrines one recommends . . . I have felt how necessary it was to keep down many and many sharp and telling things that rise to one's lips, and which one would gladly utter if one's object was to show one's own abilities."

Not the critic only, but many another writer as well, must recognize, then reject, an obstrusive cleverness. Often indeed the censor is not on guard; when E. A. Robinson pictures Seneca Sprague's sparse hair—

> an atoll, as it were,
> Circling a smooth lagoon of indignation—

one is tempted to retort that though he now has an atoll of hair, he soon will have no hair at all . . . Such sentences should be given only when the punishment fits the crime.

(3) Some things of practical value to reviewers may be said; first, about faults in the writing. The tone of the review, its degree of personal inflection, as stressed by the use of "I", "one", or the editorial "we", is likely to be determined by the custom of

453

the paper. But subtler influences play upon the reviewer. The reputation of the author usually far exceeds his own—however he hopes to surpass it soon; he must guard alike against the tendency to kowtow and the desire to rebel. If the author of the book chance to be unknown, there are again the devil and the deep sea he ·must avoid: the assumption that in these days of wide publicity anything unknown is thereby known unworthy, and the over-enthusiastic praise likely to result from finding beauty in hidden places. If, in addition, the reviewer be a writer of books, he may have an honest inability to tolerate novels or poems of a type different from his own, as we have recently seen among writers of metrical or of free verse; or he may labor under an unrecognized jealousy of others of his own type. The pressure of publishers, through advertising, or letters requesting "prompt reviews", is a less honorable though direct influence everyone who has done much reviewing is likely to have felt, or heard of in many a rumored story. Even so apparently independent a matter as prior reviews may bend the writer, either toward encomiums of a book all seem to hailing, or toward a refusal to echo the bays and the brays of the throng.

Another large group of faults may rise from the reviewer's impulse to display his thoroughness, or his wit. If he is considering a translation, he may feel it incumbent upon him to indicate his knowledge of the original; the natural way to do this is to find fault with the rendering; space taken for this may then be justified by calling these errors typical. In the fields of non-fiction, there is a similar tendency for the reviewer-as-expert to overstress errors in details. The desire to display one's wit often leads to a disregard of the purpose of a review, as when one writer says: "Mr. Cummings is not a writer; he is a stage other writers go through. When will the young men learn this obscurity business is out of style?"—of which the taste is matched by the expression, and the idea.* Somewhat the same impulse leads to the indiscriminate application of superlatives; many reviewers phrase their comments in the hope of being quoted in publishers' advertising; a few of our most prominent editors of "literary sections" owe their rise to this practice. In 1928, according to the pages of one literary weekly, there were one hundred and forty-three "best" novels of the year, forty-five "best" of the decade, and twenty-one "best" of the age. Not only do readers come to allow

* See, also, Note 2

for this exaggeration, but the dithyrambic reviewer finds his terms exhausted when the really great arrives—if he has not, indeed, rendered himself incapable of recognizing greatness. The more difficult it grows to attract attention, the louder the vapid cry "Wolf! Wolf!"

One example should suffice to make credible the figures just presented. The publishers of *God's Stepchildren* quote one Lawrence Stallings as affirming of the book:

It has these two qualities which Anatole France demanded of great fiction, the qualities of irony and pity. *God's Stepchildren* has the quality of *The Way of All Flesh* or *Of Human Bondage,* in its dark unflinching grasp of life. But it has a color and swiftness in writing, a rhythm in its sweep, a pathos and mysticism, that neither Samuel Butler's sardonic comprehension nor Maugham's sullen writing achieves.

In the same issue of this magazine, the same reviewer is quoted by the publishers of *Paul Bunyan:*

This book admits him to the company of Carl Sandburg, Sherwood Anderson, Vachel Lindsay, Ring Lardner, and the other present fableurs of the structure begun by Washington Irving, added to by Bret Harte, and ennobled by Mark Twain. It is a first requisite for any American library. The American book of the season.

And in another magazine of the same week, the same writer assures his readers:

Boyd is certainly worth the watching . . . *Drums* is rightly called "the best novel written on the period of the American Revolution" . . . A work which restores with infinite patience and delicacy the actual fabric of Revolutionary days . . . *Drums* is this reader's pick of the American fiction on the new lists.

It is pleasant to know that the erudition and enthusiasm here displayed had already won the reviewer a high place on a great metropolitan daily—then, to consider the observation of an obscure German thinker, that "men call others by the name of genius, as wood-lice are called thousand-leggers. Not that they have a thousand legs, but that folks won't take the trouble to count."[4] The author thus distinguished should keep in mind the reflection: "To flatter and to abuse, it is all one, for it is the one kind of man that is capable of both".

A number of more drudgery faults are likely to lose the editor's imprimatur. Slipshod and incorrect English, trite phrases or their obvious avoidance, indeed too often escape the waste-basket. There, too, should be consigned reviews disproportionate to the value of the book to the readers of the periodical: art is long but space is short. Less likely to be banned, but more unfair, are discussions of general ideas suggested by the book, instead of the work itself, and comment on the jacket blurb as though it were part of the book, or as though the reviewer were bound to disprove its often extravagant claims. Many more faults into which the reviewer will fall, he will discover and rise beyond as he continues writing.

The initial problem a prospective reviewer faces is to persuade an editor to give him work. Several suggestions may be made, none of which is likely to avail; in entering the crowded field of reviewing, as elsewhere, an ounce of friendship is worth a pound of skill. One may, however, study the style of a particular periodical and the type of book it reviews; then, in a letter approximating that style, request a not too important volume from the list of forthcoming books. It is as well to send no samples of earlier work, such as reviews in college magazines, but to rely on the letter. Dropping in for a talk with the editor has succeeded; but unless one come with proper introduction the interval between crossings of the threshold is likely to be brief. One may send a review of a current book, in the hope that the editor's fancy will be caught; but by the time the outsider reads and reviews it, in all probability the volume has been assigned. This method, however, is more satisfactory with an important work in a foreign language, for such a book may not have reached the editorial rooms, and the review be welcome. Once accepted, the reviewer will find less difficulty in securing other books. The present writer's first printed review was of a foreign book, mailed to an editor, and accepted; as a sample (though in no sense a model) of what has opened the door to reviewing, I shake off the dust and here reprint it: *Goha le simple,* By A. Ades and A. Josipovici. Paris: Calman-Levy.

Simple Simon walked wondering through Vanity Fair. "Show me first your penny". So simple Simon continued on his way, saddened. But a smile gradually spread from his lips and eyes until his very flesh was radiant: he had glimpsed the pieman's wares

and was thriving on the memory. Vanity Fair flared on; a magic
carpet had swept him far away, off to the winding pathway of his
dreams. Princesses under purple sunshades tipped back the silk
to peep at him; they called lightly to one another and joined hands
to dance a ring about the lad. Legs outspread, swaying gently to
the rhythm of their round, Simple Simon watched complacently
—then walked indifferently on. The ring broke before him, to
reveal tall negroes, yellow-turbaned, in crimson loincloths, bearing great kegs and caskets: oil of cinnamon, dates cooled with
palm-leaves, squares of sugared gums. They bent for Simple
Simon to partake; and as he munched leisurely he stumbled over
a bawling child, felt the smart of a buffet on his mouth—
and awoke on Main Street, Vanity Fair.

Such is the book of *Goha the Simple*. Cheik-el-Zaki, wisest of
Islam, feels the burden of the hopes of his disciples, and the
problems of the world are heavy. Beyond his wall dwells Goha,
Goliath of form, David of glances; submissive he is to the taunts
and torments of the world, because his eyes are fixed upon the
stars. In him the Cheik finds a symbol of happiness; the simpleton accepts without question the intimacy of the professor—until
el-Zaki learns that his young wife too has found the solution of
her problem in young Goha. The misfortune that overwhelms his
fellows leaves Goha sublimely aloof, eternally freed by his visions
from a permanent share in the miseries of earth. His woes are
transient, for he dwells afar.

A series of exquisite portraits, finely etched; a flash of colorful
moving scenes; the Orient in its truth is spread for the beholder.
Not the romantic East of al-Raschid, not the furtive Orient of
Kipling, but the Orient of Asia of the earth, dusty, busy, noisy,
finding merriment in the multiplying affairs of the day: laughing
crowds; dry, lonely stretches where strange idols stare; and a
dream . . . a dream . . .

Still one returns to Goha. Goha crying his wares through the
unpeopled desert, returning—he knows not how—with a pair of
sheep instead. The episode recalls (but surpasses in simplicity
and vividness) Goldsmith's affair of the green spectacles. Goha
lying on the balcony at night, watching the shooting stars, while
she who loves him waits; Goha the simple, Goha the wonderer,
mankind. Mankind, blundering, dreaming, snatching himself from
the round world to a fairyland where his square shoulders find
pillowed rest.

The publishers who make this volume available in English will
be presenting to us one of the most vivid pictures and engrossing
stories of recent years.

(4) The pretense of publishers at times makes for similarly hyperbolic claims. A full-page advertisement of Ellen Glasgow's *They Stooped To Folly*, for example, headed *The Art of Literary Criticism*, begins by lamenting the loss of that art, qualifies: "but occasionally a book appears so soundly conceived, so brilliantly and suavely written that it inflames the critical imagination. Then book-reviewing becomes criticism, and criticism a fine art"—and briefly quotes examples. The six specimens of "criticism, a fine art," are perhaps no worse than the usual review. One says "Until then, *They Stooped To Folly* should remain the most delectable mingling of ironic wit and tolerance yet done this side of the Atlantic"; another, "a vivid simile" yet does awkward mingling of two images; a third begins "No one of our female writers has her wit" and makes us wonder as to Ellen Glasgow's sex; a fourth says "The importance of Miss Glasgow's story is negligible compared to the way she tells it", though to compare an "importance" with a "way" is as hard as to subtract three oranges from four cucumbers; a fifth tells us that "Life in such a world . . . offers its creator a spectacle . . ." confusing the book-life with the real, or the creator with the reader; the other example of book-reviewing become criticism is pompous, but grammatically correct. All six, of course, express high praise of the book being advertised.

As a consequence of such an attitude, the critic discovers, says Cabell, that "familiarity with what mankind has in the main agreed to accept as great . . . will handicap him without fail, and ultimately will lessen the market value of his paragraphs by mitigating the infallibility of his tone".

(5) To temper the thoughts suggested, the discussion Alain offers, of *The School of Judgment*, may well be conned:

Man has scarcely any judgment, but humanity is infallible. Who goes to the Salons, is lost; who goes to the Museums, is restored. There is nothing more amusing than the sort of bewildered frenzy that overcomes a man of taste when he constitutes himself a critic. For it is true that the great body of treasured works uplifts the spirit and yields it the gift of beauty; but it is no less true that this mass of work reveals not the slightest inkling of a rule by which to judge. I can readily recognize the beautiful, in Beethoven, in Michel Angelo, in Shakespeare; but I cannot in the least discern it in this new piece of music, in that fresh painting, in yesterday's play. Our imagination is too strong;

judgment lets fly in the moment's humor, and this first opinion covers the whole work as with a veil. Hesitant at first, wavering; then suddenly firm, obstinate in the chance verdict: thus the spirit of man. The painters of the Institute are harshly treated in the current word of criticism; doubtless they were praised in other times. And often, high prices are paid for daubings of which one could easily say most anything ill. There is a grain of madness in all these judgments. Why, indeed, wish to judge at first sight, as though by instinct? Prejudice always watches, and slips between. Why not wish to be predisposed, but favorably predisposed?

I was once asked to listen to a short, unfamiliar piece by Beethoven, copied out by hand, without the composer's name. I was prudent, I said nothing irreparable; but my judgment lacked assurance. There is but one means of guarding against such surprises: that is, to know everything. But it is better to recognize that the great works are always more powerful, more wholesome, in the brightness of glory. Who mistrusts himself only half judges, in a manner withholding. As though one resisted a dancing-master. Stiffness is not dancing. Or a riding-master. . . . It is a common fault to want to invent while learning. Michel Angelo, while hardly more than a child, was found copying an ancient statue; thus he toiled in grace and love, without resisting or withholding. It is in this way that one grows strong.

This paradox is striking in the fine-arts; and perhaps it is only the beautiful that humanizes. In all research, in spite of appearances, whether it be politics, physics, or even geometry, one must know how to go to school, and go again, and not throw oneself upon the first objection that comes to hand; but always in that which is human to seek oneself; in short, to move in harmony with grandeur. Epicurean if I am reading Lucretius, Stoic with Marcus Aurelius, follower of the physics of Descartes. The errors of Descartes are sound; they are on the right path. Leibnitz has not understood the "infinitely small" in their true sense; it's precisely among them that I am learning, imitating that human activity properly harmonized between the upper and the nether. The combined grace of body and mind which leaps in its inventions far ahead of proof, I shall win to by obedience. And I consider sublime the words of Michel Angelo, in his last years, when asked "Where are you hurrying, through such a snow storm?" "To school", he responded, "to try to learn."

(6) Examples of the Greek straightforward brevity, in contrast with the more repetitious color of English poetry—the native tendency fortified by the Biblical decoration—are engagingly set

down by Edith Hamilton: "The English method is to fill the mind with beauty; the Greek method is to set the mind to work". Naturally Miss Hamilton does not mean to deny beauty to Greek poetry; rather she admires its direct presentation of "facts". The examples she gives might be multiplied; a glance at the Greek anthology provides these:

Already the white violet is in flower and narcissus that loves the rain, and the lilies that haunt the hillside; and already she is in bloom, Zenophila, love's darling, the sweet rose of Persuasion, flower of the meadows of spring. Why laugh ye joyously, ye meadows, vainglorious for your bright tresses? More to be preferred than all sweet-smelling posies is she.

Why, shepherds, in wanton sport, do you pull from the dewy branches me, the cicada, the lover of the wilds, the roadside nightingale of the Muses, who at midday chatter shrilly on the hills and in the shady copses? Look at the thrushes and the blackbirds! Look at all the starlings, pilferers of the country's wealth! It is lawful to catch the despoilers of the crops. Slay them. Do you grudge me my leaves and fresh dew?

The secretly creeping flames, on a winter night, when all were heavy with wine, consumed the great house of Antagoras. Free men and slaves together, eighty in all, perished on this fatal pyre. Their kinsmen could not separate their bones, but one common urn, one common funeral was theirs, and one tomb was erected over them. Yet readily can Hades distinguish each of them in the ashes.

These examples are perhaps even more figurative than those Miss Hamilton selects, as these are complete poems, while her illustrations are portions of flowing narratives; yet contrast the matter-of-fact imagery of these with almost any English poem:

Shall I compare thee to a summer's day?
Thou art more lovely and more temperate:
Soft winds do shake the darling buds of May,
And summer's lease hath all too short a date:
Sometime too hot the eye of heaven shines,
And often is his gold complexion dimm'd,
And every fair from fair sometime declines,
By chance, or nature's changing course, untrimm'd.
But thy eternal summer shall not fade. . . .

The Greek theory of imitation, to which Miss Hamilton does not refer, is in all probability the basis of this unembroidered beauty.

The concomitant attitude toward symbolism is well portrayed in Socrates' answer (quoted by Miss Hamilton, but again without this stressing) when asked if he believes that Boreas had carried off the maiden Orithya:

The wise are doubtful, and I should not be singular if, like them, I too doubted. I might have a rational explanation that Orithya was playing when a northerly gust carried her over the rocks, and therefore she was said to have been carried off by Boreas. Now I quite acknowledge that these allegorical explanations are very nice, but he is not to be envied who has to make them up: much labor and ingenuity will be required of him; he will have to go on and rehabilitate Hippo-centaurs and chimæras dire. Gorgons and wingèd steeds flow in apace, and numberless inconceivable and portentous natures. And if he would fain reduce them to the rûles of possibility it will take up a deal of time. Now I have no leisure for such enquiries; shall I tell you why? I must first know myself, as the Delphic inscription says; to be curious about things not my concern while I am still in ignorance of my own self, would be absurd. And therefore I bid farewell to all that sort of thing. I want to know about myself. . . .

(7) It may be wondered, here and at other points, why matters seemingly not strictly relevant to a survey of criticism should be discussed. One answer might be that "literature" is today so inclusive a term that all knowledge is the critic's province; another, that much information not readily available in digest may prove most valuable to the critic, even though a fine alignment would mark it but adjacent to his field.

(8) Recognizing the emotional appeal of all the arts, Plato did not note that the arts depending on sound, (oratory, music, poetry, drama) move us more strongly than the others, for "the hearing is suspicious, being a nocturnal sense".

Indeed, the arts might be classified, according to the definitness of their imagery—sight and touch vs. hearing, smell, and taste— as plastic or musical; as Benda calls the 1830 Romantics plastic, and the late-century Romantics (stung by Baudelaire!) musical. (Though of music itself, as Chateaubriand declares, "according to the listener's temperament, the harmonies are thoughts or caresses.") This distinction presses further reasons for the stronger effect of the "musical" arts:

The sensations of sight and touch are more definitely localized, inseparable from the idea of the object that has roused them;

What of color?

bosh!

the sensations of hearing grow more easily apart from their cause, into a state of vaguer, "pure", sensation. Sight brings the sense of an object outside oneself, and suggests therefore one's own limits, the separation of the ego and the world; hearing seems in contrast to come from within, to extend the boundaries of the self, to blend the ego with the universe (as in the breast of symbolism). Most strongly, the sensations of hearing, smell, and taste, stir nervous responses more deep-set than those of sight. This may be a result of their vaguer reporting and our consequent mistrust; but it combines with the other characteristics of sound to give the arts that employ it a greater initial hold upon the feelings.

(9) In 1539 Francis established French as the official language of the law courts; the church, however, maintained a classic solidarity; and it is not until twenty years later that we even hear the advocacy of French as the language of university instruction. Montaigne, at the end of the century, declared that he would have used Latin for his essays "if there were any question of their lasting". (Yet he carefully revised the later editions!)

(10) It seems strange, in the light of such words, to hear E. E. Kellett developing his thesis:

Now once more it is to be observed that, in this chaos of contending opinions, a knowledge of the character, circumstances, and upbringing of any combatant would have enabled students of human nature to foretell with exactness the side he would take: nay, to mark even the waverings of each before he came out finally on his proper side . . . Anyone knowing Gabriel Harvey, his pedantry, his vanity, his scorn of the rascal many, could have prophesied that he would endeavor to constrain the fiery stream into a narrow and "classic" channel: that he would be an advocate of the absurdest mimicry of the ancients, and that he would endeavor, regardless of the true genius of the language, to do for English what Ennius did for Latin. Had he prevailed, we should have had what there was in Rome, a learned class of poets, writing for the learned few, and despising the native and popular bards, who, probably in consequence of this very contempt, would have gradually degenerated into vulgarity and barbarism.

When, a few pages later in *The Whirligig of Taste,* Mr. Kellett offers the triumph of native English literature, over the classical themes and forms advocated by the "highbrows", as proof of the strength and the good sense of the groundlings, of the fact that "untutored appreciation is often juster than philosophical analysis"

—he is curiously self-betrayed. Not only is the opposition (of course without intent) unfairly stated, "philosophical analysis" being a paltry phrase to characterize the ardor and zeal of the Elizabethans' wide search for something better than the doggerel of the late years; but the fight for that vigorous expression in terms of the native genius was led, before any fiat of popular favor, any test of what would be clapper-clawed by the palms of the vulgar, by men cultured and learned as were the proponents of imitation or adaptation of the classics. Furthermore, before the Elizabethan surge of native vigor, Mr. Kellet has himself stressed the example of Rome, where a cultured few changed the very structure and tone of the language, forcing an accentual tongue into quantitative strains, driving into obloquy and oblivion the early Latin literature, and through its subsequent course making it, in form, theme, spirit, in all but actual diction, almost wholly Greek. Less inclusive, but as tight, was the hold of the classics fastened by learned authority on the French . . . As knowledge of psychology increases, it seems more generally true that—though the public may get what it wants—the wants, the feelings, of the public are prescribed and dictated, and the makers of literature are at the mercy of the anonymous makers of taste. And these, of course, are interested primarily in other things than art. In other words (to anticipate) æsthetic values may be based largely on non-æsthetic criteria, whatever the surface standards to which a critic may appeal*.

(11) That in Elizabeth's day England was indeed a "nest of singing birds" may be realized by the fact that when Shakespeare was finishing his last play, *The Tempest*, in the spring, apparently, of 1611—when, that is, he himself was aged 47 (and his Queen had been eight years dead), Sir Walter Raleigh was 59, Anthony Munday 58, Samuel Daniel 49, Michael Drayton 48, Thomas Campion 44, Thomas Dekker (?) 41, John Donne and Ben Jonson were 38, John Fletcher was 32, Frances Beaumont 27, William Drumond 26, John Ford 25, William Browne and Robert Herrick 20, Francis Quarles 19, George Herbert 18, Thomas Carew (?) 16, James Shirley 15, and John Milton (and Sir John Suckling) were 2. It was seven years before the birth of Richard Lovelace and Abraham Cowley, ten before Marvell's and eleven before Vaughan's. Edmund Spenser had been twelve years dead, Sir Philip Sidney twenty-five—and Chaucer 211.

* See also pages 37f. and 441f.

So Walter de la Mare, adding the wish that any year again "could leave to the future one-tenth part of such a legacy as did 1611—the English Bible!"

(12) *Laocoon:* "establishing forever the supremacy of the antepenult".

(13) The following is a page (the selections are of graduated difficulty) from *Exercises in Judging Poetry,* prepared by Allan Abbott and M. R. Trabue, and published by the Bureau of Publications, Teachers College, Columbia University.

Read the poems, A, B, C, D, trying to think how they would sound if read aloud. Write 'Best' on the dotted line above the one you like best as poetry. Write 'Worst' above the one you like least.

Set 12.   The Creation of Light

A (. . . . .)
Let there be light, said God, and forthwith Light
Ethereal, quintessence pure, first of things,
Came from the Ocean deep, and from the east
Began to travel through the gloomy air,
Hid in a glowing cloud; until the Sun
Should be created, in the cloud she had
To stay. God saw the Light, that it was good.

B (. . . . .)
Let there be light, said God, and forthwith Light
Ethereal, first of things, quintessence pure,
Sprung from the Deep, and from her native east
To journey through the airy gloom began,
Spher'd in a radiant cloud, for yet the sun
Was not; she in a cloudy tabernacle
Sojourn'd the while. God saw the Light was good.

C (. . . . .)
And God said "Let Light be", and there was Light.
The first ethereal created thing
To being sprang, and daily from the east
Began to travel through the darksome air;
Until the golden sun should be created
She sojourn'd in a radiant, shining cloud.
God look'd upon the Light and it was good.

D (. . . . .)
Let there be Light, said God, and lo! the Light

Sprung from Tithonus' bed in darksome gloom,
Deck'd her fair form in garments rich and rare
And scattered smiles along the mournful sky.
Her chariot of the Sun not yet created,
Upon a cloud the nymph ethereal rode,
And when the cloud wept raindrops down, she flung
Comforting rainbows from her shining tent.

The objection to this type of test, that a given variation might be better than the original version, was guarded against by submitting a large number of sets to a chosen group of English professors and critics, and using only those of which the original form was unanimously chosen as best.

There seems no way of overcoming a second difficulty, namely, that it is impossible to debase the poetry in one way without also afflicting it in the other two respects. The choice is therefore always relative; and while in the specimen here adduced it is not difficult to determine that D is the sentimental perversion, nor to win agreement that in C the meter is made too regular, in A the imagery more prosaic, in some cases (in addition to the free verse sets) the results are less readily agreed upon. The intention of the authors of the test is of course no guide, and its validity in determining a critic's specific weakness—though not his general competence—is considerably impaired.

(14) There is a tendency in some quarters today to seek to merge, to identify, subject and object: the actor become the character, the author living the persons he creates—that must not be confused with the recognition that the concept of good involves that of evil, that the existence of an object predicates that of a subject, that these are entities *inseparable yet distinct*. This should be kept clear, especially in an age when Collingwood warns against the frequent fallacies that rise from a mental separation of these complements, while Julien Benda storms against the confused blending of them (as in the theory of empathy) as the chief fault in contemporary thought and writing.

(15) A. N. Whitehead says of the growth of science:

It has remained predominantly an anti-rationalistic movement, based upon a naïve faith. What reasoning it has wanted, has been borrowed from mathematics, which is a surviving relic of Greek rationalism, following the deductive method. Science repudiates philosophy. In other words, it has never cared to justify its faith or to explain its meanings; and has remained blandly indifferent to its refutation by Hume. *

This amounts to saying that inductive science is based on faith, while deductive science—mathematics—is based on reason. Yet increasingly all the sciences tend toward mathematics, or the statement of relationships apart from the mere elements of matter actually involved in such relationships. Later, indeed, Professor Whitehead adds:

Induction presupposes metaphysics. In other words, it rests upon an antecedent rationalism. You cannot have a rational justification for your appeal to history until your metaphysics has assured you that there *is* a history to appeal to; and likewise your conjectures as to the future presuppose some basis of knowledge that there *is* a future already subject to some determinations. The difficulty is to make sense of either of these ideas. But unless you have done so, you have made nonsense of induction.

Other objections to the logical bases of reasoning have earlier been advanced; but the final test of scientific law, of science, is pragmatic, practical: an idea is valid if it "works". This turns the eyes of science toward utility.

The words of F. H. Bradley in regard to the basis of induction may also be pertinent:

Sudden at this crisis, and in pity at distress, there leaves the heaven with rapid wing a goddess Primitive Credulity. Breathing in the ear of the bewildered infant she whispers, The thing that has happened once will happen once more. Sugar was sweet, and sugar will be sweet. And Primitive Credulity is accepted forthwith as the mistress of our life. She leads our steps on the paths of experience, until her fallacies, which cannot always be pleasant, at length become suspect. We wake up indignant at the kindly fraud by which the goddess so long has deceived us. So she shakes her wings and, flying to the stars, where there are no philosophers, leaves us here to the guidance of—I cannot think what.

And—to narrow the instances—in the field of light, as Sir William Bragg confesses, "no known theory can be distorted so as to provide even approximate explanation. For the present we have to work both theories. On Mondays, Wednesdays and Fridays we use the wave theory; on Tuesdays, Thursdays, and Saturdays we think in streams of flying energy, quanta, or corpuscles." On Sundays we fervently pray for light.

* cf. the attitude of the modern humanists toward the "dogmatism" of science.

(16) Self-knowledge (conceived as including knowledge of all else) as the proper goal of human activity is posited or implied by many. So far as æsthetics is concerned, this direction is pointed in the notion of art as an exercise of the intelligence; it is overtly taken in such comments as this of Ludwig Lewisohn:

Are we beginning to see the causes of things? Then, in God's name let us tell wiser, broader, deeper, stories, stories with morals more significant and rich. Yes, morals. If a story does not teach by example it is no story; it has no truth. For let men see truth and they will hasten to apply it to themselves. All but the utterly child-minded among them read for such truth as touches them, their lives, their moral difficulties, their station and their moment amid the sum of things.

Here—combined with a confusion between the presentation of truth and its recognition, with a moral fervor, and an abuse of all who disagree, that will render the thought suspect even to those unacquainted with Mr. Lewisohn's recent books—is a conception of the end of reading and living antipodal from that of the hedonist, and reconcilable with still other views of life's destined or desired fulfilment only because of the elasticity of the word *truth*. Also, when men do see truth in works of art, especially if it be what is commonly called "the bitter truth", they hasten to apply it, not to themselves, but to their neighbors.

There seems no reason why a doctrine of knowledge for knowledge's sake should hold higher esteem than that of art for art's sake; and if the retort come that the knowledge is for life's sake, one discovers on inquiry that "life for life's sake" is far from the speaker's mind, so circular a notion being avoided by thoughts of "the good life". Why knowledge for goodness' sake, is no easier a question; one is thrown back, in this search of an ultimate purpose, on such considerations as the religious reward and punishment, or the doctrine of harmony and intensity as the utmost life can give. From this spill into metaphysics one climbs out again to æsthetics, and it seems as though one has clambered from quagmire to quicksand. For just as our drive for an æsthetic ultimate led us to ethics, so now our search for the end of ethics brings us to æsthetics. These are, in truth, as spirit and body of our ideals . . . parallel lines of human functioning, which meet therefore in the infinity where their source and their goal lie concealed. For this doctrine of harmony and intensity as the test of value, this final criterion of human conduct, whether reaffirmed by Gilbert Murray or assumed by the "Ancients" of Shaw's *Back To Methuselah* (who do not act, but contemplate), is close to that which guided the Greeks to glory: for the sake of the beautiful. (See page 206.)

Those who feel that in walking the pathway of knowledge toward beauty man is treading a blind alley, may take consolation of Lord Haldane:

No systematic knowledge is sufficient in itself unless it leads up to and points to first principles.

—or of Browning:

> Just when we're safest, there's a sunset touch,
> A fancy from a flower-bell, some one's death,
> A chorus ending from Euripides,—
> And that's enough for fifty hopes and fears
> As old and new at once as Nature's self
> To rap and knock and enter in our soul. . . .

The one points knowledge toward religion; the other leaps from denial at beauty's call.

(17) And in the sphere of speech, continuing the categories, some critics declare that what appeals primarily to the intellect is prose; to the will, oratory (or rhetoric); and to the emotions, poetry.

(18) The term synæsthesis, or synæsthesia, has been employed, also, to designate other recently studied phenomena. It is applied to overlappings of the senses, the chief of which is "colored hearing", the intimate association of color and sound which some of the symbolists developed, and which in certain individuals assumes pathological vividness and insistence. June Downey lists Gautier and Alfred de Musset as "undoubtedly" genuine examples of this synæsthesia, without indicating the authority for the attribution; but in examining twenty thousand lines of Shelley, Keats, Blake, Rossetti, Swinburne, Meredith, Browning, and Poe, she finds "only one unambiguous" instance—Poe's note "I have often thought I could distinctly hear the sound of the darkness as it stole over the horizon". One hardly needs Professor Downey's warning, on the same page, that poets may make deliberate literary use of the concordance, to recognize in Poe's remark a quite unambiguous instance—of analogy pressed into metaphor.

Synæsthesis may, again, denote a more literal "clang association", between a color and the vowel sounds in its name, as "green seas meet fleet the beaked boats, where between——". It is this sense of the word that Amy Lowell praises, and John Gould Fletcher, in his color symphonies, develops. (See also Note 47.)

(19) A similar union may be posited in the artist. Distinguishing "the typical Elizabethan poem" from the product of such writers as Sidney, a man of feeling, and Greville, a man of thought, Agnes M. C. Latham says that it

contains no jot of personal emotion: as often as not it is translated from a Frenchman, who had it from an Italian, who found it in Plato; and the author is perhaps a literary hack, like Robert Greene, living squalidly—and for all that the poem is as fresh as a flower. It is baffling and beautiful: baffling because it is beautiful and nothing else. Thought is not permitted to distort it nor feeling to betray it into incoherencies.

At the other extreme from such distortion or incoherence soars the prophetic aberration Ruskin describes: but equally remote from this imagined "baffling" beauty-and-nothing-else is the harmonious flow of strong feeling and deep thought, in such interplay as to produce respondent beauty.

(20) This conception, which I would not press, explains many lapses of judgment, from the mutual likings of lovers to various tastes in art: the man who enjoys burlesque, for example, is held to the sexual aspect of love; the many who attain adventure, wealth, and happiness through the person of the cinema hero or heroine, are drawn by self-love. Each of these is an aspect of love tinged with desire. Beauty is love content to contemplate, desiring only to understand, only to enter more fully into the beloved. When the lover desires, not to possess, but to be possessed, (note that the feminine desire "to be possessed" is really—as the mantes show, killing the mate after copulation—a variant desire to have, to hold) he is approaching the mood in which thinkers today claim that one gives oneself to a work of art, to be moulded by its compelling spirit. Baudelaire was in his most devout mood when he spoke of Christ as the divine prostitute, asking of all men that they take Him into their bosoms; and if He seems to seek, it is but their own salvation, their fuller intensification and exaltation. Of art as of divinity it may be said, it restoreth the soul.

(21) The old Count in Norman Douglas' *South Wind* stirs this point about:

There is yet another element of classical beauty which is equally at variance with your modern conception of it: the element of authority. Beholding the Praxitelean *Eros*, the veriest ruffian feels compelled to reverence the creator and his work. "Who was the man?" he asks; for he acknowledges that such things impose themselves upon his untutored mind. Now a certain Monsieur Cadillac builds the most beautiful motorcars. Who is this man? We do not care a fig about him. He is probably a Jewish syndicate. Such being the case, I cannot bring myself to reverence Monsieur Cadillac and his cars. They are comfortable, but that factor of authority, which compels our homage to the *Eros,* is lacking. Yet both things are called beautiful. That we should apply the same word to products so different, so hopelessly conflicting, as those of Praxiteles and Monsieur Cadillac—what does it prove? It proves our poverty of invention. And what does it explain? It explains our confusion of thought.

(22) To those who are inclined to scoff at a theory of the imagination that denies them the celebrated power of contemplating the form and color of absent objects, Alain suggests three tests. The first of these (and enough) is that you look in memory at the Pantheon—or what you will—and count the columns. Easy as this is with the building before the eyes, in fancy you cannot even start to try. Imagine a glass of water; can you reach out to take it to your lips? Concentration, instead of fixing, destroys the vision. You can remember that a porchway has four steps—you cannot climb them; that a dress is green—you cannot see it; that a flower is sweet—you cannot linger over its fragrance. You can revive the concept, the emotion—the image fails. It is the idea, not the object, that you hold. Alice, you remember, had no eyes at the back of her head, so she looked at the shelves as she came to them. "The shop seemed to be full of all manner of curious things—but the oddest part of it all was that, whenever she looked hard at any shelf, to make out exactly what it had on it, that particular shelf was always quite empty, though the others round it were crowded as full as they could hold".

Testimony crowds upon us, in opposition to this theory, of persons who have "seen" with amazing fulness of detail many imagined objects. When such visions occur in dreams and hallucinations, their reality is not afterwards asserted by psychologists;

but many "expert introspectionists" insist upon the actual presence in the mind of the scent they savour, of the green grass they see and tread in waking fancy. A "trained introspectionist", however, may be a person who has trained himself to believe he experiences what he has learnt the investigator desires to hear. His expertness may consist in his ability to weave and maintain a coherent, plausible story—which ability is quite consistent with Alain's idea (which the behaviorists here support) that the mind seizes upon and gives imaginal life to expectancies and incipient movements. "How often is a bush supposed a bear!" "He that is giddy thinks the world turns round." The psychologists who discuss these images—even making a special class, "eidetic", of those whose images are of intense vividness, and listing the dozen points of view (before, behind, amid, afar, etc.) from which the image may be mentally seen—are themselves constantly though perhaps unconsciously making reservations in their descriptions— though none has dared to cry the king is naked. One reminds us that the most momentary vision, the veriest flash of an image, may serve to start the chain of thought. Another points out that images occur more frequently to women and children than to men. One fears to describe his images in any detail, because they develop as he pursues them for presentation. One warns us that "the image must not be conceived as a material copy or thing but merely as the content of a thought in which attention is centered on sensory quality of some sort". This is tantamount to describing the image as no more than a summoning of memory; its movement may then follow the meandering ways of reverie, or the more direct—or at least concentric—course of association. The term "wish-thinking", often used in characterization of these mental visions, further indicates the ease with which one may drift along them, and desire to accept them as actually seen. As, however, artists declare not only that they have had such images, but that in dreams and in wakeful visions they have found the material for their works, or even the work entire; and as readers state (at least to psychological investigators) that in contact with works of art they experience these images, it is necessary for the critic to take account of them—warily, warily. He should guard, for instance, against such a solemn trustfulness as led one collector of mental statistics to accept a man's statement that, after contact with a certain work, he took delight "in picturing himself sitting demurely on the North Pole, waiting to welcome derisively whatever bold explorer should win his way thither with the proud consciousness of his being first on the spot". Other more serious victims of experimentation delude themselves as well. The insistence upon visualization, upon the power of pursuing an image, may lead to dangers of interpretation. Too literal an acceptance of a figure often destroys its value, especially if the poet has used it for the sake of feeling rather than idea. The image, too closely and lengthily followed, may lead to summonings quite irrelevant to the poem, especially to the easy introduction of the stock response, emotions or thoughts habitually induced, as by such words as *mother, moonlight,* and *the flag.* The blank spaces of a questionnaire offer subtle invitation to the fancy; one dislikes seeming mentally bare, and may at once provide—and therefore believe one has—colorful clothing. The point Alain presses is that these imaginal promptings conduce to reverie and idle flow of fancy, "wish-thinking", and are of value to the artist only when, as grasped memory and bound association, they are given form in the process of the work.

(23) The symbolists more often, however, stress the other element in poetry, which may indeed be seen as a resolved opposition or harmonious blending of the pictorial and the musical, the ability to create images, and the power to stir emotional rhythms, the stimulus of meaning and the arousal of form. Which of these is emphasized may depend, in poet and in receptor, upon distinctions the psychologists press, upon whether the mind works in predominantly visual or auditory channels, whether one has a plastic or a diffluent (emotional) imagination. Symbol and sound: hermaphrodite of art.

—I might have added Dryden's word of the imagination, which, he says in defending rhyme,

is a faculty so wild and lawless that, like an high-ranging spaniel, it must have clogs tied to it lest it outrun the judgment. The great easiness of blank verse renders the poets too luxuriant. . . . Certainly that which most regulates the fancy and gives the judgment its busiest employment is like to bring forth the richest and clearest thoughts.

But I did not bring this to the discussion, for (as Dryden's brother-in-law—Crites in Dryden's essay—answers him, and as the over-Donne poets show) "he who wants judgment to confine his fancy in blank verse may want it as much in rhyme, and he who has it will avoid errors in both kinds". It is clear, however, that imagination is one of the many words that require constant definition. And it is one of the preservatives of the dying art of conversation, that such requirements are seldom met.

(24) Frost has evidently overlooked the statistics of divorce. Furthermore, just as some arranged marriages, at first formal if not frigid, ripen into loving union, so does the mating of poem and public sometimes require the preliminary services of a matchmaker, and reach its true quality only in slow growth. Poems perhaps coolly received in their day, and soon forgotten, revived, say as in Percy's *Reliques*, become the object of sincere admiration —for quite other virtues than the author's contemporaries might have found. We who (many of us) call Dryden's form artificial and his diction unreal, love the writings of Chaucer and of Spenser Dryden thought it necessary to translate into English—into the "rich, life-giving" English the Romantics were soon to disdain. How much of our love of the King James version of the *Bible*— for further example—is æsthetic? rather, has not the devotedness, for three hundred years, of all who speak and write English, made its phrases, its diction, its very mistranslations, beautiful?—so that we not only resent changes Biblical scholars may offer, but have unconsciously sunk its style somewhere in the sea and the seasoning of our taste: allusions to its stories strike instant spark, and offer rich imagery and true "æsthetic shorthand"; and caught graces of its style win ready approbation. The recent current of skepticism has correspondingly been accompanied by attacks upon the *Bible* as literature, and upon its themes and style as aids to authors: Maxwell Bodenheim, for instance, has said: "I am not one of those who turn to the *Bible* to hide the exhaustion of their intellect". This remark leaves undetermined, of course, the question as to where he does turn—but that would be a digression from the present points, that the writings of the very rebels are rooted beyond extraction in Biblical soil (the devil *must* quote scripture); and that time may not only change one's attitude toward a poem, but may inculcate quite new tastes.

Contrariwise, a loved poem may lose its lustre, through growth of the receptor, or through some quite trivial shift. The effect on one editor of the perversion of *bonnie lassie* into *bony lassie*, in Harry Lauder's song, led him to reject an otherwise desirable poem in which the word *bonnie* occurred. A friend of mine can no longer enjoy *Kubla Khan* because there sticks in his mind a columnist's distortion of the idea "in short thick pants". The lapse of a term into slang, the use of a quotation by a person one dislikes, or in a disagreeable hour, may destroy what had seemed an imperishable power. Frost's remark cannot, indeed, serve as more than a registering of what is felt by me-now: any-one-else-now, or I-at-another-time, may be stricken with quite other wounds.

(25) Children, today, are taught to read by phrases and idea-groups; spelling no longer precedes but follows reading. Psychologists, pointing out that we think in sentences, or even paragraphs, remark that the analysis of sentences into verbal relationships requires considerable exercise of thought. Every teacher of grammar will nod vehement approval of the statement. Asking a boy to dissect his phrases may tangle him as the self-conscious centipede.

Where the idea comes to its being ahead of the form, we meet one of the two artistic aberrations. Manner and matter are, at every stage of their sound growth, a constant couple: body and mind of the work, and so interacting. A poem in which it seems evident that the idea existed before the form that the poet has given it, we call *didactic*. That, on the other hand, is a *precious* work of which the reader feels the form came first, to be later given content. In great (perhaps, in true) works of art, the thought and the expression always were, and always will be, one.

(26) Paul Claudel declares that the universe is a machine for marking time; and indeed there are many who see in modern movement (more manifestly pervasive than the ancient flux) the stir that determines art. The ideas of evolution and relativity have broken down standards, which seem no longer absolute and fixed, but at any time merely one stage of a continuous unfolding; and the great speed our days have attained, the rapid succession of vogues quick communication and wide publicity effect, have impressed upon men's minds the ephemeral nature of all things. The man in the street, about whom landmarks give way to further crowding hives of swift exchange, is more conscious than his forebears that not only the glory, but all things, of the world—yea, all worlds—are passing.

To most ages, the true trial of art has been in the court of appeals: does the work repeat the thrill? Goethe erects art against the ceaseless passing of natural things:

What we see in nature is power, devouring power, nothing sta-
tionary, everything transitory; a thousand germs destroyed, a
thousand born, every moment; great and full of meaning, infinitely manifold, beautiful and ugly, good and evil—all existing
side by side with equal rights. And art is the exact opposite: it
springs from the individual's effort to maintain himself against
the destructive power of the all.

André Gide writes that his problem is not to succeed, but to
endure; to the young writers of the time, this betrays him as essentially of another age. Permanence is a pre-war delusion. Perfection is a pre-war dream. "Perfection is nothing but exceeding
cleverness; it annoys me", says one vociferous defender of the
modern mood. For there has risen a deliberate cult of the temporary, an acceptance, an embracing, of the moment ere it pass.
The Egyptians sought permanence through submission, their
pyramids taking the downward lines of the stone-heap, of nature's crumbled piles that yet endure. The Greeks fought for the
years with defiance, upright in the columns that still hold gravity
toward the sky. Our moderns seek permanence by relinquishing
the quest. The arts, which seemed once to build toward architecture as their model, now seem to move toward music as their
guide. No longer withstanding, but flowing. Permanence through
union with time. "Not for an age but for all time" these men protest is false description: all art expresses its period—that greatest which reveals it best. He is for longest time who most is of his
age. But all art with its age becomes history: record rather than
rapture. The works of other ages stir us only as we have not
grown beyond them, or as we deliberately—scholars and pedants
—put ourselves imaginatively into the ancient ways. (Try reading
the *Æneid*, they say, or *The Divine Comedy*, or *The Faerie Queene*.
You may appreciate the lifeless form, but what of the living
spirit? That spirit does not come to life unless you relive the age
—an effort scarcely worth the labor, since our own day so richly
yet so swiftly runs nearby.) We must therefore more wisely renounce, they cry, a posterity that will use us but for climbing: we
are concerned with ourselves.

Such feelings (not always organized into thought) are responsible in part for the concentration of the artist upon his own ego;
more, for the deliberate use of the strictly contemporary, of the
current slang, the timely allusion. A key to *Ulysses* shows the de-

tail of local reference to men and happenings Joyce had been aware of in Dublin. John V. A. Weaver's verses *In American* display the columnist's capture of the morning's platitude in the week's wording. The dominant arts in America, the comic strip and the movies, run their daily course to oblivion. Time has us on its tail. Our age is, perhaps—snaring a thought from the unhelpful scientists—seeking to apply the new notion that the one way to attain timelessness is to equal the speed of light! The mass of objects at that pace should give the artist halt.

Baudelaire once asked, what matters an eternity of damnation when in a moment one has reached an infinity of bliss. To Goethe, the devil has conquered when one wants the instant to last. To Shaw, the "average man's" hell is the place where he gets what he desires. But our new moderns feel, with Proust, that "a minute freed from time creates in you a man freed from time"; it becomes the goal of man's striving to give the moment the feel of eternity. This comes with complete absorption in the moment, which [apart from drugs] may be achieved through two forces: passion, and æsthetic contemplation, which is the passion of the intelligence.

(27) Those interested in details of feet and meters and stanzaic forms may pursue them through the bibliography. It is assumed that the reader knows the basic foot of most English poetry, the iamb—if not the pyrrhic; the sonnet and the Spenserian stanza— if not the haï-kaï and the pantoum. As for the origins of the poetic forms, here be content with Coleridge, of the sonnet:

> It is confined to fourteen lines, because as some particular number is necessary, and that particular number must be a small one, it may as well be fourteen as any other number. When no reason can be adduced against a thing, Custom is a sufficient reason for it.

Then, of course, we wish to add Coleridge's expository jingle:

> Trochee trips from long to short,
> From long to long in solemn sort
> Slow spondee stalks; strong foot! yet ill able
> Ever to come up with Dactyl trisyllable;
> Iambics march from short to long;
> With a leap and a bound the swift Anapests throng;
> One syllable long with a short at each side
> Amphibrachys hastes with a stately stride;

First and last being long, middle short, Amphimacer
Strikes his thundering hoofs, like a proud high bred racer.

(28) Some meters seem to dictate their mood. In the poem
there is concordant growth of words and mood and form; but
often the versifier tries to pour a theme into a taken mould. For
a brief instance, Thomas Campbell selects a lilting meter for
The Soldier's Dream, the gay movement of which continuously
struggles against its lingering sorrow:

Then pledged we the wine-cup, and fondly I swore
From my home and my weeping friends never to part;
My little ones kiss'd me a thousand times o'er,
And my wife sobbed aloud in her fulness of heart.

'Stay—stay with us!—rest!—thou art weary and worn!'—
And fain was their war-broken soldier to stay;—
But sorrow returned with the dawning of morn,
And the voice in my dreaming ear melted away.

In proper hands, however, meter is no set swing-song, but
infinitely variable; as Campbell in one line—'Stay—stay . . .'—
slows the movement, a poet will be more constant in his union of
substance and form.

A few technical points in regard to rhyme may be noted.
Exact rhyme, *meet, mete, meat,* while valid in French, is not good
practice in English, which approves of identity only through the
accented vowel; though the repetition of a rhyme-word, as an
echo or a refrain, is frequent. The refrain appears in all periods. It
occurs as repetition in unrhymed poetry, in the Egyptian *Book of
the Dead,* in the Hebrew *Bible,* in the Greek idylls of Theocritus
and Bion, in the Latin *Vigil of Venus*—rare, indeed, in Greek and
Latin, and in Anglo-Saxon a single extant occurrence, in Deor's
Lament; more frequent in the songs of the American Indian. It
abounds in early Renaissance verse, in the set forms that Provençal
troubadours drew from the middle ages, and throughout modern
poetry even into the recent *vers libre*—as in Carl Sandburg's "in
the dust, in the cool tombs". The echo is less often but more
subtly respondent, woven through an entire poem, as in Swinburne's haunting calls of *Itylus:* "O sister swallow", or as Ernest
Dowson scales passion's monotony in *Cynara,* or changing with
each stanza, as in this memory of *Orpheus:*

One broken-hearted evening after rain,
When the clouds lifted from a single star,
And he was more than weary with his pain,
He walked among the grasses poised with rain
And from his listless lute let fall one plaintive bar.

Assonance at line-ends, which has grown popular of late—often mingled with rhyme, though at hazard in single variation in a poem otherwise strictly rhymed—is, being half-rhyme, of two sorts: it may be vowel rhyme, as in *slack, bag, cad;* or consonant rhyme, as in *back, peck, brick*—though in either case the varying sound will probably differ but slightly. Assonance may also occur in double rhyme,—*argues, cargoes; vessel, wassail;* and in triple rhyme—*mincingly, entrancingly;* though triple rhyme itself is seldom used save in humorous verse, as the songs of musical comedy.

A new form of line-end, which may prove fruitful, has been introduced lately by Frank Kendon, who calls it analyzed rhyme. This device consists in taking any two words that fall as line-ends—say, *down, trees*—and building the next two line-ends by transferring the final consonants of the one to the final vowel of the other—e.g., *drowse* and *scene.* To the immediate objection that this is most artificial, it may be replied that likewise is ordinary rhyming, as the practice of chasing rhymes through the alphabet, and the existence of rhyming-dictionaries, make clear; and that facility in rhyming is the result of long tradition of reading and writing rhymes. (The distaste many readers feel for assonance, indeed, may rise in part from their own early efforts to rhyme, and the emphasis lent by the pains of the search. It is of course complicated, among other causes, by the fact that rhyme, like other formal elements in art, may be grasped, may be checked, without understanding, and made therefore to serve as a convenient—though false—standard of judgment.) That rhyme itself is artificial, however, does not quite meet the facts, as is shown by the spontaneous rhyming of children; but any device is legitimate that leads to beauty; analyzed rhyme may be judged by the poems that employ it. A small body of these as yet exists; I offer as specimens four lines from a poem by the inventor of the device:

Dew upon dew condenses; from the city
Chimes of faraway bells the hours attune.

> The silver landscape, no man walks wherein,
> Unto itself is sweet, a secret beauty.

—and the last stanza of a poem by Ada Boden Stevens:

> Let there be springs where no man yet may cool
> His lips—their lakes safe for the wild duck's mate;
> Unmarked by axe or heavy, trampling boot:
> Let there be forests left when temples fail!

(29) Onomatopœia may be in the phrase as well as in the word; witness Tennyson's

> The moan of doves in immemorial elms,
> And murmur of innumerable bees.

Professor Downey calls attention to onomatopœia that reaches other senses. One may think it a rather unusual mind for whom the word *laugh* appears to grin; but the association of word with color, sound, and sight * runs through all recent poetry; it is emphatic in such lines as Thompson's on the sunset:

> Thy visible music-blasts make deaf the sky,
> Thy cymbals clang to fire the Occident,
> Thou dost thy dying so triumphally,
> I *see* the crimson blaring of thy shawms!

Keats' line,

> And lucent syrops tinct with cinnamon

is advanced as gustatory in its evocation; his words, we are told, tingle on the lips. Of vocal onomatopœia Professor Downey speaks more directly, averring that after Poe's lines:

> For every sound that floats
> From the rust within their throats
> Is a groan

she invariably feels "a dull ache in my throat, a dark green roughening, extraordinarily persistent". We should be loath to question the Professor's dark green roughening; and Gautier mentions a tactile onomatopœia, speaking of words that "sparkle when they are rubbed, like phosphorus". Of "murmur", one of Professor Downey's friends declares "You can pick up this word and stroke it". Kinæsthetic onomatopœia, the impulse to move-

* See Notes 47 and 48.

ment, which—words aided by rhythm—is probably the most frequent of these summonings (and the most real) is not instanced by Professor Downey; but it is unnecessary to adduce further examples of the tendency to motion poetry promotes.

Beyond the colorings of associated ideas and sound-suggestions, other elements add overtones to the sense. Most prominent among these, and already mentioned, is the feeling aroused. The attitude toward the listener, present or implicit, also helps determine the phrasing and the movement of a passage, whether the writer is conscious or not of any such adaptation in tone. Intimacy, formality, condescension, respect, play through the wording. The intention of the author, furthermore, affects his product. Whether he is avowedly, or secretly, or unwittingly, directing his work toward an end—convincing or expounding or merely pleasing— his choice of words will be modified, and his emphasis laid on sense or feeling or tone, according to that purpose, which combines with these other, and more, shades and subtleties of meaning to bring into being the chosen expression, in the work of art.

(30) This is the opening of *Four Saints In Three Acts, An Opera to be Sung,* by Gertrude Stein:

To know to know to love her so.
Four saints prepare for saints
It makes well fish.
Four saints it makes well fish,
Four saints prepare for saints it makes it well well fish it makes it
    well fish prepare for saints.
In narrative prepare for saints.
Prepare for saints.
Two saints.
Four saints.
Two saints prepare for saints it two saints prepare for saints in
    prepare for saints.
A narrative of prepare for saints in narrative prepare for saints.
Remain to narrate to prepare two saints for saints.
At least.
In finally,
Very well if not to have and miner.
A saint is one to be for two when three and you make five and
    two and cover.
A at most.
Saint saint a saint.

Forgotten saint.
What happened today, a narrative.

And lest you deem this a not grossly exaggerate burlesque of the usual libretto, try this poem of hers, entitled

Conscience

Racket is a noise. Noise is a poise. Boys with the b spelled like a p
    is poise. Boys is poise.
And then I read the men. Men say. Leave me and be gay.
Men say tenderness today. Men say go away.
And leave me.

A potato field and the promised land. It is a very pleasant burning
    smell.
Armandine Armandine yesterday noon. Armandine Armandine
    what is the tune.
Devotion. What is devotion. He is devoted to that. She is devout.
    And an opening. An opening is covered by Cæsars.
Sharp wire. Do sharpen wire. Devotion. Devotion is determined
    by design.
When this you see remember me.
I do mean to replace crockery with furniture. I do mean to organize
    victory. I do mean to say grace.
I am not a bar tender.
Automatically but not silently.
Little fool little stool little fool for me. Little stool little fool
    little stool for me. And what is a stool. That was the elegant
    name for a cow. Little stool little fool little stool for me.
    Little fool little stool for me.
Let us let us conscience.
Let us conscientiously renounce the sense of reticence.

One line of the poem seems to betray the secret of its creator's method. Here is a small fragment of Blümner's pure poem, *Ango Laïna:*

        Oiai laéla oia ssisalu
        Ensúdio trésa súdio mischnumi
        Ia lon stúaz
        Broor schatt
        Oiázo tsuigulu
        Ua sésa masuó túlú
        Ua sésa maschiató toro

In even this small portion, a sound pattern may be perceived.

Of course, the consideration of any work of art involves intricate associations; while Gertrude Stein's works are likely to be more confusing than Blümner's, in that she uses real words, she has the advantage of being able (as the orthodox poet uses sound as a grace-note over sense) to employ meaning to shade her tonal progressions. *Conscience,* just quoted, gives instances of such use.

Blümner is by no means the only writer of poems of pure sound; Tristan Tzara has fashioned them; and others may be found in issues of *transition,* which, under the editorship of Eugene Jolas, came to the fore in support of experiment in art, and which contributed to literary development with its preaching and practice of the "revolution of the word".

The process of inventing words, hitherto largely limited to manufacturers, scientists, and nonsense-writers, is being developed for more serious artistic purposes. The Carrolls and the Lears of recent times had their predecessors. Apuleius indulged in linguistic experimentation; the Dark Ages were thick with vocabularian vagaries, from Abbo's poem on the siege of Paris to that most fantastic *Hisperica Famina*—even in the solemnities of old English charters; Burchiello was most prominent of the many Italians who in the fourteenth and fifteenth centuries wrote *verbiage verses;* and sixteenth century France gives many examples of *poèmes en galimatias, poems in pishpartout.* The riffruffroaring Rabelais had his counterpart in his English translator, the ururursterous Urquhart, whose original works vie with the most recent products of James Joyce. The Provençal poets, to represent the distraught state of the unrequited lover, mixed languages haphazard in their lines. But there seems, in the newer difformations and inventions, if not a more deliberate, a more earnest, endeavor.

The various impulses to this word creation in art are classified by Benjamin Crémieux (in *transition,* June 1930, the final issue, which has many examples of the deed.) He suggests, as simplest cause, such a "verbal drunkenness" as leads children [in whom it is rather a quest or a display of power] to run sounds along: *humlumdumbum.* It may, *per contra,* be a sophisticate effort to create an esoteric tongue, a language for the initiate. This again has its parallel in childhood, in the various disguise tongues, with their twisted consonants and added endings: *I'llglee gloglee lafterglee youglee,* and the like. Beyond this, nearer the level of art, is the use of words for values other than meaning, for musical or plastic possibilities, for palatal conformations and other motor impulses. Verlaine, Mallarmé, Gertrude Stein have made this use. The word with them has become "an instrument of percussion not precision", leading toward the individual Volapuk of Joyce, the "panaroma of all flores of speech".

Still more complicated uses of new forms are found in the work of Léon-Paul Fargue and James Joyce. Paul Valéry points out that

Fargue has been led by quite accurate observations to establish, here and there, certain phonetic deformations which curiously disfigure the words employed and constrain us to picture in our imagination the absurd and inhuman beings in whose mouths we are obliged to put them; for they suggest the activity of thick tongues, twisted lips, or monstrous nostrils. Fargue is the first to have invented and used what might be called phonetic caricature.

Joyce, though frequently combining syllables for the purposes already mentioned, seeks also to break through the abstract symbol of the word to a closer reproduction of thinking in process: as the stream of consciousness technique seeks to follow the sudden shifts of attention in consciousness, so Joyce attempts to snare the half-starts, hesitations, blunders, glimpsed offshoots, of ideas as they grow and gather and pass to word-forms in the active mind. Joyce works on the basis of sound, not spelling; he assumes a cultured audience, appreciative of intellectual play: by interpenetration and combination of several words, English or foreign, by displacement of letters, by deliberate *lapsus linguae*, by the addition of word-fragments, he shapes his thoughts.

We may come, touch and go, from atoms to ifs, but we are presurely destined to be odds without ends.

From "atoms to ifs" imagination rounds Adam and Eve; as putting "all space in a notshall" further engages the fancy; as "mielodorous is thy bel chant" brings smell and taste to fort the other sense; or as "Joepeter" for Jupiter dethrones the gods. . . . Hans Arp and Kurt Schwitters in German, Henry Michaux in French, may also be noted as prominent in these questings.

Gelett Burgess, in his *Burgess Unabridged,* offered many builded words—*penaninkumpoop, whimpulse;* but suggested that the best new words would be full-sprung from their creator's

brain, without traceable association: *gloogo, persuetude, xenogore.*
What he and the other nonsense-writers probed for humorous
possibilities, is not, thereby, screened from use for other ends. It
has always been a way of genius, to lift the scorned, the ridiculed,
the neglected, into art.

Those who refuse merit to these experiments may remind us
that the road from hell to heaven is a progress of increasing
clarity, from the stony rebel Nimrod, who in his verbal confusions
knows no word and howls brute sounds, to the silent splendor of
God, whose quiet love knows and informs all hearts. Yet to those
who object that these created forms lack precision and clarity, it
may be answered, as Eugene Jolas retorts, that precision and
clarity are necessities when one's aim is to give information, but
perhaps in some works of art are even obfuscatory to the intent.
Maeterlinck prefers the vagueness of twilight. Max Eastman, discussing the revolt against the idea of art as communication, demands for the artist "freedom to play by himself". The retort is
obvious; but the artist himself may rejoinder: If you aren't interested, you needn't come around.

(31) One of the few exceptions is the "English Aristophanes",
Samuel Foote, whose plays are something like the modern revues
—Foote's Follies of 1775—and as swift in their capture of local
happenings. In *The Tailors, The Maid Of Bath, The Devil Upon
Two Sticks, The Minor, The Nabob,* and more, Foote provoked
frequent attack by the deftness and point of his satire. He defined
comedy as

the exact representation of the peculiar manner of that people
among whom it happens to be performed, and a faithful imitation
of singular absurdities and particular follies, which is openly produced, as criminals are publicly punished, for the correction of
individuals and as an example to the whole community.

And it must be confessed, though our *Garrick Gaieties* made
merry with Grover Whalen only after he had resigned as Police
Commissioner of the City of New York, that one and another of
Foote's flayed fellows was thereafter made by public feeling to
atone. Ridicule is perhaps not a deterrent; but it may serve as a
corrective, when the fault or folly is ripe and ready to fall.

Foote's definition of comedy, moral justification and all, may
as well be applied to the Greek. Voltaire spoke of true comedy as

"the speaking picture of the follies and the foibles of a nation". . . . And of course there is W. S. Gilbert.

(32) An interesting attitude toward the writing of history is quoted in Norman Douglas' *South Wind,* from Monsignor Perelli, author of the *Antiquities of Nepenthe:*

Portraiture of characters and events should take the form of one gentleman conversing with another, in the easy tone of good society. The author who sets out to address a crowd defeats his own object; he eliminates the essence of good writing—frankness. . . . History deals with situations and figures not imaginary but real. It demands therefore a combination of qualities unnecessary to the poet or writer of romance: glacial judgment combined with fervent sympathy. The poet may be an inspired illiterate, the romance-writer an uninspired hack. Under no circumstances can either of them be accused of wronging or deceiving the public, however incongruous their efforts. They write well or badly, and there the matter ends. The historian who fails in his duty deceives the reader and wrongs the dead.

Anatole France would doubtless have found the *Antiquities* cocklewarming.

Perhaps a general notion about the informal essay calls for contradiction. The idea that one may ramble at glorious haphazard in the essay has recently been given countenance by Philip Guedalla, who calls the form "one of nature's accidents, like wild-flowers or Mr. MacDonald's cabinet"—a statement only literally true. Writing really "at random" is probably confined to the da-da-ists and the superrealists—and the insane.

Two quotations from *Byron,* by André Maurois, leading exponent of the "fictionized biography", should suffice as examples of the technique. The book begins:

Through the enchanted Sherwood Forest, close to Nottingham, a little band of black-habited monks, canons regular of the Augustinian order, came wandering among the oaks. King Henry the Second of England, threatened with excommunication for the murder of Thomas à Becket, had promised the Pope to do penance and to endow monasteries. A site was chosen in a valley, close to a spring and lake; the trees were felled, to the glory of God and for the salvation of the King's soul.

The justification for this passage is that the Byron home had once been the Augustinian monastery. Speaking of Byron's walks with a maid, Maurois says "Sometimes during these excursions their bodies touched, or hand brushed hand; the contact made the boy's blood leap." Thus records give rise to fancied deeds, and estimates of character spring into reported moods and actions. A wary and a wise reader he, who knows the fact from the fiction! (The writers themselves, as James Stuart Montgomery reveals, make their fiction fact, by virtue of "the secret master-word which historians and biographers have handed down, one to another, since the days of Herodotus and Plutarch".)

(33) That very murder trial, it may be remembered, was reported for various newspapers by the dramatist Maurine Watkins, the philosopher Will Durant, and the divine John Roach Stratton. Indeed, when "Scarface" Capone was released from a Pennsylvania jail, and his killing was daily expected—and tabloid readers disappointed as uneventful days dragged on—the New York *Daily Mirror* published a serial entitled *Scarface, A Fictionized Romance of the Prince of the Underworld*. A rival sheet, not to be outdone, offered $25 apiece for three "letters from readers" weekly, and from them printed a serial: *A True Composite Story Written From Graphic Readers' Letters*. The vogue of fictionized biography may be noted again, in connection with this avidity for the personal. Science, with many authors in its train, has moved more ardently toward the objective; the great reading public (with seeping silt of Freud) is beginning to rush (along the trodden path of exciting deeds) toward the depths of the ego.

(34) Such was the proportion of about a thousand New York city high school lads; elsewhere, the number of readers is perhaps a bit larger.

(35) It is suggested by Wilson Follett, in his discussion of romantic literature as (what he thinks but does not call) wish-dreaming, that when the wish dies the book fades with it, or "will remain to later ages as the property of unmature or restless minds who know not what they want." The case of Dickens, alone, suffices to prove the inadequacy of this explanation. There should be considered, however, the fact that literary, like scientific, developments seep gradually into public consciousness. Neither Verlaine nor Browning is as formidable today as to his contemporary reading public; the impressionistic painters are now in every art museum. The new vocabulary of the new school has been learned; our time has its own incomprehensibles.

(36) Distinguishing *the emotion of sympathy* from *the æsthetic emotion*, Benda declares that the former is satisfied chiefly in the theatre, whence the great popularity of the drama (and of the cinema); and consists in a sharing—noted by Bossuet in the seventeenth century—of the feelings of the characters. So, too, (remember Flaubert's empathetic stir) du Bartas, while planning his description of a horse, used to get on all fours, gallop, neigh, and buck—yet Vergil probably did not; and *The Red Badge of Courage*, unlike *All Quiet On the Western Front*, was written by a youth who had never been to war. Aristophanes laughed at the notion that a poet wishing to portray women must contract their habits. . . . The æsthetic emotion, Benda indicates as the feeling that rises from the appreciation of the "truly artistic" qualities of a work, as emotion based on intelligence. See Note 45.

(37) Returning for a moment to the actor, one may inquire to what extent he, too, should feel the mood appropriate to the whole. The emotion a player has to present may be quite the reverse of that which is drawn from the situation—as the discomfiture of a butt is cause of amusement; of a villain, cause of delight; should a consciousness of the single desired impression spur on or restrain his playing; or will the acting of the part for itself, as though the character were a living personality, supply the proper tone in the symphony? To the author each rôle may be as an instrument in the orchestra, variously carrying the theme or supporting it—and indeed the analogy with the musician invites pressing. For it would seem that the player of the bass-viol, now sustaining a motif for five bars, now waiting ten until he fingerthrums an echo to the brass; or the man who thrice during the movement slides the cymbals together and four times clashes them at the close—it would seem that each musician can enter more than mechanically into the spirit of the work only if he grasps it as a whole, and consciously subordinates and orders his part: yet the intensity which one observes in the kettle-drummer, the absorption of his striking and the fervor of his constant retightening of the stretched skins, seems indeed to rise from a concern with the particular rôle. Concordance among the instruments, or the actors, is (one always hopes) secured by the director of the orchestra or of the play; probably, if the composer, the author, has worked well, a correct interpretation of each part by a player absorbed in the part would effect an harmonious whole. Most

performers, other than actor-directors, of course play their rôle
"for all it is worth"; the history of the theatre tells a paltry tale
of jealousy and struggling for the spotlight, where the "star" system has prevailed; repertory tends to induce more balanced co-
ordination. It may be doubted, however, that even the most detached performer can at once participate in a work and derive
from it the mood appropriate to the receptor; yet it seems likely
that a sense of the total desired effect will help him to contribute
his proper part.

(38) Even when talking of care, writers are frequently careless: Mr. Montague's word *wary* begs the question, and destroys
the value of the last sentence. . . . Dr. Reuben Steinbach has
compiled, and discussed in a series of articles in *American Speech*,
a long list of "errors" in rhetoric made by professors of rhetoric
in their very text-books on the subject: violations of "rules" by
their formulators. One should keep in mind the fact that "rules"
are merely convenient summaries of general practice, and should
ponder a certain warning that mentions a mote and a beam.

(39) More than the Middle Ages, indeed, show that man believes what he hears much sooner than what he touches and sees
for himself. Priestcraft and prophecy rest upon the fact that men
seek authority, want to be told. The news-bringer bears also conviction. What the eye takes in is at once set down as dangerous or
harmless; if the former, there is instant action; if the latter—or
if suspect—there is casual survey or close examination. The ear
is suspicious, as has been said, and uneasy; its alarms cannot find
basis or remove; therefore does it clutch assurance, and messengers are accorded instant credence . . . especially if the news be
of high import. Something of this readiness to belief remains when
a story is put into the mouth of a narrator. (See Note 8.)

(40) Regional fiction, the story of local color, has a wide appeal; small countries like France and Spain have their many sec-
tional novelists, even as the various parts of the United States
have their several celebrants. There is in such books a pleasing,
exotic savour; there is possibly, as well, these days of feminine
readers, a parental sense of safety. When M. Perrichon (in Labiche's play) stops at the railroad station to buy his daughter a
book, he is afraid. Reading is dangerous; it may turn a girl's
head. Perrichon hesitates, looks about, and chooses—*The Banks
of the Saone*. Such expectation of virginal innocence comes, how-

ever, if at all, with stories of different sections of our own or similar
lands; distance, as tales of the Orient or the Gold Coast reveal,
permits one to imagine barriers burned away, especially in torrid
climates.

(41) For Caliban aping his god see, not Shakespeare, Browning.

(42) There is, of course, no chronological chain in the development of these attitudes; each rose, and persisted, and declined,
with but vague regard to artistic sequence or logical demolishment.
Indeed all, once awakened, have persisted side by side; nor is it impossible to trace them as tendencies throughout every period
of art, responses to the desires of perennial types of man.

From their persistence, indeed, rise many attitudes and fashions that engage the observant mind; the reënforcement of the
romantic stress on the individual, for example, by Freud's Psychanalysis, Adler's Individual Psychology, and other currently
popular probings (which, reducing man's impulses to universal
forces—sex, inferiority, neglect—are ultraistic in trend: see page
434f.) helps to account for the vogue of biofiction, as many of
the readers of today forget the product in the man.

The tendency of all the arts, in the more fixed ages toward
architecture, in these more fluid days toward music, springs also
from a desire to give garment to the spirit. Professor Parkhurst,
indeed, declares that "architecture is the only complete embodiment of the forces that pervade the physical being of man", and
music is "at once the symbol and the realization of the unresting
tides whose impalpable waters wash ceaselessly over the sands of
consciousness. . . . And because it is thus reproductive of the
rhythms actually of emotion itself, and is able to transcribe them
in unalloyed purity, it, more than any other form of human creation, is the reconciler and healer of human conflict." Such remarks are emotive, expressions of a wish and a welling, rather
than a literal fact; they betoken the resurgent claims of the spirit,
upon tracts where essence has been forgotten in surface maze.

(43) "One must always be drunk", says Baudelaire; "on wine,
on poetry, on virtue—what you will. But get you drunk". Psychologists concur in the thought that, especially in our crowded
yet controlled era, an "occasional relaxation" of the social inhibitions may be helpful toward the maintenance of appropriate
conduct during the remainder of one's social contacts.

This should comfort the countryman in New York, the New

Yorker in Paris, and others who take advantage of freedom from observation to enjoy regressive emotional excess. In this connection, too, should be remembered the English gentleman, the only white at a post in the African jungle, who was (if possible) even more meticulous than at home, in dressing for dinner, in observing all the formal proprieties of his social group. These equally, however, disagree with Carlyle.

(44) The term Puritan, usually with a capital P, first applied to one sect of protestants in religion, has had such varied extensions and tones of meaning that it may at one time refer to the sturdy, sound, basic elements of the best American life, and at another to sanctimonious pretense, to formal hypocrisy, or to whatever grates on Mr. Mencken. As Kenneth B. Murdock says, speaking of the Puritan contribution to American literature, "Unfortunately even the Puritans disagree as to the meaning of the name Puritan, and no one of their definitions covers all the groups, all the shades of thought, all the human aspirations which contributed to the making of Puritanism in the broad aspect that alone matters where literature is concerned." In the present use, removing the capital, the term puritan is employed (with no depreciatory implications) to describe one of two contrasted states of mind, without regard to territorial or historical graduations.

(45) The fact that most writers have been men does not weaken the force of this classification, for many feel that an artist is likely to be great in measure as his imaginative sympathy reaches out to include the other sex. Every true artist is <u>Tiresias</u>. Clemence Dane, indeed, claims that, while the great, Miltonic character, who moulds his destiny, is a masculine creation, the dynamic character, changing with the events, comes prominently into English fiction with woman writers, Jane Austen and the Brontë sisters. As a matter of fact, the shift of emphasis came earlier, with the women readers. At the end of the seventeenth century, the rising middle class in England was taking the theatre from the Court, and women became important in determining literary success. (Women, more than men, are readers of books.) Comedy is no longer brilliantly heartless, but moves, through moral implications and social sympathy, toward the problem play. (The people, more than the prince, demand a moral: when Faust, in his early appearance as a folk-figure, was in his second, the wandering, period, he played his pranks—devil's man though he was—on the

greedy, the garrulous, the good-for-nothing; not on the pious and the pure.) "Bad" characters are villains instead of gallants, and are punished instead of granted the heroine's hand. Tragedy no longer deals with the fate exclusively of kings and of empires, but—in the words of Nicholas Rowe, who quite knowingly initiated the change—presents "a melancholy tale of private woes". Those who deem *The Doll's House* (1879) pioneer drama may ponder the words of Calista, victim of the gay Lothario ("dearest of libertines" to the fair sex, and not Shakespeare's man):

> How hard is the condition of our sex,
> Thro' ev'ry state of life the slaves of man.
> In all the dear delightful days of youth
> A rigid father dictates to our wills
> And deals out pleasure with a scanty hand;
> To his, the tyrant husband's reign succeeds;
> Proud with opinion of superior reason,
> He holds domestic business and devotion
> All we are capable to know, and shuts us,
> Like cloistered idiots, from the world's acquaintance
> And all the joys of freedom. Wherefore are we
> Born with high souls, but to assert ourselves,
> Shake off this vile obedience they exact,
> And claim an equal empire o'er the world!

The epilogue to the same play (*The Fair Penitent*, 1703) attacks the "double standard" of sex-morality, of which Rowe's *Jane Shore* further emphasizes the evils. The great contemporary success of these plays, the weeping audiences that indulged in emotional debauches with "soft, complaining Rowe", show that the "fair reader" had begun to assert the empery she now unquestioned holds.

A similar ascendancy developed in France, even in courtly circles. Racine's *Andromaque* (1667), his greatest success, attained twenty-seven performances, whereas eighty were given of Thomas Cornellie's *Timocrate*, of which the hero (turned Penelope!), loving the princess whose town his troops besieged, went out each night to repair the damage his army had done. So strong have the women grown, Julien Benda protests, that

all the literary attributes exalted by the contemporary æsthetics are those that women possess to the highest degree, and that form as it were a monopoly of their sex: absence of general ideas; worship of the concrete, of the circumstantiated; swift, wholly intuitive perception; a solo of sentiment; interest absorbed in the self, the most intimate, the most incommunicable, etc. . . . *The whole of modern æsthetics is framed for the woman.* The men struggle. Many of them try to imitate the literature of their rivals. Alas! They must grow resigned to it: there is a degree of unintellectuality and of shamelessness they will never reach.

Yet it may be remarked that few women have so deeply probed their sex as Joyce in the final pages of *Ulysses,* and that perhaps the best description of an accouchement is by a man.

The feminine influence flows even into such fields as folk-lore. For years the orthodox origin of the phrase "He'll never set the Thames on fire" lay in the *tems,* a small cake of sieved flour such as King Alfred the Great allowed to burn—the phrase referring to a person who's not wise; recently however, the emphasis has shifted: the *temse,* we are reminded, was a nub of the old spinning-wheel that a fast worker could overheat with the friction, and the phrase, in its feminine aspect, refers to one who's not industrious.

(46) The term symbolism, it is wise to remember, has a meaning other than that of a certain understanding about art and life. It has been applied earlier in this volume in the "scientific" sense, to denote the use of a word as representing a specific concept (e.g. *thirteenth* means *one after the twelfth*) as opposed to emotional evocation. It is this sense, probably, that Santayana intends, when he states that man's "simian chatter becomes noble as it becomes symbolic"—though the context does not permit one to feel sure; it is probably in the other sense (though, considering Fry's emphasis on the significance of form, again one must reserve a doubt) that Roger Fry applies the term when he says "In proportion as an artist is pure, he is opposed to all symbolism". A person who understands the two meanings need never confuse them, at least, in his own application.

The second sort of symbol is subdivided by Helen Flanders Dunbar. The first sort she calls arbitrary, or extrinsic: that which, though once perhaps a fancied or perceived association, is now a mere sign or emblem, with meaning because we agree beforehand to give it such; here lie the letters of the alphabet, and the shorthand marks of the sciences; from these any. original emotional power is usually quite gone. The aim of these symbols is to express the idea aptly and concisely. Next, she distinguishes the descriptive, or intrinsic, symbol, which aims to enhance that which is symbolized, to give it vividness or distinction; this sort is achieved through recognized similarity, as when we speak of a man as a tiger, or a river as "a silver ribbon flung across the green tapestry of the countryside". Beyond these, the interpretative, or insight, symbol, "the union of silence and speech", is a "semblance of a reality greater and truer than the symbol in all its aspects, a sort of initiation in which thought may be led through meaning to deeper meaning". Thus, Miss Dunbar illustrates, the palm, from having been strewn in the triumph [but why was it thus employed?] is the emblem of victory; it may be, as in the *Song of Songs,* a metaphor to enhance the bride; and, when contemplated in the oasis, it may become "as it were a veil behind which the desert dweller may discern the faithfulness and the mercy of God, and the justice of the righteous man". The last type tends to become a sensing personal to the author, who, striving to express the inexpressible, often produces merely the incomprehensible. Yet, in ways each artist learns,

Instinctive Art
Must fumble for the whole, once fixing on a part
However poor, surpass the fragment, and aspire
To reconstruct thereby the ultimate entire.

Among those who see less pervasive values in the use of symbols, Lowell remarks that he looks upon "a great deal of the modern sentimentalism about nature as a mark of disease. It is one more symptom of the general liver-complaint." And Anatole France, long idol of the literate American, declares: "Symbolism will rule the future, if the nervous condition that produced it becomes general. Unfortunately, M. Ghil says O is blue, and M. Rimbaud says O is red. And these exquisite invalids argue under the indulgent eye of M. Mallarmé." Later, André Gide observes: "Rimbaud and Mallarmé have become Adam and Eve. The apple was offered by Cézanne. And we shall always bear the burden of this original sin." Yet no Stylites pillar (seclusion that keeps him in the public eye) of esoteric assumption, no picture painted by a donkey's tail, nor music fit for a donkey's ears—no scoffing of amiable or witty observers can override the influence of symbolism on contemporary art. As Browning says of it all:

> Art hangs out for sign
> There's finer entertainment underneath;
> Learn how they ministrate to Life and Death—
> Those incommensurably marvellous
> Contrivances which furnish forth the House
> Where Soul has sway.

(47) The most active literary pursuit of this idea has been along the line of the concordance of color and sound. The French, in particular, have sought to link word, even letter, and hue—the poet René Ghil, the psychologist Rossigneux, Arthur Rimbaud in the sonnet *Vowels:*

> A black, E white, I red, U green, O blue,
> Vowels; some day I shall reveal your birth:
> A, black velvet swarm of flies that over earth
> Buzz to the foulest stench, abyss of hue
> Sombre; E frank with smoke and fierce intents,
> Spears of proud glaciers, white kings, blossom-dips;
> I purple of spitting blood, laugh of fair lips
> In anger or in drunken penitence;
> U cycles, divine rhythm of the seas,
> Peace of beast-strewn pastures, wrinkles that crease
> Brows whereon the furrow of learning lies;
> O great lightning, with strange clamors hurled
> Over the quiet of angels and the world,
> O omega, violet ray of her eyes.

This is a more subtle, and a much more individual sensing—since few indeed, as Anatole France and Lafcadio Hearn complain, will associate the same colors and letters—than that developed in John Gould Fletcher's poem *The Vowels,* in which each vowel is amplified in figures the words whereof repeat the vowel-sound.

While English poets have developed no theories of color concordance, English poetry, though never (despite Marvell)

> Annihilating all that's made
> To a green thought in a green shade,

is rich in association of color and sound. Oscar Wilde has written a *Symphony In Yellow;* also:

> The Thames nocturne of blue and gold
> Changed to a harmony in gray.

The linking runs throughout nineteenth century verse (many instances are given in Chapter XI of Professor Downey's *Creative*

Imagination), and continues with the blendings of today . . . as in E. A. Robinson:

> And it was then that like a spoken word
> Where there was none to speak, insensibly
> A flash of blue that might have been a bird
> Grew. . . .

and

> So great a silence there among the flowers
> That even their fragrance had almost a sound,
> An accusing voice of color.

In *A Rebours*, Huysmans suggests other concordances and substitutions, as when Des Esseintes savours symphonies of perfume, or sips music of blended drinks. One recalls Francis Thompson's "Who girt dissolved lightnings in the grapes?" . . . Powerful effects, outside of literature, have been obtained by drenching an auditorium in color while playing such compositions as Scriabine's *Fire Music*, or by the arresting patterns and developed themes played on Wilfred's color-organ. Motion picture palaces revive, in perfumes, the incense of ancient temples of worship. The notion of an intermingling of the arts, or, rather, the idea that all the arts make common appeal, is by now commonplace. Spengler says: "A 'singing' picture of Claude Lorrain or of Watteau does not really address itself to the bodily eye any more than the space-straining music since Bach addresses itself to the bodily ear"; the aim of all art is directed—by the varied appeals of the different art forms—upon perhaps uniform inner responses.

This transfer of the zone of appeal Professor Parkhurst has made the basis of a classification of metaphors: the simplest are those wherein the two terms are of one category, as

> All the world's a stage
> And all the men and women merely players;

next are those that invade two sensory domains:

> Heavy with bees, a sunny sound;

beyond these are a group that draw the ineffable (abstract, essence, spirit) into the concrete sensuous:

> And seal the hushèd casket of my soul. . . .
> Some shadows of eternity;

finally, fourth and "most momentous of all types"—as a breath
of first creation—"it is the sensory world of inanimate objects
that is lifted into the mysterious recesses of the invisible kingdom
of consciousness"—a rather purple picture of personification:

> The moving waters at their priest-like task
> Of pure ablution round earth's human shores.

This use of literary figures, valid insofar as it is associated in
the mind (as white with purity) with what is intended, must be
distinguished from the employments of symbolism, a sort of fifth
degree of metaphor, which seeks to convey a deeper significance,
that can be received only by those ready to lose themselves with
the author in wide, far visions, in moral or mystic raptures, or in
unutterable contemplation of cosmic or divine powers and essences.
André Berge gives many examples to press the point that metaphors, which used to drive from the concrete object to vaster,
vaguer implications, now frequently linger in the second group,
bring the abstract or the immense down with a concrete homeli-
ness:

> the skylight of an hypothesis. . . .

joys like tart fruits plucked over-fence by the road.

So, in the drama today, abstractions become concrete (as in the
moralities); and Pirandello sets æsthetic problems and metaphysical doubts walking the stage. See Note 51.

(48) Experiments, such as those of R. C. Givler, seem to support the symbolist reliance upon sound. This investigator, in ac-
cordance with the frequency with which poets have employed and
stressed the various sounds, has constructed their characteristic
tonal patterns, as, for Keats,

> ni rul su vēēd ri nest it el ith rēēn
> la māz mō kif de poth la pām wē hō.

Asking his subjects to indicate their responses to such lines, and
to similarly pi'd sounds from single poems, he reaches the conclusion that the sounds, devoid of meaning, rouse in the hearer
"a mood congruous to that of the original poem". He finds, furthermore, that even meaningless words, beaten as iambics, carry
suggestion: ne-rol repeated twenty-five times, to a number of
listeners "implies the joys of rustic work and pleasure; visual

imagery of the fields in summer". Most of the subjects felt, through the line

> Shun dōle ow rod thū nark blōre ō land ēēp,

the call of the sea, faintly as in a shell borne from its source:

> Roll on, thou dark and deep blue ocean, roll.

(How much of this, as in the shell, is the roar of the listener's nerves, it is hard to say.) Almost invariably, too, they record a stronger motor impulse with the transmogrified, meaningless line than with the original.

As (says F. Y. Eccles) "the emotion which symbolism pursues bears no constant relation to the objects represented or the ideas expressed; rather it aims at the recovery of vanished moods by curious incantations, by the magical use of verbal atmosphere"— if the meaning (or his quest of it) does not actively withhold the reader, the sound may of itself waft him to the poet's port. It seems therefore reasonable of the symbolist to claim that, as every musical sound should have an echo, and every painted figure, a sky, "we who sing with thoughts and paint with words should give to every word and every phrase its echo and its horizon."

While sound effects are as the sunset sky to the orb of the poet's theme, they are sought often in drama, and not neglected in the novel. Jane Austen, Meredith, Hardy, are among those who effectively employ sound to strengthen the feeling and the movement of their stories; Dickens, striving toward it, at moments of emotional pressure betrays himself in verse. Sound explains much of the post-Ulyssean Joyce. Of which more in the text and Note 30.

(49) A specimen of the work of the da-da-ists may not be out of place, being elsewhere not easily obtainable. This, by Picabia (insofar as translation can indicate), is

Ninie

Perfumes, flowers, love, dancing, music,
Sleeping under the fair star,
The naked Aphrodite,
A child that's beginning to walk,
The Spartan
Biting his lower lip,

The cithern's sound:
I am the man who's inventing the new cement.
The brooklets become rivers,
Inns palaces;
The sensibility overstimulated by the underside,
Is looking for new chimneys, new elegance,
Whose ovens' goal is to melt the chains of liberty.
The air is not white,
Rich men do not love war.
My service is gold, and I eat from a plain dish.
Coast lands are not like the mountains.
Intelligence is the apple of Adam
Stupidity that of Wilhelm Tell.
The game of dominoes was invented by Menander.
There are not enough dominos for me to like the game.
The backside is always the same;
The sun is always the same;
The moon too,
Art, too.
Novelty is only a drawing-room masquerade;
There is wit
But wit is Italian
And the finest thing in Italy
Is the mandolins.

P.S. Don Quixote is an example.

The unanimist's sense of a bond between all things glimmers,
probably without intention, through these lines.

(50) Appended to Breton's manifesto is a novel entitled *Soluble Fish*, of which the following is a typical specimen:

Once upon a time there was a turkey-cock on a dyke. This turkey-cock had but a few days left to warm himself in the sunlight, and he looked mysteriously at himself in a Venetian glass arranged for that purpose on the dyke. It is at this point that there intervenes the hand of man, that flower of the fields you have not lived without hearing of. The turkey-cock, which answered to the name of * * * —just in fun, you know—no longer knew what to do with its head. Everyone is aware that the turkey-cock's head is a seven- or eight-faced prism, just as the high hat is a prism of seven or eight surfaces.

The high hat balanced itself on the dyke like an enormous mussel singing on a rock. The dyke had no reason for being there, since the sea had retired, very forcefully, that morning. Besides, the harbor was all lit up by an arc-lamp as large as a child on his way to school.

The turkey-cock felt that he was lost if he could not attract this passer-by. The child saw the high hat, and, as he was quite hungry, undertook to empty it of its contents in the shape of a fine jellyfish with a butterfly beak. Can butterflies be assimilated by lights? Evidently; that is why the burial stopped on the dyke. The priest sang in the mussel, the mussel sang in the rock, the rock sang in the sea, and the sea sang in the sea.

So the turkey-cock stayed on the dyke, and since that day it frightens the child on his way to school.

(51) Such associations as of color and sound (to which attention is called in Note 47) may be extended. One recalls the chapter on the horror of white, in Melville's *Moby Dick*. Motion is suggested, in sculpture and painting, by setting various parts of the body in positions they can occupy only successively: Rodin's *St. John the Baptist*, in its stride, has both feet flat on the ground. A man chopping wood is endowed, in a painting shown in an exhibition of *The Independent Artists* in New York, with six pairs of arms, spread from high up, with the axe overhead, to down, with the axe in the wood-block. Brahman statues of the dancing Shiva have many curving arms. Music (through title and program note) tries to tell stories and paint scenes: instead of *First Symphony* and *Etude 34*, we hear *The Sorcerer's Apprentice, The Afternoon Of a Faun, New World Symphony, Rhapsody in Blue, An American In Paris;* and once numbered compositions are rechristened by ductile minds. De la Mare's poem *Silver* is a landscape evoked in music. With broken lines and words dismembered, poets endeavor to have the appearance of the page contribute to the poem's summoning. The effects of one art are sought in another, with frequent absurdity and excess, but possibly with ultimate finding of new powers.

(52) *Der Bettler*, by Reinhard Sorge, awarded the Kleist prize; produced by Max Reinhardt in 1917. The London *Times* (*Literary Supplement* on Germany, 18 April, 1929) in an excellent survey of recent German literature, names the following plays as also presenting this theme: Walter Hasenclever, *Der Sohn* (also pre-war); Rolf Lauckner, *Predigt in Litauen;* Franz Werfel, *Spiegelmensch;* Fritz von Unruh, *Ein Geschlecht;* Arnolt Bronnen, *Vatermord;* Joachim von der Goltz, *Vater und Sohn;* Georg Kaiser, *Die Koralle;* Ernst Toller, *Die Wandlung.* This

conflict is, of course, a recurring theme of many times, even outside of expressionism; a recent English instance is St. John Ervine's *The Ship*.

(53) Analogous is the feeling Berge stresses, that "the whole bookly production of recent years, though quite individual, even individualistic, is the manifestation of a single, collective soul". "The thirst for the absolute" is a phrase that recurs in his pages, linked with such flares of mysticism as mark Maritain and D. H. Lawrence, and with the many conversions to Catholicism that have studded the years of symbolism since Baudelaire's alternate blasphemy and devotion. Thus T. S. Eliot, and many both of ultraists and of humanists, seek the church.

The quest of symbolism is akin to that earlier known in the rule of allegory. Although the Greeks to some extent submerged secondary meanings in their *mimesis*, the dark ages found them the one way of preserving the classical literature, beneath the pagan doctrines and doings discerning a moral intent. The *Metamorphoses* of Ovid was thus transmoralized; Fulgentius was followed by Petrarch, who tells us Æolus is Reason, controlling the winds of passion, and the true subject of the Æneid is the Perfect Man. In the original works of the time, as well, allegory flourished, on into the renaissance—as *The Faerie Queene* reminds us—and beyond into the days of Chapelain's *La Pucelle* and Pope's *Iliad*. High-school text books of today explain the allegory of *The Idylls of the King;* but after the Victorians the concept is largely replaced by that of symbolism. As between the older *translation* vs. *adaptation*, the difference is that allegory implies a definite undermeaning; symbolism leaves the receptor free to feel whatsoever summoning true.

(54) An excellent example of this in sculpture is the tapering, bare, curved form of Brancusi's *Golden Bird*, (on which, it may be remembered, United States Customs officials tried to collect duty as metal in bulk, and) which Mina Loy has celebrated:

> The toy
> become the æsthetic archetype
>
> As if
>
> some patient peasant god
> had rubbed and rubbed
> the Alpha and Omega
> of Form
> into a lump of metal

A naked orientation
unwinged unplumed
    the ultimate rhythm
has lopped the eccentricities
of crest and claw
from
the nucleus of flight

The absolute act
of art
conformed
to continent sculpture
—bare as the brow of Osiris—
the breast of revelation

An incandescent curve
licked by chromatic flames
in labyrinths of reflections.

(55) However a free will may be regarded by philosophers out-side of the Society of Jesus, it is asserted or sought by many novelists. At all times the popular hero has of course hewn out his own career; but now in the tide of deterministic fiction are signs of a turning. One of Soupault's novels bears as a rhythmic beat the recurrent cry "a gratuitous act, if you please". André Berge, one of the founders of the periodical *Cahiers du Mois,* planned a sym-posium on the subject; though this did not eventuate, because the contributors parted, "joined in a mutual negation", Berge tells of them:

For Maritain, grace is the one gratuitous act; Soupault admits the possibility, but claims that his logical habits prevent his realiz-ing it. . . . The hypotheses multiply, but only one thing matters, and is striking: the desire for that gratuitous act which will give us the sense of liberty. This no doubt brings to mind those abso-lute monarchs who sheared off heads at random to convince them-selves of their omnipotence. The author in his work may realize his dream, at the cost of later finding all his disappointments again.

It has been said that a sound system is to assume free will in de-ciding one's own conduct, and determinism in considering the acts of others. To most, perhaps, free will is a truth felt beyond knowledge; and the author who exhibits it helps restore man's consciousness of his own importance.

(56) The Inquisition—and the Crusades. According to this theory, hell and heaven are the natural creation of the child; purgatory—which is of later coming—is an invention of the adolescent. It was an adolescent who, hearing a sermon on the tortures of hell-fire, cried in the depths of his soul: "No! No! If there are damned in hell, Christ is beside them suffering there!" Whence the adolescent atheism. Agnosticism marks the mood of the mature.

(57) Galsworthy, indeed, has been accused of subtly taking sides; this charge, if valid, makes his plays not tragedies but problem plays or melodramas; that is, this defect holds them from what is generally deemed highest art. Of *Justice* and *Loyalties* is the statement most often made.

And if I have done well, and as is fitting the story, it is that which I desired; but if slenderly and meanly, it is that which I could attain.

II MACCABEES.

BIBLIOGRAPHY

Where are your books?—that light bequeathed
To beings else forlorn and blind!
Up! Up! and drink the spirit breathed
From dead men to their kind.

WILLIAM WORDSWORTH.

BIBLIOGRAPHY

It would not be difficult to make a separate volume of names of books to be read in connection with literary criticism. (It has, indeed, been done: *Literary Criticism*, by C. M. Gayley and F. M. Scott, is a series of brief outlines and extensive bibliographies.) The present list avoids such fulness by omitting the works of authors discussed in the text, when they can easily be traced from such reference—save in the case of important recent works, or when the various editions of a work make specification advisable. Titles of foreign books are given in English whenever translations are available. The books are listed in the section to which their material is most pertinent, though many, of course, touch on other fields as well. The list is in no sense more than a partial selection, indicating books that have stirred the present writer to thought (though not always to assent) and that will carry the reader farther along any relevant path he may choose to follow.

Certain works are of such wide applicability as to require mention outside of special sections. Several series of essays are interesting:

Essays and Studies, by Members of the English Association.
Essays by Divers Hands, Transactions of the Royal Society of Literature.
Tracts of the Society for Pure English.

These English studies often combine original criticism with scholarly exposition in bolder (if more dogmatic) fashion than American essays of the same type, which will also repay consultation:

American Journal of Philology.
The Modern Language Journal.
Publications of the Modern Language Association of America.
Studies in Philology.

* * * * * * * *

Alain: *Les Idées et les ages.*
  Propos.
  Propos sur l'esthetique.
  Système des beaux-arts.

507

Alain, little known in English as yet, is one of the most terse and pointed of contemporary writers on æsthetics, especially valuable by virtue of his reasoned insistence on the work itself—work in the sense not of the finished product, the work of art, but of the creative process.

BOSANQUET, B.: *A History of Æsthetic*. A survey of the metaphysics of beauty, historically considered.

RICHARDS, I. A.: *Principles of Literary Criticism*. A provocative statement of the modern approach.

SAINTSBURY, GEORGE: *A History of Criticism*. The three volumes of this work constitute the fullest survey of literary criticism, presented in vigorous, though at times opinionated, style.
Loci Critici. An anthology of representative writings from the period covered by his history.

SCOTT-JAMES, R. A.: *The Making of Literature*. A more "popular" and argumentative survey than Saintsbury's, discussing the great figures in the history of criticism.

I

DISTINCTIONS AND PRECAUTIONS

BRIDGMAN, P. W.: *The Logic of Modern Physics*.

BURTT, E. A.: *The Metaphysical Foundations of Physics*.

CANBY, H. S.: *Definitions*.

EDDINGTON, A. S.: *The Nature of the Physical World*.

GARD, WAYNE: *Book Reviewing*.

GRUDIN, LOUIS: *A Primer of Æsthetics*.

JONES, LLEWELLYN: *How To Criticize Books*.

KELLETT, E. E.: *The Whirligig of Taste*.

MATTHEWS, BRANDER: *Twelve Good Rules for Critics* (in *Americanisms*).

MOORE, T. STURGE: *Armour for Aphrodite*.

OGDEN, C. K. and RICHARDS, I. A.: *The Meaning of Meaning*.

PAVLOV, IVAN P.: *Conditioned Reflexes*.
Lectures on Conditioned Reflexes.

RIGNANO, EUGENIO: *The Psychology of Reasoning*.

RUSSELL, BERTRAND: *Philosophy*.

SIDGWICK, ALFRED: *The Application of Logic*.
The Use of Words in Reasoning.

SMITH, L. W.: *Current Reviews*.

WATSON, JOHN B.: *Behavior*.
    Behaviorism.
WHITEHEAD, ALFRED NORTH: *Science and the Modern World*.

Further reading along the lines of this section may be profitably carried on in The International Library of Philosophy, Psychology, and Scientific Method, which includes such studies as Broad, C. D.: *Scientific Thought*, and Richie, A. D.: *Scientific Method*, as well as several others here listed—and more.

II

THE GROWTH THROUGH THE GREEKS

ARISTOPHANES: translated by J. Hookham Frere (and Introduction).
ARISTOTLE: edited by Lane Cooper.
BALDWIN, C. S.: *Ancient Rhetoric and Poetic*.
COOK, SIR THEODORE: *The Curves of Life*.
EGGER, E.: *Essay on the History of Greek Criticism*.
GHYKA, M. C.: *La pensée contemporaine, II Esthetique*.
HAMBIDGE, JAY: *Dynamic Symmetry*.
HAMILTON, EDITH: *The Greek Way*.
LIVINGSTONE, R. W.: *The Greek Genius*.
PLATO: especially *The Republic, Philebus, Phœdrus, Gorgias*: translated by B. Jowett.
ROBERTS, W. RHYS: *Greek Rhetoric and Literary Criticism*.
SHEPPARD, J. T.: *Æschylus and Sophocles*.
ZIMMERN, ALFRED: *Solon and Crœsus and other Greek Essays*.

III

THE RENAISSANCE

For a general survey of the literature of any age, the volumes of the series Periods of European Literature, under the editorship of George Saintsbury, may be consulted.

BRAY, J. W.: *A History of English Critical Terms*.
CLARK, D. L.: *Rhetoric and Poetry in the Renaissance*.
KLEIN, D.: *Literary Criticism in the Elizabethan Dramatists*.
LANGDON, IDA: *Milton's Theory of Poetry and Fine Art*.
RIGAULT, H.: *Histoire de la querelle des anciens et modernes*.
SMITH, GREGORY, Editor: *Elizabethan Critical Essays*.

SPINGARN, J. E.: *History of Literary Criticism in the Renaissance.*
Editor: *Critical Essays of the Seventeenth Century* (English).
SYMONDS, J. A.: *The Renaissance in Italy.*
TAYLOR, H. O.: *The Classical Heritage of the Middle Ages.*
VOSSLER, KARL: *Medieval Culture.*

IV

RULE AND REVOLT

ALDEN, RAY M., Editor: *Critical Essays of the Early 19th Century* (English).
BRANDES, GEORG: *Main Currents In Nineteenth Century Literature.*
BROWN, J. E., Editor: *Critical Opinions of Samuel Johnson.*
DRYDEN, JOHN: *Essays* (edited by W. P. Ker).
DURHAM, W. H., Editor: *Critical Essays of the Eighteenth Century* (English, 1700–1725).
LOWES, J. L.: *The Road to Xanadu.*
SAURAT, DENIS: *Blake and Modern Thought.*
TISSOT, E.: *Les évolutions de la critique française.*
WYLIE, LAURA J.: *Studies in the Evolution of English Criticism.*

V

THE WIDENING VIEW

ABERCROMBIE, LASCELLES: *Progress In Literature.*
BABBITT, I.: *Masters of Modern French Criticism.*
BALL, A. H. R., Editor: *Ruskin as a Literary Critic.*
BAUDOUIN, CH.: *Psychoanalysis and Æsthetics.*
BOURNE, RANDOLPH: *History of a Literary Radical.*
BOWMAN, J. C., Editor: *Contemporary American Criticism.*
BREWSTER, WM. T., Editor: *Modern English Literary Criticism.*
BROOKS, VAN WYCK: *The Ordeal of Mark Twain.*
BURGUM, E. B., Editor: *The New Criticism.*
CALVERTON, F. V.: *The Newer Spirit.*
CAZAMIAN, L.: *Criticism in the Making.*
CRUSE, AMY: *The Shaping of English Literature.*
DOWNEY, JUNE E.: *Creative Imagination.*
ELIOT, T. S.: *For Lancelot Andrewes.*
The Sacred Wood.
FOERSTER, NORMAN: *American Criticism.*
Editor: *The Reinterpretation of American Literature.*

(HARCOURT BRACE, Pub.:) *Criticism in America, its function and status*.

ICKOWICZ, MARC: *La littérature à la lumière du matérialisme historique*.

KOSTYLEFF, NICOLAS: *Le mécanisme cérébral de la pensée*.

LEWISOHN, L., Editor: *A Modern Book of Criticism*.

LIPTZIN, S.: *Lyric Pioneers of Modern Germany*.

MACKENZIE, AGNES M.: *The Process of Literature*.

McLAUGHLIN, E. T.: *Literary Criticism for Students*.

MORDELL, A.: *Notorious Literary Attacks*.

MUMFORD, LEWIS: *The Golden Day*.

NOVAK, M.: *The Bases of the Science of Art*.

(OXFORD UNIVERSITY PRESS, Pub.:) *Tradition and Experiment in Present-Day Literature*.

PAULL, H. M.: *Literary Ethics*.

PAYNE, W. M.: *American Literary Criticism*.

POSTGATE, J. P.: *Translation and Translations*.

PRESCOTT, F. C.: *Poetry and Dreams*.

RICHARDS, I. A.: *Practical Criticism*.

RICKERT, EDITH: *New Methods for the Study of Literature*.

ROBERTSON, J. M.: *Essays Toward a Critical Method*.

TRENT, W. P.: *The Authority of Criticism (and other essays)*.

VAUGHAN, C. E., Editor: *English Literary Criticism*.

VICO, G.: *The New Science*.

WEST, REBECCA: *The Strange Necessity*.

WILKINSON, MARGUERITE: *The Way of the Makers*.

WILLIAMS, ORLO: *Contemporary Criticism*.

WINCHESTER, C. T.: *Some Principles of Literary Criticism*.

WOOLF, LEONARD: Editor: *The Hogarth Essays*.

WOOLF, VIRGINIA: *The Common Reader*.

WORSFELD, W. BASIL: *Principles of Criticism*.

Of individual studies in the new scientific technique, almost any of the journals of psychology will afford many examples. Much material of interest, and probably many methods that can be elsewhere profitably applied, may be gleaned from the volumes of such periodicals as

The Journal of Applied Psychology.
The Journal of Philosophy, Psychology, and Scientific Method.
The Psychological Review.

VI

NATURE AND ART

ALLEN, M. CECIL: *The Mirror of the Passing World.*

BELL, CLIVE: *Art.*

BLAKE, VERNON: *Relation In Art.*

BOSANQUET, B.: *Three Lectures On Æsthetics.*

BREWSTER, WM. T., Editor: *Representative Essays on the Theory of Style.*

CARRITT, E. F.: *The Theory of Beauty.*

COLLINGWOOD, R. G.: *The Mind in Æsthetics* (in *The Mind,* Edited by R. J. S. McDowall).
       Speculum Mentis.

CROCE, B.: *Æsthetics.*

DUCASSE, CURT JOHN: *The Philosophy of Art.*

EDMAN, IRWIN: *The World, the Arts, and the Artist.*

FAURE, ELIE: *The History of Art.*

GROOS, KARL: *Das Spiel als Katarsis.*

HEGEL, G. W. F.: *The Philosophy of Fine Art.*

LADD, HENRY: *With Eyes of the Past.*

LANGFELD, H. S.: *The Æsthetic Attitude.*

LEE, VERNON (VIOLET PAGET): *The Beautiful.*
       The Handling of Words.

LIPP, THEODORE: *Psychologie des Schönen und der Kunst.*

MACCOLL, D. S.: *Nineteenth Century Art.*

MARVIN, F. S. and CLUTTON-BLACK, A. F., Editors: *Art and Civilization.*

MÜLLER-FREIENFELS, RICHARD: *Psychologie der Kunst.*

MUNRO, THOMAS: *The Scientific Method in Æsthetics.*

OGDEN, C. K., RICHARDS, I. A., and WOOD, J.: *The Foundations of Æsthetics.*

PARKER, DE WITT H.: *The Analysis of Art.*

PARKHURST, HELEN H.: *Beauty.*

PRALL, D. W.: *Æsthetic Judgment.*

STACE, W. T.: *The Meaning of Beauty.*

STEIN, LEO: *The A B C of Æsthetics.*

STRZYGOWSKI, J.: *The Origins of Christian Church Art.*

VALENTINE, C. W.: *The Experimental Psychology of Beauty.*

VOLKELT, JOHANNES: *System der Æsthetik.*

WELLS, HENRY: *The Judgment of Literature.*

WÖLFFLIN, HEINRICH: *Kunstgeschichtliche Grundbegriffe.*

WORRINGER, WILHELM: *Abstraktion und Einfühling.*
       Form in Gothic.

VII

POETRY

Lyra Graeca.
The Greek Anthology.
Elizabethan Lyrics (Edited by NORMAN AULT).
Seventeenth Century Lyrics (Edited by NORMAN AULT).
The Golden Treasury.
The Oxford Books of Verse.
The English Poets (Edited by THOMAS H. WARD).

ANDREWS, C. E.: *The Writing and Reading of Verse.*
BAUCHE, HENRI: *Le langage populaire.*
BAUM, P. F.: *The Principles of English Versification.*
BRADLEY, A. C.: *Oxford Lectures on Poetry.*
BREMOND, HENRI: *Poésie et Prière.*
BREMOND, HENRI et DE SOUZA, ROBERT: *La Poésie pure.*
BREWER, R. F.: *The Art of Versification.*
BROWN, W.: *Time In English Verse Rhythm.*
BUCHANAN, SCOTT: *Poetry and Mathematics.*
CHAPIN, ELSA and THOMAS, RUSSELL: *A New Approach to Poetry.*
COLLINS, H. P.: *Modern Poetry.*
COWL, R. P.: *The Theory of Poetry in English.*
DRINKWATER, JOHN: *Victorian Literature.*
EASTMAN, MAX: *The Enjoyment of Poetry.*
ELLIOTT, G. R.: *The Cycle of Modern Poetry.*
(EVERYMAN'S LIBRARY): *The Prelude to Poetry* (poets on their art).
GARROD, H. W.: *The Profession of Poetry.*
GRAVES, ROBERT: *Another Future of Poetry.*
                    On English Poetry.
GROOM, BERNARD: *Some Kinds of Poetic Diction.*
HAZLITT, WM.: *The English Poets.*
JESPERSON, OTTO: *Language.*
KENT, R. G.: *Language and Philology.*
KER, W. P.: *Form and Style in Poetry.*
LALOU, RENÉ: *Vers un alchimie lyrique.*
LOWELL, AMY: *Tendencies in Modern American Poetry.*
LOWES, J. L.: *Convention and Revolt in Poetry.*
MOORE, GEORGE, Editor: *Pure Poetry.*
MURRAY, GILBERT: *The Classical Tradition in Poetry.*
NEIHARDT, J. G.: *Poetic Values.*

POWELL, A. E.: *The Romantic Theory of Poetry.*
RAYMOND, G. L.: *Poetry as a Representative Art.*
RICHARDS, I. A.: *Science and Poetry.*
RIDING, LAURA and GRAVES, ROBERT: *A Survey of Modernist Poetry.*
ROMAINS, J. et CHENNEVIÉRE, G.: *Petit traité de versification.*
SAINTSBURY, GEORGE: *A Historical Manual of English Prosody* (1 vol.).

> *History of English Prose Rhythm.*
> *History of English Prosody* (3 vols.).

SAPIR, EDWARD: *Language.*
SMITH, L. P.: *Words and Idioms.*
SONNENSCHEIN, E. A.: *What Is Rhythm?*
TINKER, C. B. *The Good Estate of Poetry.*
TREVELYAN, R. C.: *Thamyris, or Is There a Future For Poetry?*
UNTERMEYER, LOUIS: *The New Era in American Poetry.*
VENDRYES, J.: *Language.*
VERRIER, PAUL: *Essai sur les principes de la métrique anglaise.*
VITTOZ, R.: *Essai sur les conditions de la poésie pure.*
WILSON, K. M.: *The Real Rhythm in English Poetry.*
WYLD, H. C.: *Studies in English Rhymes.*
YOUNG, SIR GEORGE: *An English Poetry on Inductive Lines.*

VIII

DRAMA

ARCHER, WM.: *The Old Drama and the New.*
> *Playmaking.*
ARMSTRONG, MARTIN: *Laughing.*
BAKER, G. P.: *Dramatic Technique.*
BAKSHY, A.: *The Theatre Unbound.*
CLARK, BARRETT, Editor: *European Theories of the Drama.*
A Century of Essays (EVERYMAN'S LIBRARY):
> DEKKER: *How a Gull Should Behave in a Playhouse.*
> DE QUINCEY: *On the Knocking at the Gate in "Macbeth."*
DIXON, W. MACNEILE: *Tragedy.*
DUKES, ASHLEY: *Drama.*
EASTMAN, MAX: *The Sense of Humor.*
GRIEG, J. Y. T.: *The Psychology of Laughter and Comedy.*
HAMILTON, CLAYTON: *Studies in Stagecraft.*
> *The Theory of the Theatre.*
HUGHES, GLENN: *The Story of the Theatre.*
LEGOUIS, EMILE H.: *The Bacchic Element in Shakespeare's Plays.*

LUCAS, F. L.: *Tragedy.*

MANTZIUS, KARL: *A History of Theatrical Arts.*

MITCHELL, ROY: *Creative Theatre.*

MONTAGUE, C. E.: *Dramatic Values.*
> *The Literary Play;* and *A Note on Dramatic Criticism,* by J. E. SPINGARN: in *Essays and Studies* by MEMBERS OF THE ENGLISH ASSOCIATION.

MOULTON, R. G.: *Shakespeare as a Dramatic Artist.*

MURRAY, GILBERT: *Hamlet and Orestes.*

NICOLL, ALLARDYCE: *The Development of the Theatre.*
> *Introduction to Dramatic Theory.*

POLTI, G.: *The Art of Inventing Characters.*
> *The Thirty-six Dramatic Situations.*

STUART, D. C.: *The Development of Dramatic Art.*

THEATRE (Essays reprinted from *Theatre Arts,* perhaps the best monthly magazine of the dramatic arts).

THORNDIKE, A. H.: *English Comedy.*

TISDEL, FREDERICK M.: *Symbolism in the Theatre.*

WALKLEY, A. B.: *Dramatic Criticism.*

WHITMORE, C. E.: *The Supernatural in Tragedy.*

YOUNG, STARK: *The Theatre.*

IX

PROSE

BREWSTER, D., and BURRELL, A.: *Dead Reckonings in Fiction.*

CARRUTHERS, J.: *Scheherezade, or the Future of the English Novel.*

CHEVRILLON, A.: *Three Studies in English Literature.*

CROSS, WILBUR: *The Development of the English Novel.*

DANE, CLEMENCE: *Tradition and Hugh Walpole.*

DAWSON, W. J.: *The Makers of English Fiction.*

FOLLETT, WILSON: *The Modern Novel.*

FORSTER, E. M.: *Aspects of the Novel.*

GALLISHAW, J.: *Twenty Problems of the Fiction Writer.*

GOODMAN, THEODORE: *Narrative Structure and Style.*

HAMILTON, CLAYTON: *Materials and Methods of Fiction.*

HORNE, CHARLES F.: *Technique of the Novel.*

JAMESON, STORM: *The Georgian Novel and Mr. Robinson.*

JOHNSON, R. BRIMLEY, Editor: *Novelists on Novels.*

LUBBOCK, PERCY: *The Craft of Fiction.*

MARBLE, A. R.: *A Study of the Modern Novel.*
MUIR, EDWIN: *Plot In the Novel.*
MUNSON, GORHAM B.: *Style and Form in American Prose.*
NEWMAN, FRANCIS: *The Short Story's Mutations.*
RALEIGH, SIR WALTER: *The English Novel.*
READ, HERBERT: *English Prose Style.*
SLOSSON, E. E., and DOWNEY, JUNE: *Plots and Personalities.*
SPEARE, M. E.: *The Political Novel.*
STODDARD, F. H.: *The Evolution of the English Novel.*
THOMSON, J. A. K.: *Irony.*
TURNER, F. McD. C.: *Irony in English Literature.*
WAGENKNECHT, ED.: *Utopia Americana* (in the University of Washington Chapbooks, many of which are provocative).
WALKER, H.: *English Satire and Satirists.*
WEYGANDT, C.: *A Century of the English Novel.*
WOOLF, VIRGINIA: *Phases of Fiction.*
ZOLA, E.: *The Experimental Novel.*

X

SCHOOLS AND SCHEMES

ABERCROMBIE, LASCELLES: *Romanticism.*
ARAGON, LOUIS: *Traité du style.*
BAHR, HERMANN: *Expressionism.*
BAILLY, A.: *L'Ecole classique française.*
BENDA, JULIEN: *Belphégor.*
              Sur le succès du Bergsonisme.
              The Treason of the Intellectuals.
BERGE, ANDRÉ: *L'Esprit de la littérature moderne.*
BERL, EMMANUEL: *Mort de la pensée bourgeoise.*
BRETON, ANDRÉ: *Manifeste du surréalisme.*
CABELL, JAMES BRANCH: *Beyond Life.*
CHARPENTIER, JEAN: *Le Symbolisme.*
DUNBAR, HELEN F.: *Symbolism in Medieval Thought.*
EATON, R. M.: *Symbolism and Truth.*
ECCLES, F. Y.: *La liquidation du romantisme.*
FERNANDEZ, R.: *Messages.*
FIDAO-JUSTINIANI, J.-E.: *Qu'est-ce qu'un classique?*
FONTAINAS, ANDRÉ: *Mes souvenirs du symbolisme.*
GIDE, ANDRÉ: *Incidences.*
GRIERSON, J. H.: *Classical and Romantic.*
JACKSON, HOLBROOK: *The Eighteen Nineties.*
LAIRD, J.: *A Study in Realism.*

LASSERRE, P.: *Des Romantiques à nous.*
MACHEN, ARTHUR: *Hieroglyphics.*
MARTINE, F.: *Le naturalisme français.*
MORE, PAUL ELMER: *The Drift of Romanticism.*
PATTEE, F. L.: *Tradition and Jazz.*
PFISTER, OSKAR R.: *Expressionism in Art.*
READ, HERBERT: *Reason and Romanticism.*
ROOSBROECK, G. L. VON: *The Legend of the Decadents.*
SCHEFFAUER, H. G.: *The New Vision In the German Arts.*
SYMONS, ARTHUR: *The Symbolist Movement in Literature.*
VALÉRY, PAUL: *Variety.*
          Varieté II.
WALDMANN, EMIL: *Die Kunst des Realismus und des Impressionismus.*
WATERHOUSE, F. A.: *Random Studies in the Romantic Chaos.*
WHITEHEAD, A. N.: *Symbolism.*

INDEX

How index-learning turns no student pale,
Yet holds the eel of science by the tail.
ALEXANDER POPE.

INDEX